ADVANCE PRAISE

"What do people do while living between historical periods?
They talk about the past and try to imagine the future. This book
by Vadim Makhov is invaluable precisely because it represents a
collection of timely reflections, an attempt to give a prologue to a new
historical period. The central point of the book, as I see it, is search
for the meaning of social and biological evolution and for answers to
questions of concern to all of us: what change will occur next, what
new things will happen to us? To answer these questions, the author
puts forward what I have called 'the Makhov hypothesis'."
Alexander Auzan, DSc (Economics), Professor,
Dean of the Faculty of Economics of Lomonosov Moscow State
University, Scientific Director of the Institute for National Projects

"This is truly a big-idea book that is, at the same time, free from
distorting and juggling facts. Vadim has created a unique body of
knowledge about humanity, seen through the prism of his original
'lucky clover' theory, which can be disputed as rather ambiguous,
but cannot be denied grace."
Arild Nerdrum, Co-Founder of Fjord Capital Partners

Published by
LID Publishing Limited
The Record Hall, Studio 204,
16-16a Baldwins Gardens,
London EC1N 7RJ, UK

524 Broadway, 11th Floor, Suite 08-120,
New York, NY 10012, US

info@lidpublishing.com
www.lidpublishing.com

A member of:

www.businesspublishersroundtable.com

SKOLKOVO
Moscow School of Management

© Vadim Makhov, 2018
© LID Publishing Limited, 2018

Printed in the Czech Republic by Finidr
ISBN: 978-1-911498-94-0

Cover and page design: Caroline Li

VADIM MAKHOV

HUMANITY'S LUCKY CLOVER

A HISTORY OF DISCOVERIES, TECHNOLOGIES, COMPETITION AND WEALTH

LONDON   NEW YORK   SHANGHAI
MADRID   BARCELONA   BOGOTA
MEXICO CITY   MONTERREY   BUENOS AIRES

CONTENTS

FOREWORD

Dear Readers,

I am pleased to introduce the book of my dear friend, Vadim Makhov. I am sure that after you have read this book, you too will change your view of where we as a species came from and the challenges we face in the future. Vadim's book is full of fascinating insights.

For example, we all understand that a drastic shift in our lifestyle took place 10,000 years ago when humanity started farming and left gathering behind. Vadim Makhov highlights the fact that humanity had to pay quite a price for the innovation – the reduced biodiversity of food resulted in a sharp drop in life span.

Then, food production efficiency gradually increased, causing the emergence of cities and urbanization. Again, the price that humanity had to pay for increased comfort in human life was epidemics and mass viral diseases – these being the first weapons of mass destruction on earth.

Three centuries ago, a number of industrial revolutions allowed us to switch from human muscle force to machines driven by steam. However, the industrial revolution gave rise to financial inequality that has today become not only a critical part of social life, but also has evolved into a powerful engine for change in society.

Just like differences in the salt level of water give rise to powerful currents in the ocean, inequality results in 'cross-flows' and stirrings in human society.

Humanity's Lucky Clover presents the experiences of real people, such as inventors, scientists, financial experts, and public figures. They are the ones who changed our world for the better and in their turn brought innovations to enable our lives. These people, diverse in their occupations, are united by a common theme – at the beginning of their work they had to change their attitude on certain critical issues.

This is the fundamental point of this book. Those who cannot change their mindset cannot change anything. George Bernard Shaw drew our attention to this fact in the previous century. This century is much more revolutionary, since we see that everything is changing globally.

In the past, poor countries demonstrated low economic levels and reduced economic growth, since the economies of these countries were desperately stagnant due to inefficient central planning. The better-off counties attributed their progress to their democratic set-up and the personal economic freedom offered by capitalism. For example, the more democratic South Korea superseded communist North Korea by all indicators. Cuba is another example of a country where the continued experiment of the introduction of a centrally planned, allocation-based system resulted in a deeply unmotivated population.

For the last two decades, things have changed substantially. Communist China, being strongly committed to its old ideology, has shown impressive growth (7-9% yearly), without the demolition of their Soviet-type planning system. Russia has given up the planned economy but is still having a hard time catching up with its nearest more advanced Western neighbours (e.g. Poland). Tiny Singapore, the former colony of Malaysia, was an unremarkable Asian fishing village not long ago, but has grown to be the world's lead cargo transhipment port and the world's largest financial centre. How come?

The answer is not that obvious. Under the pressure of daily news, with an unsophisticated setting of 'Open Your Mind to New Ideas!' attacking us from everywhere, we struggle to maintain our common sense to cope with the ever-growing flow of information. We need personal information filters for our inquisitive minds to prevent them from overloading. We want to touch solid ground after an exhausting information rollercoaster.

Vadim offers the reader his own solutions. His model, called the Lucky Clover, is comprised of four closely interrelated components – science, society structure, business practice and institutions, allowing us to save and increase our accumulated wealth. Where these components are well balanced, supplementing one another and feeding from their synergy, such societies are prospering. Wealth and wellbeing is growing. Sciences are developing, and inequality in these societies is shrinking. If one of the clover's leaves fades, prosperity gives way to stagnation.

It sounds slightly simple and naïve. Not so! The author's style and easy-to-read text considerably enhances understanding of the most complex issues. This is undoubtedly a strong point of the book, given the fact that it narrates quite serious issues.

Generally, economic growth is slowing down at a global level. Inequality within countries is growing, thus giving rise to migration flows. The globalization project is suffering heavy criticism. Constructive accusations come down to two points. The first point, the opening of economic borders for free movement of capital, goods and services, has failed to bring the expected prosperity for most of the world's countries and has caused currency wars. The result is everybody is against everybody, and within this setting inequality continues to increase. The second point is that globalization cannot solve economic issues. The controversies between counties are too strong and the time to take reasonable 'steps without regrets' is ever decreasing. Consequently, the issues related to the greenhouse effect, decreased biodiversity, drastically disappearing languages and cultures are not being addressed. Following the logic of the Lucky Clover model offered by Vadim, all these factors result in decreased possible interactions between the key elements. Fewer interactions mean less freedom of choice and more dictatorial behaviour, since incompatible elements just won't fit in the market.

Since the time of the first industrial revolution, the key consequence has been that it has become possible to perceive progress as the speed at which the society is ready to perceive technological innovations and discoveries. Vadim Makhov makes it clear that this approach is one-sided. What is the use of the speed at which innovations penetrate our life, if they do not give added value to society, and end up reducing employment? The impetuous attack of the digital world not only has significantly decreased the value of information, but destroyed whole industries and areas of knowledge, together with their researchers. Vadim Makhov illustrates his thought with examples of eliminated jobs in the publishing and newspapers industries. Even now, you can actually see how digitalization destroys high-quality journalism. Publishers cannot afford it anymore; it is replaced with 'cheap' bloggers, and tomorrow free-of-charge feed aggregator apps will arrive instead.

Confucius said that thinking without learning brings destruction, and learning without thinking results in a waste of time. This is what this book is about. Thinking over the situations and stories described by the author, you will learn how to perceive circumstances differently.

This book is not flawless. Having become accustomed to quality economic literature, I miss the discipline in the narration such as that observed in *Capital in the Twenty-First Century* by Thomas Piketty. The author here methodically proves that there are no natural ways to reallocate wealth. So, the wider the spread of knowledge in society, the more effective that becomes as the tool of the fair distribution of wealth. Vadim Makhov welcomes this line of argument.

Overall, the strengths of the book greatly outweigh its weaknesses. As for the disputable points, I hope the author will provide his e-mail address for readers' feedback. I think that the energy, intuition and generosity of spirit of the readers will be a genuine gift for Vadim, to inspire him towards new achievements!

Basically, a remarkable capturing of knowledge, leading to guidelines on how to conduct our future. Well done, Vadem Makhov!

Andrew Kakabadse, Professor of Governance
and Leadership at Henley Business School,
University of Reading and Emeritus Professor
at Cranfield University School of Management

WHAT THE LUCKY CLOVER LOOKS LIKE

"Though endless exponential growth is impossible, it could, presumably, be approximated to infinity..."

– Kenneth Arrow,
an American economist and a 1972 Nobel laureate in Economics.
From a lecture delivered at the Higher School of Economics
in Moscow, 31 March 2013

INTRODUCTION

Studying epochs and industrial revolutions, and giving lectures on innovation to business people, I noticed some common traits that distinguish successful societies and states from unsuccessful ones. This observation fascinated me and inspired me to conduct a more detailed investigation. Further examination showed that in all historical periods the differences manifested themselves in four integrated elements: knowledge, systems for 'embedding' the knowledge into society, labour management, and money circulation. This discovery led to a number of questions and speculations: Why is this happening? Why do these four elements manifest themselves most vividly in successful societies, regardless of the epoch? Would the correct combination of these elements produce a universal formula for success?

The more I pondered, the more closely I studied the various remarkable historical facts and analysed the ideas of prominent scientists, the more questions arose. How did we happen to come here, to our planet Earth, at all? At what point of our development are we now? In the process of gathering information, accumulating and analysing knowledge, and correlating scientific and historical facts with hypotheses and ideas put forward by philosophers of both antiquity and modernity, a unified logic system was gradually forming in my mind, which I have set out on the pages of this book. In the basis of the system lies a model for assessing the success of the development of this or that society based on the analysis of the four above-mentioned elements: knowledge, society, business, and wealth. I called this model a Lucky Clover model, and I will explain why a little later.

In this book, we will contemplate together why some countries develop faster and more successfully than others and how the former are similar in many ways to successful commercial companies. Applying the Lucky Clover model, we will observe how it was actualized in different countries and societies in different periods of human civilization, and will finally try to work out whether there is such a thing as a universal formula for success.

In his last work, *The Statistical Theory of Global Population Growth*, the famous Russian scientist Sergey Kapitsa said that the explosive growth of world population is the most important of all global problems. Sure, there is scarcely anything new in this statement, since already long ago, Thomas Malthus, one of the founding fathers of demography, deeply frightened the world by showing that population growth, taking place in a geometrical progression, was critically at odds with food production, which was only increasing in an arithmetical progression. Kapitsa himself wrote that exponential growth up to the point of full depletion of resources is a trend we can observe in the majority of living beings, because the growth of most of the animal species is limited by the availability of resources, such as food.

Fortunately, man has proved to be a special, or even a different, living creature. We are very different from all other animals, and this is why Malthus was proved wrong. We have enough food, and sometimes even more than enough. However, this contentment only confirms the fact that we ourselves still do not fully know or realize the laws of our own development.

In his work, Kapitsa, building on the findings of the Scottish demographer Paul McKendrick, came to the conclusion that the 'normal' number of people on Earth should be about a mere 100,000. But "it is developed consciousness, language, and culture that make us different from animals, and that is why we are 100,000 times more plentiful" (Kapitsa 2013, 15).

Kapitsa went far beyond professional demographers. Having examined the concept of factual hyperbolic increase in the global population (according to which the population growth rate is proportional not to the number of people living on Earth, but to the square of this number, i.e. very slow at first and accelerating sharply later on), he concluded that the global population is bound to stabilize soon.

Having considered the history of mankind with utmost abstraction by having taken the growing number of people as a mathematical function developing at a 'ten-billion step pace', he found that we have almost reached the limit of explosive population growth, i.e. have come to the point of 'compression of historical time'. The hyperbolic increase in the global population will no longer continue, as the human population growth function is destined to change. Soon we will enter a phase characterized by a global demographic transition from unrestrained to smooth and slow population growth. When exactly, no one yet knows. Kapitsa himself maintained this would happen rather soon.

If so, a radical change in the pace of growth in the global population living on the planet will definitely affect the world economy, as soon as within the lifespan of our generation. Some of these changes can already be seen today, if we look at the history of human progress and the dynamics of gaining, preserving, developing, and applying knowledge. I was also curious to explore this history using the already mentioned Lucky Clover model.

THE FOUR LEAVES OF THE LUCKY CLOVER

It was not by accident that the name 'Lucky Clover' appeared. It owes its origination to a variety of ancient legends that glorified a rare, four-leaved plant which had magical properties and brought good luck to anyone who found it. The Lucky Clover model I use in this book as an aid to studying the development of human civilization suggests that a society that has found a lucky clover will have good luck and success in its development.

Before I start explaining the Lucky Clover model in detail, let's define, in order to get a better understanding of the issue, the terms 'innovation' and 'innovation cycle'.

The word 'innovation' came into the economic mainstream vocabulary from a 'lateral' flow owing to Joseph Schumpeter, an Austrian and American economist (Schumpeter 1934), and has acquired a variety of interpretations since then. The most appropriate definition of innovation in terms of revealing its meaning is 'invention necessarily followed by its subsequent commercialization'.[1]

Having become acquainted with the concept of long-term cycles in market conditions, put forward by Russian scientist Nikolai Kondratiev, Schumpeter introduced the notion of 'Kondratiev waves' in economic science, combining his own ideas about the role of the entrepreneur in the process of economic development with Kondratiev's theory of long-term fluctuations in the economic dynamics generated by the innovation process.

**A FOUR-LEAF CLOVER,
A SYMBOL OF LUCK**

LEGENDS ABOUT THE FOUR-LEAF CLOVER

Legends about the magical properties of the four-leaf clover are so old that no one knows how or where they appeared first. According to one myth, Eve, when expelled from paradise, took a four-leaf clover flower with her to remember life in Eden. Since the quatrefoil was a plant from the Garden of Eden, anyone finding it on this sinful Earth was considered to have been given a sign of good luck.

A belief held by druids (Celtic priests) about the four-leaf clover as a revered and rare plant species was one of the primary sources of such legends. For druids, the quatrefoil symbolized the essence of the universe as represented by the four elements of nature: earth, air, fire and water. According to tradition, the finder of such a flower received the patronage of all druids. A four-leaf clover was believed to bring good luck both to its holder and to those who were close to them, and render any potion doubly strong. In addition to commanding elemental powers, each of the four leaves was credited with characteristics of its own: hope, belief, love and good luck.

Other nations have also long since considered the four-leaf clover a magical plant possessing great natural strength. In ancient Egypt, its images were put on mirror surfaces to prevent dark forces inhabiting the reflected world from penetrating our world and hurting the person looking into the object. The four-leaf clover had a mystical significance in India. To ward off evil spirits, the Indians used its images to decorate the walls of buildings and to embroider their clothes and carpets. In China, the clover is a symbol of spring and awakening.

Our Slavic ancestors believed this rare plant to symbolize the open world – its four directions, one for each leaf. It was also believed to have a powerful charge of vitality and to enable its holder to retain youthfulness and attractiveness. The lucky finder of a four-leaf clover would dry it and carry it around in a special bag, never showing it to anyone. Such a talisman was believed to protect its holder against the evil eye and malicious spells and to attract good luck.

Christians attribute a symbolic meaning to the four-leaf clover, associating it with the Holy Cross and the four Gospels.

The belief in the magical power of the four-leaf clover still exists, and there are whole companies that specialize in cultivating four-leaf clover plants for the production of gifts and good luck charms.

The four-leaf clover is the result of mutation of the usual three-leaf clover. This mutation can be caused either by a rare combination of recessive genes or by external factors. Most interestingly, such mutation is not restricted to four leaves. Five-leaf clovers exist too. The more leaves a clover plant has, the more singular and the more difficult to find it is. There is only one quatrefoil in 10,000 clover plants. However, if you believe in your luck and know how to look for this unusual variety, finding it will not be as difficult as it seems.

In this model of the economy, it is those who manage to 'commercialize innovation' before others that reap the lion's share of the profit. As the innovation becomes disseminated, the production costs level out, and profit becomes harder to make. In making profit, the most important factor is not competition on price or quality anymore, but competition between new products, new technologies, new sources of provision, and new organizational forms. Making profit through the use of these tools is the economic essence of innovation.

Profit thus becomes a matter that is here today and gone tomorrow. It is cyclical. Once it starts to ebb, the old business structure falls into ruin and is replaced by a new one (in the so-called process of 'creative destruction'). This results in a complete innovation cycle.

Our Lucky Clover model is based on innovation cycles that rest on four key elements. These elements can be compared with the four leaves, because it is growing and evolving.

These four elements are:
- Science as a source of discoveries and inventions;
- Society as the recipient and custodian of newly created goods; changing society determines the content and form of wealth at any given moment;
- Business practices (entrepreneurs who set up 'innovative charges');
- Wealth (capital, the material basis).

To have a successful innovation cycle, it is required that all four of its key elements – knowledge, society, business, and finance – successfully interact with each other and develop consistently. In other words, just as in nature, a plant can be considered healthy if the development of all of its leaves match each other agreeably. A healthy organism of this sort is a 'lucky clover'.

However, any organism must fade after the flowering phase. This means that a new lucky clover must take root and emerge somewhere else.

Now let's see how the Lucky Clover model works (Figure 1 on p12). The first leaf, knowledge, enables us to understand how the world works, and helps us to get new knowledge. Innovations are needed to ensure that new scientific knowledge is converted into production opportunities and brings commercial profit. With the arrival of profit, production grows, and as a consequence, so does people's wellbeing. Innovation is closely associated with invention, with new ideas or methods, because it implies their practical application. The renowned inventor Nikola Tesla, whose work we will consider later on, demonstrated his first model of the electric motor back in 1883, while still in Strasbourg. But Europe at that time would not find a use for his invention. It was only five years later, in the United States in 1888, that he created his first commercial motor. In just three or four years after that, thanks to commercialization, the market was flooded with hundreds of thousands of electric motors, from the sale of which Tesla received his royalty payments. Thus, an innovation process is a way of gaining knowledge and transforming it into an equivalent of public recognition.

But knowledge alone is not enough, since it does not work on its own. To make proper use of it, high-quality human resources are needed, created in the presence of developed and well-functioning social institutions in society. Therefore, society is the second leaf of the lucky clover.

Human society is characterised by interaction between its individual members and groups within social institutions. As has been observed, there is a stable relationship between the density of settlements and the intensity of innovation-based growth. However, a simple increase in the population does not result in a fabulous upsurge in the level of collective consciousness. Even if we ensure the same population density as in Macao, where there is only 49 square metres of land per inhabitant, this will still bring us no more brilliant minds (D'Efilippo 2013, 91). A greater population density expands the boundaries of the possible for brilliant minds that are able to generate remarkable ideas. The interaction between such minds increases the probability of useful discoveries being made and disseminated among the general public.

It is exactly this that makes modern global market society valuable. An invention is the creation or realization of an idea. Inventions are always plentiful, but not all of them come to be used in practice, and not all of them produce surplus product in the economy and provide added value. This means that they cannot be integrated into the market. Some people must take this risk of implementing innovation. These people are entrepreneurs, people who form a special class, without whom the scheme does not work, and the clover does not blossom. Business is another leaf of the lucky clover.

The fourth leaf of the lucky clover is wealth or money, an element that brings into focus the interesting question about the measure to be used to evaluate the success of innovation. In modern economic theory, this measure is economic benefit, which performs the function of maximizing shareholders' means, and also serves to achieve a satisfactory level of economic development (featuring sustainable annual growth, an acceptable level of unemployment, etc.) on the macroeconomic level. Nature uses another, tougher measure – viability. Different organisms have different survival strategies, but the main result must be continuation of life in a particular environment. If you want to survive, you will have to adapt. In the Lucky Clover model, money works as a kind of 'amplifier' by making it possible to obtain and combine resources to produce new knowledge and successfully take commercialized inventions to the next development cycle.

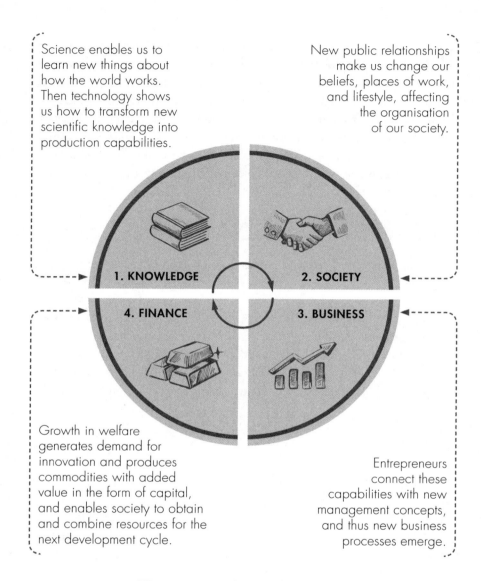

Science enables us to learn new things about how the world works. Then technology shows us how to transform new scientific knowledge into production capabilities.

New public relationships make us change our beliefs, places of work, and lifestyle, affecting the organisation of our society.

1. KNOWLEDGE

2. SOCIETY

4. FINANCE

3. BUSINESS

Growth in welfare generates demand for innovation and produces commodities with added value in the form of capital, and enables society to obtain and combine resources for the next development cycle.

Entrepreneurs connect these capabilities with new management concepts, and thus new business processes emerge.

FIGURE 1. THE LUCKY CLOVER MODEL

KNOWLEDGE AS A SOURCE OF WEALTH AND THE MEASURE OF SUCCESS OF INNOVATIONS

Would it make sense to invent other measures of success for companies and industries? Is the viability criterion applicable to entire countries, or does the absence of such a measure mean that there is an undisclosed desire to circumvent delicately the fact that sooner or later all systems will see the same fate? I think that this is the reason why the term 'competitiveness' is used more often than 'viability' in the economic domain.

In each cycle of innovation, at each new loop of evolution, the same functions are put into action in order to make the four-leaf clover blossom – creation, integration, competition, and filtration (selection). This results in accumulation of social wealth, represented by one of the leaves of the lucky clover, the leaf that makes it possible to create a reserve of 'energy' for the next phase of adaptation.

The process itself is interesting and captivating, as it requires people at each loop to create something completely new – something that will define what wealth itself will take. In advance of further narrative, I will say that the process is not linear, and takes place with a time lag. Sometimes an innovation is implemented decades after the invention was made. Innovations penetrate into other areas step by step, gradually accumulating a certain critical mass.

The process may be either slowed down or speeded up by exchange and dissemination of knowledge. This can be affected by such factors as openness, compatibility of scientific schools, the evolution of knowledge itself, the globally dominant language of communication, the level of development of mathematics in society and, of course, the presence of a wide network of contacts which provide circulation of information.

WHAT THIS BOOK IS ABOUT

This book will take a close look at the history of mankind and discover interesting facts and patterns. The Lucky Clover model will help us to do this. For convenience of perception and thought, I have divided the whole continuum of mankind's history into four key stages.

The first stage covers biological evolution and humankind's departure from it. It is a sort of prehistory. These 'subjects' per se are so vast that it would take dozens or hundreds of volumes to address them. I will only briefly outline them in the first chapter, limiting the description to some general notions of how the basic ideas around which the whole book is constructed were conceived and formed. We will hypothesize about the origin of life on Earth, the evolutionary algorithm, and what can actually be considered as a unit of natural selection. We will get a notion of the concept of 'the selfish gene' and follow the anthropological chronicle of man. Here we will reflect on what distinguishes man from an animal and why humankind is so populous on the globe, totalling more than 7 billion, and not 100,000 like other animal species of similar sizes.

The second stage is the period from the Neolithic Revolution and the first settlements to the emergence of cities, states and empires – in other words, the period of evolution of civilisations. The second and third chapters of this book are devoted to reflections on this period. We will familiarize ourselves with the 'Great Man' and consider his role in society, bring in the notion of a static society, a society that features characteristics of all states of that period, and see why their traditions and customs hindered humanity's transition to a new stage of evolution. We will see how the new way of life that came with the arrival of the Neolithic Revolution made it possible for people to create and accumulate wealth in a much more efficient way. The arrival of commodity-money relations played an important role in this transition. The sophisticated arrangement of the first states changed society over time, and specialization increased the productivity of labour. The existence of large numbers of people called for interstate exchange, and hence the need for an exchangeable material medium – gold – was instigated. The development of world trade, in turn, became the main growth driver in the ancient world. Using the examples of various states and empires, we will see how the lucky clover bloomed in different parts of the ancient world, identify some regular patterns that were typical of that world, and find out the reasons for its fading.

The third stage is the period from the Renaissance in Europe to this day. It is to this part of history that the main part of this book, comprising chapters 4 to 13, is devoted to. This period begins with the scientific revolution and the emergence of new ways of acquiring knowledge based on critical thinking and hypothesizing. In my opinion this period saw key changes that have made it possible for humankind to come to where it is now and be able to reach new heights. This is a period of dynamic societies that are the opposite of static societies, and we will see how this characteristic affects the dynamics of human history.

The fourth stage, covered in the last chapter of this book, is the period that starts today and goes on to 2050 and beyond. Delving into it, I will try to visualize technologies expected to emerge in the foreseeable future by looking into an innovations kaleidoscope. Within this viewable prospect (let's call it 'the horizon'), we can make predictions and, therefore, figure out how humanity will develop, based on the analysis of today's achievements. Looking ahead I will reflect on what awaits us beyond this horizon, what our society will be like, what will surround us and make part of our everyday life, what the next innovation cycle will be about, and where mankind's demographic development curve will go. In the conclusion, we will once again consider the significance of the Lucky Clover model as a link. We will generalize – this time at a new level of thinking – our ideas about the past, and take a look beyond the horizon.

I wish you an easy and fascinating read – which I sincerely meant it to be, in any case.

CHAPTER 1

HUMANKIND'S DEPARTURE FROM BIOLOGICAL EVOLUTION

Watch, learn, and work.

— Michael Faraday's credo

IN THE BEGINNING WAS THE WORD...

Hypotheses and constructive criticism are important elements of the process of acquiring new knowledge; the latter, in turn, sooner or later changes our ideas about the world.

Knowledge gives us not only the idea of how life began, but also how knowledge itself originated from the very first moment – the birth of everything in the world, the Big Bang theory. The modern scientific conception of the world is presented in the following hypothesis.

The early universe was very hot, as well as homogeneous and uniform during the first few billion years of its existence. However, the interaction of gravity and pressure forced areas where there was more matter than in the surrounding space to oscillate, emitting waves, like a tolling bell. Then the universe cooled, and 'imprints' left by those sound waves 'congealed' in the form of galaxies, stars, gas, and dust. Five billion years ago, a cloud consisting of dust and gas came into contact with a galactic formation whose core was rotating faster than its peripheral wings. The cloud was subjected to a wave of compression, as a result of which the Sun and the planets of the solar system emerged. The whole stock of chemical elements presented on our planet (the primary alphabet of the planet Earth, as it were) was made up during that turbulent period. Some million years later, the Sun and the planets turned out to be located in a more deserted part of the cosmos. Thus, the planets of the solar system appeared, due to planetary activity, while life on Earth originated due to a temporary respite. Then, approximately four billion years ago, after some turbulent processes, the surface of the Earth cooled so much that water and oceans appeared, where volcanic activity formed a natural laboratory in which a variety of molecules were created and developed so as to give rise to flora and fauna on our planet.

We all, nevertheless, realize that even this hypothesis provides no answers to many of the obvious questions. For example, what was there before the early universe? Who created it? Does it have limits, and what is behind these limits? There are enough clever heads in modern physics that quite rightly criticize the Big Bang theory. But currently there is no better explanation available based on our existing knowledge.

Humankind's eagerness to find more meaningful answers results in the formulation of new hypotheses based on more and more advanced explanations. This is how our knowledge develops. We make wild guesses first, propose hypotheses, and through analysis select the best theory. This hypothesis will prevail until a better one appears to change our views and ideas.

This we proudly refer to as new knowledge. We need new knowledge in our development, applying it in technology and the transformation of the world around us. We have no firm knowledge yet of how the universe was formed and how it is evolving, but we know quite a bit about how the evolutionary process takes place.

UNIVERSAL CONSTRUCTOR

Biological evolution is similar to programming. The nitrogenous bases (adenine, guanine, thymine, and cytosine) serve as a kind of alphabet in genetic codification. Letters come together to form words and phrases, as the nitrogenous bases (chain) are connected with the nitrogenous bases of another. This is how the genetic code is formed, a language that nature used to create a new replicator – deoxyribonucleic acid (DNA).[2] Since then, DNA has been storing large amounts of information, having surpassed ribonucleic acid (RNA) – messengers that carry instructions from DNA for synthesis of protein – as its competitor and constituent part at the same time in respect of reliability (stability). As a result, something like a double entry is produced.

The genetic code has become all-purpose, and has a phenomenally broad scope of application to determine characteristics of organisms and ways of their behaviour; it is present in organisms ranging from primitive single-celled creatures to beasts and birds. The genetic code itself does not develop further, while new organisms born on its basis continue to create new knowledge and carry it in themselves!

EVOLUTIONARY ALGORITHM

The evolutionary algorithm (Figure 2) starts with the creation of a DNA molecule according to the design. Evolution creates the design without a designer. The algorithm quickly and reliably finds a good design, which is coded with a specific pattern that makes it possible to implement and decode while carefully reading out its description. Organisms, embodied in reality thanks to the 'anonymous' designer, are not only integrated into the ecosystem, but also interact with each other. More organisms are born than can survive – and this is where competition begins (natural selection), ensuring that it is not the strongest organisms or species that survive, but... the best designs – the best genes!

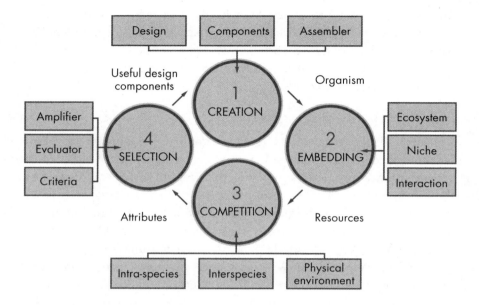

FIGURE 2. THE FOUR KEY STAGES OF THE EVOLUTIONARY ALGORITHM

1. CREATION

To assemble an organism, a specification is needed, as well as the components to compile the design and a skilled reader and assembler. The task of the latter is to assemble the new organism precisely and accurately in accordance with the design using the specified components (the four nitrogenous bases). The genius of nature lies in the fact that DNA is both the design and the assembler. In fact, it is a universal constructor that can, in addition to assembling (copying), sustain and modify the design. The subsequent operation of the evolutionary algorithm takes place subject to the presence of the design reader and assembler and with the help of natural selection.

2. INTEGRATION

When the newly created DNA is integrated into the natural habitat, the living organism must occupy a niche in a certain ecosystem where it will begin to interact with other organisms. As a result of intra- and inter-species interaction between organisms and their interaction with the environment, the population of the species to which the given organism belongs grows and gradually changes the environment itself.

3. COMPETITION

Having integrated into the ecosystem, the organism begins to interact with other individuals within the species, with organisms belonging to other species, and with the environment. As the population grows, this interaction increasingly takes the form of competition: vitally needed resources are not sufficient for all, and habitats with optimal conditions for existence are also limited. Not all individuals are destined to survive and leave progeny in a competitive environment. This is the third step of the evolutionary algorithm. Neo-Darwinists assert that competition is not always to the benefit of that population. Quite often, a particular individual achieves its ends at the expense of its species' wellbeing.

Richard Dawkins, in his book *The Selfish Gene* (Dawkins 1976), gives the following example. Common gulls settle in large colonies, making nests at a distance of about two metres from each other. Some birds come for nesting earlier so as to occupy the most convenient places. Accordingly, they are also the first to start hatching. As it turns out, these birds obtain better places to nest in, but the less favourable weather conditions they have to endure while hatching significantly increase the percentage of unhatched chicks. Dawkins concludes that the selfish gene, while allowing a single individual to obtain certain benefits, is generally detrimental to the population as a whole.

The history of human evolution provides numerous examples of this phenomenon, which I will attempt to address in more detail later by discussing some traps which destine civilizations to failure.

4. SELECTION

The fourth step of the evolutionary algorithm is selection. It is not organisms, nor species or populations that are selected, but the genes that create them!

This is what Dawkins writes about – the development of the first replicators: "Do not look for them floating loose in the sea; they gave up that cavalier freedom long ago. Now they swarm in huge colonies, safe inside gigantic lumbering robots, sealed off from the outside world, communicating with it by tortuous indirect routes, manipulating it by remote control. They are in you and in me; they created us, body and mind; and their preservation is the ultimate rationale for our existence. They have come a long way, those replicators. Now they go by the name of genes, and we are their survival machines."

At the same time, Dawkins points out that the theory of the selfish gene is the commonly known "Darwin's theory, expressed in a way that Darwin did not choose".

Dawkins is even convinced that Darwin would have recognized the relevance of the selfish gene theory: "It is in fact a logical outgrowth of orthodox Neo-Darwinism, but expressed as a novel image. Rather than focus on the individual organism, it takes a gene's-eye view of nature. It is a different way of seeing, not a different theory."

It is genes that are subject to selection, and not interacting organisms as it may appear. Apparently, evolution is a process of selecting possibilities out of a huge number of options, and this process unthinkingly grinds information about the design of things. Evolution selects mainly what works best and this process is repeated many times. A cycle does not have a predetermined end point, since the beginning of the next cycle is based on the result achieved in the previous one.

KNOWLEDGE PRODUCED BY BIOLOGICAL EVOLUTION

The connection between DNA and its environment is very close. As such, the evolution mechanism can act in various modes. Its toolkit contains adaptive steps and research leaps, as well as combinations of the two. First, when a local optimum is required, the genetic code makes adaptive steps: if one adaptive step improves the situation, the next step is made; otherwise, the original location is reverted to. But there are some adverse environmental conditions in which 'the ante has to be upped', so to speak, in order to survive, and then research leaps are made.

A direct analogy can be drawn between this technique and the active use of supportive and disruptive innovation principles in modern business models. Supportive innovation aims to improve continuously the quality of goods and services and to satisfy the most demanding clients. Such innovation is given the highest priority by companies that lead in their respective markets. Such companies have stable positions and loyal customers, i.e. the external conditions are generally favourable for them. The only thing they need to do is constantly monitor the situation and make timely adaptive steps.

Disruptive innovation works differently. Entrepreneurs whose business is focused on such innovation produce completely new products, and their main problem is not competition in the existing markets, but lack of demand in general. If successful, they form a new market. The market of 'classical' products is very difficult to enter for a start-up, and is already divided between its leaders with their popular brands, solid reputations, well-adjusted sales channels, and smoothly running production processes. In such harsh external conditions, evolution makes research leaps.

HUMANKIND'S DEPARTURE FROM BIOLOGICAL EVOLUTION

This biological process of obtaining and accumulating knowledge in genes remained almost unchanged until the appearance of man as a species. We were the first to be different from all other species, as until that time, all knowledge animals might need had been encoded in their brains genetically. We proved to be able to acquire knowledge ourselves.

Of course, this did not happen in a flash. First, mirror neurons appeared in the brains of the first humans and apes as a result of 'ordinary' mutations; then animal gesture became accompanied by sound. Later, we acquired a new ability, speech, and as we began to work with more objects, the more important this ability became. The need to associate movements with situations gave rise to the need to assign names to objects that existed in the external world. People developed a sign system. Animals also have it, but in a limited way – it is sufficient for them to distinguish between several dangerous situations and several types of cry signals. Man, on the other hand, increasingly got into new situations, and required new words. This is how our language became combinatorial in nature: individual sounds formed words, which were then combined into sentences. We outstripped the apes because we could invent new words, and thus introduce new concepts. Then, according to the well known statement by Friedrich Engels, work developed man from an anthropoid ape. Furthermore, according to Konrad Lorenz, the ability to produce complex objects accurately following a certain ideal model turned our mind into a universal constructor for conversion of anything into anything that is possible under the laws of nature. Thus, our brain as a new medium for storing information emerged. The human brain proved to be able to store information of any type.

This new information environment enabled the creation of a new way of learning. Man began to act by means of guessing, testing guesses by experiment, and criticizing, having left recombination by gene mutation and selection to nature.

The difference was huge. The human body became the first to be able to function outside a friendly environment. Moreover, mankind proved to be able to transform the terrestrial biosphere around it into its own vital provision system. In information terms, this means that we turned out to be a function capable of changing its own code. All this became possible thanks to the human brain and the development of communication skills!

Human knowledge is abstract replicators, information that has come into a suitable physical system (the brain) and remained there. Biological knowledge, in contrast, is only built up by preserving mutations. It is limited in terms of preservation and use, because it has no explanatory nature. Speaking in modern language, it is not cross-platform. Unlike explanatory human knowledge, it is difficult to transfer to another physical medium. Natural variations, or mutations, are random, while man purposefully presumes and builds hypotheses, having set a specific purpose first.

Aiming to preserve and disseminate knowledge, man invented an ancient writing systems, cuneiform, and then other forms of writing, then books. Mankind then carried out a revolution in the dissemination of knowledge by introducing the printing press, and, ultimately, made exchange of knowledge instantaneous through the internet.

In our world, all knowledge is produced in just two ways: in the process of biological evolution and through the use of man's creative thinking. However, I will say that in the final chapter of this book I suggest the possibility of a third method for producing knowledge – through artificial intelligence. In the last chapter, I will deliberate on the characteristics of future unnatural and superhuman knowledge.

MEMES AND CREATIVE THINKING ISOLATE MAN FROM THE BIOLOGICAL ENVIRONMENT

For lack of specific facts, taking a look at prehistoric human existence and the origins of human creative thinking is not a simple task. Its contours are hidden in the thick mists of time. Writing originated at about 3000 BC. Samples of early text are also very scarce, represented mainly by copies of the most famous works of their time. Where no written records of events were made, information was passed on from generation to generation through the human networks of inhabitants of early settlements and towns.

Scientists believe that Homo sapiens as we know it today appeared about 30,000 BC. By that time there were, according to various estimates, 3 to 4 million human beings on Earth, and this magnitude was maintained until about the 10th millennium BC, i.e. until the glacier began to retreat. This discrepancy between the number of humans and those of other large mammals serves as evidence that as early as from the time of its appearance, Homo sapiens in fact had no serious competition from any other species. Of course, one person, or even a small tribe, could be threatened by a pack of predators, but on the whole people could cope with any animals. In addition, with the help of tools, fortified homes, and fire, humans were able to expand significantly the range of their habitat. Any other species would need thousands or even millions of years of biological evolution to populate such areas. Man, however, did it much faster since he was the first not only to evolve as a species, but also to adapt his habitats to suit his needs, with the help of his revolutionary ability to create, use, store, and transfer knowledge, forming thus the sphere of human thought – the noosphere.

Today, our population is somewhere near 7 billion, although naturally this figure should not have exceeded 100,000. This is the natural limit for mammals of about the same weight and size as humans, since biology dictates that species closer to the top of the food pyramid must always number less than that of a species of smaller animals they feed on. Such was the population of our ancestors hundreds of thousands of years ago.

CAUSES FOR FUNDAMENTAL DIFFERENCES BETWEEN BIOLOGICAL EVOLUTION AND HUMAN EVOLUTION

What makes us different from animals? One of the most common answers to this question is the way we move, our bipedalism. A monkey can walk on two legs too, and so can bears in a circus. Of course, a human can do it for a longer time, but this is clearly not the point.

Another answer is language. However, many animals communicate using various sounds, and parrots can even mimic human speech. Does this mean that the only difference is that humans have a much more extensive vocabulary?

A third answer is the size of the brain. Yes, we have a brain that is larger than that of other animals similar to us in size. But it's obviously not the size of the brain that distinguishes a human from an ape. The argument that we use tools is not very coherent either, since apes and monkeys are also deft at using stones and sticks.

A fourth suggestion is organized society. But here we promptly recall ants – they also use other species to achieve their ends.

Another interesting hypothesis is that humans are different from animals in that they are able to disseminate knowledge through ideas (memes) and complexes of interrelated ideas (meme complexes). However, some animals also use memes, being able to imitate them (e.g. parrots). It should be noted though that imitation is not about repeating memes, but simply about copying behaviour. Replication is different from imitation, since it copies knowledge, and it is knowledge that prompts change in behaviour, not imitation.

To explain humankind's departure from the animal world, science has also proposed a climate hypothesis. Initially, this theory was put forward by

Charles Darwin, who rightly noted that large-scale climate change in any region may significantly affect the availability of conventional sources of food and other resources. This causes the extinction of some species whilst encouraging others to adapt. To obtain a climate record for ancient times, modern geologists are exploring the Earth's surface (hundreds of metres in depth) to obtain data for as far back as over a million years ago. According to the resultant geological data, on average, climate change has occurred every 20,000 years. It is known, for example, that North Africa had a period of wet climate some 5,000 to 10,000 years ago. The Sahara was covered with grass and vegetation. The Nile was affluent and brought its waters to the Mediterranean, where soil enriched with organic matter and sapropel accumulated.[3] Thus, man has repeatedly had the opportunity to make a qualitative leap in his development over the last three million years.

There are many hypotheses but, to me, one seems to provide an answer that can truly be considered the best of all: the main thing that distinguishes man is creative thinking. But what is creative thinking?

CREATIVE THINKING AND MEMES

It is interesting that until recently this question had been studied rather superficially. Wikipedia, when searched for information on 'creative thinking', refers to the concept of 'creativity', although the term 'creative thinking' is already in active use both in scientific communities and at the common level. David Deutsch, a British physicist known to the world not least due to his works on the theory of explanation, also uses the term 'creative thinking'. But he gives no clear definition to it either, only mentioning that it is a certain ability to think abstractly.

In his book *The Beginning of Infinity* he describes the processes associated with creative thinking (Deutsch 2011): "In prehistoric times it would not have been obvious to a casual observer... that humans were capable of creative thought at all. It would have seemed that we were doing no more than endlessly repeating the lifestyle to which we were genetically adapted, just like all the other billions of species in the biosphere. Clearly, we were tool-users – but so were many other species. Closer observation revealed that human languages and the knowledge for human tool use were being transmitted through memes and not genes. That made us fairly unusual, but still not obviously creative: several other species have memes. But what they do not have is the means of improving them other than through random trial and error. Nor are they capable of sustained improvement over many generations... Although we do not know exactly how creativity works, we do know that it is itself an evolutionary process within individual brains. For it depends on conjecture (which is variation) and criticism (for the purpose of selecting ideas). So, somewhere inside brains, blind variations and selections are adding up to creative thought at a higher level of emergence."

Thus, on the one hand, we have a kind of abstract thinking, while on the other, we only think logically at some level of our consciousness (emergence). To put it simply, while possessing emergent thinking, a person can think in abstract categories only within a certain system of concepts.

In fact, this is what differentiates us from animals. This actually is creative thinking. It is precisely through creative thinking that we use fire and tools and create communal organizations. Thanks to creative thinking and the knowledge of how to cooperate with their own kind, human populations reached 3 million back in 10,000 BC instead of staying within 100,000 as prescribed by the laws of evolution.

THE NEURAL NETWORK, THE CAPABILITIES OF THE BRAIN, AND THE WORK OF HUMAN CONSCIOUSNESS

Let's be clear: we still do not know how clusters of neurons generate consciousness in the human brain. We know only that consciousness and creative thinking are closely related. Moreover, there is no separate science today that studies consciousness only, despite the fact that many branches of knowledge touch upon this issue. There is no coherent concept. Some scientists study the activity of neurons, while others try to analyse the functions of the various parts of the brain, and very few attempt to combine several levels of brain study to find the solution to this difficult task. It is difficult to visualize intricate webs of neural connections, let alone recreate a structure that consists of the 100 billion nerve cells involved in processing information and passing it via thin fibres, whose total length adds up to 165,000 km, with over 150 trillion synapses.

It is known that the size of the human brain increased significantly in the process of natural selection. For example, three million years ago, the brain of an Australopithecus had a volume of about 450 cubic centimetres, which is comparable to the size of a chimpanzee's brain. 1.6 million years ago, Homo erectus had a brain whose volume was already 930 cubic centimetres on average. This species ate meat, was flexible and agile, and had a skeleton that looked similar to that of a modern human being. About 800,000 years ago, the ancient humans acquired fire and the first stone implements. Our predecessors left behind very little evidence of ingenuity. The oldest finds date back to about 3.4 million years ago, when our ancestors began to split rocks to create cutting implements. The next 1.6 million years were a lull period in terms of creativity, during which multi-functional hand-axes were made in the same old way without modification (Pringle 2013, 38). Then, 70,000 years ago, Homo sapiens' brain reached 1,300 cubic centimetres and according to some scientists, this increase resulted in an increase in the number of neurons activating recollection, which improved the species' memory and capability to think associatively.

With time, other changes took place in the human brain. Katerina Semendeferi, a physical anthropologist at the University of California, compared the prefrontal cortex of modern humans with that of chim-panzees and discovered that the distance between neurons on the level increased by about 50%. This, she believes, made it possible to create more complex links in the brain and increase significantly the level of interac-tion between neurons (Pringle 2013, 42).

It is impossible to say how these changes resulted in our consciousness taking control of gathering information about the external environment and the internal condition of the body, processing the collected infor-mation, and being able to create new information and provide adequate responses. Our consciousness is our coordinating centre.

In his book *Flow*, the American psychologist Mihaly Csikszentmihalyi uses a "phenomenological model of consciousness based on information theory". The model is called phenomenological because it deals directly with the phenomena of consciousness – events which we realize and inter-pret, rather than with the anatomical structures, neurochemical reactions or unconscious intentions that have determined these events. These are pure information theory principles which include knowledge of the pro-cedures of processing, storing, and reading out sensor information, i.e. the operation of attention and memory.

In this model, 'realize' means the ability to control or direct information flows from certain events we become conscious of (sensations, feelings, thoughts, intentions).

For a better understanding of this model, Csikszentmihalyi gives the following example: a person sees in a dream that his or her relative has had an accident and is highly upset by the fact. Despite being able to perceive information, experience feelings, think, and make decisions in the dream, the person does not affect these processes. In dreams, we are part of a single scenario, and cannot change it arbitrarily. But acting consciously, we can control our thoughts and the information we receive about the world from our senses.

But from the point of view of physics, we are a very limited biological machine. According to scientists' estimations, the human brain processes information at the rate of 126 bits per second. The speed in conventional computer channels is several hundred megabits per second. In other words, some of the already existing computers are millions of times faster than human consciousness. Nevertheless, we have our own advantages over computers.

EVOLUTIONARY ALGORITHM IN CONSCIOUSNESS

So why do we surpass computers at intelligence? After all, they can analyse millions of scenarios simultaneously, while a person can process no more than a dozen. I am sure that the reason lies in creative thinking again. The evolutionary algorithm works in the same way – a human simply selects a few scenarios, analyses them as far as possible, selects the best on a competitive basis and then, using his or her creative thinking abilities, amplifies it, moving on to a new cycle. Schematically, this process is shown in Figure 3.

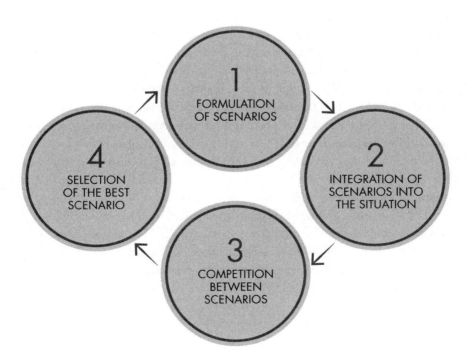

FIGURE 3. EVOLUTIONARY ALGORITHM IN HUMAN CONSCIOUSNESS

The power this unique ability gives to the best of our kind is demonstrated by the outstanding scientist Nikola Tesla. On one occasion, Tesla explicitly described the operating method of his former employer, another famous American inventor and businessman, Thomas Edison, in this manner: "If he had a needle to find in a haystack he would not stop to reason where it was most likely to be, but would proceed at once, with the feverish diligence of a bee, to examine straw after straw until he found the object of his search. His method was inefficient in the extreme, for an immense ground had to be covered to get anything at all unless blind chance intervened and, at first, I was almost a sorry witness of his doings, knowing that just a little theory and calculation would have saved him 90% of the labour. But he had a veritable contempt for book learning and mathematical knowledge, trusting himself entirely to his inventor's instinct and practical American sense." (Rzhonsnitsky 1959)

Nikola Tesla himself had an incredible imagination. In his own words, his ideas were not his brainchildren – he just drew knowledge from the vast library of the universe. He wrote about his method: "The moment one constructs a device to carry into practice a crude idea, he finds himself unavoidably engrossed with the details of the apparatus. As he goes on improving and reconstructing, his force of concentration diminishes and he loses sight of the great underlying principle. Results may be obtained, but always at the sacrifice of quality. My method is different. I do not rush into actual work. When I get an idea, I start at once building it up in my imagination. I change the construction, make improvements and operate the device in my mind. It is absolutely immaterial to me whether I run my turbine in thought or test it in my shop… Invariably my device works as I conceived that it should, and the experiment comes out exactly as I planned it. In twenty years there has not been a single exception. Why should it be otherwise?" (Rzhonsnitsky 1959)

Tesla sincerely believed that an idea could not be embodied until the project had been thought out down to the last detail. This does not mean that he insisted on paying attention to every smallest detail, but merely that the basic principles of the invention had to be thought out thoroughly.

MEMES, NETWORK DENSITY, AND THE CREATIVITY OF ANCIENT PEOPLE

Knowledge is passed from person to person via memes. A meme is transferred from one generation to the next without change until someone improves its concept. It is reasonable to assume that the larger the group of people in which a meme is kept (the so-called 'network'), the more opportunities arise to improve its concept. In larger groups, individuals have numerous social ties and, therefore, more chance of obtaining new information than in small, isolated groups.

Mark Thomas, a Professor of Evolutionary Genetics at University College London, has built a model for studying the impacts of demographics on the progress of mankind. Using the model, he compared the density of population in Europe during the Upper Palaeolithic (between 50,000 and 10,000 years ago and characterized by paleontological evidence of an increase in man's abilities) with that in Africa 100,000 years ago. The model made it possible to predict periodic progress in the manufacture of tools depending on the density of population. Artefacts found in sub-Saharan Africa confirmed the suggestions made by the model, i.e. evidence of human progress in that area was seen at a time when its population reached a density comparable with that in Europe in the early days of the Upper Palaeolithic. The message is clear: broad social networks dramatically increase the creative activity of its members (Pringle 2013, 43).

The results of Thomas's research are consistent with the views held by many scientists. Thus, according to Curtis Marean, a professor of archaeology at Arizona State University, Homo sapiens almost completely populated the African continent and learned how to use the abundant food resources of the coastal ecosystems approximately 160,000 to 120,000 years ago. Some 70,000 years ago, man invented projectile weapons, left Africa 70,000 to 55,000 years ago, entered Europe, and exterminated the Neanderthals almost 45,000 years ago (Marean 2015, 10).

According to Canadian journalist Heather Pringle, the presence of archaeological evidence of early technical and cultural inventions made by humans supports the idea that human creativity manifested itself 90,000 to 60,000 years ago in Africa and about 40,000 years ago in Europe. This suggestion is evidenced by finds of man-made beads of shells, highly artistic petroglyphs of animals, and new types of stone and bone implements. However, much more ancient evidence has been discovered in the last few years, indicating that human species were able to create new objects before Homo sapiens appeared – some 200,000 years ago.

Pondering on the origin of human creativity, Heather Pringle believes that "humanity had a spark of creativity smouldering for millennia before it burst into full blaze in Africa and Europe. Apparently, the ability to create new things did not emerge suddenly in the later stages of evolution, but was gaining momentum for hundreds of thousands of years, fuelled by a complex mixture of biological and social factors" (Pringle 2013, 38).

In terms of creative accomplishments, the difference between the modern humans and the first Homo sapiens is enormous. This difference is a subject of study for many researchers who are trying to understand what exactly distinguishes our brain from our ancestors', and when humankind's creative thinking reached the critical level of development that made it possible for our civilisation to start advancing.

HOW THE HUNTER-GATHERERS FELL INTO THE FIRST TRAP

It was discovered recently that the ancient humans that inhabited today's Europe, China, and Africa appeared to be on the brink of extinction about 60,000 years ago, as their numbers had fallen sharply. The glacial climate had made large areas of Eurasia inhospitable for a large number of animal species. But the ancestors of modern humans were able to withstand the low temperatures, and began to proliferate and inhabit new areas rapidly, as the widespread use of new tools facilitated their advancement.

Ian Tattersall of the American Museum of Natural History in New York believes that it is since then that man has been processing information about the outside world in a completely new way. In his opinion, as far as one can judge, we are the only creatures that can visualize the environment and their own experiences in the form of abstract symbols they can play with in their minds, creating new versions of reality: in addition to what has been, we can imagine what could have been as well (Vishnyatsky 2010).

Although humanity successfully passed the cold test, it was only the glacier retreat (10,000 BC) that created favourable conditions for human proliferation throughout the majority of the world. At that point, hunting and gathering laid the foundation for the 'prehistoric' human economy.

Hunting proved to be the first 'ecological' trap for man, as the development of new tools and food production techniques led over time to a food surplus, the consequence of which was that the natural balance that limited our species' population was upset.

By the middle of the Stone Age, people had adapted to the climate and developed new tools for the procurement of animal and plant resources. Fishing emerged, as well as marine mammal hunting and clam collecting.

Knowledge was accumulated and tools improved through the whole of the Stone Age. At some point in their development, people, united in tribes, were able to deal with any animals and cope with minor natural disasters. The hitherto traditional threats became less important. After bows and arrows, spears, and traps for animals had been improved, clashes between tribes became the most likely source of danger for people, and this factor gave a strong impetus to the development of social relations. Further development of communication skills in the form of speech brought considerable success in this area.

The first people hunted large animals, but took from nature no more than they needed for their subsistence. Their numerous descendants, who were equipped much better, killed wildlife in huge numbers.

The invention of the driven hunt was the first innovation that changed humankind's primitive 'economy'. At Solutré, a town on the territory of modern France, the remains of 100,000 horses were found, and at Przhedmost, the Czech Republic, the bones of more than a thousand ancient mammoths. Thus, the first economic crisis in the world was provoked, causing hunger. Nikita Moiseyev, a prominent Soviet and Russian scientist, wrote, "…Having improved weapons, people very quickly… exterminated all large ungulates and mammoths that had formed the basis of their diet in early Neolithic times, and now hunting could no longer ensure enough sustenance for them. Humankind was on the verge of starvation, and doomed to degradation. It was really facing the threat of disappearing from the face of the earth at all, as many other species had before. Apparently, many of our ancestors' populations were on the verge of extinction. And some of them did become extinct, unable to cope with the difficulties, or were exterminated by other human populations in their struggle for the resource base which they all shared." (Moiseyev, 1990)

American biologist Edward Divey estimates the world population at that time (approximately 10,000 BC) to have totalled about 5 million (Mellaart 1965).

The invisible inner work of our brain, which merely watched and studied the world around it for a long time, has made us who we are now – humans.

CHAPTER 2

NEOLITHIC REVOLUTION AND THE FIRST CIVILIZATIONS

" A nation is born stoic and dies epicurean... "

– Will Durant

Early man managed to escape from the hunger trap by moving to sedentary life and creating agriculture. So considerable is the significance of this phenomenon that in order to characterize it, V. Gordon Childe, a renowned Australian archaeologist and prehistorian, introduced a special term, 'the Neolithic Revolution', in 1949. In his view, the agricultural revolution which began about 10,000 years ago transformed the human economy, giving man control over his own food reserves (Childe 1950). However, there are also alternative versions of how the innovation entitled 'agriculture' was assembled.

Apparently, the advent of agriculture caused the appearance of a range of subsequent cultural phenomena that were united by the fact that they were all based on symbols. With symbols, 'cultural filters' that separated man from his experiences emerged. The domestication of animals and plants laid the foundations of agricultural production, intensified the division of labour, and paved the way for primary stratification of society. With agriculture, man acquired 'work'. Hunter-gatherers had had no work as such, as there was not much need for them to toil every day to accumulate reserves.

Now that humans had started to work, they needed not only to accumulate food reserves and find methods for their preservation, but also to accumulate information about stocks, as well as to develop methods to account for work done. With this division of labour, antagonisms appeared.

Interestingly, no images made before the Neolithic Period depicted people killing other people. According to estimates, the average population density at the time of hunters and gatherers was just one person per 100 square kilometres! There were not enough people to fight other people, since nature posed much greater threats to humans. In fact, the first images of battles between people, as well as early prototypes of urban layouts, appear in the Neolithic Period.

The emergence of the phenomenon of forced labour gave rise to rituals, hierarchy, violence, and political institutions. At the same time, the transition to sedentary life prompted an increase in birth rates and contributed to reducing the age difference between the children of one mother. This was because a nomadic woman could only carry one child, while the rest of her children had to follow the tribe on their own feet. Children could only move quickly on their own feet if aged four years or older, and it was this factor that caused the age difference between the children of one mother at the time. Obviously, this advantage offered by sedentary life alone contributed to a significant increase in population. The ensuing population growth created an even greater surplus of food, and the process went on with increasing momentum.

As a result of this positive feedback, the gap between the 'fed, numerous, and technically advanced' and the 'hungry, sparse, and backward' sharply increased over time. Exterminating their own kind, depriving them of arable land, sacrificing the natural environment, reducing the life span of many generations of descendants, Neolithic man started the mechanism of accelerated exploitation of nature for quick extraction of wealth. Agricultural production led to the creation of new products that did not have analogues in nature and whose production very soon exhausted its capabilities.

The production of food surpluses brought numerous benefits to their owners, and humanity as a whole managed to grow in number. The population density increased significantly, by tens of times, as people only cultivated plants they needed. In agriculture, up to 90% of the biomass was edible, and one hectare of arable land provided enough food for up to 100 times more people than before. Animal husbandry caused a further increase in the quantity of calories produced per unit of area of farmland, as livestock produced offspring and manure and could be used as draft animals. However, there were problems too. On the one hand, with the invention of agriculture, our ancestors partially insured themselves against starvation, because now they could grow food for themselves even within a limited area of land. On the other hand, crop production within limited areas created a potential for rapid destruction of the environment, and led to changes in vast areas which invariably become more and more arid, since natural processes could not keep up with agricultural production. Scientists call this a mismatch between social and natural processes.

Today, deserts occupy a considerable part of the areas where ancient civilizations had once flourished. There is plenty of historical evidence demonstrating that these civilizations inevitably destroyed the environment. Throughout history agricultural progress has, as a rule, been accompanied by environmental setbacks.

Jared Diamond describes these processes in great detail in his book *Guns, Germs and Steel* (Diamond 1997). Diamond explains how the production of food surpluses created a vicious circle in society. The 'agrarians' constantly modified their tools, and accumulated and applied knowledge, which led to developments that enabled them to warm their homes and gave them confidence in providing steady sustenance for their tribes. Animal husbandry gave people new materials – wool, cotton, and bone – which in turn gave rise to the development of crafts. But each time, having got out of one trap by exploiting nature, humanity fell into another.

With the growth of population, more and more pasture was needed to feed the growing numbers of animals. The emergence of settlements in which people could live comfortably meant at the same time the tethering of those people to certain areas.

PEASANTS AT WORK. GUAM, THE MARIANA ARCHIPELAGO.
An engraved copy from a painting by Denis-Sebastien Leroy,
included in the World Tour series, 1817-1820

ALTERNATIVE VERSIONS OF THE EMERGENCE OF AGRICULTURE

Note that not all historians consider the appearance of agriculture to be a consequence of a severe food crisis.

Tim Flannery, an Australian palaeontologist, believes that there is no evidence to suggest that the emergence of agriculture was due to overpopulation. The famous explorer Carl O. Sauer, who believed that agricultural activity was not brought about by an increase in food supplies or a chronic lack of food, based his conclusion on the fact that ancient agriculture could not guarantee a stable food base due to the imperfection of the ancient agricultural technologies. So, how did agriculture emerge after all?

There are many theories, including some most unexpected ones. For example, according to Khan and Isaac (Zerzan 2016), food production began on the basis of religious activity. Some scientists believe this to be the most plausible hypothesis.

ARATRO, SEMINATOJO EC.

WHAT HUMANITY PAID FOR THE TRANSITION TO A SEDENTARY LIFE, AND WHAT IT GAINED

Our civilization is now based on the cultivation of several varieties of plants, including wheat, barley, millet, rice, maize, and potatoes. For the sake of repletion, we have reduced the biological diversity of our food.

Biologist Peter Farb concluded that "agriculture provides humans with food of lower quality, since it is based on the production of a limited number of foodstuffs". For a long time it was believed that our ancient ancestors died aged 30 to 40, and that this life expectancy continued until the industrial age. But now, many scientists recognize that during the Palaeolithic Period, once certain threats had been eliminated, people lived long lives, and life expectancy only dropped sharply when humanity created an agrarian civilization.

Jared Diamond, an American scientist and author, has called the emergence of agriculture a catastrophe which we have never managed to recover from: "Tuberculosis and diarrhoea had only to wait for crop farming to come, and measles and bubonic plague, for the emergence of large cities. Malaria and virtually all other infectious diseases are heirs to agriculture. Degeneration-related diseases appeared when domestication came to power and culture developed. The spread of cancer, coronary thrombosis, anaemia, dental caries, and mental insanity are just a few examples of the negative effects of agriculture; women used to give birth much easier and with less pain, if any at all" (Diamond 1997).

What did humanity gain? James Mellaart, one of the most prominent British archaeologists, calculated (with reference to Edward Divey) that following humankind's transition to agriculture, the world's population grew 16 times over 1,000 years, surpassing the 80 million mark!

People could no longer, as before, leave their fields and set off in search of a better life. The process of obtaining food became purposeful production rather than spontaneous action. This brought people stability and orderliness, but made them work to live. Agriculture enabled humanity to escape from the hunger trap, which led to a dramatic increase in population and, consequently, to an increase in the number of interconnections between them. Humanity remained in this situation until the first known civilization was created (approx. 5800 BC) (Mellaart 1965, 48).

The increase in population density and the complexity of relations could not proceed without conflict. Ancient people would resolve issues and abstain from killing each other by determining consanguinity during general meetings in their settlements. Such communities still exist in some countries. The so-called 'Great Man', a highly respected distinguished member of the community, would decide how to resolve conflicts within the tribe without bringing the matter to a blood feud.

In a primitive economy, the selection process was fairly straightforward: a tribe that hunted better and used their food more rationally would survive and lead to further generations. But as the economy and society grew and became more interdependent, the feedback from the natural selection process became less significant. The first conflicts in such societies emerged when the Great Man began to allocate resources to his own benefit and to the benefit of his family rather than taking decisions guided by the interests of the whole tribe. When the tribe's main task was to survive, such decisions led to either the extinction of the opposing tribe or the removal of the individual in question from his position. As settlements grew, civilization emerged, and wealth accumulated, people became even more dependent on their social groups, and less on nature.

In extreme cases, such situations hindered economic evolution and even led to famine over substantial periods. Thus, society was faced with a huge problem: the bigwig began to distort the function of natural selection.

Still, apart from the need to solve personal problems, there was a great need for structural centralized solutions. The economies of the first states depended on the collection of taxes in kind and their subsequent distribution in a rational way. Bigwigs became the centre, around which segmented and small autonomous communities united to provide food. From this all tribal structures originated.

At the time of the first settlements, a pronounced adaptive nature became typical of human society. It acquired features of statehood, and mechanisms for administration, and coercion. Thus, as population density grew, a need to construct large irrigation systems for arable farming arose.

In Table 1, a functional and historical classification of the typology of early social formations is provided, demonstrating how the growth of a social group affected the development of relationships between its members and led to the emergence of the first states.

	BAND	TRIBE	CHIEFDOM	STATE
Number of people	Dozens	Hundreds	Thousands	Over 50,000
Settlement pattern	Nomadic	Fixed: 1 village	Fixed: 1 or more villages	Fixed: many villages and cities
Decision making	'Egalitarian'[5]	'Egalitarian'	Centralized	Centralized
Bureaucracy	None	None	None, or 1 or 2 levels	Many levels
Conflict resolution	Informal	Informal	Centralised	Laws, judges
Food production	No	No, or begins to emerge	Gradually intensifies	Intensive
Division of labour	No	No	No, or begins to emerge	Yes
Exchanges	Mutual	Mutual	Redistributive ('tribute')	Redistributive ('taxes')

TABLE 1. TYPES OF EARLY SOCIETIES[4]

According to Diamond's classification, though the populations of the states that existed around 5000 BC did not exceed 50,000, the density of the human network was already such that it stimulated the creation of centralized decision making and the emergence of bureaucracy, laws, courts, and money.

There are many theories explaining the emergence of the state as a social innovation. Philosophers and public figures have put forward new ideas on this subject since antiquity. But a more original theory suggested that states were formed around vast irrigation systems.[6] There is, however, growing evidence demonstrating that states appeared first and that irrigation systems followed. Even in ancient Egypt, there was a large number of channels that were controlled by numerous tribes rather than by a central government headed by a pharaoh.[7]

One of the main theories of the origin of the state explains its emergence by the necessity to coerce people into maintaining order. As soon as people began to store food reserves, taking foodstuffs from others by force became the most obvious and easiest way of provision. But such gains had to be protected from both external and internal enemies, distributed, and even used to generate additional revenue. This idea is well known, and it was first formulated by Thomas Hobbes, who believed that war was a manifested consequence of the selfish nature of man who was focused exclusively on his own interests.[8] From this Hobbes drew the conclusion that war of all against all would be inevitable if there were no state. The state, according to him, normalized people's aggression, putting it on a rational track.

THE FIRST IN HISTORY: THE ROLE OF THE SUMERIAN CIVILIZATION

The Sumerians were one of the oldest nations that emerged in southern Mesopotamia (modern-day southern Iraq), in the mid-6th millennium BC. The first civilization formed where the climate was less severe. At the time when the European hunter-gatherers still fished and hunted small predators, the Sumerians already had an advanced civilization.

Sumerian inscriptions, represented on clay tablets, appeared around 3500 BC, and give a certain idea of what the Sumerians looked like, what type of economy they had, what gods they worshipped, how they brought up children, and much more. The famous British historian Arnold J. Toynbee wrote that the Sumerian society had inherited nothing from its predecessors, but all societies that came after it turned out to be inextricably linked with it. In essence, he argued that the Sumerians were the first highly developed civilization (Toynbee 1934).

They knew how to drain swamps, build dams, and dig canals to bring water to arid regions. They were the first to achieve high yields from arable land and to grow date palm trees, mimosas, willows, and many other plants in irrigated areas. In their numerous cities, they built palaces and temples and decorated them with colourful mosaics made of coloured clay.

The Sumerians showed an amazing zeal for science and possessed unique knowledge in mathematics and astronomy. Their achievements in geography, physics, chemistry, medicine (healing fractures and classifying diseases), history, philology, warfare (building fortresses), and agriculture amaze modern scientists. The Sumerians invented the wheel, schools, a calendar, a bicameral parliament, and a scientific journal ('farmers' almanac').[9] They were the first to produce a collection of proverbs and aphorisms, and books (in the form of clay tables), introduced taxes, laws, carried out social reforms, and made the first attempts to achieve peace and harmony in society. The Sumerians invented the diamond drill and the waterwheel and devised and started to use the 'Archimedean screw' for irrigation (a mechanism for lifting water from low-lying bodies of water to irrigation canals) long before Archimedes. They built the first aqueduct in the world and erected ziggurats – amazing towers that were the forerunners of the future pyramids.

The first kilns and smelting furnaces appeared in Sumer too. Historians were extremely surprised to find that the Sumerians had methods for ore beneficiation and metal smelting and casting. They mastered these advanced technologies just a few centuries after the emergence of their civilization.

Moreover, they invented the concepts of capital and interest! Interest to be given as a surplus product to cover the risks of when priests, who owned storage facilities, gave portions of their stockpiles to merchants to take and trade in faraway lands. The Sumerians' mathematical knowledge enabled them to do such calculations, and later this practice was extended to commodity loans – allowances that priests gave to hired peasants in grain, to be returned later with a surplus. But how did they do it without money? They would produce clay tablets with information about debts and once the debt had been repaid, the tablet would be broken. So essentially, the first clergymen were also merchants and bankers.

The economic basis of the Sumerians' state was the country's centralized and state-owned land stock. Communal lands, cultivated by free peasants, were considered property of the state, and the populace was obliged to carry out various duties and pay taxes in kind.

What did they use to pay taxes if money in our sense did not yet exist? Here is what David Graeber, an American anthropologist, writes in his highly interesting book *Debt*: "…Credit systems… actually preceded the invention of coinage by thousands of years. As it happens, we know a great deal about Mesopotamia, since the vast majority of cuneiform documents were financial in nature… Temple administrators already appear to have developed a single, uniform system of accountancy – one that is in some ways still with us, actually, because it's to the Sumerians that we owe such things as the dozen or the 24-hour day. The basic monetary unit was the silver shekel. A shekel was subdivided into 60 minas, corresponding to one portion of barley… It's easy to see that 'money' in this sense is in no way the product of commercial transactions. It was actually created by bureaucrats in order to keep track of resources and move things back and forth between departments. Peasants who owed money… settled their debts mostly in barley, but it was perfectly acceptable to show up with goats, or furniture, or lapis lazuli. Temples and palaces were huge industrial operations – they could find a use for almost anything. We did not begin with barter, discover money, and then eventually develop credit systems. It happened precisely the other way around. What we now call virtual money came first." (Graeber 2011)

So, this is how it began: credit, work, interest, debt, and money – these all emerged a long time ago. Once in place, these engendered a surprising phenomenon: slavery.

In the societies of the first settlements, it was land that served as the main asset that brought profit. If a war broke out and enemy territory was captured, any captives taken were simply killed. It was economically inefficient to keep them alive, as slaves did not produce a surplus product, being able to only feed themselves.

In the Sumerian society, however, representatives of the ruling dynasties and priesthood (a relatively small percentage of the population) became the class of decision makers, implementers and the main agents of change. Due to a high population density and productivity having increased considerably as a result of breeding plants and introducing progressive agricultural practices, slavery became profitable at some point.

The Sumerians' view on slavery was significantly different from that of today. At that time, a poor harvest and the inability to pay out debts meant that a peasant, or his wife and children, could be taken as slaves if there was no livestock to be taken away in repayment. Children who were born into slavery were also deprived of freedom. In fact, people served as a kind of money, and their work, as well as their progeny, were born into slavery, as interest. With the advent of slavery, the first fully fledged economic crises came. During years of harvest failure, slaves became so numerous that slavery turned out to be inefficient as a form of debt repayment and an amnesty was declared (with all debts forgiven or cancelled), and the accumulated stocks (collected as in-kind taxes) reduced the risk of mass starvation and extinction. In Babylon, such amnesties took place in spring, during the annual celebration of the New Year: debt tablets were broken, detainees released to their families, and land that had been taken away for debts was returned.

Having fallen, Sumer left after itself a number of notions that were taken over by many other peoples. Among these notions were religion, commodity and credit relations, and the inexplicable love for silver and… Egyptian gold.[10]

THE SECRET OF THE EGYPTIAN CIVILIZATION[11]

The history of ancient Egypt begins around 3000 BC. The two-volume book, *History of Egypt*, written by Egyptian priest Manetho, who lived during the time of Alexander the Great's campaigns, tells us that there were three main periods: the Old Kingdom, the Middle Kingdom, and the New Kingdom (ruled by 30 dynasties altogether). Although no precise knowledge is available about that time, new information is constantly being gathered, as archaeologists unearth more and more artefacts each year.

For millennia, people lived in Egypt because of the fertile floodplain of the Nile River. The Nile's floods provided four harvests each year. Cereals, legumes, and various vegetables were grown. Apart from the usual wine made from grapes, wine was also produced by fermenting dates or palm juice. Papyrus served as a reliable material for ship rigging, cane and date palm fibre were used for weaving mats and baskets, and linen was grown to produce fabrics that ranged from sackcloth to the finest textiles.

Cattle, sheep, goats, geese, and pigs, whose skin could be tanned and dyed, laid the basis for dozens of branches in the ancient economy. The abundant production of dairy goods, honey, and fish, as well as the wide availability of sun-dried products and salt as a natural preservative, allowed for the creation of significant reserves.

There were no horses in Egypt until the end of the Middle Kingdom, when Asian nomads, the Hyksos, penetrated the valley of the Nile on horses and chariots. Before that, donkeys had been used as the primary transport vehicle, and cows harnessed for ploughing.

Thereafter, chariots and ships (another Hyksos innovation) formed the basis of expansion led by the pharaohs of the New Kingdom (Ramses II, Akhenaten, and Thutmose III). Chariots proved to be a manoeuvrable weapon similar to the role tanks played in the twentieth century. The Egyptians terrified their enemies by swift breakthroughs, and battles quickly turned into a pursuit to exterminate.[12]

As Egypt lacked good timber for construction, it was imported from Lebanon. It would seem that the Egyptians had developed credit arrangements at around the same time as the ancient Sumerians. However, no data is available about trade crediting in ancient Egypt, and all loans, as far as we know, took the form of mutual aid agreements between neighbours (Graeber 2011, 218). No interest was charged either. To resolve disputes, courts were consulted. A debtor who had failed to pay would have received lashes as punishment or would have been ordered to pay double the outstanding amount.

Why did foreign trade not trigger the development of credit relations? This was because the rulers of Egypt had an exclusive product, gold, which enabled them to trade successfully with other countries, enjoying a sort of monopoly on liquidity. The first gold in the world was found in the Arabian Desert. Throughout the Copper Age (3900-2100 BC), gold was mined only in that region. During that period, about 700 tonnes were produced. Since gold had to be panned out, significant numbers of slaves were required for its production.

Soon after, it was found that Egypt possessed another incredibly rich gold-bearing region, Nubia and South Sudan. The precious metal occurred there in various forms – from pure gold to white gold, which Egyptians thought to be silver.[13] Gold brought Egypt indisputable authority. Other Middle Eastern societies developed aphorisms that the Egyptians had more gold than dirt. Egyptian tombs dated as far back as 2400 BC demonstrate this, with pictures of gold smelters busily working at ancient metallurgical furnaces.

Plentiful natural resources and local production made ancient Egypt rich and powerful. The birth rate had increased, although infant mortality had also grown. By the reign of the 11th dynasty (XXII-XX centuries BC), the country's population totalled about one million.[14]

By 1090 BC gold mining in Egypt virtually declined to nothing, and the country lost its monopoly as alternative major mines opened in areas occupied by Spain and France today, as well as in the Balkans (Marfunin 1987, 14).

Gold and a high turnover of generations account for the longevity of the Egyptian civilization.[15] Only with the advent of the Iron Age, shortly before the Persian conquest of Egypt, did the first debt crises break out, similar to those seen by the Sumerians earlier. Historians believe Pharaoh Bocchoris to have been the first to provide a serious debt amnesty in Egypt (720-715 BC). He felt that it was "ridiculous to send a soldier to fight for his homeland while he was threatened by a lender because of having failed to repay the loan" (Graeber 2011, 219). Soon after, however, Egypt was conquered by Rome, and the role gold had played in its history was taken over by wheat.

CHINA'S MYSTERIES

Although numerous studies have been conducted to elucidate the origin of the Chinese, as far as we know, the question still remains unanswered. Regardless, the first Chinese tribes arrived on the banks of the Yellow River in 2500-3000 BC, and certainly differed from the natives, having a more advanced culture. Once there, the early Chinese started to wage bitter wars with the indigenous tribes. About a million people had lived there in different tribes (predecessors of the Tibeto-Burman peoples), and the figure doubled after the Chinese invasion. As the new arrivals from the north spread, the tribes of indigenous population were exterminated, assimilated, or displaced south, to areas unsuitable for residence. Gradually the ancient Chinese' character changed, and the aggressiveness gave way to a deep inner sense of the superiority of the Chinese race.

China's landscape is shaped by three mountain systems and huge alluvial plateaus with fertile soils in the northern, western, and southern parts. The mountains appeared to be rich in natural resources, containing coal, iron, gold, silver, copper, lead, and tin. China's territory is crossed by three great rivers and numerous others; it is not surprising therefore that rice was the main crop grown there in ancient times. In his book, *Why Europe?* Jack Goldstone, an American sociologist, says, "Rice plants have many more seeds or kernels per plant than wheat; thus, much less of the crop had to be kept for seeding the next harvest, and more edible food could be harvested per acre. In addition, because flooding the fields helped fertilize the soil and keep down weeds, and far less animal power was needed for ploughing, rice cultivation needed no fallow period and required little land for grazing" (Goldstone 2009, 11).

The monsoons made it possible, as in Egypt and Mesopotamia, to bring in harvests several times a year. But sometimes droughts and floods brought terrible famine for millions of people. As in Egypt and Mesopotamia, these events led to the emergence of a new relationship between large groups of people in China. David Graeber explains in his book *Debt* that "…China's rulers instituted the custom of retaining 30% of the harvest in public granaries for redistribution in emergencies. In other words, they began to set up just the kind of bureaucratic storage facilities that, in places like Egypt and Mesopotamia, had been responsible for creating money as a unit of account to begin with."

Referencing the ancient Chinese political and philosophical text Guanzi, Graeber mentions a severe famine where people were forced to sell their children. To rescue these people, Emperor Tang began minting money out of copper. This money was called 'merciful', and it appeared a thousand years before the official origins of coined money in China (Graeber 2011, 220).

As a result of conquests, China's borders moved considerably during these times. In the 11th century BC, ancient China was conquered by the Zhou dynasty, and by the 7th century BC, the whole country was divided into provinces, with the emperor acting as the guarantor and the head of the legislative and administrative power. Each subordinate ruler replicated this structure within the boundaries of his province. The Chinese created an excellent legal system. The entire population was divided into four groups: administrators and academics, peasants, craftsmen and artisans, and merchants. China's tax system followed this division: peasants paid land and taxes, artisans and merchants paid tithes, and administrators collected taxes. Similar to Native American civilizations, the Chinese imposed special taxes on the tribes they conquered.

With the Chinese having transformed its aggressiveness into a profound sense of superiority, its rulers avoided any political alliances, believing in their own invincibility, even when suffering defeat by invaders. This was because the Chinese had a special cultural code rooted in the national education. Advancing into public service would be absolutely impossible without knowledge of the works of Confucius or Mengzi, or without calligraphy skills or the ability to write poetry. Education had a high value because its owner could hold public office and thus had prospects of improving the standing of his family.[16] Career paths began at an early age, and the tradition still exists, having lasted for millennia.

Of particular importance are special 'Chinese ethics' and a special racial theory. The advantages of a Chinese man, such as patience and reserve, honesty and commitment to obligations, were valued only when displayed towards Chinese people. Cheating a stranger could, on the contrary, be regarded as a virtue in some cases. The arrogant attitude of the Chinese towards other nations continued for centuries, and was only superseded by way of inheritance by the Manchu people who conquered the Chinese.

It is known that Chinese emperors subjected ambassadors of inferior races to humiliating ceremonies called the Koto.[17] The ambassador had to crawl on all fours into the hall where the audience was to be held and then, kneeling, prostrate himself nine times before the emperor. In the early 20th century, Sun Yat-sen (Former President of the Republic of China) indicated that the loss of Chinese nationalism centuries earlier was the cause of China's deplorable state...

An important fact about China's economy at that time is that production solely depended on the efficiency of the workforce and the exploitation of animals. Machines as an important economic factor appeared in China only in the 20th century. For many years, two-thirds of the country's population were involved in farming, which kept peasants busy most of the time, with two harvests collected every year in the north of the country and up to five every two years in the south.

Chinese merchants traded with West Asia, Greece, Rome, Carthage (Tunisia), and Arabia, and later, starting from the 17th century, mostly with European countries, while the major trade routes did not change in 2,000 years! Trade was based on barter transactions, and European goods were exchanged for fabrics, tea, and porcelain. At some point in time, Europeans began to give silver bullion as payment for goods.

It appears that it was tradition based on deep interconnection between the resources of the land and the dominant culture that enabled Mesopotamia, Egypt, and China to take good care of their civilizations. These nations were dynastic empires, where change was slower, which meant that in periods of economic decline, the environment had time to recover. Conservatism in the development of agricultural technology naturally limited the growth of the population in these territories.[18] For a long time, the populations of these countries were sufficient to feed themselves without the need to exploit natural resources.

Ironically, these same reasons led to the regression of these countries in the 19th-20th centuries.

UNHAPPY FAMILIES

Not all ancient civilizations developed harmoniously. The lesson to be learned from history and the first civilizations is the importance of correctly selecting a cultural code for the society and preserving it to support the culture and, therefore, the health of the soil, water, and forests for future generations, and thus create auspicious conditions for the accumulation of wealth. Otherwise, the inconsistency of the pace of economic development launches a series of destructive cycles, and the lucky clover languishes and wilts. In Egypt and Mesopotamia, a series of food crises were brought about solely by droughts and floods. In later civilizations, it was the people themselves who quarrelled with their own bread and butter.[19] As noted earlier, pasturing of the first domesticated ruminants was the main factor in the desertification of the Roman Empire, as well as the reason for entire regions (Greece, Lebanon, and North Africa) having lost grass cover almost completely (Diamond 1997).

Plato described the damage very vividly in his unfinished dialogue *Critias*: "There was abundance of wood in the mountains, of which the last traces still remain, for although some of the mountains now only afford sustenance to bees, not so very long ago there were still to be seen roofs of timber cut from trees growing there, which were of a size sufficient to cover the largest houses; and there were many other high trees, cultivated by man and bearing abundance of food for cattle. Moreover, the land reaped the benefit of the annual rainfall, not as now losing the water which flows off the bare earth into the sea, but, having an abundant supply in all places, and receiving it into herself and treasuring it up in the close clay soil, it let off into the hollows the streams which it absorbed from the heights, providing everywhere abundant fountains and rivers, of which there may still be observed sacred memorials in places where fountains once existed; and this proves the truth of what I am saying" (Kukal 1988).

Similarly, in ancient Rome, with an increasing demand for wood in the capital and other cities, a massive deforestation began. Swamps formed in several watersheds due to loss of connection between the slopes and the estuaries. Although Rome existed for several centuries, it became obvious over time that its economy and agriculture had already been significantly undermined by continuous deforestation and massive pasturing.

Rapidly growing civilizations meant that humankind had fallen into another trap which further enslaved people and distanced them from nature, making man and nature antagonists.

The same laws of development manifested themselves in the New World (the majority of the Western Hemisphere, specifically the Americas). David Webster, a researcher and the author of a book on the fall of the Mayan civilization (the indigenous people of Central America), explains its collapse by overpopulation and agrarian failure to cope with all the concurrent political implications (Webster 2002). The rulers of the Tikal kingdom, now Guatemala (Kukal 1988), faced an impending crisis and were compelled to take measures to reduce government and military spending, and either make efforts to develop land through terracing or stimulate a decline in fertility.[20] But the Maya rulers did not want to change the general policy and proceeded with environmentally destructive activities on an even larger scale. This decision resulted in higher pyramids, more power for leaders, more work for people, and more wars. In this way the Maya government elite deprived their own people of the last gifts of nature.

The New World was less fortunate in a number of other respects as well. Diamond believes that the slow population growth in the New World can be explained by the original lack of large-seeded cereals in America (where only maize was known) and animals suitable for domestication (Diamond 1997, 114).

The origins of the world's key animal and plant species potentially suitable for domestication proved to be distributed rather unevenly over the planet. Most of today's animals and plants come from the environs of the Fertile Crescent (cows, horses, sheep, goats, barley, oats, and both one-grained and two-grained wheat), from China (pigs, hens, rice, and millet), and, in some cases, from India, Egypt, and Abyssinia (Ethiopia).[21] Some large regions, on the other hand, had nothing to breed at all. But since the Eurasian continent had no insurmountable obstacles dividing it into isolated parts, livestock and agricultural techniques could easily migrate, forming a 'common agricultural belt' that ranged from Japan to Ireland.

Webster believes that if the Americas had been more populated, progress would have proceeded at a different pace, but this low density of the human network did play a negative role. But then again, we do not know what course history would have taken otherwise, since the Europeans discovered the continent and changed the course of its development by the unintentional introduction of diseases that the indigenous people had no natural immunity against. It is quite probable that highly developed civilizations would have arisen in the Americas, as they did in Europe and Asia. Likewise, it is probable that the Native Americans would have fallen into a trap from which there would be no escape. History knows such an example – Easter Island.

Before people came to Easter Island, it was densely covered by subtropical forests filled with various flora and fauna. In the 17th and 18th century, a terrible war broke out on the island between the two tribes that populated it – the long-eared and the short-eared tribes. These peoples had come to the island at different times and had different racial characteristics. As a result, the long-eared were defeated by the short-eared who burned the enemy in a huge, two-kilometre long trench, and then destroyed the whole forest as a result of slash-and-burn agriculture. After that, the island went into a period of very harsh decline, hunger, and regression. As a result, the short-eared became extinct themselves some time after their victory.

It appears that the Easter Island and Maya civilizations went into a decline as a result of devastating activities following a peak in their development. The potential of those civilizations (based on the level of technology available to them) and the environmental capacities of their habitats were exhausted. At some point in the progress of ancient civilizations, self-destructive and self-sustained sequences of tragic events commenced. Perhaps the ancient Sumerians were right when they measured out a strictly defined period for their own civilization – Zod.[22]

––––––––––––

The above historical facts provide valuable insights into the mechanism that enabled mankind to make a qualitative leap in its development, which gave rise to a significant increase in the Earth's population. Hunting brought about improvements in labour techniques and provided for accumulation of knowledge as early as the Stone Age. Communication skills and fullyfledged speech, once developed by humanity, enabled it to stand out 'culturally' from the animal world. The transition to sedentary life caused a concentration of human networks and stimulated the development of interpersonal relationships. Man began to act rationally with regard to his own future. The integration of people into settlements and later into cities contributed to the development of opportunities for knowledge preservation and initial specialization in human activities. In fact, it is the more sophisticated structure of society that created new notions: business as an occupation and, as a consequence, commodity-money relations between people, although there was no money in its traditional form yet.

The first 'urban' civilization, the Sumerians, created a system for distributing foodstuffs through temples and one of the earliest forms of 'commodity-money relations', though different from modern ones in that it was people, livestock, and grain that played the role of money at that stage. This marked the growing power of city-states. The complex structure of such states changed society over time, and specialization emerged, increasing productivity. At the same time, environmental crises and diseases that came with agriculture led to a reduction in life expectancy. Therefore, the most significant civilizations of ancient times flourished as long as the land could feed the people and was sufficient to survive famine crises in unity.

However, in the first civilizations progress was very slow, primarily because of the natural character of their social systems. It was the ruling dynasties that acted as the main agents of change; specifically, Great Men were designated as independent mediators in solving disputes.

Eric D. Beinhocker, in his book *The Origin of Wealth*, estimated the level of annual earnings per capita in a hunter-gatherers' society to be within 90 international dollars (Geary–Khamis dollars) in 2000 prices (Beinhocker 2006), whereas by the time of the first settlements (before the Roman Empire), a person's earnings, according to the economist Angus Maddison, already came up to US$450 (Maddison 2007). How this indicator changed over time we will consider in detail in the next chapter, but for now let's note that the development of agricultural productive forces made it possible, as hunting had done before, to move from a lack of resources to their abundance. This abundance proved to be so attractive that no one at the time thought about its possible negative consequences, which led mankind into another progress trap. As noted by Will Durant, the author of *The Story of Civilization* and a Pulitzer Prize winner, a nation is born stoic and dies epicurean (Durant 1993).[23]

Not much changed with the advent of the next generation of empires, when people became more numerous, and life more comfortable. For further convenience, humanity 'invented' money and began to live even more comfortably.

CHAPTER 3

THE POWER OF EMPIRES, THE POWER OF GOLD – HOW DID IT ALL BEGIN?

"He sees men come, he sees men go
crawling like ants on the rocks below
The men who scheme, the men who dream
and die for gold on the rocks below
Gold gold gold
they just got to have that gold...
Gold gold
They'll do anything for gold"

– The lyrics for the theme song from *Mackenna's Gold*,
a 1969 American Western film

THE POWER OF GOLD

Gold is a unique and tangible 'string' that connects us with our remote ancestors. Gold was a major innovation and made it possible for the first civilizations to accumulate and preserve and store their wealth.

For as long as 700 years, a huge stone statue of Buddha stood in the Thai capital Bangkok. When it was decided some 50 years ago to move the statue to another place, the stone broke, and metal glistened through the cracks. The 'stone' proved to be a thin covering of plaster, and as soon as it was removed, a gold Buddha, weighing 5.5 tonnes, appeared.[24]

How much gold has mankind extracted and collected throughout history? The answer to this question is both complicated and interesting. Having studied the locations of ancient gold mines, estimated the amount of remaining gold, and made some calculations, scientists[25] came to the conclusion that almost 103,000 tonnes of gold has been mined in the world throughout history.[26] Today, around 45% of this is stored in the vaults of various countries as gold reserves.

Yet about one third of the world's gold is in the form of jewellery. Interestingly, for a considerable period of human history, gold was not used as a means of payment, but rather as a symbol of high social status and power, particularly royal power. For example, it was believed in India and China that gold was not meant to be owned or held by mere mortals. Unlike in Europe, the Chinese did not mint gold coins and only used it for decoration.

103,000 tonnes of gold (Bernstein 2000) – is this much or little? Given that each cubic metre of gold weighs 19.3 tonnes, it is easy to calculate that all the gold produced by mankind would occupy a little more than 5,000 m^3, and would fit in a cube measuring 17×17×17m.

Before the discovery of America, most of the gold was produced in the Arabian-Nubian province of Egypt.[27] Whoever controlled this region at that time controlled the gold currents too, and held the global economic power in their hand. The ancient Egyptians used gold bullion as a means of payment in international trade. Unlike today, bars of gold had no markings; their value was determined solely by weight, and they easily changed hands.

Abundant historical data indicates that the ancient Egyptians actively mined for gold and other minerals, and managed to create a large gold production industry. According to records, there were some mines that had been operated for millennia. Evidence shows that gold was mined by the Egyptians throughout Africa as long ago as at the end of the Bronze Age, around 1200 BC.

Gold mining was, and still is, a tough trade. When the industry first emerged, slave labour was used actively in the most unsightly forms at the mines. But for the Nubian and African regions of ancient Egypt gold made it possible to establish international trade, and thus create a state economy, albeit a primitive one. Gold mining brought about the creation of smelting, and later people learned how to separate silver from gold and smelt copper and tin together to make alloys. Of course, it was a slave economy, and gold served as a means of reinforcing the central government and the pharaohs' ornaments, and as an asset in inter-state commercial transactions. Thus, it is the presence of gold that enabled Egypt to become one of the greatest ancient civilizations. Thanks to this, Egypt survived for thousands of years, restoring its power even after poor harvests, wars, and natural disasters, while many other nations disappeared. It is not surprising that the ancient Egyptian civilization ended with the Assyrian and Persian conquests at the time when the Arabian-Nubian gold-bearing province had been virtually exhausted. Later, those mines were taken over by the Romans, and afterwards by the Byzantine Empire.

Over time, gold mining moved to Europe, where a new gold mining technique – hydraulic mining – was introduced for the first time. Gold produced in Europe strengthened the economy of the Roman Empire, but very soon European mines became depleted, and with the depletion came the fall of the empire itself.

During the period from 500 to 1500 AD, only 2,500 tonnes of gold was produced in the world – for the most part in Africa, and only partly in Asia.[28] In the 16th century, gold mining in the Old World declined, but increased significantly on the newly discovered American continent.

Amassing gold meant strengthening the economic power of the state and the real power of gold manifested itself when it turned from a luxury commodity into a measure of value, and thus one of the greatest innovations of mankind – money – along with silver, copper, and bronze. Even before money was created, gold had served empires in developing international trade and, therefore, made societies and economies more developed.

How did the arrival of money change things? As Niall Ferguson, a British historian, notes, money plays multiple roles in our world (Ferguson 2008, 23). Its main role, he believes, is that it acts as a medium of exchange, eliminating all the drawbacks associated with barter – direct exchange of goods for other goods. As a unit of account, money simplifies the evaluation, and hence calculation of turnovers. Ultimately, money makes it possible to store or preserve value, and hence paves the way for economic transactions that are often separated by time and distance.

Ferguson writes: "To be used as a means of performing all these functions, money should be an affordable commodity, relatively inexpensive to use, durable, easily scalable (i.e. capable of being divided and aggregated), convenient to carry, and reliably protected against forgery." He notes that in Sumer, people used clay tablets to record operations. However, metal, being more robust for the above purposes, was the ideal material for cash for thousands of years thereafter. This lasted until the arrival of the Dutch securities and the French innovations of John Law.[29] We will come back to this in Chapter 13. In the course of our current narrative though, coins become the most important innovation.

The oldest of the known coins date back to around the 6th-7th centuries BC, and were discovered during the excavation of the temple of Artemis at Ephesus (an ancient Greek city now in modern day Turkey). The Lydians (Iron Age people) used oval-shaped coins with an image of a lion's head and made of a special alloy of gold and silver called 'electrum'.

LYDIAN GOLD COINS

Thanks to Herodotus (a 5th century BC Greek historian), we know that the Lydians were the first to learn how to mint and use coins.[30] The town of Sardis, the capital of Lydia, had a market square with rows of shops offering a wide range of products, from meat and grain to jewellery and musical instruments. At the beginning of the 7th century BC, the first Lydian money appeared. Termed counters, these were inconvenient for exchange, as they had no standard size, weight, or marking that would determine their price.

This is what Peter L. Bernstein wrote about this period in his work *The Power of Gold: The History of an Obsession*: "Gyges, the first king of the Mermnad dynasty, carried out a revolutionary monetary reform in Lydia by suppressing private issuance of metallic money, especially coins made out of pieces of electrum, and establishing a state monopoly over the issuance of money" (Bernstein 2000, 37). At the beginning of the 6th century BC, the Lydian kingdom culminated in its development.[31] Croesus, the last Lydian king, introduced a bimetallic monetary system which continued to prevail in most countries for many centuries thereafter.

According to Bernstein, silver coins were used as equivalents of values that were too low for measuring in gold, while most of the state-owned gold was needed to finance international trade. "Like the Egyptians, Croesus set the ratio of gold to silver at 10:1 as a matter of convenience, although he made no legal ruling to that effect. This bimetallic system had its useful features, but monetary systems based on two metals were seldom stable, because changing supplies of the two metals over time caused their relative values to fluctuate" (Bernstein 2000, 39).

But that was not Croesus's only financial innovation. He also invented the first imperial currency in history. These were gold and silver coins that came into circulation in the entire territory of Asia Minor (western Turkey), as well as in Greece. This currency attained a wide circulation and played a crucial role in advancing the welfare and economic development of the Mediterranean region. It contributed to the development of trade within the Lydian empire, as well as foreign trade with countries in the East, West and South, which, in turn, stimulated free exchange of people and ideas. Croesus's reform is on a par with the introduction of the euro in Europe in the 20th century. The euro was revolutionary in Europe; it created a single currency for numerous nations and intensified trade, increased mobility of the population, and promoted a strong economic upturn. This looks all the more surprising given the fact that Croesus, while aspiring only for personal enrichment, carried out financial reform that made an impact on the course of history that has lasted to this day.

The Persian king Cyrus[32] defeated Croesus at the Battle of Sardis in 546 BC, but spared the Lydian king's life and kept his financial innovations. Cyrus's successor, Darius (who reigned 522-486 BC) also quickly took over the Lydian international monetary system and ensured its use throughout Persia. Moreover, Darius took Croesus's concept a step further: instead of using local hallmarks, he had his own image minted on all coins.[33]

The Persian government was also the first in history to collect taxes in cash rather than in kind. This was another turning point in the history of global finance. Since then, money increasingly became the most common and widely circulated means of payment.

Why, in fact, did such an innovation as coinage emerge? "The period when the Greeks began to use coinage, for instance, was also the period when they developed their famous phalanx tactics, which required constant drill and training of the hoplite soldiers. The results were so extraordinarily effective that Greek mercenaries were soon being sought after from Egypt to Crimea. An army of trained mercenaries needed to be rewarded in some meaningful way. These new armies were under the control of governments, and it took governments to turn chunks of metal into genuine currency. Large quantities of coins made the task of provisioning large standing armies much easier. Actually, one theory is that the very first Lydian coins were invented explicitly to pay mercenaries" (Graeber 2011, 227).

Why did coins turn out to be so attractive for both mercenaries and the public alike? Graeber argues that coins became attractive due to yet another innovation: taxes. As he notes, conflicts over debt had two possible outcomes. The first involved the conversion of poor debtors into slaves of the rich. States that followed this model were, as a rule, militarily ineffective. The second was popular states that took decisive action against debt peonage, thus creating the basis for a class of free farmers whose children would, in turn, be free to spend much of their time training for war. "The fiscal policy was, in fact, an extensive booty distribution system. The requirement to use coins for payments to the state ensured that coins were in sufficient demand so as to promote the development of other markets. Large amounts of silver, gold, and copper were dishoarded[34], as the economic historians like to say; it was removed from the temples and houses of the rich and placed in the hands of ordinary people, was broken into tinier pieces, and began to be used in everyday transactions" (Graeber 2011, 224, 226).

This can be summarized using the Lucky Clover model. The four-leaf clover, which bloomed in the previous civilization cycle, induced the emergence of government, financial relations, and loans, as well as accumulation of products and precious metals. These savings became the subject of numerous wars, resulting in military science appearing and giving rise to innovation in this area, thus forcing the rulers to change the nature of public relations and pave the way for the appearance of two new classes: free peasants and professional armies. With society developing, economic relations expanding, and gold being introduced into circulation as a means of payment, the structure of assets held by the population changed. Human labour became the main profit-generating factor of production, and slavery was the price that the people paid for the mistakes they or their leaders made. At that stage, another stratum of society – professional soldiers – became actively involved in the decision-making process.

With the development of society, the structure armies changed – they became one of government's most important institutions and were required to perform both external and internal functions for the state.

The external functions involved forcibly attaining foreign policy goals set by the state, and the internal included preserving, strengthening, and protecting the foundations of the existing state system. As a result, the need to maintain a standing army increasingly appeared. In turn, the role of the military expanded to cover not only protection and safety, but also conquering other states' territories. All of this required finance (through taxes), owing to which coins became a major part of the fiscal relations.

ALEXANDER OF MACEDON

Alexander the Great is commonly known as a brilliant commander. The financial aspects of his victories are less well known, though his achievements in this area have been surpassed by no one thus far. At the peak of his reign, Alexander the Great literally owned all of the world's wealth.

Alexander's father, Philip II of Macedon, took the Macedonian throne in 359 BC at the age of 23. He was king of a mountainous and sparsely populated country inhabited by tribes that were constantly at war with each other. Philip began with the only activity he was in control of, farming, and proved to be successful in solving the problem of increasing agricultural production in his land. By constructing irrigation facilities and canals, draining wetlands, and establishing control over the water levels in the rivers, he turned the alluvial plains of his kingdom into a powerful resource – a vast corn granary, as Peter L. Bernstein notes. "The abundant and constantly increasing food supplies enabled him first to appease the restless subjects, then ensure an increase in the population of southern Greece, and then start the construction of new cities and multiply the manpower for his army" (Bernstein 2000, 47-48).

Along with the agricultural improvements, Philip also carried out a military reform, creating a standing army for Macedonia. With the army restructured and provided with all necessary supplies, Macedonia quickly gained strength, enabling Philip to conquer Greek cities one after another. With the subjugated territories, Philip took over rich sources of precious metals – mines – and was thus able to replenish the coffers.

Having an unmistakable financial instinct, Philip produced more coins than was necessary to cover transactions and military costs. He kept the remainder in a reserve that could be used to finance the potential deployment of military operations against the Persians, who had begun to threaten the Macedonian boundaries.

Over time, Philip managed to turn Macedonia into a powerful force and assumed control over the whole of Greece.[35] In 336 BC, after a 23-year reign, Philip was assassinated. His son Alexander found the right words for his people: "My father found you nomadic and poor. Clad in sheepskins, you tended your meagre herds on the mountains…he made you citizens and brought order and law into your life"[36] (Bernstein 2000, 48).

Alexander continued the large-scale minting of coins at all the mints founded by his father, in addition to the production of coins in Greece, Asia Minor, Syria, Egypt, and Mesopotamia. With multitudes of slaves available, mining gold and silver for coinage was not a problem. To the stocks inherited from his father and the production of precious metals at the mines of Macedonia and Thrace, Alexander added the enormous treasures he captured in the course of his victorious campaigns in the East.

THE ROMAN EMPIRE

The Roman Empire took full advantage of the innovations made by Alexander and his father. The Romans formed their gold reserves in full compliance with the principles set by Alexander the Great.

According to historians, the Romans did not prospect for gold themselves. They preferred to take control of mines that had already been discovered and developed by others, seizing them together with the outlying countries and attaching the latter to the Roman Empire as provinces. For example, Spain became a Roman province in 197 BC as a result of the Second Punic War, which was fought against Carthage (modern day Tunisia) (218-201 BC). The same fate befell Gaul (Western Europe), and then Egypt (in 31 BC). Then, in the 1st century AD, Britain, with its minor amounts of accumulated and prospected gold, was conquered, and then Thrace.[37]

By the 4th century BC, the Romans had already established the custom of storing their treasures in an important temple in Ancient Rome, the Temple of Jupiter. We can say that the temple played the role of a savings bank at the time. Of course, money was kept there primarily for security reasons, but the temple was also a public treasure house and a religious institution. One night in 390 BC, as legend has it, some geese that were kept near the temple started to cackle, and thus warned the Romans of an unexpected attack by the Gauls, preventing Rome from being raided. The Romans were so grateful to their guardians they built a sanctuary for Moneta, the goddess of caution. Later, the English words 'money' and 'mint' came from this Latin name.

"The Romans introduced their own currency, called the Libra ('pound' in Latin), from which the symbol '£', designating the pound, originated. The first letter of the Latin word 'denarius' (d) came to be used to refer to the English penny. The word 'solidus', indicating that the coin is made of pure gold or silver, became the name of a coin worth 1/12 of a pound of silver, and equivalent to 12 denarii. Later these relations were put in the basis of the English currency system. The pound was equal to 20 shillings, and the shilling to 12 pence" (Bernstein 2000, 49-50).

This system was maintained from the time of the Norman conquest of England until as late as the 1980s. To mint coins, the Romans made use of different metals: gold for aurei, silver for denarii, and bronze for sestertii. The lower the reserves of a metal, the higher the denomination of the coins it was used to mint. The emperor was depicted on the obverse of each coin, and the figures of the legendary founders of Rome, Romulus and Remus, on the reverse. Coinage was regular practice in the ancient world, but it was in the Roman Empire that coins were put into mass circulation.

The empire's policy to expand its borders led to its coins becoming widely distributed as a means of payment. Initially, when the Roman Empire had an effective political system and kept its imperial bureaucracy to a minimum, it easily assimilated the residents of the conquered territories. There were no manifestations of racism or nationalism, and a person of any nationality could become a Roman citizen. The authorities were tolerant of all religions and made sure that no conflicts or wars would flare up on religious grounds. The Roman network of stone roads, whose total length was 78,000 km, was so successfully laid that modern roads in Italy follow its contours.[38] Only one other civilization, the Incas in America, were able to create something similar.

Thanks to this network and innovations in mining, "the Romans took the organisation of works on ore fields and the mining technology to new levels (particularly applying hydraulic mining in Iberia), and thus achieved the highest possible ore production outputs in all gold-bearing areas" (Marfunin 1987, 33).

The hydraulic mining mentioned by Marfunin required the development of large gold mining sites at which tens of thousands of slaves worked. The conditions of their work remained as appalling as they had been in ancient Egypt. No progress was made in this respect, and the labour efficiency remained the same. However, slave labour ensured progress in the life of the citizens of Rome. In Julius Caesar's time, the wealth of the Roman Empire was estimated at 25,000 bars of gold and 40 million gold sestertii, roughly approximate to weigh one and a half tonnes of gold.

It can be said that the ancient history of gold is directly related to the first empires – ancient Egypt and Rome. The Egyptian stage of human civilization was based on African gold deposits, whilst the Roman stage was based on deposits of the Iberian Peninsula. Historians point out that by the 1ˢᵗ and 2ⁿᵈ centuries, large Roman cities had aqueducts, public baths, fountains, amphitheatres, libraries, churches, and other public facilities. By that time, the Roman Empire had also reached its peak in terms of political organization. It had a territory that stretched from the Scottish border to Egypt and a population that consisted of 20 million residents in the European part, 20 million in West Asia, and 8 million in North Africa.[39]

The Mediterranean Sea was a sort of inland lake for the empire and was widely used to deliver grain from Alexandria and Carthage to the port of Naples, and another near Rome. Gold played a special role in these shipments: "Trade between Rome and its provinces was domestic trade, and for bread and papyrus from Egypt, dates from African oases, ore from Iberia, etc. Rome paid with wine and olive oil, ceramics and metal products. Gold as a means of payments was only used in trade with distant Eastern countries, thus irrevocably disappearing in India and China. Jewellery and spices – these were the commodities that required payment in gold. A pound of silk from China at the time of Augustus cost a pound of gold" (Marfunin 1987, 33).

As in the days of Alexander the Great, much gold was spent to keep the army, but the use of its coins for military ends was wider in Rome, in that Germanic tribes were paid to defend the northern borders of the empire.

It was then (for the first time in history) that huge masses of people moved to cities. The urban residents comprised about 15% of the empire's total population. Later, Europe would only attain this percentage again by the beginning of the 19ᵗʰ century. The Romans left us a legacy of beautiful architecture, advanced urban development, and an effective education system. A legal system was created, and to this day Roman law is applied in modern jurisprudence.

Rudolf von Jhering, a German jurist and legal theorist, remarked that ancient Rome had conquered the world three times: the first time through its armies, the second through its religion, and the third through its laws (Graeber 2011, 198).

However, as you know from the previous chapter, society paid for social progress with environmental setbacks. Early degradation was not a serious enough factor to topple the economy, but a reduction in agricultural production, a growing dependence on imports of grain, and an agricultural decline in the very heart of Italy turned out to be the weak point of the Great Empire.

The growth of the city of Rome itself and the accumulation of wealth caused a boom in demand for land within the capital. People of noble birth and people who had acquired wealth alike bought land, and Roman soldiers received allotments as a reward for their service. This new growing class of property owners removed farmers from their land and forced them out to locations unsuitable for farming. Negative environmental consequences quickly followed.

Land reforms carried out by the rulers of the empire were, for the most part, unsuccessful; control over public land was actually lost, and the state could only appease the lower strata of society in one way – by distributing free wheat. During the reign of Emperor Claudius, 200,000 Roman families lived virtually on the dole. On top of that, Rome was desperately short of gold: "With the annual gold production adding up to at least five tonnes, there was still never enough metal for coinage" (Bernstein 2000, 52).

One of Rome's historical incongruities was that its city-state democracy proved to be very frail. Before long the real power was taken over from the Senate by warlords, such as Julius Caesar, who controlled the army and the provinces. The empire defeated the institutions of power on which the city-state concept was founded.

Transition to authoritarian rule always means the beginning of the end of the empire (Spengler 1926). Even though Emperor Augustus and many other Roman emperors who followed were enlightened people, they could not cope with large-scale problems. All pre-industrial cities were extremely dependent on being provided with resources and having their stockpiling systems running efficiently. With the growth of urban population, food supplies started to dwindle in Roman cities. There was not enough gold; the logistics were becoming a serious limitation, with roads falling into disrepair and horses and carts being in short supply.

A sudden sharp decline in population created a no less serious problem. In Rome, several serious pandemics broke out.[40] Pestilences, lead poisonings via water delivered by pipes, confusion caused by emperors changing one after another, barbarian assaults, growing religious oppositions, and corruption – all these undermined the empire. The spending on provisioning and protecting the empire was growing and becoming more and more onerous, and the system of imperial power degraded and returned to primitive forms of organization. By the time of Constantine, the first ruler of the Eastern Roman Empire, more than half a million-people served in the imperial army. But without a constant influx of slaves, merchants, and migrants, ancient Rome could neither maintain its population nor its economy, since the economy relied on the number of its citizens paying taxes.

**ANCIENT BIBLICAL MANUSCRIPTS DISPLAYED
AT *THE BOOK OF BOOKS* EXHIBITION.**
Jerusalem, Israel

HOW KNOWLEDGE BECOMES IMMORTAL

History could have taken a completely different path had it not been for the Library of Alexandria. The significance of this library for science is comparable with that of money for finance. The principal library stock, which consists of 200,000 scrolls, was collected by Demetrius of Phalerum, advisor to King Ptolemy I Soter, during the first 10 years of the library's operation. The hardest part of the whole enterprise was to convince the sponsor (the king) of its value. Demetrius' decisive argument was that "books say what friends would not dare to say to a king in his face". That attempt to collect all the books of the world in one place nearly succeeded.[41]

The Bibliotheca Alexandrina was created, complete with a catalogue. Each scroll had a plate attached to it, essentially similar to a modern catalogue card, on which the authors and the names of the works contained in the scroll were indicated.

The library had no reading rooms, but had desks for scribes who made copies of original scrolls, thanks to whom many of the books have survived to this day, despite the fact that the library has suffered two major fires during its existence. The fate of the Library of Alexandria was decided by Caliph Omar. In response to the question about what to do with the books, he said: "If they are consistent with the Koran, the only divine book, they are not needed; if inconsistent, they are undesirable. Therefore, they should be destroyed in any case." At his command, the scrolls perished in hot water at the city bath. But the knowledge was saved through its distribution in copies.

The decision to lower the minting standard (to melt down existing coins and mint a greater number of smaller ones) resulted in inevitable inflation. A measure of wheat, which used to cost half a denarius in 338 BC, cost 10,000 denarii in the empire's heyday. A gold solidus cost 4,000 silver coins at the beginning of the 4th century, and several orders of magnitude more by the end of the century.[42] The problem reached such a pitch that Roman citizens, overburdened by the inflation and exorbitant taxes, began to move to the Goths.

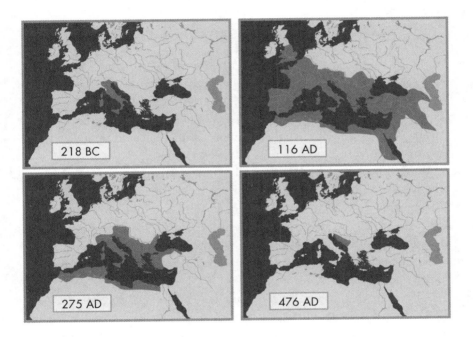

FIGURE 4. THE RISE AND DECLINE OF THE ROMAN EMPIRE

Figure 4 represents the Roman Empire in different periods of its existence starting from 218 BC; the highest point in its development was passed in 116.[43] Then came a recession – the division of the yet undivided empire into two parts and the seizure of the former capital by the Barbarians. The once great city was pillaged and half-destroyed by endless barbaric and papal wars.[44] The lucky clover wilted.

The strength of the empire moved to its periphery, where German, Gothic, Frankish, and British tribes founded small ethnic states in northern lands which had not yet been exhausted by the Roman civilization. But the small feudal principalities were not able to carry out large-scale mining operations, did not have a significant workforce, and were exhausted by constant internecine conflicts and wars. As for the demand of gold, not only did it fail to weaken or disappear, but on the contrary, it strengthened, as lack of money in Europe during that period caused the replacement of land rent by money rent. The lucky clover wilted in Europe, but the torch of civilization was picked up by the Byzantine Empire, a new Eastern empire that lasted until the fall of Constantinople in 1453.

BYZANTIUM

While in the West many urban centres were in ruins as a result of a succession of barbarian conquests, the Byzantine cities entered a period of economic prosperity once again. The Byzantine Empire did not emerge out of nowhere. Its inheritance consisted of numerous economically prosperous parts of the once mighty Roman Empire, located on a vast territory of over one million square kilometres.

Since the Roman state had ceased to be a republic, its emperors repeatedly wanted to move the capital from Rome to the East. When Emperor Constantine decided to establish a new capital, he did not immediately opt for a small and remote settlement located on the Bosphorus called Byzantium. Initially, his choice fell on the site of the city of Troy, for which the emperor personally drew the outline and basic structure of the future metropolis.

City gates had already been built in Troy when, according to the 5th century Christian historian Sozomen, the Lord himself appeared before Constantine in his dream at night…and persuaded him to find another place for the capital (Vasiliev 1998). After that Constantine chose the place where Byzantium subsequently rose. From then onwards, 'the presence of God' as the underlying cause was the dominant explanation for decisions made by Byzantine emperors.[45] Constantine's second step, which was destined to determine the fate and longevity of the empire, was associated with the choice of religion.

Although Constantine himself, like most Romans, was a pagan for many years, he eventually became a Christian.[46] Many historians defend the sincerity of Constantine's conversion, emphasizing his religiousness and asserting that he had been a Christian without ever realizing it, even before adopting the faith. Researchers' opinions on why Constantine chose Christianity differ. Deciding to become one of the Christians, who were very much in the minority in the empire at that time, was a very risky move.

However, the emperor's conversion to Christianity made it possible to confiscate gold from the empire's pagan temples – the gold had been accumulating there for many centuries – and put it into circulation. This was a strong economic measure. Constantine the Great ruled Byzantium from 306 to 337 AD. During his reign, Byzantine coins became the main means of payment and, moreover, a prestigious commodity. The standard unit of currency was first called the gold 'solidus', just as it had been the monetary unit of the Western Roman Empire formerly, and later became known as the 'bezant'. The first bezants weighed 4.55 grams – more than any other gold coins that had ever existed – and had a pure gold content of 98%. With the troy ounce of gold set to cost US$1,484 recently, the gold contained in one bezant would cost US$213.[47] However, the purchasing power of gold was much higher in Constantine's time than it is now.

Constantine's main coin, the gold solidus or the bezant, was minted, with its weight and purity kept constant, for almost 700 years, i.e. long after the fall of Rome. This is why it is made reference to in the *Guinness World Records*. No other coin in history can be compared with it for duration of use.

This monetary unit of the Byzantine Empire was the central financial pillar that supported the entire world trade for a whole millennium! The bezant in those days was, as the US dollar is today, a perfect means of payment in international trade. Its circulation remained unchanged and suffered no degradation for many centuries; hence it is the monetary system of the Byzantine Empire that the world's economy is based upon.

The famous Byzantine merchant and traveller Cosmas Indicopleustes wrote in the 6th century that a faraway Indian ruler, looking at a solidus and comparing it with a Persian silver drachma, uttered: "Indeed, the Romans are brilliant, powerful, and wise!"[48]

What role did gold play in the Byzantine Empire? As historians note, gold came to Byzantium from different sources: from derelict parts of the former Western Roman Empire, from gold mines in the Balkans, but mostly from Northeast Africa and Caucasian and Central Asian countries, thanks to advanced and intensive trade.

As we can see, Nubian gold still continued to play an important role in the world economy after the decline of the pharaohs' kingdom.

As long as the Islamic onslaught in Nubia could be contained at least partially, and bread continued to come from Egypt (the empire's bread basket), Byzantium could maintain its political independence.

THE HEYDAY OF THE BYZANTINE EMPIRE

Byzantium's auspicious geographical position, coupled with a strong financial system, ensured success for the empire's trade. Positioned at a crossroads of trade routes connecting Europe and the East, the country preserved its economic superiority over other European countries up until the 12th century. Innovations, such as Greek fire (an extremely effective incendiary weapon), and the fore-and-aft sailing rig (borrowed from the Arabs) which enabled vessels to sail against the wind, ensured naval domination for the empire. Rapid development of construction machinery and considerable progress in exact and natural sciences enabled Byzantium to overtake many states of the East and the West in economic development.

All international trade flowed through Byzantine ports, with fabrics, jewellery, and other items of refined luxury being offered for sale on a large scale only there. Under the influence of vestiges of Greek culture, Christian-Greco-Eastern culture, known as Byzantine culture, emerged. The empire's population totalled up to 30-35 million at that time and was very multi-national, largely including Syrians, Jews, Armenians, Georgians, Egyptian Copts, Greeks, and settlers from the Caucasus. True Romans were few from the very beginning; soon there were practically no native speakers of Latin left, and Greek came to be the empire's main language.

School was the most important social institution in Byzantium. The system of education was very similar to the antique instructional set-up, with reading, grammar, and numerical literacy taught, which set it apart from the western system.

Moreover, Constantinople had considerable food supplies and high-quality raw materials enriched by local craftsmen. Byzantium's economy was more advanced than Western Europe's, and all Europeans who visited the country believed it to be fabulously wealthy. Active trade was conducted with Italian city-states and with Germany through Italian ports; the main imported commodities were metals, linen, carpets, and Spanish wine.

The famous Silk Road to China also went through Constantinople, as did the Incense Route – the trade route through the Arabian Desert to

Red Sea ports, and then by sea through the Persian Gulf to the Indian Ocean.[49] Through Arab sailors, Byzantium received silk from China, precious stones, pearls, groceries, and spices from India, and expensive carpets and wines from Syria.

The level of economic development of the different parts of the Byzantine Empire varied.[50] Egypt was considered the 'granary', and its capital, the city of Alexandria, a cultural and craft centre. Red Sea harbours linked the country with Ethiopia and other African countries. Through the Persians and the Arabs, on whom Byzantium depended and with whom it constantly fought, the empire traded with Ceylon (Sri Lanka) where goods from India and China were stored for further shipping west.

On the other side of the Strait of Constantinople, on the Balkan Peninsula, Byzantine goods reached the Danube via river trade routes (located in present-day Macedonia) and then came to Central Europe through areas that make part of present-day Hungary. The empire's imports from Europe included pickles, flax, honey, fish, and other foodstuffs.

Constantinople also maintained relations with the southern part of Russia through Crimean harbours. From there, bread, salt, honey, eggs, and furs were imported. Through Crimean ports, Byzantium gained access to the Caspian Sea and reached Asian oasis towns. This channel was used to import leather, wool, and metal goods. For a very long time, Byzantium was a very self-sufficient state.

DECLINE OF THE BYZANTINE EMPIRE

A fundamental change in the Byzantine Empire's economic development came in the 12th century as a result of agricultural policy failures. In that century, economic superiority was finally taken over by Western Europe's states, where feudal relations began to emerge at that time, and land rent was replaced by more efficient cash rent. Whereas medieval Europe's urban population had by that time already begun to develop as a conscious civic institution that opposed secular and ecclesiastical authorities, the stability of the Byzantine civilization and the rigidity of its traditions played a cruel joke on the empire.

Following the peasants, the Byzantine merchants and artisans found themselves in a tight situation. The empire had for a long time been governed by Roman law, which promoted commodity circulation, but gradually the state began to exercise more and more control over commerce and handicrafts. Taxes rose sharply and became exorbitant, while officials tightened penny-wise supervision even over its own production.

At one point, Constantinople became a place where huge ugly weeds – monopoly, privilege, and protectionism – began to flourish, instead of the lucky clover. No room was left for free labour and personal initiative. Each Byzantine corporation operated within certain boundaries which it could not trespass, but within which it had a monopoly. Other regulations were imposed specifying everything from working conditions and payments to workers. Only monopolies were allowed to buy raw materials and sell finished products in each sphere of production. As a result, internal competition gradually disappeared.

Not surprisingly, no powerful guild-oriented social strata, capable of gaining recognition of their rights at the national level, emerged in the cities.[51] Moreover, a fatal blow was dealt to crafts and commerce in the 12th century, when the emperors suddenly granted enormous benefits to Italian merchants, thus making them formidable competitors of domestic trade. The Byzantine craftsmen, who had grown used to being taken care of by 'their' authorities, lost the competition. There was a clear understanding in Italian port cities, especially in Venice, of how much profit could be earned in Byzantium.

Exempt from inspection and duties in all Byzantine harbours, the Italian merchants managed to have their trade affairs brought under a special court jurisdiction. On the shores of Constantinople's Golden Horn inlet, they founded an entire settlement where they built a church, houses, and depots. There they were totally independent and felt completely at home. However, consumed with greed, the Italians took a dismissive attitude towards imperial decrees, and thus set both the authorities and the populace against them. In 1171, Emperor Manuel I Komnenos ordered all the Venetians to be arrested, and all their property and all Italian ships confiscated. A long war broke out. In retaliation, the Venetians caused the route of the Fourth Crusade to be redirected to Constantinople.

Instead of fighting with the Muslims, the crusaders sacked Constantinople in 1204. Having been defeated, the Byzantines were no longer allowed to export goods, and could only sell them to foreign merchants at Constantinople markets. All major commerce had been completely taken over by the Venetians and the Genoese. Their formidable fleet came close to Constantinople's shores each time when they felt it necessary to impose their will on the Byzantine emperor.

Starting from the end of the 13th century, signs of economic decline began to show clearly in the Byzantine Empire. When Emperor John VI Kantakouzenos (1292-1383) tried to re-establish the former Byzantine merchant fleet, at least to some degree, the Italians simply burned it. Thus, a full stop was placed in the empire's history, and the former glory and power became myths.

THE HIDDEN CAUSE OF THE CRUSADES

As Niall Ferguson points out in *The Ascent of Money*, "Demand for money was greater in the much more developed commercial centres of the Islamic Empire that dominated the southern Mediterranean and the Near East, so that precious metal tended to drain away from backward Europe. So rare was the denarius in Charlemagne's time that 24 of them sufficed to buy a Carolingian cow. In some parts of Europe, peppers and squirrel skins served as substitutes for currency; in others *pecunia* came to mean land rather than money." (Ferguson 2008) Europeans had two options to solve this problem: they could export labour and goods, or a more radical option suggested going to war against the newly emerged Islamic world and bringing heaps of precious metals home as trophies.

The conversion of the pagans to Christians as the declared objective of the Crusades and the ensuing conquests was hardly more important for European kings than the prospect of plundering money to fill the coffers. Otherwise, why would the Crusaders suddenly invade the capital of the Byzantine Empire instead of fighting the Muslims?

In fact, the inability of rulers to solve this problem has always led to a reduction in the precious metal content in coins in the past, which is analogous to modern devaluation of money, or inflation.

THE FALL OF THE EMPIRE

The decline of the Byzantine civilization began when the empire's rulers lost control over the supply of gold and wheat from Egypt. Islamization and colonization of Egypt by Arab tribes deprived the empire of the funds it needed to pay the army.

The Byzantine territory was diminishing drastically, and the Muslim influence in the region had been growing from the 8th century. Cruelty in the levying of taxes (which became exorbitant due to failures in the agricultural and trade policies) frequently went to such extremes that the Muslim penetration seemed less frightening for taxpayers than the arrival of representatives of the Byzantine fiscus.[52] Villages on the outskirts of the empire slid into poverty and were deserted. Gold mining decreased. Uprisings broke out in various places. As a result, the 'eternal engine of trade' was gradually taken over by the Arabs.

Having conquered the Byzantine East, the Arabs still permitted free circulation of Constantinople's coins on their territories despite the fact that their religion prohibited any depiction of people. The first Arabic coin die was an imitation of a Byzantine stamp (the 'Arab-Byzantine' die), and only the appearance of the image of Christ, totally unacceptable to the Islamic world, on the empire's gold and silver coins at the end of the 7th century prompted the caliphate to start minting its own coins.

Constantinople was in desperate need of funds. Under the pressure of financial difficulties, the Byzantine emperors began to resort to devaluating money and issuing substandard coins. Lack of funds caused the empire to reduce the strength of the troops employed to protect its borders and delay wage payments. Since the troops mainly consisted of mercenaries, failing to receive payment, they themselves rebelled and took revenge on the defenceless populace. As a result of these problems, the borders were not guarded vigilantly, and Arabs infiltrated the Byzantine territory. Unable to resist the Arabs militarily, Constantinople paid up, but to do that, more money was needed. The empire was caught in a vicious circle: due to lack of money, the army had to be reduced; due to lack of soldiers, more money was needed to pay off the adversary.

History is ironic in a way. The rise of Constantinople, as a political, cultural, religious, and military centre, played a bad trick on the empire. Drained of finance, the millennial civilization shrank to the limits of its capital and finally fell as a result of a powerful artillery strike carried out by the Turkish army led by Mehmed the Conqueror in April 1453.

KEY FACTORS IN THE RISE AND DECLINE OF THE BYZANTINE EMPIRE

It was not at the end, but rather at the beginning of Byzantium's history that its cities peaked in their development. The territory of the Eastern empire consisted mainly of areas with well-developed agriculture, where fertile soils enabled the farmers to gather two or three harvests a year. But Byzantium succeeded mainly as an open state. It conducted large-scale foreign trade and was a monopolistic mediator in trade between the East and the West. Gold provided a basis for the empire's prosperity.

To guard its borders, Byzantium hired mercenaries, who had often served powerful enemies in the past. For a long time, the Byzantine Empire served as a buffer for Christian states, protecting them against Islamic incursions and Tatar raids. But as a result of the failure of an agrarian reform, and due to deterioration of relations between various strata of society in the cities (primarily in Constantinople), life in the Byzantine Empire became harder and more dangerous. The state lost its merchant fleet and control over key resources (gold and wheat), and literally became very enclosed (legends were told about a triple wall that allegedly surrounded Constantinople, and about a gold chain barring entrance into the Golden Horn).

As a result of the successful Turkish conquests, many Greeks (who considered themselves Romans) began to relocate actively to the West before the empire finally fell. In this way, the cultural heritage of Byzantium spread to the territory of modern Western Europe.

The accumulation of world treasures in Italy (thanks to Byzantines) created exceptionally favourable conditions in the West for the advent of the Renaissance later on. Moving cultural and material assets further to Europe, saving them from destruction by the Turks, the Byzantines promoted the beginning of the next era – the Renaissance and the scientific revolution. It is no coincidence that the year when Constantinople fell nearly corresponds with the year when the scientific revolution began.

CHINA

During the reign of the Song Dynasty (960-1279), China's role in world trade increased dramatically. At the same time, Hangzhou, a town located south of the Yangtze River, was made capital of the country. The town was sited in a prosperous and densely populated area where rice was grown. The Song began to rely on tax collection more than most Chinese dynasties before them, and thus encouraged the development of ports and foreign trade. In order to protect settlements located in the Yangtze River basin and coastal areas from Mongol raids, a professional fleet, the first in China's history, was founded in 1232. Based in Shanghai, in the span of only one century it grew to include 20 squadrons numbering 52,000 hands. The ships were equipped with powerful catapults capable of throwing heavy stones as projectiles at enemy ships.

Maritime trade in China was always carried out through a small number of port cities where a few thousand merchants from India, Persia, and the Arabian Peninsula lived (Meliksetov 2002, 215). The main trade routes ran along the coast of Indochina, reaching Japan in the west and India in the east. Chinese merchants exchanged textiles, porcelain, and jewels for spices, incense, and precious woods. Gradually, the centre of the country's economic life shifted to the southeast of the country, where maritime trade had come to dominate. It's difficult to say whether the emergence of large ships was the result or the cause of this increase in maritime links.

This activity, however, did not secure the Song Dynasty in power. The Mongol Yuan dynasty of rulers (descendants of Genghis Khan) replaced the Songs and continued to build ships on yet a larger scale, both for foreign trade and for internal transportation of grain to their new capital Beijing. In 1274 and 1281, two huge fleets (comprising over 900 vessels) were collected for military intervention in Japan. The invasion did not succeed. To compensate for the failures in the East, the rulers reopened overland trade in the West, with Europe and the Middle East, along the Silk Road.

But soon an anti-Mongol uprising arose and strengthened in Central China, and the second emperor of the dynasty, Yongle, who came to power in the turmoil, lead several naval expeditions outside China's traditional zones of influence in the Eastern World Ocean.[53]

These naval companies were intended to demonstrate the power and wealth of China as well as to extend its influence into new areas. Korea had already fallen under the influence of China by that time, and Yongle managed to persuade Japan to accept similar relations in 1404.[54] In support of these initiatives, the emperor offered an initial exchange of gifts (silk, gold, lacquer, porcelain).[55] However, Yongle immediately banned private trade.

Yongle had a powerful navy at his disposal. Warships were used to protect settlements on islands. Treasury ships were the most important ships in maritime expeditions to the western oceans. These ships were about 120 m long and 50 m wide. Each of them consisted of 15 or more watertight compartments, so that even a partially damaged ship would not sink and could be repaired directly at sea.

The crew on each ship was accommodated in 60 compartments, i.e. much more comfortably than the sailors on Portuguese ships. The expeditions required enormous investments. The total number of their members exceeded 30,000, and included (apart from seamen) officials and scholars.

China's main political objective was, as today, to establish domination in Southeast Asia. China had always relied on its ethnic communities in Malaysia, Sumatra, and Java, as well as on the Philippines. However, the routes of the Chinese ships went far beyond Southeast Asia, reaching the coast of India, the Gulf States, and even the east coast of Africa.

However, with the death of Yongle, the maritime strategy lost support. Oceanic diplomacy was done with – treasury ships were not needed any longer, coastal defence forces were reduced, and the number of large warships decreased from 400 to 140 by 1474. Most of the shipyards were closed, and naval forces quickly sank into degradation as a result of desertion. Termination of active foreign policies in the southward direction signified the creation of the first 'iron curtain' in world history, and in 1446, China deported the ambassadors of all foreign states. From 1552, the country ceased to build large vessels, and the ships that already existed returned to their ports.

One of the most important lessons that can be learned from medieval China's history is that isolationism is the worst practice a country can adopt. Nobody can stop time. China survived in isolation for four or five centuries (until the Opium Wars began). By isolating itself, China missed out on the advantages of being part of the industrial and scientific revolution.

Most researchers believe that the financial crisis that curtailed the maritime expeditions was triggered by the exorbitant obligations the government took in order to move the capital from Nanjing to Beijing, and to construct the Grand Canal. To cope with the challenge, Yongle decided to increase the government's revenue by printing vast quantities of paper money. The result was predictable: inflation, and total refusal to use paper money in the private sector. After this, silver became the dominant instrument of exchange and tax payments. And this, as we remember from the history of ancient Rome, signifies recognition of currency as the basic means of payment.

China preserved an ancient concept of external relations that was based on its dominance and dictated that a country wanting to trade with China and have access to the East Sea, including Japan, had to pay tribute to China. Silver was brought from Japan by sea for a long time, but then Yongle imposed a ban which quickly wiped out both private trade and interstate exchange. Even seagoing junks with more than two masts were prohibited.

The rejection of international relations caused large-scale development of illegal private trade and piracy. China's coast guard was completely corrupted. By that time (1557), the Portuguese had already established their base in Macau. They were well aware of the trade situation and easily came into contact with Chinese and Japanese pirates. In 1567, the Chinese government lifted the ban on private trade, but prohibited its subjects from trading with Japan. This gave the Portuguese an incredible commercial opportunity. Only Venetian merchants had more freedom in trade during the last years of the Byzantine Empire.

Requests made to grant Japanese merchants access to China in 1513, and again in the period from 1521 to 1522 were rejected. In 1539, the Chinese seized cargo from Japanese vessels that were used for transporting tribute to China. In 1544, Japan's attempt to resume trade with China was again rejected. That was enough for Japan to feel hostility towards China.

These political events were taking place after rich reserves of silver were discovered in Japan in 1530 and it had become the largest producer of silver. The Chinese market suffered a shortage of silver. Since the Chinese had prohibited Japanese ships from entering its ports, Chinese pirates and Portuguese dealers became the main suppliers of Japanese silver to China. There was no trade between Japan and China until 1557, so it was very easy for Portugal to take over Macau.

The gains of the Portuguese rose spectacularly. Portuguese merchants shipped Indonesian spices from Malacca to Macau, sold them in China, bought Chinese silk and gold, and sailed on from Macau to Hirado and Nagasaki, ports in southern Japan. With the proceeds from the sale of the Chinese commodities, Japanese silver was bought, brought back to Macau and resold. The proceeds were once again used to buy silk for shipment to Japan or Goa. Thus, the Chinese gave away the lucky clover with their own hands.

JAPAN

The Portuguese trade was accompanied by missionary activities carried out by the Jesuits (the Society of Jesus, a religious congregation of the Catholic Church which originated in 16th century Spain). Francis Xavier (a Roman Catholic missionary) was in Japan from 1549 to 1551, when the Jesuits were successfully converting heathens to Christians in southern Japan. The number of Japanese Christians soon rose to 300,000. The Japanese were interested in Portuguese ships, maps, and navigation skills. They were even more interested in Western weapons. Portuguese technology of that era was even portrayed in Japanese 'Nanban' ('southern barbarian') art. Firearms were brought to Japan by the Portuguese in 1543, and were quickly appreciated by the military. The Japanese managed to copy the weapons and organised their manufacture domestically.

In 1596, the Spanish authorities in Manila tried to replicate the Portuguese' success and sent Franciscan missionaries to the region. The missionaries acted so aggressively that the indigenous population was under the mistaken impression that Spain wanted to conquer their land.

The Spanish missionaries and 19 new believers were crucified in Naga-saki. That same year, Toyotomi Hideyoshi (lord and chief Imperial minis-ter who completed the 16th century unification of Japan) confiscated the Spanish galleon *San Felipe*, and thereafter, Japan perceived any missionary activity with hostility. Soon, the Japanese established contact with British and Dutch traders, who did not seem to have burning religious ambitions. Eventually, Christianity was outlawed in Japan, and the Portuguese were expelled from the country in 1639. From then on, Chinese and Dutch merchants held Japan's trade with the mainland (and hence the supply of Japanese silver) in their hands.

OPEN AND CLOSED SOCIETIES

Of course, retold stories are entertaining and instructive in themselves. Drawing on historical experience, I would like to direct the reader's attention to the emergence of innovations such as money, taxes, and for-eign trade. The phenomenon of money not only encouraged commodity exchange between existing states, but also contributed to the creation of new ones. The next step involved transition to the payment of taxes and dues with money. In history, many conflicts, successes, and inade-quacies are presented as consequences of religious conflicts or ingenious solutions bestowed on society by individuals. In truth, much depended, and still does, on the size of taxes and its collection practices. These factors did and still motivate people to support the government, or, con-versely, to minimize their economic activity to a far greater extent than it may seem.

Very often, the inability of rulers to maintain the rates of currencies led to depreciation of money, and in turn to mass riots, hunger, and prob-lems with controlling armies. In such circumstances, the lucky clover would quickly wilt, just as it would, conversely, bloom in the conditions of intensive exchange and foreign trade derived from tax revenues and a growing national wealth.

We are therefore considering two types of society that formed in var-ious states: open societies and closed societies, as they have been defined by Karl Popper.[56] In an open society, people are motivated by their own interests and calculation – factors that are necessary for the development of market relations and entrepreneurship; they are inclined to risk and innovate. Speaking modern languages, such societies have many more agents of change. In traditional (or closed) societies, important deci-sions are made by the heads of dynasties or a narrow circle of autocrats, while open societies have whole classes numbering hundreds of thousands of people for every million. An open society is based on meritocracy, a good financial system, extensive foreign trade, and market relations, and cannot exist without these factors. As we can see, open societies could over time degenerate or transform into closed ones (Popper 2007, 10).

Such societies develop in a smooth and evolutionary way, since preservation and further augmentation of the accumulated wealth is one of their goals. Another of its goals is to sustain (protect) the population. For the purpose of protection, a professional army is created and recruited. Conflicts with other nations lead to changes in the economic and political systems, since the economic system usually goes far beyond the limits of such a society.

The ancient Greeks created one of the first open societies, which took the form of, speaking in our modern language, a civilization of venture capital and small business. Ancient Rome was also an open society and had a monetary system that was accepted far beyond its borders. The Byzantine Empire was an open society as well – it was open for international exchange while having an army powerful enough to defend its interests at the same time. China was also such a society during the era of geographic expansion. These periods were auspicious for the lucky clover, making it bloom.

However, beneficial changes were followed by rapid growth of the country's wealth as a result of favourable international exchange. Such growth often misled state leaders into making inadequate assessment of the causes and effects, which led to erroneous conclusions being made.

A closed society is an immobile, static, frozen society. It consists of castes or classes, and the transition of a member of an inferior part of society upwards only takes place in exceptional cases.

The economies of the highly populated city-states of the first civilizations were unable to cope with either external or internal shocks, and slid into a closed state for various reasons. In China, it was self-imposed isolationism which excluded export profits from being among the possible sources of investment. As a closed society the economy of the Chinese empire relied in its development only on domestic savings and smuggling silver from Japan. Serious crop failures brought the empire into a state of chaos and gave rise to interruptions in food supplies to the capital, followed by peasant revolts, a weakening of the state, enemy raids, and change of rulers, and then the repetition of the entire cycle without any qualitative change.

In the Byzantine Empire, trade began to falter for internal reasons. The imperial rule had created an inadequate institutional environment. Business became unprofitable as a result of monopolization and over-regulation. Trade, worse still, was monopolized by another nation. The state found it impossible to devalue the currency. The bezant was, like the dollar today, a universal legal tender. Attempts to reduce the content of precious metal in it caused public irritation (merchants refused to accept it as a means of payment). Taxes increased, and business went under Muslim jurisdiction, taking advantage of the fact that the Arabs did not yet intervene in the economic life of the empire's provinces, preferring to collect a fixed tribute. The lucky clover slowly began to wilt.

In the Roman Empire, the extensively developing cities and the established standard of living came into conflict with the inefficient wealth distribution system of a slave-holding civilisation. To have more slaves, an army was needed, and the army required money for its maintenance. The money was spent on imported spices and luxury goods, as well as on political projects, while the army dispersed, joining the ranks of barbarian forces that were hostile to the empire.

Still, on the whole, even the low rates of development of the first civilizations ensured considerable progress for humankind. What gives us reasons to be confident about this? We have this confidence thanks to the serious work of Angus Maddison (a historic economist) who took a long-term view of the above events, and did it with the utmost degree of abstraction.

ANGUS THE GREAT

In ancient times, population grew slowly, and so did wealth. If we try to assess wealth the way it is assessed today (by the growth of the GDP, equivalent to the global earnings for a certain period), we will find that it has been formed as the total consumption by all households in the world and the total expenditure by all governments and rulers.

The economic strength (GDP) of ancient states that existed in different epochs can only be compared by using adequate measures. There are not many sensible methods that can be used for this purpose, and only three of them are applicable in practice. These are assessments with reference to gold, with reference to another product (wheat as a measure of the cost of all other goods), or with reference to a society that still exists today. Let's take, for instance, Rome and its money, sestertii and aurei. 100 sestertii made one aureus. An aureus contained 8 grams of gold.

We know about Rome's population thanks to numerous and well pre-served historical evidence – censuses for a number of years. People have been counted (for fiscal purposes) for a long time, and people evading a census can sometimes be threatened with substantial penalties.

The first method for determining GDP per capita is to calculate it in the gold equivalent. If we set the price of one ounce of gold at US$300 in 1990 prices, the GDP per capita in ancient Rome would make US$780, and the worldwide average for that period would add up to US$400-500.

The second way is to use a universal commodity – wheat – as a meas-ure of value. Wheat prices are also well documented historically. By taking consumption per capita in wheat equivalent, researchers obtain a rough estimate of expenditures on household items, consumables, and government spending. By multiplying the resulting equivalent by the price of wheat in sestertii, we can easily calculate the price of one kilogram of wheat. For example, in 1688, wheat cost US$1.80 per kilo-gram in today's money. If we use this method to calculate the GDP for different countries at that time, the results would range from US$200 to US$1500.

The third way is to assess GDP by making reference to a society that still exists today. Societies similar to ancient ones can still be found today in Africa, Latin America, and Asia. These are tribes with primitive communal arrangements. By assessing the value of their consumption in current prices, we arrive at approximately the same figures as were typical for peoples of ancient times. A general graph of world GDP (Figure 5) shows us that economic growth has been quite compara-ble with population growth. This implies one simple consistency: the average person worldwide became neither richer nor poorer over a very long period of time. Inside nations, processes were uneven. To compare individual states, another very important indicator is needed – the GDP per capita. Indeed, in China and India, countries with large populations, the public wealth is divided between vast numbers of people.

Maddison's time series have given a powerful tool to researchers, sci-entists, and economists. With this tool, it can be seen that some coun-tries developed better and faster than others.

The main question that researchers of these series are concerned with today is "Why did some countries suddenly begin to develop more 'upwardly', i.e. showing a more energetic GDP per capita growth, while others more 'flatly', with their populations growing in conditions of continued mass poverty? Why did only a few countries manage to grow

ANGUS MADDISON

ANGUS THE GREAT

I am convinced that Angus Maddison (1926-2010) deserves this title. His autobiography, written at the age of 68, is titled *Confessions of a Chiffrephile*. The word 'chiffrephile' is Maddison's coinage, composed of 'chiffre' (French) – 'figure', and 'phile' (from Greek philé) – 'love'.

In 1978, Maddison left the Organization for Economic Cooperation and Development (OECD) to work at the University of Groningen (Netherlands). There he set a daunting task for himself – to calculate the population of the world as a whole, and of particular regions and nations in past epochs down to the 1st century BC, and estimate the gross product for these entities. Fortunately he was successful. Today all economists around the world use this giant time perspective of global economic development unfolded from ancient Rome to the present day.

Why are his calculations so valuable? The task of comparing financial indicators for various years poses a serious problem due to the value of money changing over time. Comparing data for different years requires expressing the GDP in prices for a certain year. Thus, it is only owing to Maddison's rigorous estimates that we know that we are 40 times richer today than the citizens of Rome during its heyday.

Accumulated wealth was distributed very unevenly in empires. Until 1500 AD, both population and accumulated wealth (earnings) grew very slowly. The graph in Figure 5 shows two curves: one represents the global population, and the other the global gross domestic product (GDP) expressed in Geary–Khamis dollars[57] since Anno Domini and to the present day. The curves are gentle and almost coincide, and there is virtually nothing worth noting until the first inflection point (about 1500 AD). Even if the lucky clover bloomed in some countries, as it did in 'the world trade centre' (Byzantium), 'the world factory' (China), and 'the abundant granary' (Egypt), only accelerated development of trade was noticeable, which prompted growth in the population of those countries. From around 1500 AD population begins to grow faster. Trade does not enable the economy to grow at an equal rate with the population growth rate anymore. Thus the trend starts to change around 1870 and the two growth rates become equal in our time only.

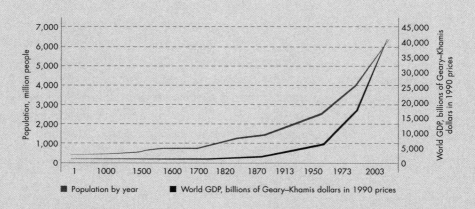

FIGURE 5. POPULATION AND GLOBAL WEALTH GROWTH

in both directions at the same time?" Closer consideration of the GDP per capita in various countries brings more fascinating questions.

Why did some countries develop and grow much faster than others? For example, China showed nearly no change and kept to a constant level of earnings (within US$600 per capita) for nearly 2000 years until 1963. It then experienced a sharp rise. Owing to what? And how long will it last? Considering humanity as a whole (in fact, combining two graphs, one for GDP and one for population), I have produced a very informative visual representation of this (Figure 6) which represents the period from the beginning of our era to the present day.

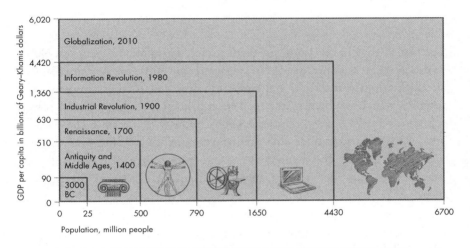

FIGURE 6. WEALTH AND POPULATION GROWTH THROUGHOUT HUMAN HISTORY

Time on this chart is presumed to be projected along a diagonal axis. Along the vertical axis, the GDP per capita is shown. All GDP per capita figures are presented in the equivalent units known to us as Geary–Khamis dollars (in 1990 prices) while taking into account the reconstructed purchasing power. Along the horizontal axis, the world's population in millions is shown.

Let's recall how things were in 3000BC. The average earnings per capita added up to US$90 and the world's population was just over 25 million by the beginning of the Christian era. The dynamic chart in Figure 6 clearly illustrates how the global population and the GDP per capita increased in the days of Egypt and Rome and how these indicators changed during the Renaissance, the Industrial Revolution, the Information Revolution, and the globalization epoch.

How have these things changed since the ancient times? The population has increased 268 times, and the GDP per capita has increased 67 times. The global GDP indicator in Geary–Khamis terms has increased from US$2.2 billion to US$40.3 trillion, or almost 18,000 times!

We owe our science and modern technological advances, as well as our freedom and democracy, to those periods when societies were open; where gold played a twofold role in ancient civilizations and its circulation ensured economic progress, while the lack of it often turned into a problem that led to societal degradation.

The use of gold in international trade enabled empires to create stocks of materials that were not produced domestically. With the position of gold strengthening in international trade, empires began to accumulate gold reserves which enabled states to hire and keep well-trained and robust armed forces. In order to increase their mobility and reduce the costs of army logistics and maintenance, coins were introduced into everyday life.

For the public, the attractiveness and importance of coins was connected with the need to pay taxes. Coins quickly became the primary means of payment that facilitated the conduct of transactions. Monetized businesses quickly grew in number.

As gold and silver coins were introduced, the importance of temples, where the stocks were held, increased, but wide circulation of money required inflows of gold. Mining was developed in Egypt and Rome. Gold became as important for the functioning of the Roman Empire as bread. The well-functioning supply system ensured a high degree of urbanization. The first, democratic forms of ancient Rome were adaptive and ensured growth for the state, despite an ever-increasing density of human networks. These factors combined and brought efflorescence for the culture and prosperity for the public. Adaptive networks with higher density also provided better conditions for the emergence of innovation and contributed to preserving the achievements of human culture with the help of literature and books.

However, later, when masses of people were involved in the process of adopting economic decisions, Rome actually transformed from democracy into an empire ruled by warlords, and fixed its borders.

Centralization of power, tightened control over the public, the introduction of stern mechanisms of state coercion, and suppression of initiatives combined to make the Roman society static.

The resulting order was due to an increased adaptability of human society. New ideas began to form and grow in the minds of the first people. Pros were replaced by cons, since urbanization did not only result in accumulation of knowledge, but it also led to overpopulation, pandemics, and devaluation of money if there was not enough food for the population at large.

The environmental degradation and internal imbalances brought the slave-driven economy of the Roman Empire to a collapse and thus contributed to the creation of the Byzantine Empire, which was driven by the gold solidus and world trade. The population of the Byzantine Empire in its prime reached 35 million people. But the loss of control over such key resources as gold, wheat, and merchant fleets, brought the thousand-year empire to a collapse.

Then the lucky clover bloomed in China until the middle of the 15th century. But there, the accumulated wealth created a false sense of exclusivity and led to isolationism. Knowledge suddenly became a useless toy. Discoveries were forgotten, inventions lost relevance. The lucky clover languished and wilted.

Such were the results. Discoveries and inventions are usually much more numerous than innovations. Inventions become innovations when they are incorporated into an economic system that generates wealth. Innovative processes only work if there are niches in which inventions can be installed and used, there is competition, and the evaluation and remuneration system adequately corresponds with the interests of the public.

CHAPTER 4

SCIENTIFIC REVOLUTION: HOW THE WORLD CHANGED OWING TO THE PRINTING PRESS

> *Of course, scientific truth will always find a way into life, but it is people, not the truth, that can make this way short and direct.*
>
> — **Pyotr Kapitsa,**
> a Nobel laureate and Cryogenmash founder

LITTERA SCRIPTA MANET[58]

Geniuses rarely receive recognition during their lifetime. The death record of inventor Johannes Gutenberg is very modest and says: "On St. Blasius Day in the year 1468, Venerable Master Johannes Gensfleisch zur Laden zum Gutenberg died by the grace of God."[59] And this is all despite Gutenberg's invention, the printing press, fundamentally changing the process of transferring information and disseminating knowledge. German emigrant printers and their foreign apprentices quickly spread the printing technique outside Germany. By 1480, printing shops had been opened in Denmark, Sweden, and Norway (Eisenstei 1993, 17). In Russia, the first printed book, *The Apostle*, was published by the first state printing house through the efforts of Ivan Fedorov in 1564 (Saidasheva 2014, 48-49).

Science had existed in medieval Europe before the invention of the printing press. But, unfortunately, we know little about it. The labour of a scientist was hard before the invention of printing. Tremendous efforts had to be made to obtain the required information and many manuscripts were simply worn out over time, while many were deliberately destroyed in the fight against the then dominant ideology.

Medieval culture replaced that of the Roman Empire, but a hierarchical society nurtured by castles and monasteries meant that large volumes of information were recorded by monks and therefore suffered from excessive orderliness. The distribution of towns in medieval Europe, sparse in comparison to the Roman Empire, caused a reduction in the rates of development of new ideas. In this way, a step back was made in the process of societal evolution.

Some estimate that the Great Men (kings, margraves, barons, etc.) of medieval Europe controlled up to 80% of economic turnover. It appears that it was the Great Man who dominated the selection of business plans and transfer of new ideas, while markets played a secondary role. To transfer skills, successful channels were established in workshops, guilds, and creative groups set up by artists, architects, jewellers, military, and others. The applied nature of such small creative groups enabled them to preserve merely basic techniques and skills rather than scientific knowledge. This is why many historians note that the achievements made by 'medieval techies', such as the clock, the telescope, and measuring instruments, are quite significant in history.

Why did typography manage to survive despite the dominance of church dogmas? The answer is simple: printing appeared to be

GUTENBERG'S PRINTING PRESS, MAINZ, GERMANY, 1450S. Hand-painted wood engraving, 19th century

WHAT GUTENBERG INVENTED

Gutenberg is also credited with the invention of an oil-based ink which was more stable than the water-based paints that had been used before. A jeweller by profession, Gutenberg skilfully used his knowledge of the properties of metals. However, the typographical alloy that came to be used to produce more durable printing characters was invented by Peter Schiffer, Gutenberg's colleague. To produce his 'proprietary' letters, Gutenberg used a special mould with which he could cast new letters very quickly and with extraordinary precision.

advantageous to the church at that time. The Catholic Church was discontented with numerous errors that proliferated in the process of manually copying church books, which then gave rise to different interpretations. In addition, Gutenberg's invention reduced the cost of books by dozens of times (De la Mare 2007, 207). John Andreas, a scientist and Bishop of Aleria, wrote to Pope Leo II in 1468: "How fortunate we are that this blessed gift has been given to Christianity during your lifetime: now even a poor man can buy a library for pennies." (Vernadsky 2007)

However, the invention of printing as such had a surprisingly broader impact. Now large numbers of books could be made available to the public, and ideas could spread throughout various areas, and even countries. This was truly a turning point. Even during Gutenberg's life, it became possible not only to record new observations but distribute them too, and thus constantly update, improve and develop the scientific worldview.

Several centuries later, Academician Vernadsky called typography "a powerful tool that has preserved individuals' thoughts, increasing their power by hundreds of times, and made it possible to overcome imposed alien worldviews in the end" (Vernadsky 2007).

It is not inconceivable that that the starting point of the scientific revolution might be eventually reviewed and moved to the time when the printing press was created. After all, the introduction of printing did not just change the world – it regularized it. Since then, the lucky clover would bloom in every country where the power belonged to books and science.

A HELIOCENTRIC SYSTEM: EARTH CHANGES PLACES WITH THE SUN

A scientific revolution started in 1543 with the publication of a work by Nicolaus Copernicus on the arrangement of a heliocentric system. This work is officially recognized as the event that opened the era of experimental knowledge.

However, nothing comes out of nowhere. History is always a chain of interrelated events and a movement where one step brings about the next. The roots of what we know today as the Copernican heliocentric system are well ramified and go far back into much earlier centuries.

A Greek Pythagorean named Philolaus showed that the Earth moved around the centre of the universe, along with the other planets. In fact, Copernicus had several predecessors who had expressed similar views on the arrangement of the celestial system. The works of Nicolaus Cusanus

(1401-1464) had the most profound effect on Copernicus. Cusanus, for the first time since the ancient Greeks' time and a century before Copernicus, had suggested that the Earth moved both around an axis of its own and around a point in space (which Copernicus took to be the Sun afterwards). Cusanus argued that the universe was infinite and had no centre, with neither the Earth nor the Sun nor anything else occupying a special position in it, and that all celestial bodies were composed of the same material as the Earth, and, quite possibly, were inhabited. He also argued that all celestial bodies moved in space and that any observer was at liberty to consider themselves motionless.

However, written too much ahead of their time, the astronomical works of Cusanus did not attract public attention in his day. Still, Cusanus' ideas were lucky enough to have been born in an era when printing existed. This saved them from extinction and distortion through religious counter-propaganda. Cusanus' manuscripts were published in Rome in 1501, at a printing house built through his own efforts. Cusanus paved the way for the emergence of a heliocentric system; his books came into the right hands, and had a direct effect on the views of Copernicus, Bruno, and Galileo. Only 12 years after the publication of his book, Copernicus fully explained the new theory in a letter to a friend.[60] Copernicus was an atypical representative of his time, and a unique person. His interests included mathematics, law, taxation, medicine, and, of course, astronomy.

Printing gave an innovative push not only to science, but also to other qualitative changes in all the elements of the lucky clover, launching a new, powerful cycle of innovation. After another 40 years of continuous observations and a number of discoveries, Copernicus's work, titled *On the Revolutions of the Heavenly Spheres*, was published.

Copernicus made a significant portion of his astronomical achievements in the 1520s. Watching the planets, the scientist made a number of discoveries, and most importantly, found that the position of the planetary orbits in space did not remain fixed as had been thought previously. In 1523, Copernicus discovered that the apses line – the line that connected the point of the orbit where the planet was closest to the Sun and the point where it was the farthest from it – changed its position in time. He continued observation, and had basically completed the creation of a new theory by the early 1530s. The world system proposed by the ancient Greek scholar Claudius Ptolemy had dominated science for almost one and a half millennia. The system argued that the Earth rested motionless in the centre of the universe and that the sun

INDIAN MATHEMATICIAN SRINIVASA RAMANUJAN (1887-1920).
An Indian postage stamp, 1962

HOW TO FIND A GENIUS

This is the true story of a boy born into a poor family in a small Indian village near Madras on 22 December 1887. Aged seven, he showed an extraordinary ability to memorize numbers, and when he was 16 he was awarded a student grant and enrolled at a local college. One day, several prominent European mathematicians received a letter that said the following: "Dear Sir, I dare to write to you while being an accountant at the Madras port on a salary of only £20 a year. I am 23 years old. I do not have a university education, but I have graduated from high school. I dedicate all my free time to mathematics. I have been studying divergent numerical series, and I have received what Indian mathematicians call amazing results. I am poor and cannot publish the thesis I attach to this letter, but if you find anything of value in it, you are free to publish it. Sincerely, Srinivasa Ramanujan."

Of all the mathematicians he wrote to, only Godfrey Harold Hardy from England responded. Hardy, a very talented mathematician himself, wrote: "I have never seen anything like it. One page is enough to say that this is a piece of mathematics at its highest. These results are correct, because if they were wrong no one would have enough imagination to invent them!" Thanks to Hardy, Ramanujan came to Cambridge. In 1919, aged 33, he died of tuberculosis. He left behind 4,000 theorems. Most of them were found in his letters and three notebooks.

American mathematician Bruce Berndt asserts that the results of Ramanujan's theorems are widely used today in polymer chemistry, computer design, and cancer research, though his works have not yet been studied in full by anyone. Hardy said that he considered his 'discovery' of Ramanujan his greatest contribution to mathematics.

and the other planets revolved around it. Ptolemy's theory failed to explain many of the phenomena that were well known to astronomers – in particular, the meandering movement of planets in the visible sky (especially the 'reverse' motion of Mars, although in reality Earth just overtook Mars in its motion around the Sun). But the provisions of Ptolemy's system were considered inviolable, as they were in perfect agreement with the teachings of the Catholic Church.

Watching the movement of celestial bodies, Copernicus concluded that Ptolemy's theory was not so much wrong as inaccurate. After 30 years of hard work, continued observations, and complex mathematical calculations, he convincingly proved that the Earth was just one of the planets, and that all the planets revolved around the Sun. Having discovered that the Earth and the planets were satellites of the Sun, Copernicus managed to explain the visible motion of the Sun across the sky, the strange inconsistency in the movement of some of the planets, and the visible rotation of the sky. Copernicus's astronomical works were not appreciated by his contemporaries. On the genius scale suggested by Stanislav Lem, they are closest to the 'absolute genius' level.[62]

The first edition of *On the Revolutions of the Heavenly Spheres* was published by the Lutherans, and only a few copies of it came to Italy, England, and other non-Lutheran countries. The second edition was published in Basel in 1566 and sold out all over Europe. By the end of the century, Copernicus's views were well known, but the heliocentric doctrine could not be taught openly, and was only referred to, if ever, as a hypothesis.

Copernicus based his heliocentric system on clear deduction. A very small part of the book is devoted to the solar system, most of it containing mathematical calculations. It was from Copernicus that the countdown to new science, a science based on experiment, research, and recognition of nature as the main creator of all things in the universe, began.

CHANGING THE PARADIGM

With the appearance of Copernicus's mathematically proven hypothesis, humankind's perception of the outside world began to change gradually but fundamentally. In fact, a radical change had taken place in the scientific view of the world. Nature and Science (logos), previously obliged to obey Religion and Ideology (myth), were now in the vanguard of progress. Such a cardinal shift simply could not have been assessed accurately by Copernicus's contemporaries. For thousands of years,

NICOLAUS COPERNICUS.
Illustration from Meyers
Konversations-Lexikon,
a German encyclopaedia
published in 1905-1909

NICOLAUS COPERNICUS

Nicolaus Copernicus (1473-1543) was a Polish astronomer who studied mathematics, medicine, and theology at the University of Krakow, the largest European academic centre at that time. Upon completion of the university course, Copernicus travelled in Germany and Italy, attended lectures in various universities, and even held professorships in Rome and Krakow, making astronomical observations. The main work of his life, titled *On the Revolutions of the Heavenly Spheres* (1543), was banned by the Catholic Church from 1616 to 1828.[61] Copernicus is mostly remembered as a great astronomer.

people had construed the world under the influence of their cultural (i.e. established as historical tradition) perceptions. And then suddenly an obvious and generally accepted requisite as the revolution of the Sun around the Earth was absurd. And there was proof of this too, though in the form of mathematical calculations that could only be understood by one in a thousand.

Later, in the 20th century, this phenomenon was adequately explained by the American philosopher Thomas Kuhn. He introduced the term 'paradigm shift' in modern language (Kuhn 1962). Some years earlier, the Russian scientist Vladimir Vernadsky called such historical phenomena 'changes in the scientific view of the world'.[63]

In *The Structure of Scientific Revolutions*, Kuhn presented the development of scientific knowledge as an intermittent, revolutionary process, the essence of which is represented by the concept of paradigm shift (Kuhn 1962, 11).

The 17th century is called the century of genius and many European countries experienced a peak in their development. Science witnessed the appearance of Galileo Galilei in Italy, Blaise Pascal and René Descartes in France, Francis Bacon and Isaac Newton in England, and Christiaan Huygens in Holland. The names of many others who raised the prestige of European universities could be added to this list. In Germany, the brilliant mathematician and astronomer Johannes Kepler (1571-1630) continued the scientific revolution, writing works on the orbits of planets and the laws of motion, and developing scientific methods of research. His discoveries laid the foundations of modern theoretical astronomy.

Kepler's achievements are truly surprising for those who are familiar with his biography. He was born into a poor family and had poor health, suffering from fever attacks, gastric disorders, skin diseases, and a congenital defect of sight. Being a Protestant surrounded by a Catholic majority, Kepler was persecuted for his faith all his life and even forced to leave his house twice, leaving all his property behind. Many troubles befell his family too: his first wife died early, and less than half of his 12 children lived beyond the age of 10 (Bely 2013).

High-ranking nobles often delayed payment of his salary. He had the misfortune of living during the Thirty Years' War (1618-1648), one of the most violent wars in Europe's history. For the last 12 years of his life he worked in warfare conditions, his house being occupied by soldiers and his life hanging by a thread. Still, despite all the difficulties, he continued his work, became one of the greatest astronomers, and kept his faith (Banville 1981).

BRAVE ACROBATS.
Rob Gonsalves, 2009

WHAT A PARADIGM IS

The word is often used in modern language in the sense that American historian and philosopher of scientific knowledge Thomas Kuhn (1922-1996) gave it. Kuhn's main work, *The Structure of Scientific Revolutions*, was published in 1962. It was there that the Greek word paradigm ('example' or 'sample') acquired a new meaning: an initial conceptual method, a model for stating and solving problems. Since then, a paradigm shift has meant a scientific revolution. This is how the word paradigm, which had previously been used only in linguistics and rhetoric, gained a much wider use.

Today we understand an academic community as a community of people who accept a certain paradigm. In the 17th century, a community of scientists did not only deal with 'science', but also explained the essence of theories that had been put forward, and demonstrated the fields where those theories could be applied. They took nothing on trust, but compared hypotheses with observations and experimental results.

The Scientific Revolution (1450-1730) was a period when the emergence of new scientific ideas led to the rejection of doctrines that had been considered inviolable since the days of ancient Greece.[64] Preconditions for the scientific revolution were set in ancient times: academic knowledge was developed in the Roman-Byzantine period first and then in the Middle Ages, by both Islamic and European scholars. Nearly every scientific revolutionary had brilliant predecessors. Thus, Nicolaus Copernicus was preceded by Nicolaus Cusanus, and still earlier, in the 4th century BC, by Aristotle, who had favoured a heliocentric model of the world. Similarly, Andreas Vesalius, in his work *On the Fabric of the Human Body*, developed Galen's teachings in anatomy.

New scientific methods set the course of history in each field of science for generations of scientists to follow. This was possible due to sufficient openness of scholarly works, allowing new generations of scientists to find for themselves unsolved problems of all kinds. Kuhn distinguished several stages in the scientific development of a discipline: a pre-paradigm stage (the period prior to the establishment of a paradigm), a paradigm dominance stage (normal science), a crisis of normal science stage, and a scientific revolution stage, the essence of which lies in the transition from one paradigm to another (Kuhn 1962, 5). This structuring is very similar to the categorization into stages that Schumpeter's followers used later when they described the 'technological paradigm shift' theory. We see the same S-shaped curves rising over time. I would like to illustrate this with an example from Thomas Kuhn's book *The Structure of Scientific Revolutions* (Table 2).

STAGES OF DEVELOPMENT OF SCIENCE ACCORDING TO KUHN	STAGES OF DEVELOPMENT OF ASTRONOMY
Pre-paradigm stage	No successful system for predicting the positions of planets existed before the 2nd century BC
Paradigm dominance stage	Ptolemy's system, formulated in the 2nd century BC, had extraordinary success due to being able to predict changes in the positions of stars and planets
Normal science crisis stage	Predictions of the positions of planets never agreed fully with more accurate observations (but the identification of the errors was slow due to the absence of printing and lack of communication between scientists); continued eagerness to dispose of these small differences created numerous fundamental problems (e.g. the social demand to change the calendar); at the beginning of the 16th century, many excellent astronomers realize that the existing astronomy paradigm fails in dealing with its traditional problems
Scientific revolution, paradigm shift	Publication of Copernicus's *On the Revolutions of the Heavenly Spheres*; a heliocentric model becomes the new paradigm

TABLE 2. PARADIGM SHIFT IN ASTRONOMY

The scientific revolution brought about a radical change in the ways the world was perceived and explained by people. By transforming the thought process, the revolution caused a radical reform in knowledge, explaining both man and nature in a fundamentally new way. Thinkers overthrew the authority of the medieval, classical perception of the world and in its stead, they created a new cult: science that could explain everything that existed, and not as a succession of God's mighty works, but as a logical result of the development of nature. These scientific revolutionaries overturned the course of world history, recognized nature as the ruler of the universe, and made scientific consciousness the central pillar of human existence, the key element of civilization, an idea which has continued to this day (Table 3).

Mathematics became the key for these great people. For example, Galileo Galilei believed that nature could only be questioned in the language of mathematics, but believed that mathematical analysis and theory must be based on experimental evidence. For Galileo, scientific evidence was the result of observation and measurement of the primary properties of objects – amount, shape, size, and motion – rather than the secondary properties, such as colour, sound, and smell. According to Galileo, nature only responded to questions asked in the language of mathematics, because mathematics represented the realm of measure and order.

All the great scientists (Galileo Galilei, Isaac Newton, René Descartes) had the major characteristic of an experimenter: they always sought to confirm their theories by real-life testing. Good scientific theories were expected to fit into reality absolutely naturally. Their approach cannot be described as purely mathematical: it was rather physical and mathematical, since reality was for them mathematics embodied in matter.

The most innovative idea about the essence of the scientific method was expressed by Galileo. In his book *The Assayer*, he said: "Philosophy is written in this grand book, the universe, which stands continually open to our gaze. But the book cannot be understood unless one first learns to comprehend the language and read the letters in which it is composed. It is written in the language of mathematics, and its characters are triangles, circles, and other geometric figures without which it is humanly impossible to understand a single word of it; without these, one wanders about in a dark labyrinth." (Galilei 2011)

YEARS OF LIFE	SCIENTIST	PUBLICATIONS/WORKS
1473-1543	Nicolaus Copernicus	*On the Revolutions of the Celestial Spheres* (1543) – a presentation of the heliocentric theory.
1514-1564	Andreas Vesalius	*On the Fabric of the Human Body* (1543) – refutation of Galen's views: Vesalius discovered that blood circulation was due to heartbeat.
1544-1603	William Gilbert	*On the Magnet and Magnetic Bodies, and on That Great Magnet the Earth* (1600) – a presentation of a basic theory of electricity and magnetism.
1561-1626	Francis Bacon	*New Instrument of Science* (1620) – a presentation of a new system of logic based on a process of reduction: a significant contribution to the development of the scientific method.
1564-1642	Galileo Galilei	He improved the telescope, made important astronomical discoveries, and meticulously observed sunspots. His main achievement was popularization of advanced Copernican astronomy. Three pillars of Galileo's scientific approach were intuition, reasoning, and experimentation.
1571-1630	Johannes Kepler	He published the first two of the three laws of planetary motion in 1609. He continued to carry out the scientific revolution, writing works on planetary orbits and the laws of motion, and developing scientific methods of research.
1596-1650	René Descartes	*Discourse on the Method of Rightly Conducting one's Reason and Seeking Truth in the Sciences* (1637) – a contribution to the development of the scientific method.
1632-1723	Antoine van Leeuwenhoek	He constructed a powerful single-lens microscope and made detailed observations, the results of which he published about 1660, thus discovering the microscopic world of biology.

TABLE 3. STAGES OF THE EMERGENCE OF NEW SCIENCES

THE ASCENT OF THE WEST

The brief presentation of world science history above emphasizes that before the 1500s, population growth played a direct and crucial role in a civilization gaining strength, while, as we have seen, undermining the development of civilization at the same time. After that point, a new stage began: the ascent of western countries.

In the closing paragraphs of the previous chapter I spoke about a change in the long-term economic performance of Western Europe, clearly visible in statistical series (Delong 1988). In 1000 AD, the level of earnings in Europe was lower than that in Asia and North Africa. However, a long period of recovery, once underway, enabled Europe to catch up with China (the world leader at that time) as early as during the 14th century. The graph below shows the aggregate GDP of China, India and Japan (the East) in comparison with that of the US, Europe, and Russia (the West).

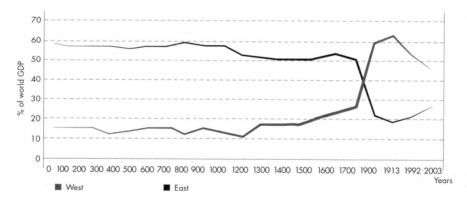

FIGURE 7. SHARES OF THE WEST AND EAST IN THE WORLD GDP

The graph presented in Figure 7 shows that before 1000AD, Asia's share in the world GDP was about 60%, and Europe's about 15%; then, from 1000 to 1500, Asia's share was 50%, and Europe's 20-25%. During that period, earnings per capita increased significantly (almost doubled) in Western Europe, whereas China's earnings increased by only one-third, other Asian countries showed a less significant growth, and Africa demonstrated regression. Even today, the growth in the levels of earnings and productivity in Western Europe during that period looks like a miracle.

The seeds sown by the scientific revolution enabled Europe to reach a level of earnings and productivity that was more than two times higher than that in the rest of the world by 1820!

Taking into consideration the population dynamics, Europe should have stayed on the side-lines of the global economy, since more people meant more probability of discovery. Asia had for a long time been an object of admiration and the worldwide centre of wealth. China was the centre of absolute wealth, but its arrogance and determination to isolate itself from the world so as to prevent the loss of the monopoly on technology set the country on a losing course.

Of course, the West overtook the East in part because the Europeans managed to discover the New World, which presented the world with evidence of the existence of something that the church and religious doctrine could not explain.

Books, science, and the era of great geographical discoveries brought about a revolution in the acquisition and dissemination of new knowledge, and in ways of doing business, by introducing innovations such as banking, which have laid the foundations of the modern financial system, and then by changing the whole social structure in Europe. This is why the graph shows Asia's share in world production going down, and Europe's going up. Europe owes its prosperity to the scientific revolution prepared and carried out by talented scientists. The advent of a new scientific paradigm created auspicious conditions for the development of key innovations of that period, such as the printing press, the scientific method, mathematization of science, the heliocentric model of the world, magnetism and electricity, the steam boiler, physics, chemistry, and even...the simple timepiece.

Several centuries after the fall of Rome, market towns began to thrive in northern Italy again. Urban development and progress in handicraft production during this period stimulated the development of commodity-money exchange and the formation of early capitalist relations. The advance of commodity production caused a significant expansion of trade and market relations. More and more agricultural produce was exchanged for urban handicraft goods through trading, thus becoming involved in commercial turnover. This instigated growth in the country's commodity production, the transformation of peasants into commodity producers, and the formation of an internal market. The expansion of trade facilitated accumulation of money and the emergence of a currency market. This period, marked by further development of the feudal system, vitalization of cities as centres of economic life, and the inception of capital-based relations, made Italy one of the centres of Renaissance culture.

The economic system, moving from feudal relations to initial forms of modern capitalism, was becoming less hierarchical, while the network was becoming denser. The Renaissance broke information impediments and facilitated free exchange of ideas, enabling scientists and innovators to breathe life into the European continent. The circle closed again, and society finally returned to the parameters of the days of the Roman democracy.

As John Desmond Bernal, an English physicist and sociologist, shrewdly remarked, the Renaissance made academic specialists look at the world in a different light. Religion, superstition, and fear were replaced by common sense and knowledge (Bernal 1954). Fear and prejudice (myth) gave way to logic and argument (logos). Renaissance scientists were not agents of absolutely new ideas, but through a shift in viewing things, aided by experiment and observation, they successfully developed the intellectual wealth that had already been accumulated by mankind.

Gutenberg's invention could not have come at a better time, since not only did it make the production of books cheaper, but also dramatically speeded it up. A new industry emerged, reproducing cultural 'memes'. Thanks to this, the best minds were able to disseminate their ideas widely.

New (or well-forgotten old) world order ideas that ran counter to the dogmas of the church changed society's views on methods of obtaining the truth, and deprived the church of the monopoly in this matter. The scientific method was rooted in society. The scientific revolution created visions based on formulating hypotheses and subjecting them to criticism. As a result, knowledge began to grow, and enabled people to improve substantially their quality of life, to settle on new territories, and to thicken community networks. As a result, prerequisites emerged in Europe for the formation of a dynamic society with a very high network density and good conditions for consolidation, development, and dissemination of new ideas, and, consequently, for innovation growth. Europe was able to overtake Asia in terms of accumulated wealth thanks to commercialization of knowledge and the development of a 'technological approach' in Western European society. The acquisition of knowledge became necessary for personal success, the popularity of universities as all-embracing depots of versatile knowledge was growing, and the scientific method was used to acquire new knowledge instead of religious revelation.

CHAPTER 5

COMMERCIAL AND BANKING REVOLUTIONS; HOW WARS WERE FINANCED

"Never loiter about the Palazzo della Signoria as if you have been called there by your business. Go there only if you have been called by others, and take official positions only if requested. Never exhibit yourselves before people, and if this cannot be avoided, try to keep your representation to a minimum. Stay away from the public, and never go against the will of the people, except when the people defend something that is fraught with trouble..."

— The last words of Giovanni di Bicci, the founder of the Medici clan, to his sons, Cosimo and Lorenzo, in 1428

The word 'accumulation' best characterizes the Middle Ages in Europe. Not 'obscurantism', not 'indulgence', not 'war', and not even 'renaissance'. Today macroeconomists call this notion 'savings', but the meaning remains the same. 'Accumulation' encapsulates the essence of the concept well. Accumulation takes place in cognitive processes, in biology, and in finances. But accumulation (savings) is impossible without a 'container' where the funds could be placed.

Tycho Brahe accumulated unique data, which Kepler inherited and used to formulate new laws.[66] Kepler's experience, made available thanks to the invention of printing, was in turn used by Newton, who discovered the basic principles of mechanics. Accumulation of gold, as discussed in Chapter 2, meant economic and physical power over people and nations. Accumulation of administration experience by empires and the emergence of national states brought about the need for coinage as a medium in commodity exchange. At that time, the quality of a coin characterized the accumulated power of the state that minted it.

The minting of the first sterling European coin – the denarius – was initiated by Emperor Frederick Barbarossa (1122-1190) in Milan in 1162. This coin received the sonorous name 'imperial', was made of gold, and used in trade between North Italian cities. However, the scale of the coinage did not permit this monetary unit to become international. At the same time, a silver coin called the 'groschen' was also put into circulation besides the golden imperial.

In the second half of the 13th century, a new coin worth 12 denarii was issued, to serve as an equivalent of the Byzantine solidus. This coin was distributed in European countries in different modifications whose names have, thanks to literature, survived to the present day: shilling, soldo, sou, and others.

Soon enough, new 'denominations' came to be minted in the northern Italian cities of Genoa, Florence, and Venice, affecting the development of the European gold coinage system.

In 1252, a gold coin was minted in Florence, which contained 3.52 grams of pure gold. Called 'florins', these coins very quickly became an international means of payment and models for other coins minted in Western and Central Europe. At first, Florence maintained a strict relation between the gold and the silver coins. However, this bimetallic monetary system proved to be (as other such systems had before) extremely unstable. The silver ratings steadily deteriorated and the florin soon cost much more denarii.

This predetermined the need for a currency reform, and the production of a sterling silver coin that had greater value than the spoiled denarius. This coin was called 'grosso'.[67] In the first half of the 13th century, the grosso, worth 12 denarii, became the main coin of the Tuscan League.

The presence of a well-organized monetary exchange system started a new wave in the development of trade relations with the Arab East and Byzantium. Thus, in conditions of medieval dictate, prerequisites for the emergence of European banking formed.

Before that, the Christian church had prescribed that only Jews could lend money at interest to people of other nationalities.[68] But development of economic relations was impossible without lending and as a result, lenders tried to get around the prohibition, using such tools as pawning, providing loans, and repayment of loans in more rewarding coins than those in which the loan was provided.

Medieval money-changers often provided banking services. However, since usury was condemned by the state and punished by the law (under the influence of the church), money was usually lent by merchants who were united in large companies. Such partnerships provided funding for both industrial production and trade and banking operations. These organizations had small offices which were often separated by a trestle table on which traders closed deals and changed coins. The word 'bank' and other modern terms in the financial industry originated from the Italian 'banco' ('bench', 'table').

THE MEDICI: THE SECRETS OF THE LIBRO SEGRETO

As a result of rapid development of trade, 'maritime loans' became popular in medieval Florence. A merchant or a ship owner, when going to sea, acquired a certain amount of money from a lender. This money had to be returned, together with the interest, when the merchant arrived at the port of destination or returned to the port where he started the voyage.

Interest on such loans was quite high. At the end of the 12th century, it was 20-25% – but only for the duration of the voyage, not per annum! If the journey was not too long but very dangerous, the interest could reach 50%.[69]

The provision of loan capital was a very profitable and very risky business, especially so for bankers who lent money to governments and the sovereigns of foreign countries. These bankers depended on the political and economic situation and on the borrowers' military victories or defeats. As a result, there were no large banks in the market for a long time.

A number of large Florentine companies went bankrupt very soon after their inception, because of the English king's inability to pay his debts as a result of having political and economic problems with Florence and the Kingdom of Naples. Thus, in place of the Bardi, Peruzzi, and Acciaiuoli families that had gone bankrupt owing to incurred risks, the more cautious Medici (Italian banking family) arrived (Strathern 2003).

BANKING

The first banks in Italy often had an 'all-in-one' structure, were thus highly vulnerable, and could go bankrupt through the fault of just one debtor. The Medici Bank, in contrast, was a partnership with multiple connections, each of which acted on the basis of a special and regularly reviewed contract. Branch managers were not hired employees, but rather junior partners who received a share of the profits. It was this decentralized structure that enabled the Medici Bank to become a thriving enterprise.

Representatives of this dynasty ruled Florence for three centuries. Two popes, three dukes (of Florence, Nemours, and Tuscany) and even two queens of France (Catherine and Marie) came from this family. The Medici became the most influential banking family in the history of Italy. It should be noted, though, that their status as the principal medieval bankers was based not so much on economic efficiency as on political shrewdness. This quality, difficult to do without even in our day, was simply indispensable at that time.

THE SECRETS OF THE LIBRO SEGRETO[70]

Giovanni di Bicci de' Medici, the founding father of Italy's most famous banking family, established the Medici Bank, stipulated the basic principles of banking, and laid a solid foundation of wealth destined to serve as a springboard for the family in its pursuit of political power. With his bank's profits growing, Giovanni di Bicci used only conservative methods to increase his capital, buying land in the Florentine valley and on the Tuscan hills that surrounded the city. Later, having become wealthier, he began buying property in the city itself. The Medici Bank was developing steadily, though the volumes of its transactions still could not be compared with those of any of its three predecessors, the Florentine banks that had gone bankrupt.[71] Di Bicci simply never tried to swallow a piece that he would not be able to digest.

The Medici's success was nearly always based on the use of techniques that had already been tested by others. Initially, the bill of exchange, an instrument that had been widely used in the Middle Ages as a means of financing trade, was of particular importance for the Medici.[72] Bankers had no cheques; instructions were given verbally and recorded in the banking books. No interest existed; investors were given 'discrezione' (these were personal deposits that yielded profit to the depositors in proportion to the company's annual profit) as compensation for putting their own money at risk.[73]

The Medici played an important role in establishing a banking system that made extensive use of branch banks. The Medici's novelty feature was transfer of financial capital and political titles by inheritance, i.e. accumulation as such. They succeeded having learned an important lesson: scale is of the essence in financial activities.

Enlarging their bank and providing a greater variety of services than any financial institution had done before, the Medici actually invented a method for risk distribution. They reduced non-payment risks by trading in currency (letters of exchange) and issuing loans. The Medici were the first to introduce diversification of risk in banking: they did not issue large loans to a single debtor and operated in many places at the same time through their branches (partnerships). Decentralization enabled them to keep their business for many centuries.

The development of the bill of exchange as a useful tool to finance trade operations only became possible thanks to the Medici, because they had the largest branch network. By selling their papers, the Medici earned good money using time and exchange rates between various currencies to their advantage. A Venetian merchant going to London would buy a bill of exchange from the Medici for Venetian ducats and the bill would indicate the sum to be issued in England in pounds and the period of time after which the merchant would be able to exchange his paper (at the London branch of the Medici Bank). If the ducat exchange rate grew during the merchant's travel, he would lose money (and the bank would earn on the difference between the rates); if the exchange rate sank, the merchant would benefit from the difference between the exchange rates. The Medici Bank would win in any case because the London branch bought out the ducats (the liability in paper form), but did it for the Venetian branch rather than for itself. In addition, the merchant's ducats could be used by the bankers interest-free during the whole period of his travel to England. In the end, the Venetian branch returned as many ducats as it received, but did it at a different branch of the bank, after some time, and interest-free.

**AN ILLUSTRATION FOR WILLIAM SHAKESPEARE'S
'THE MERCHANT OF VENICE'**
– the scene where Shylock is indicted and Antonio freed

THE DUCAT AS AN INNOVATION IMMORTALISED BY THE GREAT SHAKESPEARE

The Latin word 'ducere' means 'to lead' or 'to guide'. A commander was called 'dux' in the Roman Empire. In Italian, the word transformed into 'duca', and hence came the English word 'duke', meaning a 'high-ranked man' or 'ruler'. A duke, governing a smaller area than the king, often did so more efficiently, and could be more powerful than the king himself.

In 1140, the governor of Venice put ducats into circulation, which gained wide use. A Venetian Jew called Shylock, one of the main characters in Shakespeare's play *The Merchant of Venice* (1596-1597), grieving for his daughter who runs away from home taking his money with her, exclaims: "O my ducats! O my daughter!" In Shakespeare's comedy, Shylock is a usurer who has given a loan to Antonio, a merchant, against the pledge of a pound of flesh from Antonio's own chest, and is doggedly trying to persuade the court to impose the execution of the contract.

From a modern point of view, the play presents Shylock as a humiliated and dispossessed man who has nothing but his revenge. Even the humanity of Venetian laws does not apply to him, because he is a Jew.

Venetian ducats were widely used in the Balkans, the Mediterranean, and the Middle East. Starting from 1325, they spread throughout Europe. Since 1559, a ducat weighing 3.49 grams was the main coin of the Holy Roman Empire. The Austro-Hungarian Empire minted such ducats until 1915, and the Czech Republic and Yugoslavia stopped minting them only between the First and Second World Wars.

The Medici's branch network made it possible to accumulate huge amounts of money, changing, through paper, florins for pennies, ducats for pounds, and vice versa. In this scheme, the only question was which of the Medici partnerships would keep the profit from each particular transaction. As a result, the business as a whole was very stable.

Giovanni di Bicci de' Medici and his followers recorded all their transactions in their famous book, called the *Libro Segreto*. The book provides many interesting facts, such as, for example, that the Venetian branch of the Medici Bank was founded in 1402 and that after a short time it managed to occupy a prominent place in the extensive trading operations of the Venetian Republic, buying and selling wool on the Valencia market and participating in the shipment of spices and amber from the East to Venice.

Most of the banks employed less than 10 employees. Clerks employed by the Medici Bank earned about 50 florins a year – that sum would get one a decent living. According to the Libro Segreto records for 1397 to 1420, out of a total profit of 151,820 florins, the Roman branch earned more than half. The reason for the difference was that the Medici Bank had at that time two departments in Rome: the Roman branch per se and a branch stationed directly with the papal court. One branch always accompanied the papal court in journeys so as to cover the pope's and its court's immediate financial needs.[74] The second branch stayed in Rome, engaged in the main business of dealing with the papal revenues from abroad.

During the reign of Pope Martin V, the Medici Bank was licensed to mint coins. It was not for good appearances, of course, that the bank gained this privilege. The Libro Segreto contains interesting information pertaining to that period: the balance sheet of the Roman branch, includes a large list of personal deposit accounts, opened 'a discrezione' (secret accounts to which interest on deposits was accrued in violation of the prohibition imposed by the Church on usury). Such deposits ranged from 2,600 to 15,000 florins and the circle of depositaries included cardinals, several prelates and a close friend of the Pope.

Further the book tells us about the extraordinary generosity of Cosimo de' Medici, the son and heir of Giovanni di Bicci de' Medici. He spent 660,000 florins to support arts. For all that, it has been estimated that Cosimo inherited about 100,000 florins from his father and, in the face of all his philanthropy, left to his heirs by the end of his life more than 200,000 florins, i.e. twice as much.

THE MEDICI AS THE FOUNDING FATHERS OF STOCK MARKETS

The Greek philosopher, Heraclitus said: "War is the father of all things, the father of everything."The word 'father' appears here because the Greek word for war ('polemos') is masculine and means 'power', 'conceiving and inseminating force', or 'initiating energy'. For most of us, the notion of war is associated with extremely negative connotations, but first of all war means utmost concentration of strength in an effort to achieve economic benefits. Some time later, Niccolò Machiavelli wrote that "war is a pragmatic means of implementing the material interests of the state" (Dugin 2007, part 2, sec. 6).

During the 14th and 15th centuries, the medieval city-states of Florence, Tuscany, Pisa, Siena, Milan, and Venice waged wars against one another and emerging territories of present-day Germany and France. For warfare, Italian cities often formed unions. Most often, the initiators of such wars had them waged by mercenaries. To save its own residents from the dirty warfare business, a belligerent city would hire military contractors ('condottieri') who then recruited soldiers, seized the land of their opponent, and then plundered mercilessly. Thus, it was in 1430 too, when the Florentine army commanded by Rinaldo degli Albizzi (the future rival of the Medici) set off for Lucca, a small Italian town. This city-state had had the cheek to form an alliance with Milan, and thus had put Florence in danger of losing access to the sea in the area of the city of Pisa. For Florence, this meant loss of trade relations.

The whole of northern Italy was soon involved in this war. Venice immediately declared war on Milan, forcing it to stop supporting Lucca, and the powerful Genoese fleet went to sea and set off to the port of Pisa, so vital for Florence, in order to capture it. All these details would be superfluous if it were not for one question: how were such large-scale hostilities funded?

More powerful than Florence, Milan and Venice financed the wars from their coffers. Where could the Florentines find adequate funds? The answer is surprising. The government of Florence (the city was a republic ruled by 'signors') conducted a usurious transaction which was permitted by the church since it represented a mandatory loan.[75] According to the deal, the prosperous citizens were exempt from property taxes, but were obliged to lend money to the city government for warfare needs. In exchange for these enforced loans (called 'prestanze'), the rich were actually entitled to receive interest on the plunder in the future.

But the Florentines' brilliant plan failed. In April 1433, a peace treaty was agreed, according to which all parties were to return to their pre-war position. Considerable losses had been suffered, and many influential Florentines were furious. Emotions prevented them to assess their own invention – government loans – which, unlike the direct negative consequences of the infamous war, would survive for centuries and form a basis for many future wars. The method of financing wars through government debt was, like so many other things in the history of finance, invented by the Italian Renaissance.

Today, it looks absolutely natural when governments and large corporations issue debt securities to receive finance from a large number of people and institutions. The real importance of this point, however, should be understood well. After the introduction of loans by banks, the invention of debt securities was the second great innovation in the ascent of money. Why?

Continuing Heraclitus's proverb, we can say that if war is the father of everything, the debt system in particular, having been generated by war, is the mother... of stock markets, or 'bourses', as they were called at that time. The ability to sell loans to the public when investors needed cash was an important feature of the Florentine banking system.

The republican government of Florence made its citizens the largest investors in their own state. By the beginning of the 15th century, two-thirds of the city's homeowners had invested in Florence's debt securities. This quasi-republic, though ruled by a few wealthy families such as the Medici, was nevertheless a progressive form of government in comparison with various forms of hereditary monarchy established in many of medieval Europe's cities. While a tyrannical government could arbitrarily breach its payment obligations to creditors, in Florence, people who issued debt securities on behalf of the government would often buy them as well. The public controlled the city's government and finance. The people's keenness to have interest paid on their own loans served as a starting point for providing a solid political base for this system. It was thus this innovation that brought about the appearance of such a phenomenon as the stock exchange afterwards.

However, the history of the Italian city-state of Florence in the 15th century was not smooth. The new humanistic philosophy professed by the Medici prioritized knowledge, intellectual independence, and curiosity. Florence at that time was a place where new ideas produced further, completely new, ideas. But the progress did not last long.

A charismatic monk called Girolamo Savonarola argued that Florence must return to the medieval values and the only true moral values, and predicted that the city would perish otherwise. In 1494, Savonarola managed to seize power and succeeded in having the city rid of luxury. This, however, also meant the return of all the earlier restrictions on art, literature, thought, and behaviour. Later, Savonarola was deposed and burned at the stake, but the former optimism did not return to Florence. The flowering period of the city's lucky clover proved to be short-lived.

VENICE: MONEY ON TRUST

Other cities in Italy also contributed to the formation of a worldwide financial system. In fact, Venice developed a system of public debt even earlier than Florence, in the late 12th century. In 1171, an equity company that had existed in Venice for decades acquired the form of a deposit union.

In the 14th century, Venice's consolidated long-term debt, called the Monte Vecchio ('the Old Mountain'), played a key role in funding this city-state's wars with Genoa and other rivals. A new mountain of debt – the Monte Nuovo – arose after the protracted war with the Ottoman Empire that raged between 1463 and 1479. Like the Florentine prestanze, the Venetian prestiti were forced loans, but with a secondary market which allowed investors to sell their bonds to other investors for cash.

In Venice, banks operated under the direct control of the municipality. Even if a bank acted as an independent institution, the city council had the right to check its operations. This was because the law regarded the depositors of a bank as its actual owners. At some point, the city council ordered that all payments in the city must be processed through a single bank, which significantly facilitated debt repayment and loan provision, since Venice was at that time one of the worldwide industry and trade centres.[76] In the second quarter of the 17th century, the city set up an efficient system for multilateral debt repayment and, moreover, international loan provision. That said, Venetian banks could not provide loans via current accounts, while in other cities state deposits and non-cash payments were allowed to be made on less stringent terms.

Venetian bankers had to invent and implement new techniques that facilitated the creation of IOU money. In Venice, a lender typically did not cash a cheque, but instead requested his banker to credit his current account. If the lender did not have such an account, the debtor, in order to fulfil his obligations, could provide the lender with a certificate of deposit ('fede di credito') which could be used to make payments to a third party who had a bank account. Sometimes this passed through several hands before reaching an account, and thus served as an efficient tool for streamlining money circulation. The Venetian fede di credito represented an early form of paper money, or 'money on trust', as it were, and considerably advanced the evolution of the global banking system, showing that financial markets were the best means of distributing and raising capital, conducting monetary exchange operations, and optimizing the wellbeing of society.

Seeking to achieve equilibrium, markets stimulate the selection of projects that express the needs and preferences of most of the population. Markets are a means of reallocation of resources from less competitive to more competitive projects, acting as evolutionary machines designed for qualitative selection of projects. They are more efficient in allocating resources than a Great Man, however, they can destroy most traditional solid technological and social rents by means of innovation and creating new product niches. The strong side of a market is that it offers the best opportunity for economic growth through unbiased selection of business plans and projects.

TRANSFER OF POWER FROM DEFAULTERS TO BANKERS

Against the background of incessant wars, a banking and commercial revolution began in Europe. The situation was complicated by warfare against the Ottoman Empire, rampant plague, and lack of gold. The very development of trade was suffering the effects of more than a hundred years' deflation (from 1540-1640). There were no favourable conditions for the lucky clover to blossom.

Large-scale international trade required the presence of a fully fledged credit sector. Even before the Medici, Europe's money market had been dominated by Tuscan merchant bankers who moved their offices from Bruges (the then financial centre of Europe) to Antwerp in 1500.[77] These banks held negotiations with the King of Portugal at the beginning of the 16th century, as a result of which a monopoly was established in the city of Antwerp with a view to distributing spices in Europe, and a new financial centre emerged.

At the same time, other merchant bankers, from Genoa, occupied leading positions in the Iberian Peninsula. With their loans, they supported the great discoveries of the Portuguese and Spanish.

Considerable sums were invested in establishing sugar plantations on Atlantic Ocean islands and funding the Portuguese' trading in spices and gold with West Africa. Afterwards, the great geographical discoveries made by the Spanish conquistadors broke the monetary restrictions on economic freedom. A new source of revenue acquired by Spain – a whole continent with enormous silver reserves – created, at long last, favourable conditions for the lucky clover in Europe.

In the Lucky Clover model, finance comes in to play after discoveries and inventions have passed through the commercialization stage. So, innovations in the banking sector were themselves an invention that stimulated the development of society, contributing to its transformation on the threshold of a new round of development.

In the 16th century, the Genoese first supported the Portuguese' trade relations with India and the Far East. Later, they largely shifted their focus to the New World, which needed substantial financial support. Significant capital was required to fund the silver mines in Mexico and Peru and organize the delivery of raw materials to Europe and Asia.

The production of silver in the 16th century became so important that its arrival in Seville from Mexico and Peru had an enormous economic and political effect on the whole of Europe. The Spanish 'piastres' began to dominate in international payments. Soon the entire system acquired strategic importance for foreign policy. After 1534, bills of exchange that travelled through the Iberian Peninsula came under ferocious criticism from the authorities. The rulers suddenly identified them as hidden interest-bearing loans. At the end of the 1540s, internal bills of exchange were banned and this dealt a blow to internal promissory notes that were issued, caused considerable difficulties, and greatly complicated commercial operations in the city.

A wave of bankruptcies swept through the public sector in the second half of the 16th century, causing malfunctions in the routine payment system. The bankers and merchants' reputation was compromised. Religious conflicts, and hostilities between Spain and France also had a negative impact on trade between northwest Europe and the Iberian Peninsula.

The lucky clover wilted, and the Spanish monarchs of the 16th century found that excessive amounts of precious metal could be equally a blessing and a curse.[78] Already at that time, long before any economic discussions were held, it became clear that it was not only the amount of money that determined purchasing power, but also the speed of its circulation.

As a result of trade relations having been broken, the purchasing power of money declined (there was enough money and not enough goods). This dealt a severe blow to the now established financial structure. Castile trade fairs gradually shrank in the second half of the 16th century. In 1605, the last merchants and bankers who specialized in international banking operations finally left the city.

A powerful wave of inflation swept across Europe in the period from 1540 to 1640. In England, the cost of living increased by 7%. The vast amounts of silver and gold turned out to be a 'resource curse' for Spain.

The lucky clover had finally wilted, and now war was in the air. Hostilities began with Spain attempting to suppress the Republic of the Seven United Netherlands, a Spanish province at that time. But in spite of its considerable military power supported by all the gold and silver produced in Mexico and Peru, Spain lost the war. The ensuing financial difficulties were so serious they could be compared with the problems that the Byzantine Empire had in Egypt when it lost control over Nubia. As a result of Spain's war-induced difficulties and the exorbitant costs of the unsuccessful attempts to subdue the rebellious northern provinces of the Netherlands, the Spanish Crown found itself unable to service its debts. Defaults were declared 14 times from 1557 to 1696.

Having formed republican organizations in the course of the war, the United Provinces of the Netherlands acquired finances for warfare. The money came from a market of a completely new type, a loan market that offered life-long and perpetual annuities and lottery loans. By 1650, the Netherlands had more than 65,000 investors in debt securities, and it was this mass investment that enabled the Netherlands to finance its long-lasting struggle for independence.

The Netherlands not only won the war, but also acquired a well-developed banking system. For the first time in history, bankers took power, while kings, despite their status and ostensible power, went bankrupt.

INNOVATIONS IN THE BANKING SECTOR OF NORTHERN EUROPE

Thus, with the Spanish Crown losing its influence, the lucky clover flourished in Northern Europe. This period can be called one of 'financial revolution', being comparable in terms of its achievements with the earlier progress made by the Italians in the development of banking.

Now the banking sector came up with an important technical innovation: promissory notes were issued with an additional phrase "to pay the bearer on demand". With this addition, a payment did not necessarily have to be made in cash. A debt could be repaid by giving the creditor a third party's promissory note which could be passed from hand to hand, and sometimes the initial debtor received back his own note after a while. The addition "to pay the bearer on demand" enabled unimpeded repayment of debts and loans. As a consequence, monetary circulation accelerated, while the use of coins shrank. This was important, since precious metal was in rather short supply by that time.

The city of Antwerp became one of the early pioneers in this innovation. The ledgers that were kept by an English cloth merchant of that time contain the first signs of the present-day practice of discounting in trading securities.[79] Antwerp's progress was interrupted by the Eighty Years' War (1568-1648). In 1585, after the capture of the city by Alexander Farnese, Duke of Parma, who fought on the side of the King of Spain; trade in Antwerp was shut down, and domination of financial business was taken over by Amsterdam. After the conquest of Antwerp, numerous merchants and industrialists emigrated from that city to Amsterdam, which was already an important export market trading in fish and dairy products and a transit market trading in other commodities, especially grain and timber from the Baltic countries, Scandinavia, and northern Russia. Soon, businessmen from other cities in the south of the Netherlands joined the Amsterdam market. Thus, Amsterdam became Europe's leading trading centre.

In 1600, the city successfully replicated the so-called 'cash-desk' business. Cashiers provided their services to both Dutch and foreign merchants, on whose behalf they made payments and non-cash transfers and kept accounts that enabled the clients both to use their funds and to take out loans. The cashiers very actively traded in bearer bills ('promissory notes made out to bearer'), and bought, sold, and exchanged coins.

The war forced the northern and southern provinces of the Netherlands to use the same accounting money, florins, but there was no single minting system. In the south, the mints were under the supervision of the Spanish government.

The chasers in the north of the Netherlands minted sterling coins, and therefore could offer the suppliers of precious metals a higher price. Since imports from Baltic and Eastern countries had to be paid for in hard currency, a surge in the demand for high-quality coins occurred. Amsterdam cashiers were clearing exorbitant profits. If a payment was made in cash in Amsterdam, the cashier would select high-quality coins for resale to importers of Baltic and Asian commodities at a significant premium. Good coins were collected and exported, i.e. removed from local circulation, and this led to degradation of the national monetary reserve, for which the Amsterdam city council soon blamed the cashiers.

In these circumstances, the city council decided to change the law, and issued a decree of 31 January 1609 whereby the cashiers' trade was banned and a municipal exchange bank, the Bank of Amsterdam (Amsterdamsche Wisselbank), was instituted, and granted a monopoly on exchange operations. As a public institution, the Bank of Amsterdam maintained official exchange rates and thus made them stable. The success of the innovation was such that 'the Amsterdam model' was quickly adopted by other cities.[80]

The treasury also received massive loans in the second half of the 17th century. By 1750, the Bank of Amsterdam was the most liquid bank. The Netherlands' phenomenal success with its maritime business and crafts was largely due to this innovation in the banking sector.

The ratio between reserved and deposited amounts was close to 1:1 in Amsterdam. This was because a merchant who transferred coins to the bank received in exchange a receipt as a proof of a deposit made in the same amount. Riksbank in Sweden was the first bank that managed to overcome this limitation. As a result, money was allowed to be invested without its owner losing the right to use it on request. Most people do not need all of their money every hour of every day. Banks lend money to other people at interest, thereby earning an extra profit. Consequently, banks act as financial mediators that facilitate the investment of the funds of their depositors.

Riksbank was the first to introduce a 'fractional reserve system' whereby a bank's reserves did not have to match its obligations. At that time, the ratio between reserved and deposited amounts was reduced to 30%, and is 12% today. We can see perfectly well the multiplication effect of this innovation. Before, all krones had simply remained in the bank; now, seventy krones out of each one hundred could be lent, increasing the country's monetary stock.

The third most important innovation was the transition from short-term transferable securities to paper money. Thus, banknotes appeared in the form they exist today. This move was first made in England in 1694. The idea of the innovation was that now everybody could pay with paper money without having to have an account with the bank that had issued it.

BANK	YEAR	INNOVATION
Amsterdamsche Wisselbank, Amsterdam	**1609**	The bank was the first to create a cheque system and launch direct debiting as a means of money transfer. This expanded the choice of cashless payment options in conducting commercial transactions. The necessity to keep a 100% ratio between reserved and deposited amounts was a limitation that had not been overcome.
Riksbank, Sweden	**1656**	The bank streamlined commercial payment and lending procedures. The bank's depositors could actually make interest-bearing loans from their cash deposits, with the bank acting as a mediator.
The Bank of England	**1694**	In 1742, the bank was granted a partial monopoly on the issue of banknotes (interest-free promissory notes designed to facilitate payments without opening current accounts with banks). Banknotes could be paid by anyone who held them.

TABLE 4. THREE MAJOR INNOVATIONS IN NORTHERN EUROPE'S BANKING SYSTEM IN THE 17TH CENTURY

The changes that had been made in commerce and finance (see Table 4) affected another element of the lucky clover – society. Once a country began to fill with banknotes, a new class came into being to service the cash flows – a class of financiers. The development of new financial elites in Europe began in earnest with the arrival on the scene of the Rothschild family.

The 'Commercial Revolution' in Europe was a period of economic expansion and mercantilism, accompanied by various processes taking place: voyages in search of new lands; colonization of unknown countries; large trading monopolies and banks being established; joint-stock companies and stock markets emerging; insurance companies and debt obligations proliferating. The overall trade turnover in Europe and worldwide grew, and a mature financial system developed. It was at that moment that the lucky clover acquired a fully fledged fourth leaf.

Now humanity was ready for the next important historic step: an industrial revolution. The commercial revolution enabled European countries to grow rich swiftly and overtake Asia and the Middle East in terms of economic development. Accumulated capital and new banking techniques made it possible to convert savings into investments.

Thus, the might of a state, as well as its economic power over the people, were now characterised by the accumulated gold reserves. The Italian Renaissance and the Medici gave the world a banking revolution which in turn caused rapid development of financial instruments. Europe's new monetary system enabled the continent to enter a new stage in the development of its trade relations with Asia. This would have been impossible without credit instruments; therefore, their appearance created the preconditions for the development of banking in Europe. At that point in time, finance began to evolve, developing mechanisms for payment, accumulation, and investment, and, perhaps most importantly, the means for raising borrowed capital.

CHAPTER 6

GREAT GEOGRAPHICAL DISCOVERIES AND COLONIZATION: HOW THE OLD WORLD AND THE NEW WORLD CLASHED

" *Three paths lead to knowledge: the way of thinking is the most noble way, the path of imitation is the easiest, and the way of experience is the most bitter path...* "

– Confucius

The story of the discovery of the New World tells us that there is no alternative to technological development – you either develop and live, or do not develop, and vanish or die out. The era of colonization, which began when the New World was discovered, took place thanks to another technological loop. Prior to being discovered by the Europeans, America was a huge 'laboratory' of world history and culture, where one-third of mankind developed completely on its own from the primitive state to the first generation of civilizations. About 11,000 years ago, prehistoric man reached the southern tip of the South American continent. Development of numerous Indian tribes took place virtually in isolation from the Old World's culture.[81]

It should be noted though that many of the Indian peoples that inhabited the Arctic zone, the prairies, and most of the jungle remained forever on the tribal level – in fact, in the Stone Age. Only two regions in the whole of the Western Hemisphere, located at the junction of North and South America – now Bolivia and Peru – were populated by ethnic groups that rose above savagery. [82] By the time the Europeans arrived, the people of the Aztec Empire located in and around the Valley of Mexico and the Incan Empire in the Andes had on their own come to obtain such achievements as irrigated agriculture, stone architecture, primitive writing, and relatively developed religions with original astrological, chronological, and calendar systems. Moreover, these American civilizations already had complex religious and political rituals and public ceremonies.

Up to two-thirds of the population of the New World lived in the Inca and Aztec empires, while the lands occupied by these two states comprised just slightly over 6% of the total area of the two continents (Razdorskaya and Shchavelev 2006, 84). Agriculture and related trades formed the basis of their economies. Having achieved considerable technological successes, the ancient Americans had nevertheless only matured to the Stone Age level by European standards, since they still did not possess metal tools, draft cattle (and even domestic animals), the wheel, the plough, the potter's wheel, and many other technologies that were widely used at that time.

CORTÉS AND THE AZTECS

As we know, it was the Spaniards who began the conquest of America. In 1492, a fleet of ships, led by Christopher Columbus, crossed the Atlantic. In 1521, a small group under the command of Hernán Cortés conquered the city-state of Tenochtitlan, the capital of the Aztec Empire, and captured and killed Montezuma I, the emperor. In 1531, Francisco Pizarro with his company set sail from Panama in order to take over the Incan Empire, a territory legendary for its riches. He conquered the empire's capital, Cusco, and deceitfully assassinated its ruler Atahualpa. The shocking and formidable appearance of the intruders, who were light-skinned, bearded, clad in armour, and mounted on 'terrifying' creatures called horses, and their firearms, their courage, and their cynical deception of the Incas' leaders, helped them to secure victory. The winners got hold of mountains of precious metal and multitudes of slaves.

Why did the large indigenous populations surrender? According to Cortés's biographer Christian Duverger, during the stay on Cuba, Cortés clearly indicated that he was planning a colonization expedition rather than a rapacious raid.[83] He was a determined and intelligent man, and his first steps were to establish contacts with the local population on the island of Cozumel. Cortés established vital connections, gained allies among indigenous tribes, and studied the principles on which the Aztec government was built.[84]

On 16 August 1519, the Spaniards set off for Tenochtitlan, the capital of the Aztec Empire. While on the way to the Aztec land, the conquistadors had found a strong ally in the independent mountain principality Tlaxcala which was waging a war against the Aztec confederation (the Triple Alliance).[85] Afterwards, Tlaxcala became the centre of Spanish rule in Mexico. For this meritorious deed, the people of the principality were exempt from all taxes by the Spanish Crown until the end of colonial rule.

The Spaniards were kindly received by the Aztec king Montezuma II. He presented Cortés with numerous gifts of gold jewellery, and this immediately aroused the Spaniards, filling them with a strong desire to take over the country. The Spaniards quickly understood how the Aztec state was organized. Most of all they were astonished by the Aztec market: "Mightily were we surprised... by the huge mass of people, and the unheard piles of various goods, and the amazing order... Some of us, who had been to Constantinople, and even around the whole of Italy, claimed that nowhere had they seen such a great and orderly market" (Baglay 1998).

Aztec society, like any highly urbanized society, was dependent on the exchange of commodities. The urban population of Tenochtitlan was hardly engaged in any agricultural production, and relied on trade with other cities. The development of various sectors of production inevitably led to the emergence of a variety of goods. Aztec trade was a highly developed and complex institution, and it was thanks to this institution that the population of the Valley of Mexico increased continuously. The Aztec state was able to feed enormous numbers of urban residents – the capital's population stood at about 200,000. Only a quarter of this number lived off tributes; the other three quarters earned their living by trading.

It is evident that this ratio could only be achieved in Tenochtitlan, the empire's centre where the nobility and the military were concentrated heavily, and where the bulk of the tribute collected from the subjugated peoples came. As a result, the metropolis was reluctant to fight because this would lead to interruptions in commodity supplies. When deciding what to do – fight or negotiate (and trade) with the Spaniards – the Aztec leader chose peace… and lost. He lost because the Spaniards knew only too well that control over an urban centralized state belonged to those who controlled its financial flows and treasury.

Out of all of Montezuma's royal residences, the Spaniards quartered where the Aztecs' state coffers were found.[86] Using this fact as a means of pressure, the conquistadors persuaded Montezuma to swear allegiance to the Spanish Crown.

After no news from Spain for six months, Cortés suddenly received reports that Diego Velázquez de Cuéllar, the Governor of Cuba and his long-time foe (Cortés embarked upon the voyage in order to escape from him), had sent a detachment of 18 ships to Mexico with orders to arrest Cortés and deliver him to Cuba. With the political situation becoming critical, Cortés, accompanied by a detachment of 300 men and some natives, headed for Veracruz, leaving his deputy with a hundred soldiers to control Tenochtitlan. Using riches borrowed from Montezuma, he managed to buy off the soldiers who had been sent to capture him. After that, together with his strengthened army, he returned to the Valley of Mexico.

However, when Cortés returned to the capital, he found that his deputy, Lieutenant Pedro de Alvarado, had massacred, for no apparent reason, many members of the Aztec aristocracy. The Aztecs had chosen Cuitláhuac as the new king and begun to prepare for war with the Spaniards. In the midst of the crisis, Montezuma had died in unclear circumstances.[87] The situation was becoming tense, and on 1 July 1520, the Spaniards, having lost half of their men and the whole of the wealth they had plundered, retreated from the city.[88]

Cortés's weakened detachment was heartily welcomed into Tlaxcala, the capital of the Aztecs' opponents, where he began to prepare a proper siege of Tenochtitlan. The conquistadors' situation was strengthened considerably by an epidemic of flu and smallpox, diseases the Spaniards had brought to Mexico, which broke out among the local population. Cuitláhuac, the Aztecs' new leader, died of smallpox. While the Aztecs were fighting the diseases, Cortés received considerable reinforcement consisting of troops and artillery, and started to build the ships. In May 1521, the siege of Tenochtitlan began; the city had been cut off from supplies of food and fresh water by that time. Some indigenous peoples that had newly allied to the Spanish played an invaluable role in this military operation. A number of city-states located in the Valley of Mexico and allied to the Aztecs were taken over. On 13 August 1521, after Guatemoc, the last leader of the Aztecs, was captured, the Aztec state fell. Afterwards, Cortés ruled Mexico single-handedly until 1524.

Thus, Cortés's success was very much due to his financial and economic shrewdness and his ability to negotiate and gain allies. To understand why Cortés was so successful, let's consider the Aztec state's tribute system. The population of each tribe that had been conquered by the Aztecs paid tribute to the conquerors. Those who resisted were charged a larger tribute. Tribes that had dared to rebel were charged twice as much.

Some tribes were closer to the king and were thus treated more leniently, while others were exploited mercilessly. Cortés took advantage of this fact in order to make alliances. In fact, he offered a tax reform to American tribes, asking for a fixed tribute from each member of a tribe. Those tribes which saw the offer as very profitable sided with Cortés, judging wisely that the enemy of their enemy should be their friend.

However, this idyll did not last long. David Graeber says that after the capture of the imperial treasury, most of the plunder was taken by the officers who had credited their soldiers and the local population by billing them for everything. The people, in turn, had to take loans to pay off the debt. And what of Cortés? He had just pulled off perhaps the greatest act of theft in world history (Graeber 2011).

David Graeber explicitly says who the main 'beneficiary' of pillaging the New World was: "By 1540, a silver surplus caused a collapse in prices across Europe; at this point the American mines simply stopped functioning, and the entire project of American colonization would have foundered, had it not been for the demand from China. Treasure galleons moving towards Europe soon refrained from unloading their cargoes, instead rounding the horn of Africa and proceeding across the Indian Ocean towards Canton. Huge amounts of silk, porcelain and other Chinese products had to be exported to pay for it. This Asian trade became the single most significant factor in the emerging global economy, and those who ultimately controlled the financial levers – particularly Italian, Dutch, and German merchant bankers – became fantastically rich." Thus, joint American-Chinese capital served as the engine of the global economy long before the present-day relations between China and the US!

PIZARRO AND THE INCAS

The fall of another powerful empire – the Incan Empire – is described with reference to the adventures of a brazen gang of Spanish fortune-hunters led by Francisco Pizarro. His counterpart – the Supreme Inca Atahualpa – is typically presented in historical literature in pejorative terms. Being in possession of forces that far exceeded those of the enemy, he was too gullible, and landed in a trap. But since the Supreme Inca was too cowardly, the only thing he could do was fill the Spaniards' chests with gold and silver.

Another great empire, called the Land of Four Provinces, was founded by the Inca, in 1438, when they began a far-reaching expansion under the command of Sapa Inca (paramount leader) Pachacuti-Cusi Yupanqui (whose name literally meant 'earth-shaker').[89] Having waged an aggressive campaign across most of the Andes mountains, Pachacuti created a mighty empire, making Cusco its capital and building stone palaces and temples there. To control the empire, a multitudinous and well-disciplined caste of officials was created.

The Incas strengthened the empire and created a highly developed culture. Subjugated communities were ruled by local elders, centurions, and tribal leaders, but were always supervised by Inca chiefs. In the conquered lands, the Incas built fortresses and quartered garrisons. The population was engaged in agriculture and cattle husbandry. All farmland belonged to the communities, with arable land and pastures redistributed each year, and only homesteads were owned by families and inherited. Parts of the community land was allocated to the government and the priests.

The death of the Inca emperor from the smallpox spreading rapidly across the continent resulted in a civil war in the Incan Empire shortly before the arrival of the Spaniards. The war ended in 1532, when Atahualpa, one of the sons of the deceased emperor Huayna Capac, finally seized the throne and threw his brother in jail.[90]

When setting off on his fourth expedition, Pizarro already knew that a civil war was tearing the Incan Empire apart and that yet another small-pox epidemic had just swept through it. Moreover, in 1528 he had met with his famous relative Hernán Cortés, and evidently was well aware of how the latter had been able to conquer the Aztec Empire. Fortuitously, Roman Catholicism and the Incas' 'sun religion' were strikingly similar. This proved to be invaluable to the Spaniards when negotiating with the Incas afterwards.

Credit should be paid to the Spanish for their resourcefulness too. Pizarro's squad moved along the coast for five months, looting the Incas' imperial stores, and only then set off for Atahualpa's court. Pizarro was waiting for the emperor to make the first move. He knew that in a well-run empire, only one person could make relevant decisions, and that that person would not ignore an enemy undermining the empire's economic base for a long time.

Having heard of the Spaniards' advance, Atahualpa invited them to visit him.[91] The conquistadors lured the Supreme Inca into a trap, killing numerous servants and unarmed bodyguards.[92]

The news of the capture of the Supreme Inca and his top commanders terrorized the Inca troops. Left without their leaders and commanders, the army simply marched off towards the capital, the city of Cusco, most likely for directions.

The capture of the Supreme Inca had the most devastating impact on the fate of his empire. Tribes dissatisfied with the Inca authority rebelled, and the huge country was plunged into powerlessness and anarchy. This was only to the Spaniards' gain.

Francisco Pizarro demanded gold and silver from the Supreme Inca as a ransom for his release from captivity.[93]

The Incas were not even given enough time to collect the full ransom for their leader. Pizarro, who had already received fabulous treasures, lost his patience and broke his promise, setting up a mock trial and having Atahualpa executed. This was typical of Pizarro, who never kept his promises and always played without rules, violating all norms of war and negotiation. Such traits characterised him as a vile and dishonest person and a very skilful politician at the same time.

Since Pizarro understood perfectly well (possibly thanks to Cortés's enlightenment) that he needed a manageable figurehead to stand as the Incas' leader, Manco Inca, the son of the previous ruler Huayna Capac, was soon put on the throne. When the Spaniards arrived in Cusco, the capital city, together with the new emperor, they were met not as conquerors, but as the country's well-wishers who had restored the Incas' only lawful royal family to power.

THE ROAD OF REFLECTION AND THE ROAD OF EXPERIENCE

When the Spanish met the Native Americans, they had superiority by possessing more knowledge, a more developed social structure, more developed skills at organizing long-term commercial expeditions, and more finance (Table 5).

FACTOR	THE SPANISH	THE INCAS
Warfare	Horses, steel, firearms	No horses; the Incas' weapons could injure at great distances, but not kill
State	Unified, with a certain degree of freedom; education	Centralized; education available to a small elite only
Infections	Immunity against many diseases	No immunity; lethal epidemics resulted in the state falling apart
Finance	Gold, coins	Measurement in units of labour; gold as an indicator of the status and a means of decoration
Technologies	Sailing; printing as a means of spreading new knowledge	Small ships sailing along the coast only

TABLE 5. KEY FACTORS THAT ENABLED THE SPANISH
TO DEFEAT THE INCAS IN 1532

Faced with the overwhelming numerical superiority of the Indians, the Spaniards won the first military confrontation tactically, by breaking the Incas' customary rules of fighting. A more general picture can be seen if considering each leaf of the lucky clover individually, including the state system, the financial system, and the level of technological development.

Advantages in governmental organization. The Spanish soldiers had considerable freedom, and were motivated to take desperate actions by massive debts. The Inca state was overly centralized: the garrison would not engage the enemy without the emperor's command. The emperor had no emergency plan in case of failure of the main plan. The national elites were split in half by a civil war. Atahualpa became Supreme Inca by defeating his brother, who had the priority right to the throne, and was, therefore, illegitimate for a large part of society which supported the Spanish by providing them with food.

National health. Civil war broke out in the Incan Empire after most of the imperial court had been virtually wiped out by diseases brought to the continent by the Europeans earlier. The Indians' lack of immunity to these diseases, and advanced healthcare for the national elite, broke the state apart.

Financial capital. Money played an important role in the Spaniards' success. The Incas could not understand the strangers' passion for gold. Conversely, the Spaniards knew the purchasing power of gold all too well and, what's more, were desperately entangled in their debts.

Technology. It's easy to see why Pizarro headed for the Incas' land. He was purposefully looking for a new 'Golden Castile', fitted out ships, and hired people (i.e. both the technology and the resources were available).

Atahualpa did not carry out a preventive strike because the Incas knew practically nothing about the Spaniards' abilities and were not interested in learning about their innovations in maritime business, such as ships, cartography, and navigation with a map and a compass. The Supreme Inca did not know that the Aztec Empire had been destroyed a few years earlier, since there was no communication and transfer of experience between American civilizations. Pizarro, on the other hand, knew this story first-hand and thus envisioned the psychology of the local population and their rulers.

It was not only general knowledge of the world that gave the Spaniards an advantage, but also the printing technology and, therefore, maps and books as a special means of transmitting and reproducing other people's experiences. As emphasized in the story of Damascus steel,

'CORTÉS MEETS STIFF RESISTANCE',
an illustration depicting the Spanish conquistador
Hernán Cortés (1485-1547) fighting an Aztec warrior

THE ROLE OF HORSES AND THE BIRTHPLACE OF THIS INNOVATION

It was hunting that gave the first impetus to domestication of large animals with a view to riding them. Once domesticated, horses, unlike cows, sheep, and goats, could endure harsh climatic conditions, and could find food for themselves under the snow. According to the results of recent archaeological research led by researchers from Bristol University, specialists from the St. Petersburg Institute for the History of Material Culture of the Russian Academy of Sciences, and Kazakhstani scientists from Kokshetau University, domestication took place about 5,500 years ago, i.e. 2,000 years earlier than domesticated horses appeared in Europe.

The nomadic way of life on horseback is often seen as one of the major success factors that enabled the rise of the Mongol Horde. It should be noted, however, that the Mongols borrowed horses from peoples they had defeated, while powerful bows were their own innovation.[94]

Even Columbus sailed to the shores of America with horses aboard to assist him in his mission. As some of his conquistadors noted in their diaries, the horses immediately gave them a huge advantage over the indigenous peoples. Riders could easily kill Indian soldiers before they managed to warn their troops of the attack. By enabling the Spanish to attack with agility and high speed, the horses made the Incas, who fought on foot, helpless in direct approach.

the usefulness of knowledge is determined by its informative capacity, its practical value and the cost of acquiring the information. The Incas did not lose for military reasons, not because of their attitude towards gold, but because of lack of information. The Spaniards' interaction network was denser and more extensively branched. The leaders of their empire could not even imagine a threat of the type the Spaniards posed.

MICROBIAL UNIFICATION OF MANKIND

The outcome for the New World was sad. During the conquest of Peru, fabulous treasures hoarded in the temples and palaces were plundered. The influx of gold enabled Western Europe to mobilize forces to repel a most dangerous attempt of aggression by the Ottoman Turks. World history might have taken a different path had the Spanish Conquest taken place several decades later.

Apart from wealth, in the form of precious metals and stones, the Europeans acquired many crops from the New World. Our life today simply cannot be imagined without potatoes, tobacco, beans, tomatoes, maize, sunflowers, cocoa, vanilla, coca, quinine and rubber.

The American nations paid a double tribute to the conquerors, losing most of their accumulated wealth and, to boot, three-quarters of their population. Diseases brought from the Old World and hard exploitation in mines did their job.[95] Let's consider, for example, the population of Mexico and Peru and compare the dynamics from 1300 to 1900 (Figure 8). The population of these two countries totalled 11.5 million before meeting with the Spaniards and decreased to 3.8 million by 1700, returning to the pre-Columbus figure only in 1879. For all their cruelty, the Spanish killed only a few thousand, and the majority were killed by diseases. Similarly, when the Europeans came to the island of Fiji, it lost 90% of its local population.[96]

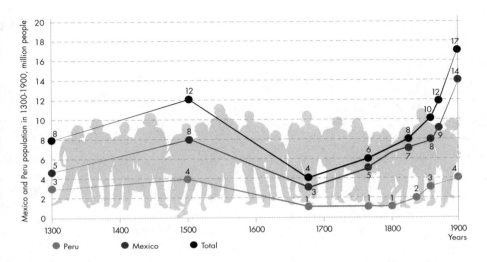

FIGURE 8. THE IMPACT OF EPIDEMICS AND DISEASES ON THE POPULATIONS
OF NATIVE AMERICANS

Bartolomé de Las Casas (1474-1566), a Spanish chronicler and the first defender of human rights, wrote that these people have a fragile physique. They do not endure serious illnesses and quickly perish from the slightest indisposition (Keram 1979). Apart from the really poor health in primitive conditions, Las Casas (Stannard 1993) was also referring to the aboriginal peoples' lack of immunity against European viruses and bacteria.

By and large, human history is inseparable from the history of epidemics. This interconnection even led to the creation of a new scientific phenomenon in the mid-20th century: 'microbial unification of humanity'.

Here I would like to return to the concept of knowledge once again. Humankind's pre-experimental knowledge in medicine, acquired through gathering facts and theoretical modelling of the nature of human diseases in the Middle Ages, was finally counterpoised with factual knowledge obtained by researchers through measurements and observation of diseases. The difference between the two kinds of knowledge is in the degree of their adequacy. A disease can be controlled effectively if there is adequate knowledge about it. It is unlikely that medical knowledge about the Black Death was adequate at the time, as the plague managed to exterminate one-third of Asia's population and half of Europe's.

GREAT MORTALITY AMONG THE INDIANS DUE TO SMALLPOX BROUGHT TO AMERICA BY THE COLONISTS.
Woodcut, 1853

INFLUENCE OF BACTERIA ON THE NATIVE AMERICANS' POPULATIONS

Alfred Crosby (Crosby 2003) and William McNeill, renowned historians, noted that the true conquerors of the New World were germs (bacteria and viruses).[97]

This biological attack on the Indians was so powerful that scientists at Stanford University have even created a new term for it: 'climate epidemics'. By and large, human history is inseparable from the history of epidemics, although the first perception of this phenomenon was recorded a century before the discovery of America – in the 14th century, when the population of Europe suffered badly from a plague that was named the Black Death for its severity.

Today we know that any new disease, whatever corner of the globe it originated in, threatens us all, due to microbial unification. For that reason, diseases are fought against jointly in the modern world. But it is poor countries that suffer from epidemics most, where there are no resources to fight infections and the population is undereducated.

Jared Diamond, the author of the book *Guns, Germs and Steel*, notes that epidemics changed the direction in which European civilization was developing. The decrease in the workforce caused an increase in wages and the importance of cities grew, as well as a demand for advanced medicine developed. These were the main reasons for the onset of the Age of Discovery.

Historian Michael Oldstone, in his book *Viruses, Plagues, and History* (Oldstone 2000), argues that human history would have been different without epidemics. He maintains it is highly unlikely that the US and Canada would have become separate states, the slave trade would have spread so wide, and the Spanish would have been able to conquer the Incan and Aztec empires.

The 'biological attacks' between the New World and the Old World were mutual. The first epidemic from the New World was one of syphilis in the late 15th century (Cortés was one of the first to suffer from this infection). Since the disease was transmitted through sexual intercourse, its wide proliferation had a remarkable and quite unexpected effect: the influence of the church in society increased. The church very successfully and profitably used this phenomenon, accusing the sufferers of sinful behaviour.

The damage caused by epidemics has always been comparable with the effects of wars and natural disasters.

THE UNLUCKY CLOVER

So far, I have discussed countries in which all four components of the lucky clover were in harmony and gave rise to rapid advances and vigorous economic development. There were very few such countries in each epoch. More often than not, one of the elements would fail to match the others and no growth would be achieved. But this is still not the worst situation. Sometimes even an ordinary clover is not allowed to, or cannot, grow.

In Europe, around the time when Pizarro was merely planning his conquest of El Dorado, the last stronghold that separated the Ottoman Empire from the Holy Roman Empire ruled by Charles V fell. It was a buffer state that occupied the land of what is now Hungary.

The defeat was caused by backward social relations. The Ottoman Empire equipped vast armies and the sultans were bold enough to give firearms to common people (simple soldiers). The outcome of the confrontation was easy to predict. Often, despite the availability of innovations, the relations within a society, when they cannot ensure security for the state, appear to be the critical element.

However, the rest of Europe quickly learned from this. Modern followers of technological determinism often assert that a fundamental discovery can only be made once and in one place, and the effect of the discovery gives the people of the country a significant advantage in a global economy. Using this advantage, the pioneering nation submits and forces surrounding nations to borrow its technology and culture. However, the supporters of technological determinism do not take into account one very important factor: isolationism. China, a country that has already been mentioned for closing itself to foreigners, never shared its most famous inventions – gunpowder and paper – with the rest of the world and deprived itself of the opportunity for rapid development for centuries. Much later, Europe had to re-invent these inventions. Isolationism is dangerous because it develops in too cyclical a manner. The periods between the cycles are marked as ones of obvious regression, when hard-won knowledge and skills are lost.

Thus it was in pre-Columbian America too, where all the stages identified by historian Arnold J. Toynbee can be traced: genesis, growth, breakdown and decay due to various factors such as barbaric invasions, internal social calamities, environmental disasters, or a consequence of the simultaneous action of several factors.[98] As a rule, each civilization cycle is followed by 'dark ages', succeeded in turn by a new life cycle.[99]

Lots of available funds and the need to expand the borders of the Spanish Crown necessitated the financing of an expedition to distant shores. Having met a new civilization, the Spaniards, who possessed both education and experience, quickly learned its arrangement. With this knowledge, they were able to find powerful allies among the enemies of the American empires and take control of the system of public administration and coercion, subjugating it by capturing the capital city and the financial and distribution institutions. Despite their modest forces, using horses and firearms mostly to prove their superiority, the Spanish gained unprecedented wealth. This did not bring wellbeing to most of them, because it was immediately spent to cover the debts they had accumulated. The biological factor, in the form of virulent diseases that had decimated the Americas' indigenous population, also contributed significantly to the conquistadors' victory and opened yet another grim chapter in human history, with the emergence of the institution of slavery.

Diseases and slavery, augmented by cruelty on the part of former Spanish soldiers, changed the natural American society beyond recognition and human history changed its course for good, almost destroying the Americas' ancient civilisations. Innovations can be disastrous for whole continents.

CHAPTER 7

THE ROLE OF THE BRITISH AGRICULTURAL REVOLUTION

"We Russians can be said to be something of an exception amongst all nations: we belong to those which exist as though they are not part of humanity, but are there to serve as a dramatic example of a nation in trouble."

– Pyotr Chaadayev,
a Russian publicist who was pronounced crazy
by the Russian government because of his writings

INTENSIVE FARMING

At the end of the 17th century and beginning of the 18th century, the ideas of Gregory King (1648-1712), a demographer and expert on national income statistics, predicted that England's population would grow from 5.5 million people in 1700 to 6.4 million by 1800, to 7.3 million by 1900, and could reach a maximum of 11 million by the year 3500 (Studensky 1968). His estimates were based on the premise that the fertility of English agricultural lands would remain unchanged, productivity would remain at its contemporary level and, consequently, the country would not have enough land to feed a larger population. Thus, he presumed that only a gradual demographic growth would be possible in the conditions of limited territory and the rates of agrarian technological evolution known at that time. However, despite all of his predictions, the population of England totalled 8.6 million by 1801, exceeded 20 million by 1820 and reached 30 million by 1900. Neither Gregory King nor anyone else could have foreseen the agricultural revolution that broke out in England in the 1730s and the consequences it brought about.

This revolution consisted of a transition to a type of farming that today we call intensive: replacement of two- and three-field crop rotations with four-field crop rotations (also known as the Norfolk four-course system named after the county where it became popular); use of various fertilizers, drainage, soil liming, etc.; emergence of a fleet of agricultural machinery; and development of new field- and garden crops imported into Europe as a result of vast geographic discoveries (maize, potatoes, pumpkins, sunflowers, tobacco, tomatoes, etc.).

As is commonly known, when using two- and three-field systems, one-third of the arable land remains fallow (unsown) in order to restore soil fertility. The Norfolk four-field crop rotation system enabled a substantial increase in production volumes since virtually no arable land was left fallow (Figure 9). Farmland was sown with wheat in the first year. In the second year, those same fields were sown with rutabaga and turnips. The third year consisted of barley together with clover and ryegrass undersown. The fields with clover and ryegrass were used for grazing or mowed for feed on the fourth year. Root crops were used to feed cattle and sheep in the winter.

This new system provided accumulating results; the fodder crops eaten by livestock increased the production of previously scarce manure, which became more enriched thanks to the improved animal feed. The grazing of sheep in the fields also provided for fertilization of the soil via animal waste, which resulted in an abundant harvest of grain in subsequent years.

At the end of the 18th century, a conventional three-field farm (of 78 acres) yielded 1,800 bushels of wheat.[100] [101] The Norfolk crop rotation system gave a fourfold production increase!

In the 16th and 17th centuries, first the Dutch and then the English actively experimented with various sowing techniques, using manure and trying different combinations of cereals and forage crops. As a result, by the middle of the 18th century, the English farmers were not only able to feed the country's population, but also exported surplus grain abroad, while employing only two-thirds of the workforce previously required.

Therefore, the revolutionary agricultural production emerged as a result of experiments with new cultivation techniques, i.e. a result of recombination: a technological approach to agriculture, focused on fostering innovation and obtaining results (i.e. commercialization), for Western society.

From 1700 to 1850, the horse population in England doubled; hence, the number of horses per unit of arable land increased by 17%. If we take into account the dynamics of the size of the population engaged in agriculture, it turns out that from 1700 to 1800, the amount of horsepower per worker increased by 34% (0.3% per year); from 1800 to 1850, it increased by 21% (0.39% per year). All of this served to steadily increase the productivity of agricultural labour in England. However, an even more remarkable event that exerted dominant influence on the growth of productivity of peasant labour was the emergence of agricultural machinery engineering.

AGRICULTURAL MACHINERY ENGINEERING

In 1701, Jethro Tull (1674-1741) radically improved the horse-drawn seed drill and later introduced efficient design alterations to the horse-drawn hoe.[102]

The so-called Rotherham plough developed by Joseph Foljambe in 1730 in Rotherham, England, is considered to be the first commercially successful plough using iron parts. It was designed based on the mathematical calculations of the Scottish designer James Small. Its fittings and coulter were made of iron and the mouldboard and ploughshare were covered with iron plates, which reduced drag and made the entire ploughing process more controllable in comparison with other designs.

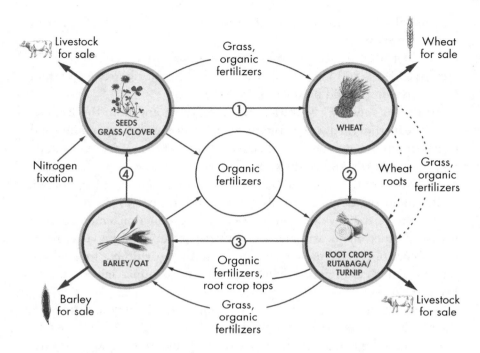

FIGURE 9. THE NORFOLK FOUR-FIELD CROP ROTATION SYSTEM[103]

The Rotherham plough was strong and light, and enabled the cutting, lifting and turning of a layer of soil. It was used in Britain all the way up until the emergence of the tractor.

With the emergence of such innovations, the demand for machinery became more and more obvious. After many unsuccessful attempts to apply mechanical force to move various types of mills, the Scottish inventor Andrew Meikle came up with the idea of using a quickly rotating drum for threshing. This idea was implemented in 1786 by Meikle's son; the machine he built is considered to be the first successfully engineered threshing machine.

In 1840, the portable steam engine was adapted for agricultural use for the first time. In the 1850s, farmers began using traction engines, predominately for threshing. They were transferred from one farm to another, while the larger farms had stationary steam engines that powered threshing machines and other farm machinery.

It is difficult to overestimate the cumulative influence this new agricultural equipment had on labour productivity. Based on statistics from the 19th century, the manpower requirement per unit of grain crop acreage was reduced by 30%.

Innovations in the social sphere also played a definitive role in increasing the productivity of agricultural labour. This was primarily called the 'enclosure' process in which common land was gradually eliminated along with the corresponding way of life and traditions.[104] Since the overwhelming majority of farmland was in the possession of nobles, the church and the crown, most peasants did not have ownership rights to their land plots. Arable land was also subject to expropriation. With reference to Sir Thomas More's *Utopia* (1516), one could say that sheep began to "devour human beings themselves". Deprived of their allotments, peasants turned into farm workers. Many lost not only the land but also their housing and thus become vagrants and beggars.

The English Reformation and the enclosure process changed English society, turning a large number of farmers into wage workers whose labour was inexpensive – many believed that England was not able to feed so many people. But the establishment of institutions of law in the country, the limitation of royal power and the separation of powers strengthened society's stability. The Norfolk four-field crop rotation system and the new Rotherham plough changed the character of peasant labour so much that England began to export its products actively, especially wool and textiles. The sale of surplus products created capital which was invested in new businesses, such as factories, breweries and mills. Keen interest in acquiring new knowledge and in scientific experiments emerged and institutions for agricultural studies were established. Stable revenues from exports boosted a further increase in production.

CHAPTER 8

THE INDUSTRIAL REVOLUTION. HOW THE STEAM ENGINE ADVANCED THE CAPITALIST WEST TOWARDS THE EAST

"The development of different parts of a system represents an uneven process; the more complex the system is, the more uneven is the development of its parts."

– Genrich Altshuller,
Creativity as an Exact Science
(the fifth law of development of systems)

THE ERA OF THE INDUSTRIAL REVOLUTION

Like the Agricultural Revolution, the Industrial Revolution also began in England. The transition from manual labour to machine production was the largest innovation, accompanied by changes in all spheres of society.

The eminent economist John Hicks defines the essence of the Industrial Revolution as an impact made by science, stimulating the development of technology and the use of new sources of energy to make machines more accurate and reliable while gradually reducing their cost and thus enabling their wide application in many fields (Hicks 1969).

An industrial revolution is not so much about inventing new machines as it is about solving the problem of finding sources of relatively cheap energy. The Agricultural Revolution in England caused the volumes of agricultural production to increase significantly. British farmers were now earning more money and began to look for new ways to use it rather than to spend it on traditional items of expenditure (purchase of land, household consumption, accumulation, etc.). Capital was used to rebuild homes and purchase industrial products, such as clothes, tools, household utensils and furniture. A strong and growing demand for industrial products developed. Moreover, the previously mentioned enclosure process resulted in the formation of a large pool of labour. This new phenomenon attracted the attention of scientists and became the subject of study for a new science. In the 18th century, Adam Smith called it 'political economy' in his *Wealth of Nations* (Smith 1776).

Against the backdrop of growth in agrarian capitalism, manufacturing then became very profitable in the 18th century. Demand for manufactured goods fell behind supply, because landowners who had accumulated wealth in the course of the Agricultural Revolution began to invest in the construction of factories (Figure 10). English capitalists actively adopted inventions from other countries. The idea of the steam engine came from the Netherlands. Blast furnaces and equipment for underground mining were imported from Germany. New silk production methods were brought from France. Innovations in glass production were first used in Venice (Italy) in the 15th and 16th centuries, spread from there to France and the Netherlands, and then were made use of by the British.

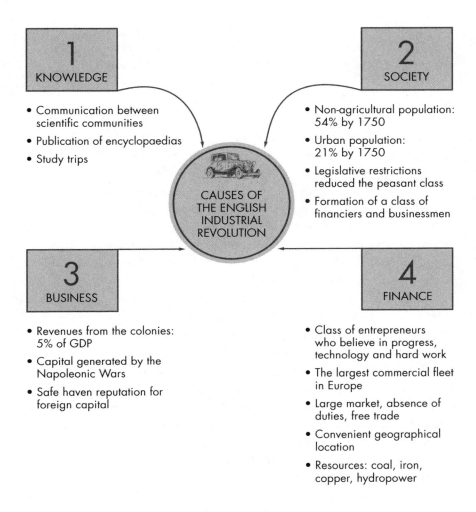

1 KNOWLEDGE

- Communication between scientific communities
- Publication of encyclopaedias
- Study trips

2 SOCIETY

- Non-agricultural population: 54% by 1750
- Urban population: 21% by 1750
- Legislative restrictions reduced the peasant class
- Formation of a class of financiers and businessmen

CAUSES OF THE ENGLISH INDUSTRIAL REVOLUTION

3 BUSINESS

- Revenues from the colonies: 5% of GDP
- Capital generated by the Napoleonic Wars
- Safe haven reputation for foreign capital

4 FINANCE

- Class of entrepreneurs who believe in progress, technology and hard work
- The largest commercial fleet in Europe
- Large market, absence of duties, free trade
- Convenient geographical location
- Resources: coal, iron, copper, hydropower

FIGURE 10. REASONS FOR THE CONCEPTION OF
THE INDUSTRIAL REVOLUTION IN THE UK

England was more successful than its European neighbours, as it ensured openness and the wide spread of knowledge. Overall, information exchange began to play an ever-increasing role in the development of industrial production, ensuring the spread of innovations.

Natural limitations served as an additional catalyst for the application of knowledge in the UK. The country was short of forests for producing firewood and the tranquil English rivers prevented widespread use of water power. Being in need of an omni-purpose fuel capable of replacing wood, entrepreneurs resorted to coal. Providing higher temperatures than firewood, coal became widely used in such production sectors as brick and paper manufacturing, and was the perfect fuel for steam engines.

THE STEAM ENGINE

The Industrial Revolution became possible due to the discovery of steam as a relatively cheap source of energy for technological wonders. The use of steam produced by burning coal removed the necessity to place factories by rivers and thereby sped up the onset of the revolution.

In 1698, British officer Thomas Savery patented a static water pump that worked using steam pressure. In 1712, in partnership with blacksmith Thomas Newcomen, Savery developed a machine that had a vertical piston whose impetus was conveyed by a simple lever to the piston of a submerged injection pump. The proper proportion of the surfaces of the pistons resulted in the production of enough force to pump water to any height.

In the UK, Newcomen's steam engine gained a more widespread use, especially in the mining industry. The machine did not cause a technological revolution in manufacturing (as it had no need for the steam engine yet) and led a quiet existence for two-thirds of a century, until the Industrial Revolution era came and James Watt transformed it into a 'universal motor' for the new production industry.

James Watt, who was a mechanic at Glasgow University in Scotland, began to experiment with steam in 1763 and his universal engine came into commercial use for the first time in 1783. What did Watt do during the 20 years in between? At first, he simply repaired one of Newcomen's engines. In 1763, Watt installed an external capacitor[105] on that machine, which enabled him to avoid massive losses of steam. Then Watt gradually increased the steam pressure. Thus, the Watt steam engine appeared in 1769, followed by, in 1782, the first double-acting steam cylinder, in which the piston was alternately exposed to steam on two sides.

Beginning in 1785, the steam engine became one of the main engines of the Industrial Revolution, since Watt's machine was able to transform the reciprocating motion of a piston into rotation motion, i.e. the engine was now able to turn the driving wheel of a mill or a factory machine. By 1800, Boulton & Watt (the firm founded by James Watt and his companion) had produced 496 such mechanisms, of which only 164 were used as pumps, while 308 were used at mills and factories, and 24 at blast furnaces.

Richard Trevithick (UK) successfully built industrial one-stroke high-pressure engines which went down in history as 'Cornish engines'.

But with steam pressure increasing, the danger of explosions also increased and so high-pressure machines needed a safety valve to release excess pressure. Such a valve was invented by Denis Papin.

In 1769, French inventor Nicolas-Joseph Cugnot demonstrated a steam cart, the first operational self-propelled steam vehicle. His invention can probably be considered a prototype of the first car (Chizhov 1838). Steam proved to be very useful as a source of mechanical energy that set a wide range of agricultural machines in motion. Thanks to John Fitch, the first steamer appeared in 1788, cruising between Philadelphia (Pennsylvania) and Burlington (NY) up and down the Delaware River with up to 30 passengers. In February 1804, the irrepressible Richard Trevithick demonstrated his first steam locomotive at the Penydarren Ironworks in South Wales.

PATENT LAW AND OPENNESS OF TECHNOLOGIES
When James Watt took out patents on his inventions, he seriously intended to capitalize on the fruit of his labour. He was not only talented as an engineer, but also invented new business promotion schemes. To demonstrate the advantages of his machine, Watt resorted to a risky plan: he began to provide his machines for free! Moreover, Watt covered the costs of dismantling the old Newcomen machines and provided free maintenance for his new engines. In return, he was to be paid one-third of the savings to be made on coal over the next 25 years of operation of his machine. Attracted by the offer and signing contracts with Watt, the mine owners did not realize what bondage they had placed themselves in with the genius inventor.

In 1779, James Watt faced competition from inventors Matthew Wasborough and James Pickard, who had taken out a patent on the use of crank mechanisms in steam engines in England (Vvedensky 1957). From then on, Watt's engines, converting oscillatory motion into rotational, violated the rights of the holders of the patent. Watt had to bypass Wasborough and Pickard's patent by connecting the piston to the shaft of the machine by means of a gear transmission (a prototype of the modern gear). Watt was able to return to the use of crank transmission in his machines only after his competitors' patent was terminated.

Not willing to be involved in such a situation again, Watt became too scrupulous in patenting his inventions. Paragraph four of the said patent reads as follows: "In many cases, I intend to employ the expansive force (pressure) of steam to press on the pistons… or any other parts that may replace it." Incidentally, Watt patented the locomotive as well (in 1784).

James Watt opened a Pandora's Box. In fact, he blocked progress through patents for nearly three decades! By taking legal action, he managed to prevent commercial use of more efficient machines.

So patent restrictions can slow down the overall development of an industry. What is more profitable: to protect inventions that have already been made or to commercialize them and thus create opportunities for new inventions?

STEAM HAMMER, METALLURGY, ROLLED STEEL, AND REINFORCED CONCRETE

STEAM HAMMER

At the end of the 18th century, the steam hammer was introduced in industrial production. The patent on the invention was obtained by the same James Watt in 1784.

The invention determined many trends in engineering for the next century, with some of the steam hammers built in the second half of the 19th century reaching remarkable dimensions. For example, the striking part of Fritz, a steam hammer that was built at one of the Krupp factories in 1861, weighed 50 tonnes.[106]

METALLURGY

By 1720, an increase in the manufacture of engines caused an increased demand for iron. The supply turned out to be scarce. The situation changed only after Abraham Darby developed a method of producing crude iron in a blast furnace fuelled by coke (a fuel made from coal). From that moment onwards, coal became the main raw material for metallurgy and metal production began to grow in Great Britain.

The revolution in metallurgy was completed with the invention of the puddling process by Henry Cort in 1784 as a result of experimenting in search of a method for producing pure iron.[107] Innovation in the industry is continuing to this day, and metal production and processing methods are continually improved so as to reduce the price of production and find new uses for metal.

ROLLING MILLS AND SEAMLESS PIPES

The production of steel is followed by rolling, which happens to be one of the most important inventions made by man. Rolling meant unification and standardisation. All products now became alike, whereas previously each forging had been individual. Rolling made such important innovations as rails and steel wheels a reality. It is not surprising that rolling supplanted forging by the end of the 18th century.[108] This happened thanks to the English inventor Henry Cort. In 1783, he patented iron production with the use of rollers, which marked the creation of the rolling mill.

However, it was only in the 19th century, when the mass construction of railways began, that rolling came to be in real demand.

In 1885, another technological breakthrough was made by brothers Reinhard and Max Mannesmann, who developed seamless pipes by rolling. This newly available economical and reliable solution in the form of seamless iron piping came to be widely used in all types of municipal engineering networks.

REINFORCED CONCRETE

Thanks to British manufacturers James Parker and Joseph Aspdin, cement, a new building material, was now available. Cement, when mixed with sand, gravel and water in certain proportions, produced concrete, a material which became an essential and indispensable component of all advanced construction. The availability of concrete paved the way for other innovations needed by society. Underwater tunnels were constructed and so were urban sewage networks (such as we know them today).

Concrete is resistant to fire and water and does not stretch, but does crumble. However, concrete beams of over four metres long did not carry considerable load, so bridges and high-rise buildings had to be built of iron at the time. Iron structures rusted and even yielded in case of fire, collapsing altogether. Concrete and iron have similar thermal expansion characteristics which means they can be used together as a much stronger combination: reinforced concrete.

The first patent on reinforced concrete was taken out in England by William B. Wilkinson, a Newcastle plasterer, in 1854. Moreover, two years later, he built a whole building using reinforced concrete. But his invention did not attract enough attention. Neither did a similar effort made by French industrialist François Coignet, who published a brochure on the use of reinforced concrete in construction. I call such situations 'the solution is already here'.

By pure chance, the laurels for the inventor of reinforced concrete went to Joseph Monier, a French gardener who overlaid with concrete an iron tub in which an orange tree grew. I believe that Monier rightfully deserved the credit and success because his efforts to commercialize the application of reinforced concrete were far more considerable than anyone else's. He built new objects and obtained new patents on pools, sleepers, floors, bridges and beams. He also realised the significance of promising markets and filed patent applications in Germany and Russia.

I would like to single out one important point. French and British industrialists were lucky enough to conduct their business in a society where entrepreneurs were the main characters. Society's moral imperative to make money and become wealthy by organizing a business nurtured inventors' talents. This was not the same thing as simply making a fortune on anything that smelled of money.

By promoting reinforced concrete, Monier became rich and society became richer, having received a material that paved the way for yet another innovation: skyscrapers.

LOCOMOTIVE AND STEAMER
LOCOMOTIVE
In 1804, British inventor Richard Trevithick built the first steam locomotive with smooth wheels and that ran on smooth rails.[109] This locomotive did not gain widespread use because its wheels skidded as a result of lack of traction with the rails. Trevithick's followers, British designers of locomotives, tried to create a steam locomotive with cogged wheels and rails, but their invention turned out to be unsuccessful: the bulky locomotive constantly broke down and was unable to move fast.[110]

Once again, the solution came through knowledge. British mechanics Blackett and Hadley developed a doctrine of friction applied to railways and trains. Trevithick's original idea of using smooth rails and wheels for locomotives finally gained universal acceptance. Nine years' later (1814-1825), George Stephenson and his son Robert created a commercially suitable steam locomotive.[111] They managed to reduce steam consumption and improve its distribution.

Commercialization of the engine began immediately. Launched in England, railway construction began to spread throughout continental Europe (France, Prussia, Italy), and then in the United States and Russia. Passenger transportation over long distances began only once the importance of railways was recognized by the military and industry. Civilian transportation expanded the boundaries of civilization in the 19th century considerably: active information exchange was established and the impelled obligation to introduce innovations gave way to constant need for them.

STEAMSHIP

Nineteenth-century Great Britain became a real global workshop. All four leaves of the lucky clover were present in unison: talented scientists could create and find means, knowledge spread quite freely in industry and society rapidly changed its shape from agrarian to industrial as a result of urbanisation, generating increasing demand for new products and inventions.

The transport sector saw the majority of advanced innovations in the 19th century. From then on, attributing an innovation to any particular country became nearly impossible. A time came when similar inventions were demonstrated in different countries concurrently. The creation of the steamer was quite characteristic of the epoch in this sense. The construction of a steamboat capable of going against the current for a whole hour, by French inventor Jouffroy d'Abbans, should be considered one of the first attempts to create a floating machine.

The first steamer suitable for shipping was designed by Robert Fulton, an American mechanical engineer and a native of Ireland. He built his first steamboat in Paris and tested it on the River Seine. In 1803, his ship steamed up the Seine for one and a half hours, reaching a speed of 5 km/h.[112] Fulton's next boat, the paddle steamer *North River Steamboat* (later known as the *Clermont*), was built in the US and made its first trip along the Hudson River from New York to Albany in 1807, covering a stretch of 270 km.[113]

It was now possible to deliver cotton to England from America or India, grain and flax from Russia, and wood from Sweden. In general, however, naval shipbuilding was developing relatively slowly until the second half of the 19th century, since the next technical leap required new technology, new materials and new engineering knowledge.

CHEMICALS

The imposition of a blockade on England by the Emperor Napoleon I of France was intended to make British industry surrender. However, quite unexpectedly, the blockade harmed France itself, as the country heavily depended on imports of manufactured goods from Great Britain. Notably, the French army, which used blue as the main colour in its uniform, was the first to suffer from the effects of the blockade.

In the 19th century, the blue colour was obtained by mixing two natural dyes. Both dyes were supplied to Great Britain from its colonies in Asia and America. Having imposed the blockade, the French were suddenly left without the necessary raw materials and began to look for an alternative way to obtain the desired colour. This began a revolution in the chemical industry in France.

Through the efforts of French chemists, factory production of synthetic soda, one of the basic chemicals, was established. The method for industrial production of sodium carbonate was developed in 1791 by French chemist Nicolas Leblanc.[114] Leblanc's method was simple and cheap and gave a much more affordable product than previous methods.

The Industrial Revolution also paved the way for industrial production of some other chemicals, which were in high market demand. Sulphuric acid had been known since as far back as the Middle Ages, but it had been created from oxides formed during the combustion of mineral sulphur in glass containers. In 1746, John Reebok replaced glass jars with more voluminous lead containers and thus increased the productivity of the process.

This also signified the beginning of a great media war between France and Great Britain, waged through the press. The increase in print production required much larger supplies of paper and it was no longer possible to make it in the traditional manual way. But like many other French inventions of that era, papermaking machines became widely used not in France, but in Great Britain, where a number of large papermaking factories opened during the first decade of the 19th century. British industry was more amenable to industrial innovation as a result of being focused on achieving commercial success.

THE ACHIEVEMENTS OF THE INDUSTRIAL REVOLUTION

In just two centuries (the 18th and 19th), and especially during the Industrial Revolution (1780-1850), the United Kingdom went through tremendous changes in agriculture, manufacturing, mining and transport, and thus greatly influenced the course of history. The revolutionary changes, which began thanks to the presence of all the elements of the lucky clover, gradually spread throughout Europe and the world.

The revolution in the textile industry laid the foundations of the factory system. The invention of the steam engine, which became the universal motor for large-scale capitalist industry, revolutionized metallurgy. This step, in turn, created the basis for a new type of industry – the factory industry.

Accordingly, a new type of capital emerged – industrial capital. Whereas the Agricultural Revolution resulted in an increase in urban population, the Industrial Revolution resulted in accumulation of technology and commercialization of inventions. A hard-working class willing to accept new risks, the class of capitalist entrepreneurs, emerged and took shape in society.

In the United Kingdom, a well-developed industrial infrastructure was created, railways and new towns were built, and the production of steel, machinery and textiles began. Moreover, the steam engine enabled the country to begin expansion worldwide, especially in India and China.

It may seem paradoxical, but shortly before the Opium Wars, China was the largest economy in the world, with a GDP close to one-third of the world's and about 10 times larger than that of the United Kingdom. Within less than a hundred years, the picture changed dramatically. And it was the steam engine that played the crucial role in the East–West balance at this turning point in human history.

OPIUM WARS

Great Britain gained a powerful impetus for the development of science, introduced new technologies and labour organization principles, and reached at some point the highest possible level of division of labour and specialisation. Further growth required expansion. England was late for the process of colonization of Mexico and Peru, and all of the New World's accumulated gold had already been taken away by Spain. The British acted pragmatically: since they were not welcome in the west, they decided to go east, towards the Portuguese and Spaniards' initial goal – the richest countries in the world, India and China.

China at the time tightly restricted trade with other countries, allowing them a very narrow field for activity. Nevertheless, at the turn of the 18th century, Western powers, and especially England, persistently tried to enter the Chinese market. In the second half of the 18th century, the whole of China's foreign trade was concentrated in the city of Guangzhou. Contacts between Chinese subjects and foreigners were punishable.[115] This, however, did not stop the trade. The British wanted tea, porcelain and textiles, while Chinese merchants prized silver. In 1784, the import duty on tea was reduced in Great Britain and the tea prices fell. There was now a surplus demand for tea, which could only be satisfied by paying for extra supplies in silver.

The British took this as a threat to their economy and tried to persuade the Chinese with some diplomacy to change trade relations. To this end, the East India Company was established, with authorization to declare peace or war as required.

RUSSIAN SHIPS AT THE BATTLE OF SINOP.
During the 1853 Russian-Turkish war,
18 November 1853, oil on canvas

SHELL GUNS, BATTLESHIPS AND RIFLES

It is difficult to imagine today why the British ships caused so much panic among the Chinese rulers, or why gunboat diplomacy dominated in the world for such a long time. These facts, however, are connected with the introduction of some key innovations in the epoch's military sector: shell artillery and armoured ships, or battleships.

Shell guns appeared as a result of improvements made on conventional guns with the use of a fuse that would, when fixed on a projectile, only ignite at the moment of the shot. A shell that hit a wooden ship and then exploded produced the combined effect of bursting into flames and sending out wooden and metal fragments which maimed members of the crew. This exceeded by far the effect of an iron cannonball capable of merely making a hole in the side of the ship.

The first to realize fully this effect were not the French military, but Russian naval mariners led by the outstanding military strategist Admiral Pavel Nakhimov. He commanded Russia's Black Sea navy fleet when it defeated the Turkish navy at the Battle of Sinop in 1853. Of key importance in that battle was the superiority of the Russian fleet's artillery.

The fear of Russian naval shell guns accelerated research and development for the protection of British and French ships. As a result, battleships were created, soon to play a fundamental role in persuading the Chinese government to open the country's ports for foreign ships.

Remarkably, the Chinese rulers viewed Great Britain as a barbaric state which could offer nothing of real value. English merchants needed a product that could be sold in China to cover the cost of importing Chinese goods. And such a product was found: it was opium from India.[116] Poppy grown in India was used as a commodity to pay with taxes. Gains in India were more important than morality.[117] The same fate awaited China as well.

Opium had been known in China even before the British came, but then it was only used as a medicine. By the end of the 18th century, drug addiction became an acute social problem in China. Whereas in the middle of the 18th century, some 400 boxes of opium were brought to China each year, by the 1840s, this fatal import amounted to about 40,000 boxes annually and the profits of the British drug trade exceeded the British profits from trading in tea and silk together. The gains of the East India Company from opium exports exceeded one-tenth of the company's total profits!

By 1836, China's elite, headed by its emperor, found itself at a crossroads. On the one hand, the opium trade brought a lot of money and a number of Chinese officials suggested legalizing it; on the other, heavy consequences and harm were an obvious danger. The Chinese decided to do away with the problem and as a drastic measure, Chinese troops surrounded an English village where some 300 merchants lived next to opium storehouses. All the unsold British opium, worth huge sums of money, was confiscated and destroyed.

Determined to take revenge, the British were now ready to start a fight against China on the slightest pretext.[118] In 1840, the tension reached its peak. Even though the English parliament did not come to a decision to declare war on China, 20 warships with 4,000 servicemen on board set off to its coasts.

The war against China turned out to be a cakewalk for the British. Rifled guns gave them a huge advantage on land, as the Chinese ground forces were armed with 200-year-old firelock muskets. The British could shoot Chinese soldiers from a safe distance. At sea, the Chinese' frustration was even more profound. English steam vessels looked pretty much like a miracle to them, being able to move in calm weather and even against the current.

Under the Treaty of Nanking, China was obliged to pay a large compensation. Furthermore, China undertook to assign five ports for British trade and pass a law under which British citizens could only be tried by British courts. Other Western countries soon requested, and received, similar privileges. Such was the essence of the good old principles of promoting 'free trade'.

The Second Opium War dragged on for four years (1856-1860). China's defeat in the Second Opium War resulted in a colossal fall of its share in the world GDP, civil wars and a temporary loss of sovereignty over most of its territory after a war with Japan. The country managed to restore its independence only after 1905. When a series of wars and revolutions began to break out in the world, the Chinese embraced the rise of a nationalist movement led by Sun Yat-sen, who very aptly described the then China as a hyper-colony, i.e. a colony that was so large that it was governed by several foreign states at once.

What enabled the United Kingdom to win so easily a trade war against the most powerful nation of the time? Was the victory only due to the achievement of the Industrial Revolution and the steam engine? Yes, the United Kingdom had seen a revolution of unprecedented force – the Industrial Revolution that changed the balance of power in the world.

Why did China fail to do the same at that time? Why did China's GDP per capita remain virtually unchanged for nearly two millennia, until 1960? Why were the great discoveries made by Europeans, not Chinese? After all, Chinese merchant ships travelled long distances, to return home filled with gold and ivory, long before Europeans embarked on similar voyages. These expeditions brought enormous profits. However, the year when Emperor Yongle died was the last year when the Chinese went on marine expeditions. Then, the Chinese authorities moved to a policy of complete isolationism, destroying the national fleet in 1552 and quartering troops in the country's coastal areas to control the coastal strip up to 50 kilometres away from the sea (Meliksetov 2002, 259).

The isolationism manifested itself in the development of technology as well. Archaeological excavations in China found blast furnaces that date back to the year 1000. At that time, China produced a total of 100,000 tonnes of crude iron per year! Europe reached a comparable level of crude iron production only in 1705, after transition to coal. In other words, the Chinese had at that time a technology that was to emerge in Europe only seven centuries later. There is quite strong evidence of this. Why did China fail to make use of this temporary advantage?

Some authors explain the failure by the Chinese authorities' determination to protect the country's original technologies, including defence secrets possessed by China at that time. Others note serious differences in the approaches to international trade: China's foreign trade system was based on honour, while the Europeans relied on laws.[119]

In China, intervention from within was seen as a negative factor that caused damage to the national economy. Until quite recently (the Mao Zedong time), the Chinese have been convinced that investment and foreign trade were harmful for national artisan production and agriculture because they took large amounts of money out of the country and thus impaired China's trade surplus. As a result, the lack of competitiveness with foreign companies left Chinese companies no chance to develop, which caused China's development to lag behind until the 1960-70s. Based on the above, we can conclude that the self-isolation policy is unlikely to have been useful for China. Mark Elvin in his book *The Pattern of the Chinese Past* undertakes a fundamental reconstruction of China's history. He proves that the country's stock of traditional technologies was exhausted by the beginning of the colonial wars and was unable to provide the country's growing domestic market with necessary products anymore. China was in any case forced to move to a new level of production and was on the verge of transforming its inefficient system of economic relations (Elvin 1973).

Gilbert Rozman in his *The Modernisation of China* suggests that late 19th and early 20th century China simply had no effective leadership able to carry out modernization of the country's economy (Rozman 1981). Thus, we can conclude that conservatism and preservation of tradition are not always good for a country. Moreover, they may cause great harm if the idea of innovation as such is rejected.

COMMERCIAL INTERESTS JUSTIFY ANYTHING

The Opium Wars were waged not by the British and French empires, but by private companies – the British East India Company and its namesake and competitor, the French East India Company. It was then that the famous British maxim 'Commercial interests justify anything', was coined. From the end of the 18th century, the British government, having found itself under pressure from the free-trade movement, began to limit the company's monopoly on trade with India. But the fact remains: the two companies were prototypes for modern multinational corporations.

Although both companies were formally controlled by their governments, in fact they had considerable autonomy and many attributes of a state, and even their own armies. The first company of this type, called the East Asiatic Company, was established in the Netherlands in the early 17th century. The company was granted monopoly on trade with the Asian region and was empowered to build fortifications, keep armed forces of its own and conclude treaties with Asian rulers. In 1602, the young Dutch company waged the first global war in history when it went to war with Portugal for colonies, forcing its opponent out of most of its territories in Asia and challenging it at the same time in South America and Africa. However, this proved to be an extremely expensive project: the government subsidies turned out to be insufficient and the company accumulated a debt that nearly equalled its market capitalization.

Similar companies began to emerge in other countries as well, but sending marine expeditions was a costly and risky business, and required pooling the capital of many participants.

Soon, the British government granted the East India Company a monopoly on trade with the East. In addition, the company was engaged in politics in the colonies, waged wars and dispensed justice. The Crown did not even have shares in the company's capital, which was all owned by big businessmen and aristocrats, and thus many military and political decisions made by the company represent a classic example of private sector involvement in global politics. In the first third of the 17th century, the company concentrated its operations in India, from where it exported such products as fabrics, yarn, indigo, opium and saltpetre to other Asian and European countries. It was also actively involved, though with varying degrees of success, in the colonization of India.

During the industrial revolution in England, the colonies were not so much considered a source of raw materials for British industry as an important market for British manufacturers. Traditional urban crafts in India (and later China) were unable to compete with cheap British goods and went into decline.

Only in 1773 did the British parliament decide that the company must report to the national government and any decisions it took would be decisions on behalf of the Crown, not on behalf of the company. The company was finally nationalized in the 19th century, after the company was accused of sparking an uprising in India.

The Industrial Revolution meant a qualitative restructuring of the material and technical base of production and transition from manual labour to machine labour, from manual to industrial production. New technology, openness to innovation, patent law, inexpensive labour force in large quantities, and James Watt's efficient and commercially attractive steam engine made the flywheel of the Industrial Revolution go at an increasing speed.

The ever intensifying innovation caused a domino effect. The steam engine entered new areas, creating new modes of transport and new plants for the production of traditional and new products, as well as for the manufacture of machines required for the production. However, accumulated knowledge and know-how quickly became property protected by patent law. An acute dilemma appeared: by protecting the commercial interests of the patent owner, law inhibited technical progress.

The achievements of the Industrial Revolution changed European society, which sought to expand its influence throughout the world. Using gunboat diplomacy, Great Britain managed to change the balance of power in Europe and then to put China, Asia's most ancient empire, on its knees.

Thus, innovation enabled one nation to gain advantage over others. It is only today that we can appreciate this lesson well, since understanding of the dynamics of a complex process only comes upon its completion.

CHAPTER 9

TECHNICAL REVOLUTION: HOW ELECTRICITY, THE AUTOMOBILE, OIL AND NITROGEN CREATED PROSPERITY

" Any sufficiently advanced technology is indistinguishable from magic. "

– Arthur C. Clarke

THE TECHNICAL REVOLUTION IN THE UNITED STATES: THE BEGINNING OF CHANGE

The UK, having found itself on the crest of the first technological wave, strived to keep the lucky clover to itself as long as it could. Retaining the competitive edge in technology at that time required keeping the structure of machines a secret, since patent rights were rarely protected abroad. Therefore, a number of laws were adopted from 1765 to 1789, expressly prohibiting the export of machines and even their drawings. However, turbulent historical events undermined these efforts. Britain, as well as the whole of Europe, was involved in the Napoleonic wars and the subsequent restoration of national governments. Another power, the US, won greatly as a result.

While wealth was destroyed in Europe, it was rapidly accumulated in the US. This country's share of world trade grew rapidly due to the export of agricultural products, especially cotton, to Europe. To support the growing export, the Americans needed a large merchant fleet.

Since the 1790s, the US bourgeoisie had conducted an extremely lucrative trade with the warring coalitions in Europe. This contributed to the growth of the US merchant fleet. US sea shipment, on top of covering the country's own export and import needs, provided almost the whole of freight transportation for the foreign trade of Holland, France and Spain. The prosperity of American ship owners and traders has always depended on wars waged in Europe: thus, during the brief respite between two wars (after the Treaty of Amiens), the volume of US foreign trade fell almost by half.[120]

As a result of the accumulation of commercial wealth, favourable conditions for a real industrial revolution formed in the US by the beginning of the 19th century.[121] The advent of machines and factories, like it had done in the UK, brought about a technological revolution. Steam engines displaced manual labour everywhere.

Steam-driven capitalism began to change agrarian America, but it was the Civil War that acted as the main factor in increasing dramatically the need for new technologies in the US. Contradictions between the North and the South played a crucial role in the fate of technical progress. The South's economy was wholly focused on supplying raw materials (cotton, tobacco, etc.) to Europe, with slavery forming the basis of competitiveness, while the North needed to construct transport links to be able to develop its natural resources and vast territories. Since the locomotive served as the engine of progress, it was this innovation that provoked, in a remarkable way, the civil war in the US. Today, it can be argued that the war was the result of a collision between two business platforms. Something that integrated well in one of them was totally unsuitable for the other!

The authorities of the northern states willingly gave large areas of land to railway companies, which in turn sold them to farmers to recoup their investments. In the South, however, farmers were a threat to the power of big landowners. The North pulled in manufacturing industries, primarily metallurgy, through the rapid development of railway communication.[122]

The South deliberately thwarted road construction plans, even such important ones as the Pacific road project conceived to connect the two oceans. The North already had a strong industrial bourgeoisie, large numbers of industrial workers and numerous strong midsized and small farms. Industrial capital was eager for further enrichment, while the cotton-growing South hindered entrepreneurial initiative. The conflict culminated on the issue of different attitudes to slavery. The South's landowners perceived the black population as property. The North's businessmen needed an influx of cheap labour, a liberated workforce free in its choice of employment. Proletarians had more rights, because they themselves decided to whom and on what conditions to sell their labour.

The North's business model was more viable and ensured a more rapid growth. When Abraham Lincoln, who was opposed to slavery, was elected president, the country finally broke into two parts. The South proclaimed themselves a confederation with Jefferson Davis as its president.

In such conflicts, demand for innovation, which comes to be perceived as a potential weapon, rises sharply. The increase in demand resulted in numerous inventions registered in various fields of the North's economy.

In the 1830s, with the discovery of a new iron smelting technology, the Union wholly covered its need in rolled steel with domestic production. This enabled the US metallurgical industry to use the country's rich deposits of iron ore. The use of petroleum products after 1840 contributed to the development of the steel industry in Pennsylvania, New Jersey and New York.

The industrial revolution resulted in huge concentration of public bodies: government offices, stock markets and major newspapers, all of which needed improved means of communication, while the army also needed modern weapons. The growing American cities required new means of lighting, and the steam-driven technology, which had come to dominate, was too unsophisticated and therefore unable to provide another qualitative leap. Such a leap was enabled by the emergence of electrical engineering, a technology that employed a completely new resource: electricity.

The electric telegraph became the first innovation of the new industrial revolution. In 1820, a year legendary for its electrical innovations, Danish physicist Hans Christian Oersted discovered the connection between magnetism and electric current and André-Marie Ampère came up with the idea to use electricity as a medium for messaging. In 1837, Samuel Morse, an American inventor, developed the concept of a single-wire telegraph, which immediately came to be used actively in the US and Europe alike. In 1855, Professor David Edward Hughes, a British-American inventor, patented a printing telegraph. Telegraphy began to develop rapidly worldwide. Large-scale military operations during the American Civil War generated a huge demand for fast and effective means of long-distance communication. The telegraph was the only method suitable for providing such communication, but it needed electrical energy. The vigorous introduction of electricity brought about another technological revolution and the outstanding inventor Thomas Edison ranked first among its heroes.

THE DEAF TELEGRAPHER

In the 19th century, children were much more independent than today. At the age of 12, Thomas Alva Edison already had a small business – a railway printing press and, moreover, a railway shop. He published a newspaper, selling it on trains and at stations, and sold sweets and sundries from a rented part of a railway car on one of Detroit's trains. One day, he tarried when selling newspapers and his train began to move. Trying to get into the carriage on the move nearly cost the young businessman his life. Fortunately, the conductor was able to drag the youth into the carriage by his ears, after which, however, Edison began to grow deaf. Then Edison himself rescued the small son of the station master from under the wheels of a railway car. To thank Thomas, the station master taught him to operate telegraph apparatus.

The hearing loss caused Thomas to stay away from the civil war and the telegraph profession then was somewhat similar to being a programmer today. There is always demand for good specialists and Edison became a brilliant telegrapher. He could memorize whole pages of text. This ability gave him the opportunity to read a lot of literature that taught him things an inventor needed to know. This same skill enabled him to be in the middle of the US financial world of the time.

Edison became head of the office for centralized notification of stock exchange prices of gold on Wall Street in New York. The operation of over 300 offices depended on telegraph apparatus being in good condition, which in turn depended on Edison's performance. Reliability of this system was the critical factor.

Edison soon realized that he could improve both the design of the telegraph apparatus and the reliability of the system. But the well-established system needed employees rather than inventors. It was, however, not the telegraph as such that attracted Edison, but what made it run: the magic power of electricity.

THE MAGIC POWER OF ELECTRICITY

Today, we hardly ever realize that we are always surrounded by magic – every day, every minute, every second of our life. Most of us are woken up in the morning by an alarm clock or some other device that uses electrical energy. Having woken up early, when it is still dark outside, a person turns on the light. This is where the magic begins… The world becomes much brighter.

Life today would be very different if electricity had not been discovered. Electricity is flexible (for example it can provide light and heat and set things in motion), it's clean and silent, it can be transmitted to be available at various consumption points, and it enables fine adjustment of the operation of various devices to be run at desired speeds and their real-time control in multi-functional industrial production. Electricity is also convenient because it can be quickly and easily delivered anywhere and transformed into any other type of energy. Fuel requires mechanical transportation to where we want to use it, whereas electricity is just available right wherever it's needed, through a wall socket. It's not just that electricity has replaced steam. There is more to this change: dangerous processes have been replaced by safe, clean and environmentally friendly ones.

The advent of electricity paved the way for the invention of new devices that could only work on electricity: hair dryers, washing machines, refrigerators.[123] Electricity revolutionized construction too: steel became much cheaper, enabling the manufacture of many new types of machinery and the construction of huge buildings – skyscrapers. The invention of sound reproduction techniques and the phonograph by Edison brought about mass production of music recordings and gave a great boost to the entertainment industry. Photography, celluloid film, radio, television, electromagnetic waves and cheap paper for mass publication of books only became possible thanks to electricity.

ALEXANDER GRAHAM BELL INAUGURATES A 1520-KILOMETRE-LONG TELEPHONE LINE BETWEEN NEW YORK AND CHICAGO.
18 October 1892.

HOW THE TELEPHONE CONTINUED TO BE... REINVENTED

The idea of vocal communication over long distances was described by Russian writer Vladimir Odoevsky in 1840, in his unfinished utopian novel *Year 4338*.

French telegrapher Charles Bursel developed a very useful principle of sound transmission over a distance and Johann Reis from Germany came up with a name for the future device: 'telephone', which in Greek means 'sound from a distance'.

In 1876, Alexander Graham Bell took out a patent on a device for voice transmission over a distance, though there were many claimants for this invention.[126]

The essence of Bell's invention was about transferring sound vibrations by means of flexible metal plates and the device was originally intended for people with hearing problems. In 1877-1878, Thomas Edison made some significant modifications to Bell's device, without which the telephone would not have received such rapid and widespread popularity.

After Tivadar Puskás, a Hungarian engineer, invented the multiplex switchboard in 1876, more than 100,000 telephones were installed in the US in just 10 years. Only 25 years later, there were more than a million operational telephones in the US.

The first commercially successful electro-mechanical telephone exchange system was invented by Almon Brown Strowger, an undertaker who, striving to stop losing customers as a result of information leaking out to his competitor, developed and installed his innovation at his funeral parlour in Kansas City. In addition, he invented rotary dialling by introducing the telephone dial.

ONE OF THE FIRST GRAMOPHONES PRODUCED BY EMILE BERLINER IN 1890, BEARING THE INSCRIPTION 'E. BERLINER GRAMOPHONE D. R. P. 45048'.

THE PHONOGRAPH, THE GRAMOPHONE AND THE EVOLUTION OF SOUND CARRIERS

The first device for recording sound was invented in 1877 by Edison, who patented it under the name 'phonograph'. The device recorded sound on a cylinder wrapped in tin foil.

In 1887, Emile Berliner, an American inventor, used a recording medium in the form of a disc and produced metal master copies from which further copies could be made. Later, gramophone records were replaced by magnetic tapes, and then by audio and video cassettes.

THE WIZARD OF MENLO PARK[124]

Edison's thinking was amazingly productive. Not only did he come up with dozens of inventions, patenting them as soon as they could be formulated, but he also quickly worked his way up from being a single inventor to establishing an invention process line.[125] He realized that he needed an industrial research laboratory with state-of-the-art equipment and a team of top-notch professionals. So, the greatest of his achievements was being both an inventor and an entrepreneur who could implement his inventions thanks to a team of specialists. Edison's father helped him in selecting the right location for his laboratory, which happened to be Menlo Park, a village in New Jersey. We can say that this was the first prototype of a modern industrial laboratory or a research and development company.

Edison was so addicted to work that he often fell asleep in the laboratory, only to keep on working on his invention as soon as he woke up. One of his first inventions was a carbon telephone transmitter (mouthpiece) (1877-1878), which was a significant improvement on the existing Bell telephone.

Edison's favourite brainchild, however, was not the telephone, but the phonograph. He repeatedly returned to this invention for almost 40 years, introducing new improvements, for which he obtained 80 patents.

So it's clear to see that a technical invention by itself is not enough; it requires further, and no less considerable or important, efforts for its integration into the market. It is through a continuous cycle of changing, becoming something else and living a new life that an invention finds a commercial application.

In 1880, Thomas Edison decided not to limit his team's efforts to the development of a primary device and set the goal of creating a whole lighting system. He designed and manufactured six types of bipolar DC generator and produced original designs for wire coils and a capture anode. In 1881 to 1882, Edison and his team designed the largest steam-driven power generator, called Jumbo, for the world's first thermal power station, and built the station for public use in New York.

Electrolytic power consumption metres, fuses with fuse links and rotary switches developed by Edison and his team were also the first devices of their kind in electrical engineering. Edison also developed a three-wire current channelling system, which made it possible to supply a lower voltage, 110v, for lighting and a higher voltage, 220v, for industrial needs. The metal screw cap and lamp holder designed by Edison were called the 'Edison screw cap' and 'Edison screw lamp holder' for a long time.

**THOMAS EDISON WITH A COPY OF HIS FIRST
SUCCESSFUL INCANDESCENT LIGHT BULB.**
16 October 1929

HOW THE LIGHT BULB WAS INVENTED AND IS STILL INVENTED TODAY

The first light bulb was created by Russian electrical engineer Pavel Yablochkov in 1876. His creation was called 'the Russian light'; however, his idea did not find enough support in Russia. In 1879, Edison improved the light bulb using his traditional method of trying various combinations of materials and designs. To make his invention, Edison used the method which Sir Winston Churchill felicitously described later, saying, "You can always count on Americans to do the right thing – after they've tried everything else." After no less than 6,000 substances and compounds, spending more than US$100,000 on the experiments, Edison got what he wanted – one of the first mass products in history, needed by everyone. Edison created a bulb that lasted for more than 1,000 hours, which meant that the invention could now leave the lab and enter the market. Such lamps were routinely used throughout the world for 30 years, though they had many competitors.

Apart from incandescent light bulbs and fluorescent tubes, the range of commercially successful sources of electric light today includes halogen lamps and LED lights. The service life of a halogen lamp is about 2,000 hours (1.8 years), a fluorescent tube lasts about 8,000 hours (approx. 7.3 years), and an LED light typically lasts 25,000 hours (22.8 years). It is likely that the bulb, just as the telephone, the phonograph and the printer, will be continue to be reinvented. Each change in dominant technology platforms gives a chance to seemingly long-forgotten ideas!

**NIKOLA TESLA
– AN AMERICAN
PHYSICIST,
ELECTRICIAN AND
INVENTOR.**
1 January 1911

THE AMERICAN GENIUS TESLA

In 1883, a young Serbian scientist by the name of Nikola Tesla successfully developed a new model of the electric motor in Strasbourg. The former mayor of the city, Mr Bauzin, was fascinated with Tesla's work and arranged for him to demonstrate a working prototype of his design to a few businessmen, but none of them ventured to finance the inventor's further work. Risky large-scale projects were of little interest at that time. In the spring of 1884, Tesla finished his work, hoping to receive a well-deserved payment from his employer. However, he soon realized that his expectations were never to be fulfilled and decided to go to St. Petersburg, where Russian electrical geniuses Pavel Yablochkov, Dmitry Lachinov and Vladimir Chikolev worked. At the last moment, Charles W. Batchelor, an inventor and associate of Thomas Edison, persuaded Tesla to go to the US instead of Russia. He also wrote an introduction letter to Edison, saying that it would be an unforgivable mistake to let such a talent go to Russia (Matonin 2014). I wonder: how would Tesla's career have developed if he had not changed his mind?

THE FIRST POWER UNIT

In 1882, Edison managed to launch on a commercial basis the world's first electric power distribution system for a whole district of a large city. Just think about it. He managed not only to conceive and develop, but also sell, a completely new system comparable in its effect on human history with, for example, a railway system, with all of its engines, junctions, semaphores, etc. And the whole project was the brainchild of one person, rather than dozens of inventors!

How did Edison manage to do what Richard Trevithick did not? The conditions in which Edison worked were not much better. The US was in the grip of one more economic depression. Edison had no money of his own to fund such an ambitious project. He managed to garner investment from Wall Street financiers by showing them a map, presenting the gas lighting network in the district proposed to be provided with electric lighting.

Edison solved an economic problem: he assessed the gas flow rate and calculated the cost of the gas lighting. His detailed business plan, verified by such compelling arguments, made the desired impression on the financiers and they agreed to invest in the project despite the adverse financial situation of the US at that time. The Edison Electric Light Company was established in 1878, with quite impressive capital totalling US$1 million.

In 1887, Edison moved to West Orange, where he built a more advanced laboratory. There, he perfected his phonograph and created a voice recorder, a device for individual viewing of moving images (Kinetoscope), and a ferronickel alkaline battery. By that time, the Edison Electric Light Company accounted for nearly three-quarters of all US production of light bulbs. Edison owned 41 power stations, which provided electric power for 100,000 bulbs. Edison energetically introduced his electric lighting system in the US, Europe and Latin America. This is how the American, and afterwards global, electrical industry was born through the efforts of one single genius.

THOMAS EDISON AND NIKOLA TESLA: GENIUSES' PRIDE AND PREJUDICE

The genius of Edison would not have manifested itself fully had he not met a person of the same calibre, Nikola Tesla (Pishtalo 2010). In 1884, having just arrived in New York and walked off the ship, Tesla headed straight for Edison's office.[127]

All of the distinguished American's inventions in the field of electricity made use of direct current at that time, whereas Tesla was enthusiastically talking about high voltage alternative current. The famous inventor saw a dangerous rival at first sight, but nonetheless offered Tesla a job in his company, putting him to work on knocking direct-current generators into shape. Edison used low-voltage direct current in his transmission lines, while Tesla advocated high voltage alternating current – which eventually became the industry standard because it solved the problem of loss reduction during power transmission. The use of direct current required building dirty, noisy and unwieldy power stations in the city, whereas Tesla's approach allowed for a fundamental change in this respect. But the better Tesla handled his work, the more he fell out of favour with Edison.

Tesla believed that a little theory and calculation would eliminate quite a bit of Edison's expensive search for technical solutions. He believed that Edison, though having a boundless, enormous stock of energy, would still be better off if he spent more time doing creative work and technical calculations before making things. It seems that Tesla did not seem to be aware of his fellow inventor's pathological dislike of mathematics.

Besides, Edison, who had built a low-voltage direct-current electrical system, was not ready to accept radical high-voltage AC power ideas. When Edison was sketching his bold plan to centralize power supply for large cities, he relied on one source of energy only – the steam engine.[128] The efficiency of a 20 MW steam-driven turbine installed in 1913 was just over 25%, which was actually a tenfold increase on the figures achieved three decades earlier, but large-scale power production required much higher performance indicators. Tesla knew how to achieve a radical increase in efficiency, but his plan required a paradigm shift. Edison was not prepared to embrace this eventuality. The two geniuses were destined to part very soon.

The invention of the induction motor by Tesla was an enormous practical contribution to the history of innovation. The induction motor, with its considerably higher efficiency, successfully replaced the steam engine. Although it is Walter Baily, not Tesla, who is considered the first inventor of the induction motor, his engine had a very low efficiency and worked on single-phase current.

For a long time, only single-phase alternating current was used in industry. In 1888, Tesla and Galileo Ferraris, a physicist from Italy, discovered the electromagnetic field rotation phenomenon and the effect produced by alternating magnetic poles.[129] Tesla took Walter Baily's induction motor as a basis and considerably simplified its design, achieving additional efficiency and reliability. Tesla's invention attracted the liveliest interest from George Westinghouse, a well known industrialist and inventor. Listening to one of Tesla's presentations, he immediately appreciated the greatness of his ideas and proved to be a shrewder businessman than Edison. In June 1888, the Westinghouse Electric Company bought up all of Tesla's patents on the two-phase motor for US$1 million and invited him to organize the production of induction motors at the company's factories. In 1895, George Westinghouse's company built the first hydro-electric power plant in Niagara Falls, thus giving birth to industrial use of alternating current.

Tesla made good money on this undertaking by selling his patents for US$500,000 in cash and acquiring 150 shares in the company, as well as receiving royalties for sales of electricity, which later proved to be a lucrative source of income. Soon enough, the number of motors sold exceeded 100,000. By 1899, 160,000 engines had been produced in the US and 10 years later that number had grown to 243,000. Most of these were powered by alternating current. Within 20 years of the launch of their series production, electric motors designed by Tesla effectively supplanted other electric devices and accounted for most of the consumption of electricity in the US. By 1900, they had been adapted for numerous industrial applications.

Tesla's two-phase motors surpassed direct-current motors by far, but still were rather ineffective in terms of design. The best design known to us today was proposed by Russian electrical engineer Mikhail Dolivo-Dobrovolsky. He reworked Tesla's induction motor beyond recognition and took out a patent on his rotor in 1889. His technical solution is still considered to be the best.

ELECTRIC VEHICLES

The differences between Tesla and Edison not only affected the development of electrical engineering, but also changed unpredictably the course of events in another industry – the automotive industry. In 1900, most cars in the largest metropolitan areas in the east of the US were driven by steam and electricity.[130]

Robert Anderson and Robert Davidson from the UK and Thomas Davenport from the US are considered to be the pioneers of the electric vehicle industry.

A SUBSTITUTE FOR A HAPPY ENDING

Thanks to his talent, Edison left his mark in all basic industries. In metallurgy, he developed a method for enriching poor iron ore by means of magnetic separation and introduced it on an industrial scale. In the building materials industry, he optimized the production of cement, making it much cheaper. This was all pioneering work in the field of construction.

In the chemical industry, Edison organized the production of a number of substances, including phenol, benzene, carbolic acid and aniline oil for dyes, thereby demonstrating his outstanding ability as a chemical engineer.

In the history of management, he is known as a founder of corporations. Having started with setting up small, specialized firms to stimulate the introduction of his inventions, Edison always knew the right time to move on to establishing large companies, such as engineering or wiring corporations. In 1889, Edison merged all of his electrical enterprises into one major corporation, the Edison General Electric Company.

Edison's lead was followed by other entrepreneurs, while his business development method (from a garage lab to a major corporation) is still used by many businessmen today. It can be said that he created a business model for transforming individual inventions into innovative breakthrough products and showed others how to build businesses.

In 1912, Tesla and Edison had been awarded a joint Nobel Prize for their achievements in physics. The prize, however, was never presented to them and finally went to Gustaf Dalén, a Swedish industrialist. It is not known what actually happened and no correspondence is known to exist on this subject. It is well established though that Tesla refused to receive the prize. He was badly in need of money at that time and US$20,000, which he would have received as his part of the prize, would have helped him to continue his work. However, other considerations were more important to him. He considered himself a pioneer and Edison an inventor. In his opinion, the inclusion of both of them in the same category completely undermined the understanding of the comparative value of their achievements and the proposal to share the prize with Edison diminished the value of Tesla's relative contribution to progress too much for him to accept it without reservation. Tesla was the first and perhaps the only scientist who refused this prestigious award (O'Neill 1944, 264).

In 1899, electric vehicles passed the 100 km/h speed milestone, which was a truly remarkable event for its time. The machine had a streamlined body made of an alloy of aluminium and tungsten, and resembled a torpedo mounted on a chassis. In 1901, another electric car, built by the Riker Electric Vehicle Company, established the first-ever official speed record by covering a mile in 63 seconds. Records were followed by records. In addition, electric cars were very reliable – they simply had nothing to break! By the beginning of the 20th century, the total number of electric vehicles in the US reached 10,000, which was several times more than the number of their petrol contemporaries.

Edison would not have been Edison if he had not attempted to finish what he had started. His efforts finally brought to the foreground of automotive history not only a car, but also a brilliant car designer, Henry Ford. Edison and Ford met in 1912, became friends and decided to flood the US market with affordable electric vehicles with the Ford logo on the hood and an Edison battery underneath it. They began to implement the idea in great secrecy. Key target parameters were selected for the future top seller: a reasonable price within the range of US$500 to $750 and a power reserve to cover 160 km. At Ford's factory at Highland Park in Michigan, engineers pored over the chassis and the propulsion unit of the future electrical Edison-Ford for two years.

It was the today well known Model T.[131] But the vehicle failed to meet the target parameters set by Edison and Ford. The reason for this was Edison's nickel-iron batteries. They showed spotless performance on the laboratory test benches, but behaved quite badly as soon as they were brought to Highland Park.

Time passed, but the promised miraculous electric Edison-Ford did not appear. Meanwhile, Ford, not wishing to lose the market, launched the world's first vehicle assembly line and began churning out petrol-driven Model T cars at a rate of one car every one and a half minutes! The electric idea just died.[132] Electricity was simply unable to compete with cheap petrol.

The electrification process was advancing unevenly across the US, whereas Standard Oil gas stations could be found anywhere. The road network grew; there were now Trans-American highways and buyers needed cars capable of covering great stretches. Petrol engines were embedded into the market before electric ones and that was their only advantage.

CARS

The automobile is 'self-propelled' thanks to the internal combustion engine. The principal invention of this engine is ascribed to Philippe LeBon, whose early death prevented him from realizing his idea. The first commercially successful internal combustion engine was developed by Belgian engineer Étienne Lenoir in 1858. It was he who came up with the idea to ignite the fuel-air mixture with an electric spark.

In 1864, German inventor Nikolaus Otto took out a patent on an original model of the gas engine and established a firm which he named N.A. Otto & Cie. Having no knowledge in electrical engineering, he discarded electric ignition. Nonetheless, the efficiency of his engine was significantly higher than that of Lenoir's, reaching 15%. In terms of efficiency, Otto's engine was superior to the best steam engines of the time and thus remarkably economical in comparison with others. As a result, there was a huge demand for the new engines. In 1877, Otto took out a patent on his new four-stroke engine. Its operation cycle forms a basis for the design of most of today's gas and petrol engines.

The end of the 19th century saw the creation of two-cylinder engines; the early 20th century was marked by the arrival of four-cylinder ones. In 1885, Daimler and Maybach assembled a light bicycle with air cooling. It was a motorcycle prototype. In March 1886, Daimler installed a water-cooled engine on a conventional carriage with wooden wheels. In 1887, he made a trip to Stuttgart at an average speed of 18 km/h.

However, the most famous person in the automotive industry – Henry Ford – established the Ford Motor Company only in 1903. So why is it he who is considered to be the founder of the automotive industry and not the German inventors? By setting up an assembly line and cutting production costs, Ford created an engine-driven coach affordable for the mass consumer. In 1913, Ford set up an assembly line at Highland Park, Michigan, for the production of his Model T. But this arrangement was only part of his system. To embed his brainchild in the market, Ford launched projects to introduce new materials and standardize engine parts, and developed a business plan for the creation of a dealer network.

HENRY FORD AND HIS ASSEMBLY LINE

It was the incredible optimism of the people Henry Ford observed at motor racing competitions that served as the main motivation for him to start a business in the automotive industry. But the idea of his assembly line was inspired by a process designed for disassembly rather than assembly. More precisely, it was the butchering process applied at Chicago slaughterhouses. William Klann, who happened to observe the methodical movements of the workers at a slaughterhouse, where each one was responsible for cutting off certain parts of the animal bodies as they moved along, shared his impression with Peter Martin, who later became head of the production department of the Ford Motor Company. The introduction of this highly technological process paved the way for the creation of the most affordable car (Figure 11). But the arrangement of an efficient assembly line was successful at the third attempt. It took years before assembly improvements enabled Ford to receive substantial profits from the economies of scale.

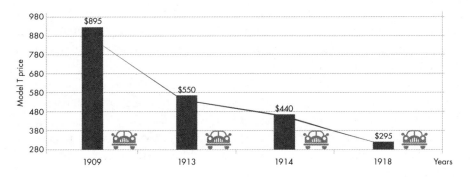

FIGURE 11. HOW THE PRICE OF FORD MODEL T CARS REDUCED OVER TIME

As a result of the introduction of a conveyor belt with a chain drive, the time required for the assembly of a car was cut by eight times, from 12.5 hours in 1913 to only 1.5 hours in 1914. Soon, a fully finished Ford Model T car left the assembly line every three minutes. The cars were produced only in black because it was the only paint that dried quickly enough so as not to slow down the assembly rate.[133]

Apart from the assembly line, Ford, in order to make his cars still more affordable, also launched a number of organizational projects to create new materials and structural elements for cars and engine parts, as well as to develop a dealer network. And although his manufacturing relied considerably on a number of technical solutions that had been developed by others before him, including the petrol engine, the magneto-electric ignition system, the rotary brush generator, the brake pads and many more, Ford nevertheless replaced a number of parts that did not suit him in the production chain with new ones. It is safe to say that Ford made a major contribution to the development of the concept of division of labour in a number of important industries in the US in the late 19th and early 20th centuries.

HUNDREDS OF MANUFACTURED REFRIGERATORS.
Hungary, ca 1959.

THE HOUSEHOLD REFRIGERATOR

In the same year Ford created the first assembly line, the world saw another remarkable invention – the refrigerator. The first prototype of a household refrigerator arrived in stores in 1913.[134] This invention, designed by Fred W. Wolf, resembled an ice box, into which a box with an electric fan was put to chill the food products in quite a natural way.

The usual cabinet, equipped with a compressor, was still to be seen later. It took six years before refrigerators became really comfortable to use and finally became part of each household. This innovation radically changed a number of industries, including food processing, food storage, logistics and retail.

The fridge as we know it today came to stay thanks to engineer Christian Steenstrup, Chief Engineer at General Electric, who designed the first durable and silent refrigerator specifically intended for domestic use.

PASSENGER AVIATION

Henry Ford also put his hand to the creation of another mode of transport – passenger aircraft. In the 1920s, planes were not especially popular with passengers. If someone dared to get into one of those flying contraptions, they had to sit on mail bags and be satisfied with a speed of 110 to 130 km/h.

In 1926, Ford took the advice of his son, Edsel, and invested, together with his partners, in the Stout Metal Aircraft Company, whose founder, William Stout, raved about the idea of creating an all-metal passenger aircraft. In 1925, Ford bought out the firm and produced an aircraft called *the Ford Trimotor*.[135] The plane had a crew of three, including a flight attendant, and the main cabin was furnished with 10 wicker chairs for passengers. This revolutionized air transport. Now travellers were brought from town to town at the speed of 150 km/h – quite fantastic for the time. In 1929, one could get from New York to Los Angeles within just one day. The trip was anything but cheap – US$338 one-way.[136]

OIL: MARKETS LOST AND FOUND

The history of the 20th century's technological revolution is also a history of humanity's self-deception about potentialities and prospects offered by new technologies. Daniel Yergin, in his famous book *The Prize*, clearly demonstrates this by referring to the history of the oil industry as an example. Oil was known a long time ago. It quickly evolved from a drug to a raw material for the production of fuel for oil lamps. Strong demand for oil remained stable until Thomas Edison invented his lighting unit, which required no oil or kerosene (Yergin 1990).

To those who had access to it, electricity was a great benefit. But its rapid development was deeply threatening to the oil industry. What kind of future could Standard Oil – with its massive investment in production, refineries, pipelines, storage facilities and distribution – look towards if it were to lose its major market, illumination?

The new technology of electricity was quickly transferred to Europe as well. An electric light system was installed in the Holborn Viaduct Station in London in 1882. So swiftly and so thoroughly did electricity – and the electrical industries – penetrate Berlin that the city was called *Elektropolis*. The development of electricity in London was more haphazard and disorganised. In the early twentieth century, London was served by 65 different electric utilities. Londoners toasted bread in the morning with one kind, lit their offices with another and walked home along streets that were illuminated by yet another kind.

To those who had access to it, electricity was a great boon. But its rapid development was deeply threatening to the oil industry. What kind of future could Standard Oil – with its massive investment in production, refineries, pipelines, storage facilities and distribution – look towards if it were to lose its major market, illumination? (Yergin 1990).

The threat of a crisis was looming on the oil industry's horizon: oil had no prospect of being used for any other purpose than heating and lubrication of coach wheels. The salvation came in the shape of the widespread use of internal combustion engines and the invention of oil cracking. Henry Ford, having got tired of waiting for Edison's new electric battery, launched the mass production of his Tin Lizzie (the popular name for the Ford Model T car) on a truly large scale.[137]

However, a series of inventions allowed the support of high levels of oil consumption. Proliferation of oil-fired boilers, a sharp increase in demand for aviation kerosene with the beginning of World War II, and growing numbers of tractors and locomotives encouraged the emergence of new markets and spurred industrial development.

Our world could have chosen the green technology path as long ago as the late 19th century, but as we can see now, the oil industry has been saved from stagnation for a long time by inventions and population growth, which opened up new windows of opportunity for the industry's traditional products. Few people think about it, but population growth would be impossible without another revolutionary discovery: nitrogen fertilizers.

THE HISTORY OF NITROGEN FERTILIZERS

Since the discovery of nitrogen by French chemist Antoine Lavoisier, we have learned about its critical role in the life of plants. This chemical element, being very common on Earth and comprising 78% of its atmosphere, is of central importance for all terrestrial life, due to its role as an essential component of proteins (18% by weight).[138] It is proteins that enable the biocatalytic activity of all living things, given that all enzymes present in their cells are based on protein molecules, while most enzymes entirely consist of proteins.

If terrestrial plants were short of nitrogen, crop yields would fall everywhere, which would make the Agricultural Revolution, and hence population growth, simply impossible. By supplying plants with additional quantities of nitrogen, we in fact intensify the synthesis of proteins in them. With nitrogen available in sufficient amounts, plants develop intensely green stems and leaves, while lack of nitrogen severely impedes the growth of plants, rendering them underdeveloped, with thin stems and smallish pale leaves.

In nature, nitrogen intake and consumption are balanced in the course of nitrogen circulation. In modern agriculture, this natural balance is disturbed: the loss exceeds the intake by far and the soil is depleted of this element. The application of nitrogen fertilizers and manure can eliminate the nitrogen deficit in the soil and create favourable conditions for the preservation and improvement of soil fertility. Intensive crop farming is founded on this principle.

It was believed until recently that a plant consumes 60-70% of the nitrogen supplied to it in the form of nitrogen fertilizers. Later it became clear that all fertilizer nitrogen applied to the soil is spent within one growing season: it is partly consumed by the plants, partly immobilised and partly irrevocably lost (Yagodyn 2004). Furthermore, soil microorganisms transform part of the fertilizer nitrogen into organic forms that cannot be taken in by plants. As a result, synthetic fertilizers provide about half of the nitrogen consumed by crops today. This is why no other innovation has had a more significant impact on humanity than artificial synthesis of ammonia, since people themselves cannot synthesize amino acids, essential building blocks of protein and have to acquire them from outside – from vegetable food.

Humankind has never had problems with phosphate and potassium fertilizers, but nitrogen fertilizers proved to be a more complex matter. Until recently, they were produced entirely by natural means. But the global population grew rapidly and the reserves of nitrogen available in the soil became insufficient. To be available in artificial compounds, nitrogen had to be 'tied up'.[139]

For a long time, humanity knew only one natural nitrogen-containing compound – saltpetre – but it soon became evident that the old ways of saltpetre production would not be able to meet the growing needs. In 1830, saltpetre mines were founded in Chile, in the form of 'guano', bird droppings that had decomposed over thousands of years.

In the 19th century, Chile became the major supplier of the substance, while the total global demand for saltpetre soared dramatically. The military industry accounted for a considerable portion of the burgeoning demand. However, by 1909, another method of binding nitrogen had been developed, whereby nitrogen was first transformed into ammonia, which was then used to produce nitrates or other nitrogenous compounds. This method was developed by German chemist Fritz Haber.

The aphorism "a scientist belongs to the world during peace time, but to his country during war" is ascribed to Fritz Haber, a Nobel laureate in Chemistry, an outstanding scientist and a part-time developer of chemical weapons. At the beginning of the 20th century, Fritz Haber, alongside Carl Bosch, successfully solved the problem of obtaining nitrogen from atmospheric air using the ammonia synthesis process which is now called the Haber–Bosch process.[140]

For the first time, Haber succeeded in synthesising liquid ammonia in 1908. He synthesised not only ammonia, but also synthesised nitrate and thus solved the problem of supplying European agriculture with enough fertilizers to enable it to feed the whole of the continent's already excessive population. The production of nitric acid as a raw material for explosives turned out to be another application of ammonium nitrate.

Haber's research into the synthesis of ammonia was funded by BASF, a German chemical corporation. Carl Bosch, a BASF engineer, streamlined the production method, enabling the corporation to launch large-scale ammonia production as soon as 1910. Thanks to Haber's invention, Germany now had explosives in unlimited quantities for the war. Soon Haber was appointed co-director of the Berlin-based Kaiser Wilhelm Institute of Physical Chemistry and Electrochemistry, where he continued his dual-use research. He personally developed methods for using chlorine in combat and was in charge of German chemical reconnaissance, instructing the troops how to use gas weapons.

Fritz Haber played a key role in the development of chemical weapons during World War I, despite the ban imposed on such weapons by the Hague Convention (1907), which had been ratified by Germany. In the 1920s, a group of scientists employed by his institute created Zyklon B, a poisonous substance produced by hydrocyanic acid being applied to a porous inert carrier. Zyklon B was used as an insecticide, and was used to kill prisoners in the gas chambers of Auschwitz and other concentration camps.

Fritz Haber defended the use of chemical weapons against charges of inhumanity and the Nazis were quick to appreciate his abilities, offering him additional funding. Soon, however, Haber received an order to dismiss all the Jews from his laboratory. In response, he sent a letter to the authorities, where he wrote: "During the 40 years of my work,

**A GARAGE EMPLOYEE FILLS A CAR WITH
A NEW 'COMPOSITE' MOTOR FUEL.**
5 September 1939

DANIEL YERGIN ON THE EFFECT OF THE INVENTION OF MOTOR GASOLINE

With the extraordinary growth of the automobile fleet, the world was already on the edge of a gasoline famine. In 1910, gasoline sales had exceeded kerosene for the first time and demand was galloping ahead. The Gasoline Age was at hand, but the developing shortage of the fuel was a great threat to the budding auto industry. The price of gasoline rose from 9.5 cents in October 1911 to 17 cents in January 1913. In London and Paris motorists were paying 50 cents a gallon, and in other parts of Europe, up to $1.

But by early 1913, within a year of Standard Oil's dissolution, the first of Burton's stills was in operation and Indiana announced the availability of a new product — motor spirits — gasoline made from thermal cracking. The thermal cracking process introduced flexibility into refinery output, something the industry had never had before. The refiner's output was no longer arbitrarily bound by the atmospheric distillation temperatures of the different components of crude oil. Now he could manipulate the molecules and increase the output of more desirable products. Moreover, cracked gasoline actually had a much better antiknock value than natural gasoline, which meant more power (Yergin 1990).

I have selected my staff judging them on their intellectual capabilities and character, and not on the basis of the origin of their grandparents, and I do not wish to compromise this principle of mine in the last years of my life." In 1933, he moved to England, but found himself unable settle there. A year later, Haber died on his way to Palestine.[141] The production of Zyklon B continued to grow during wartime.

We still should be grateful to Fritz Haber for his main invention, which made him a Nobel laureate in 1918. The Haber–Bosch ammonia synthesis process, whereby atmospheric nitrogen is bound, enabled corporations to make money... literally out of thin air. In this process, inactive nitrogen from the atmosphere is converted into useful ammonia in the presence of a catalyst. Then, nitric acid is produced by combining ammonia and oxygen at 800°C. The synthesis of ammonia from atmospheric nitrogen is not restricted geographically in terms of availability of the staple raw material, so an ammonia production plant can be located in close proximity to any consumer capable of ensuring a reasonable demand for the product. Typically, such consumers are producers of fertilizers or propellant explosives.

One of the key features of the Haber–Bosch process is the absence of waste. The reaction of the formation of ammonia from hydrogen and nitrogen is equilibrium and exothermic, and the theoretical yield at high temperatures required to achieve an acceptable reaction rate reaches 100%! The value of this process for humanity cannot be overestimated. The nitrogen fertilizer production technology, initially employed only in industrially developed nations, finally came to be applied widely in the developing world as well. The world ammonium production doubled within a decade when the developing countries adopted the technology in the 1950s. By 1975, the production had already increased fourfold and reached 130 million tonnes by the end of the 20th century, after a short recession that occurred in the beginning of the 1980s.

The paradox is that one invention by Fritz Haber killed more people than two American nuclear bombs, whereas another was one of the most important innovations in human history, to which up to 3 billion people around the world owe their lives!

Thanks to the organizational genius of the leaders of the technical revolution on the scale of Edison, Tesla and Ford, as well as of many other great managers of the early 20th century, companies as an organisational phenomenon joined in the process of accumulation of social wealth and became part of the financial world. This resulted in unprecedented progress in electrical engineering and other industries, and set the entire global economy in motion. Generally speaking, a trend was becoming more and more evident, whereby each successive technological wave occupied greater areas for its implementation than the previous one. A new use was found for oil. Refrigerators, airplanes, cars, petrol and Fritz Haber's discovery protected humanity from the threat of starvation. Inventors and scientists now perceived their own inventions in direct and indissoluble connection with the possibility of their commercialisation as some 'magic' designed to make our life absolutely perfect. Any sufficiently advanced technology is indistinguishable from magic, but, as Terry Pratchett rightly argued, nine times out of ten, magic is just the knowledge of a fact unknown to others (Pratchett 2002). From that time onwards, humankind began to grow rich rapidly, while nature began to lose biodiversity as its development base just as quickly as a result of human activities around the world! There is very little left to do now except clean up after the wizards.

CHAPTER 10

THE TECHNOLOGICAL AND INFORMATION REVOLUTION

"A man is weak and supple when he is born, and strong and stiff at his death. A tree is soft and pliable in life, and dry and brittle in death. Stiffness and strength are thus companions of death, flexibility and weakness represent the freshness of being live. Therefore, what is hard and stiff will be broken; what is soft and supple will prevail."

– **Arkady** and **Boris Strugatsky,**
Screenplay to the film *Stalker*

THE NUCLEAR INDUSTRY

The period of scientific and technological revolution of 1945 to 1980 was a golden age for Russia, and a period when science became the leading factor of production throughout the world. The world's first nuclear power station was built in the Soviet Union and was put into operation just a decade after Hiroshima. The creation of the nuclear industry in the Soviet Union was linked to another strategic goal: the creation of nuclear weapons.[142]

For the Russians, Kurchatov is what Edison is for the Americans. He managed to put together a team that was able to generate inventions on an industrial scale. Kurchatov appointed Nikolay Dollezhal to supervise the development of the industrial reactor. Dollezhal was a chemist and a mechanical engineer and had little to do with nuclear physics. The design of the reactor had only been defined in the most basic terms. Dollezhal's team, in cooperation with the Chemical Engineering Research and Development Institute, managed to build a plutonium plant by 1948. Having successfully created an atomic bomb in August of 1949, Kurchatov then directed his team's efforts to designing a reactor for the future and developing a nuclear power industry. On Kurchatov's instruction, Nikolay Dollezhal and Savely Feinberg designed a reactor for the future nuclear power station. Thus, an installation designed for the production of weapons-grade plutonium turned into a nuclear reactor similar to those existing today.

It was decided that the first nuclear power station would be built in Obninsk. There was no reactor theory (and even the capacity of the first reactor was yet to be found out in practice), no scientific staff or equipment in sufficient quantities, no housing for the employees and their families, and no pavement. There was a huge post-war enthusiasm though and the station already started to produce electricity in June 1954.

Since then, the technologies and the methods of controlling them have been developed significantly, and brought to considerably higher levels of sophistication. With the harnessing of nuclear power, knowledge not only came to play the key role in the economy, but also made a strong basis for national security.

SPACE EXPLORATION

Another important area where Russia can rightly be considered a pioneering nation is space exploration. Requiring continuous innovation, space engineering remains a catalyst for scientific research and stimulates development in a wide range of correlated sectors of the national economy.

Modern space exploration would be impossible without the creation of a carrier capable of overcoming the Earth's gravity. And there is only one carrier capable of doing that: the rocket. Its idea, conceptual design and successful implementation were authored by Russian scientists Konstantin Tsiolkovsky and Sergei Korolev.

The enthusiasm and bravery of the pioneering engineers enabled the Soviet Union to launch the world's first artificial satellite in October 1957. The creation of the first sputnik is owed, as in the case of the atomic project, primarily to three outstanding people. In 1954, Mstislav Keldysh, Sergei Korolev and Mikhail Tikhonravov wrote a letter to the Soviet government, expressing their ideas about creating an artificial satellite. On 4 October 1957, the Soviet Union successfully launched the world's first artificial satellite and a second one a month later, with a living creature, a dog called Laika, in its cabin.

The US immediately joined in the space race, but its first two attempts to launch satellites, undertaken in 1958, failed and overall only three out of 11 attempts made by the US to put spacecraft into orbit around the Earth between 1958 and 1959 were successful.

The Soviet Union was triumphant in space exploration in that period. The flowering of the Soviet Union's lucky clover meant that its scientists were in demand and motivated, the funding for space programmes was of paramount importance and the space industry's success was the pride of the whole society.

American scientists had no direct contacts with their Soviet counterparts and followed their progress instrumentally, using telescopes and radio signals. The Soviets' successes shocked them as they witnessed unimaginable things through objective observation: first the Russians targeted the Moon and sent their rocket precisely in the area where they wanted it to be and later successfully launched several satellites at one month intervals. On 12 April 1961, a rocket with a manned spacecraft on board was launched from the Baikonur launch pad in Kazakhstan. Yuri Gagarin was the first astronaut in the history of planet Earth. This launch went successfully and confirmed the supremacy of the Soviet Union in the space race.

The Americans' response followed less than a month later, when on 5 May 1961, Commander Alan Shepard became the first American astronaut. However, catching up with the Soviet Union by repeating its achievements would not be in the spirit of the Americans. It took something more ambitious, such as a lunar programme. US President Kennedy said that the Americans should be able to put a man on the

IGOR KURCHATOV, FULL MEMBER OF THE ACADEMY OF SCIENCES OF THE USSR, 1950

AN EXTREMELY SENSITIVE TOPIC

'An extremely sensitive topic' is a term used in US diplomacy to refer to sectors of science or industry in which the progress of other countries is extremely undesirable for the United States.

On 28 September 1942, the Soviet Union's State Committee on Defence issued a decree titled 'On Organizing Uranium Works', thus giving the go-ahead to the creation of a Soviet nuclear infrastructure. A special laboratory was established as a department of the Academy of

Sciences of the Soviet Union, to be provided with assistance from the Radium Institute, the Institute of Physics and Mathematics of the Ukrainian Academy of Sciences, and the Leningrad Physical-Technical Institute. Academic Abram Ioffe was put in charge of the whole project.[143] In the autumn of 1942, Igor Kurchatov, who was Ioffe's subordinate, was let in on Soviet intelligence reports that 180 kg of 'heavy water' had been brought to the Soviet Union from Norway.[144] This information was sufficient for Kurchatov to deduce that the Soviet Union had been left behind by the UK and the US in terms of nuclear weapons development. Kurchatov wrote a report to the project manager, where he formulated the main questions to which answers had to be obtained by Soviet intelligence.

On 17 June 1942, Dr Vannevar Bush, the head of the US National Defense Research Committee and one of the organizers of the Manhattan Project, sent a report to the US President, where he pointed out that the creation of nuclear weapons was quite possible. On 2 December 1942, the first fission of uranium atoms was carried out in the US by a research group led by Enrico Fermi, an Italian physicist who was to be called later the 'architect of the nuclear age' and the 'architect of the atomic bomb'.

Soviet intelligence was able to gain access to some of the documents circulated in connection with the US atom bomb project. In 1943, Kurchatov did in the Soviet Union what Edward Teller, a member of the Manhattan Project, described later, in 1962, in the following words: "The production of fissile material is the most difficult stage in the creation of the bomb. Once a country has successfully developed a process for such production, one can assume that it will have the bomb in a few months." (Nezhelskiy 1999) moon and return him safely to Earth within a decade. The primary aim of this truly grand project was to promote the image of the US. A number of Apollo spacecraft started moving towards the moon, proving the economic and technological might of the United States.

The Russians, of course, were not going to surrender. In 1965, Alexei Leonov was the first to come out of his spacecraft into open space in a spacesuit.

Starting from the 1980s, space activities began to act as one of the most important sectors of the global economy, essential to the study of natural resources and the analysis of their condition. Today, spaceflights are used to exert fire-fighting control over forest resources, search for oil spills and missing aircraft, and monitor air pollution. Satellites have become something akin to heavenly eyes. Through the artificial eyes in the sky, people are able to watch the ocean expanses every second and see where hurricanes and typhoons emerge, and thus save the lives of tens of thousands of people, assess fish stocks and ocean currents, and plot the courses of ships, keeping them away from icebergs and glaciers. The Russian GLONASS and the American GPS already provide for personal navigation, while their role in military affairs is obvious.

TELEVISION

The successes in the space sector were extraordinarily popular because, by the 1960s, TV as a new means of information dissemination had come to be widely used. In 1933, Vladimir Zworykin, a Russian scientist who had immigrated to the US, demonstrated an electron transmission tube which he called 'iconoscope'. Zworykin is held to be the father of electronic television.

John Logie Baird, a Scottish engineer and entrepreneur, succeeded in transmitting recognizable face shapes in 1924 using a mechanical television. The first electronic television suitable for practical application was developed in 1936 in the US, at the RCA research laboratory headed by Zworykin.[145] The first colour television system was developed by Zworykin as early as 1928, but its realisation became possible only in 1950.

Today, with flat LCD screens and plasma displays having become the usual devices for watching television, we perceive the first TVs as 'boxes'. The vacuum tubes on which the designs of the first TV receivers were based were later replaced by semiconductors. Then came designs based on microchips. Today's TV world is dominated by systems whose whole electronic filling is enclosed in one single microchip, but tomorrow will see the already new, digital television.

Although quite young, digital TV has already been through three stages in its development. The first stage involved research and development and the creation of experimental devices and systems, followed by the adoption of generally accepted international standards which had to be supported by all organisations engaged in television broadcasting and video content production, as well as by all TV equipment manufacturers. The second stage involved the development of digital television through the creation of hybrid analogue-digital television systems whose parameters were different from those approved by conventional television standards. This stage was necessitated by the need to compress the TV signal spectrums in order to enable their transmission over communication channels with acceptable bandwidths.

The problem of image compression for storage and transmission was so pressing that the International Organization for Standardization took over and set up two multinational working groups: first JPEG to develop methods for compressing still images, and then MPEG to develop methods for compressing moving images and sound.[146] [147]

In 1993, when it became clear that the future would belong to digital TV systems, a suite of internationally accepted open standards for digital television, called DVB (Digital Video Broadcasting), was approved.

Currently, digital TV systems are being developed at a third stage where distribution problems are expected to be solved. Digital technologies give a significant increase in transmission capacities and therefore bring about a rapid commercial effect.

SERVICE ECONOMY

The beginning of the 20th century was a period when capitalism was rapidly establishing itself. Successful entrepreneurial individualists set up industrial companies and corporations that are among the largest in the world today. The 19th century and the time up to the 1920s was a period when the happy clover of individual capitalism flourished. This phenomenon was quite accurately described by Adam Smith and Karl Marx, and economists who belonged to an alternative school of thought, the so-called 'marginalists'. The eagerness to reap a personal profit was the main motive for societal development at that time. According to classical theoretical economics, despite the fact that the capitalists generated profits by maximizing exploitation of labour (Karl Marx), the economic system as a whole transformed these individual aspirations into the public good (Adam Smith).

After World War I, the developed countries gradually transformed into capitalist consumerism economies, where the interests of individual consumers began to dominate.

Labour productivity growth put an end to the capitalism as it had been defined by Karl Marx (a system where workers earned just enough to provide a basic subsistence for their families). Franklin D. Roosevelt's New Deal was a series of programmes designed to collectivize private capitalism and put it under state control to the maximum extent in an attempt to tackle unemployment. As a result, a set of relationships was formed that some American economists called institutionalism. In a growing market economy, the adoption of key decisions was transferred from the individual to the collective level – to trade unions, business communities and the state. In times of crisis and depression, this move-ment was perceived as an alternative to the economic concept that had led society to a crisis. It was a move that caused capitalism to suffocate slowly.[148] It was in the 1930s, during the search-and-error time, that the star of John Maynard Keynes ascended. Keynes was a British economist, journalist and financier who is best known for revolutionary and con-troversial ideas that fundamentally changed the theory and practice of macroeconomics. Keynes's views popularized the idea that entrepreneurs had common desires, which were more effectively achieved once real-ized. The central desire was an increase in aggregate demand. It was this increase that the state was expected to offer to society. This simple idea dominated capitalist economic policies up to the 1980s. Capitalism was regarded as a consumer society in which the consumer's interests were protected by the state. It seemed that it was in the interests of both the workers and the capitalists.

Capitalism has changed considerably since then, giving rise to macro-economics, a science that was first to develop in theory and then to imple-ment countercyclical anti-crisis policies (designed to restrain aggregate economic growth in the economic recovery phase and stimulate it in the recession phase). A dynamic society formed, in which both the profits of the capitalists and the earnings of the workers grew. But everything has its limit and thus the post-World War II economic boom was followed by the first crisis in the 1980s. At that point in time, a new source of growth was found in addition to the production of material goods: the production of intangible goods. The last decades of the 20th century were a period when a new lucky clover flourished: the lucky clover of collective capitalism of the Western countries.

Since the beginning of the 1980s, exploiting workers to the maximum extent and expanding markets stimulated by public expenditure ceased to be the only sources of profit for capitalists. Economy, quality, service, and such intangible goods as intellectual property and brands became sources of additional value for organisational shells called 'agencies'.

In developed countries, the commodity production sector of the economy was growing very slowly and even stagnating. At some point, millions of tonnes of crude oil or crude iron started to lose their significance. The percentage of value-added production and processing depth were becoming more important in the countries' GDP. Information began to play an increasingly important role. First, it enabled businesses to save money. Production transferred to countries where labour was cheaper and local businesses also economized thanks to technology development. Manufacturers strongly encouraged consumers to replace long-term use goods (cars, household appliances, computers) with newer ones more frequently and to make more expensive purchases, ranging from green products to solar panels on rooftops, from famous brands to niche products, which greatly expanded the range of goods to choose from.[149] [150]

But if production declined in developed countries, where were people supposed to find money to buy imported goods? The West found an answer to this problem: money could be earned in the service industry and in intangible product sectors. After WWII, a new society began to form, which increasingly produced more services than goods. The share of services has long passed 50% in the GDP of developed countries. Services account for a wide range of different and specific activities, and are remarkable in that they can grow almost endlessly. New services can be invented and introduced and most (especially financial ones) can be easily imported and exported.

By the end of the 1990s, the service sector had grown to become the largest sector of the economy in the most successful countries. The total share of transport, communication, wholesale and retail trade, financial services, insurance and home, business and socio-cultural services reached 60-70% both in the GDP and in the total numbers of employed workforce. Investments in new sectors of the economy exceeded 50% of total investments.

One of the main features of that time was outstripping growth of the service sectors in comparison with industrial production. Today, one-fifth of global trade is trade in services (see Figure 12).

THE PARADOX OF THE CONCEPTS OF INTANGIBLE ASSETS AND GOODWILL[151]

The growth of the GDP of developed countries as a result of the promotion of services brought to life paradoxical and previously unknown problems related to intellectual property and the valuation of intangible assets. Modern technologies make it possible to produce any number of copies of a piece of intellectual property. The conflict is obvious: intellectual property law imposes a producers' monopoly in its purest form. In response, consumers simply 'borrow' items of intellectual property.

To make up for losses from piracy, the manufacturers of goods that make use of items of intellectual property increase the prices; this, in turn, provokes a further increase in theft. The situation is at an impasse, whereby pirate parties and programmers' open source code movements in favour of free provision of intellectual property are modern forms of the unfolding struggle. Business desperately needs an innovation, a workable business model that has to be invented.

The situation with the concept of goodwill as an indicator of the business reputation of a company remains confusing. By definition, goodwill is the difference between the purchase price of a business and its value according to the balance sheet. To put it simply, the goodwill of a company is the value of its brand. In actual fact, it's just the difference between the exaggerated estimate of the company on the part of the stock exchange and the net value of the assets it owns. This value may be high today and slump tomorrow as a result of a stock market crisis.

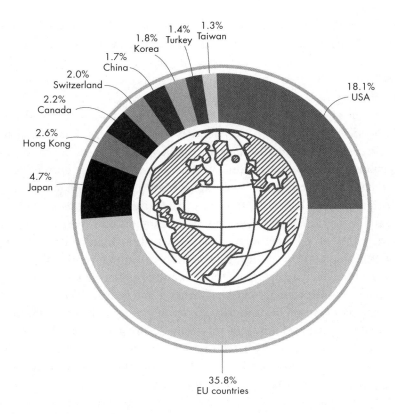

FIGURE 12. VARIOUS COUNTRIES' PARTICIPATION IN THE
GLOBAL EXPORTS OF SERVICES IN 1998

THE GROWTH OF THE CREATIVE CLASS

The growth of the share of services in the GDP of developed countries was bound to bring about major social and societal changes. New personal freedoms, quite unthinkable in the 20th century, have appeared, e.g. the freedom to dress the way you like at work. This has naturally resulted in the appearance of a whole new stratum of society, consisting of people who act as carriers of new cultural (or countercultural in some people's view) values. At the suggestion of American economist Richard Florida, this stratum was called 'the creative class' (Florida 2002).

After World War II, such people accounted for only 15% of the US population; today, they comprise up to a third of the nation. As asserted by Florida, the creative class is now becoming a major source of economic development.[152] It is this class that creates the national agenda, serves as a role model and shapes public opinion in developed countries today. Representatives of the creative class do not favour vertical hierarchical advancement through the ranks, and instead prefer horizontal movement and change of places of work in quest of more creative employment. Typically, members of this class have a strong sense of individuality and personal freedom.

The range of professions of the creative class include actors and artists, brand developers, designers, scientists and engineers, PR specialists and marketing experts, intellectuals, media people – in short, all those for whom change and subsequent innovation encapsulate the essence of their services. Many of them draw on complex bodies of knowledge and may create original ideas, but are not necessarily innovators; subclasses include healthcare professionals, teachers, lawyers, financiers and managers. They are participants of a knowledge-based high-tech economy that requires creative thinking and the ability to solve problems unconventionally.

Florida discovered a new trend: today, many companies move to regions where creative professionals cluster (rather than waiting for top-notch specialists to come to their location). Communicating with representatives of the creative class, he found out that they do not move for jobs – their choice of residence is typically based on their interests and lifestyle criteria. Such cities ('creative centres' in Florida's terminology) represent integrated systems and provide habitats where all forms of creativity can thrive. Florida describes the key characteristics of a 'creative environment' as what he calls the 3Ts of economic development: technology, talent and tolerance.

THE INFORMATION REVOLUTION

The emergence of the creative class has affected the use of a key resource of our time – information. Two processes – a social change taking place as a result of the emergence of a new class and the information revolution – ensured the transition of society into a new, more 'dense' information state by replacing old communication technologies with new ones. I would even like to draw an analogy with the compaction of neural connections in the brain (Figure 13).

The replacement of analogue and electromechanical communication devices with digital ones resulted in the establishment of new methods for knowledge synthesis and information processing. This caused an increase in the density of the information network with new ways of interpersonal communication, as well as a wide and easy access to accumulated knowledge via the internet. Since that moment, knowledge and information started to act not just as critical elements, but as the main sources of improving efficiency. Any production or service provision process is always based on a certain level of knowledge and on specific information processing methods. In my model, I call this a design scheme.

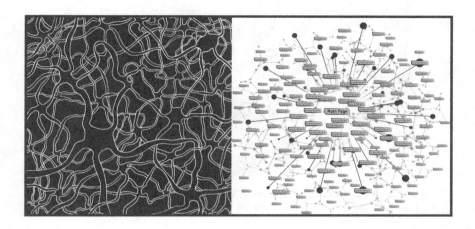

FIGURE 13. THE ARCHITECTURE OF A HUMAN BRAIN AND THE INTERNET: THE SIZE AND DENSITY OF THE WEB

Advancements in technology gave another boost to the development of the creative class in developed countries. In the Lucky Clover model, innovation is always centred on social processes which historically occur in the fields of production, professional training, or power distribution. However, the new information technologies cover the global space at uneven rates. This would seem to be a purely technological parameter, but for vast numbers of people in developing countries it appears to be a source of inequality, fraught with the risk of the exclusion of whole nations from the global division of labour due to lack of access to the information infrastructure. The situation is such because it is states today, not individual inventors as at the beginning of the 20th century, that are making efforts to become the main driver of the information revolution by funding research programmes.

Of course, large portions of the GDPs of all countries and large numbers of workers continue to depend on the liveliness of the domestic economy rather than on the global market. But in many countries, progressive sectors are already merging into global economy sectors without borders (this is happening e.g. in finance, telecommunications, media). Production around the world relies on educated people aged 25 to 50,

STEVE JOBS AND STEVE WOZNIAK WORKING ON THE WORLD'S FIRST PERSONAL COMPUTER IN JOBS' PARENTS' GARAGE IN 1976

HOW APPLE COMPUTERS BEGAN

In 1976, Steve Wozniak, inspired by the example of the Altair 8800, designed and soldered in his kitchen a personal computer which he later called Apple I.[153]

The fate of this creation would have been the same as that of many similar early pieces of handiwork by other techno geeks if it had not been for another Steve – Wozniak's friend Steve Jobs. Jobs suggested putting the project on a commercial footing. Having persuaded the owner of a local store to order 50 machines from the newly established Apple Computers Inc., Steve and Steve rushed off to find the money and buy the components of which they had no stock yet. They managed to sell about 200 computers within a year, which was a good start. In 1977, Apple introduced a new product – Apple II, which later became one of the most popular machines in the PC world. This was the first computer truly designed for common users rather than PC geeks.

which means that over a third of the workforce can be freed at the present level of development of productive forces. Resulting in widespread unemployment on the one hand, this, much more importantly, brings about ever-increasing flexibility, mobility and individualization of work, and, finally, a highly segmented social structure for the labour market.

This new 'information' society depends on new modes of information dissemination, which gives the media, the internet, the blogosphere and intelligence services abnormal power, causing a situation where it is unclear who controls whom. Government structures and political parties disappear or dissolve, acquiring the features of structures that are designed to mitigate social tensions that form in society as a result of the negative effects of consecutive waves of innovation.

The information revolution could not have taken place if a major technological innovation had not materialised by end of the 20th century in the form of computers, the internet shaping up as the World Wide Web, and the multitudes of pieces of software that people required in order to be able to communicate and conduct transactions.

COMPUTERS

Just half a century ago, the word 'computer' was firmly associated with government organizations and science fiction. However, a series of discoveries and inventions changed the computer industry radically. It all started in 1958, when Texas Instruments engineers developed the first integrated circuit based on semiconductors. Becoming smaller with each passing year, integrated circuits gradually replaced transistor modules, drastically reducing the size and power consumption of electronic devices.

Thirteen years later, in 1971, Intel combined several microchips into a big one designed to perform mathematical calculations in a calculator produced by Busicom. The innovative and relatively low-power processor 4004 had not been used previously in small (personal) computers. In fact, there was no concept of a personal computer at all. But the capabilities of Intel's 4004 processor prompted several electronics enthusiasts to come up with this concept.

The new prospects were taken hold of by creative professionals who were specifically interested in electronics and new technologies. They would sit for days in garages, creating all sorts of gadgets. While large corporations invested huge amounts of money into large computers that took up entire rooms or even buildings, the young revolutionaries came up with a completely new solution: personal computers, which though less powerful, were fully fledged workstations affordable to nearly everyone.

It did not take long for commercial ideas to catch up with technical thought. Already in 1974, a young company called MITS decided to take a risky but promising path and launched a fully assembled and ready-to-use personal computer, called the Altair 8800.[154] This seemingly unremarkable occurrence resulted in the creation of Microsoft. Its first product was an interpreter from and into the BASIC programming language, designed specifically for the Altair 8800.

IBM was the only major manufacturer of mainframe computers that showed interest in the promising market. The Big Blue could not miss such a possibility, but the company failed to identify the target audience: corporations did not understand why people needed PCs and the price of US$9,000 was just way too high for ordinary amateurs. That was exactly the price of IBM 5100, which became the progenitor of a whole line of IBM's personal computers.

It was this lack on the part of large companies of realizing the importance of this niche that gave a good chance to many small firms, such as Commodore and Sinclair. Remembered by few today, they turned out to be the most successful players in the market at that time. How did they manage to get ahead of such strong competitors as Texas Instruments and IBM? They were more flexible. Commodore's success was the result of an aggressive marketing policy. A computer priced at US$600 was sold everywhere: at specialised stores, at discount stores and even at toy stores. The composite video output enabled the user to connect the computer to any TV set, which, in fact, made it a strong rival to conventional game consoles. But Commodore's best move was to pay US$100 to anyone who disposed of any other computer or console. By doing so, Commodore simply knocked down Texas Instruments with its personal computers. Since then, Texas Instruments has been making microchips for PCs, but not PCs.

THE WORLD WIDE WEB

The satellite launched by the Soviet Union in 1957 caused activity in unexpected areas. For example, the US Department of Defense decided to create a closed communication system to be used in the event of hostilities. The US Defense Advanced Research Projects Agency (DARPA) commissioned three leading US universities to develop a computer network. Twelve years later, in 1969, these research institutions were united by a network that was called the Arpanet.[155]

All the work was funded by the US Department of Defense. On 29 October, 1969, the first communication session was held on the Arpanet.

This date can therefore be considered the birthday of the internet. After that, the Arpanet network began to grow and develop extensively.

In 1971, the Arpanet already comprised 15 communication centres and as many as 37 in the next year. In 1973, the network became international when organizations in the UK and Norway connected to it over a trans-atlantic telephone cable. Networks similar to the Arpanet but based on different technical standards began to emerge in various parts of the world. To enable communication between them, the first data transfer protocols were enthusiastically created in the late 1970s, to be finally standardized in 1982 to 1983.

Around the same time, the US National Science Foundation set up another extensive inter-university network. It was made up of smaller networks and had a greater throughput capacity than the Arpanet. During the first year of its existence, about 10,000 computers were connected to it. Over time, this network came to be called the internet.[156]

The history of the internet has demonstrated another fundamental trend, namely that of accelerating the progress of human innovations. The internet audience grew to comprise 50 million users within five years. Television achieved a comparable result within 13 years and radio within 38 years.

However, this comparison was not the only one that the phenomenal internet development rate brought about. At some point, Intel founder and executive Gordon Moore came up with this globally famous and impressive historical observation: "If the automobile industry advanced as rapidly as the semiconductor industry, a Rolls Royce would now get half a million miles per gallon and it would be cheaper to throw it away than to park it" (Azarenkov 2005, 129).

The activity of the internet community quickly resulted in a continuous increase in the number of internet users. This, in turn, gave rise to a snowballing process of resolving technical problems related to the continuous development and expansion of the network, technology and security systems. In 1987, the number of computers connected to the internet was more than 10,000. By 1989, it had increased by an order of magnitude, reaching 100,000.

Tim Berners-Lee of CERN (the European Organisation for Nuclear Research) proposed a project based on the hypertext concept, designed to enable researchers to obtain information and share it with others. In 1989, CERN had the largest intranet in Europe, and Tim Berners-Lee saw this as an opportunity to link hypertext and the internet.[157] He also created the first web browser in the world (for the NeXT platform) and,

VANNEVAR BUSH, PRESIDENT OF THE CARNEGIE INSTITUTION OF WASHINGTON, IN HIS OFFICE

THE WORLD WIDE WEB IDEA AND TOTAL CONTROL

The World Wide Web (WWW) is based on the concept of hypertext, i.e. numerous texts that are linked to each other. The concept was suggested by Vannevar Bush in *As We May Think*, an essay published in the *Atlantic Monthly* magazine in July 1945 (Chernyak 2016). The essay contained a description of a hypothetical memex machine that worked on reference principles. It was this essay that Tim Berners-Lee, the founding father of the internet, indicated as the source of his ideas. In 1945, Bush headed a US task force assigned to find materials in Germany that might be of value and interest to the US Department of Defense after the fall of the Nazi regime. As a result, Bush gained access to information about technologies the Nazis had had at their disposal. The task force found a certain machine that had been designed to facilitate the work of the security services of the Third Reich, which Bush described in his essay a few months later. It was a colossal automated file catalogue, designed by Adolf Eichmann, in which data was stored on cards kept in a filing system driven by electric motors. The machine enabled the Nazi to store and retrieve comprehensive information on the political views of any subject of the Reich up until April 1945. The information on each of the people entered in the filing system was updated every two weeks, after which Eichmann assigned a weight to each file in accordance with the category of the relevant informant. Social networks are arranged similarly today.

at the same time, the first editor (WorldWideWeb, developed using the NeXTSTEP computer, the brainchild of Steve Jobs' most commercially unsuccessful project). In November 1990, Berners-Lee created the first prototype of a WWW server. The World Wide Web as an actively functioning system did not become public until 1992. That year, the number of computers connected to the internet exceeded one million. However, the most significant event in the development of the internet in the 1990s was, undoubtedly, the creation of the World Wide Web. The whole system was based on the concept of hypertext, owing to which large numbers of individual texts could now contain references to each other.

In 1994, Tim Berners-Lee created a virtual library, which is now the oldest catalogue on the web, and also wrote a book called *The Birth of the Web* about how he created the internet (Berners-Lee 2000).

E-COMMERCE

The growth of the service sector in the US economy also acted as a prerequisite for the emergence of an entirely new phenomenon, e-commerce, since goods in the new conditions were not considered separately from their sales and service systems. The birth of e-commerce can be dated to 1960.[158]

Once data transfer networks had been created, stock management became a separate type of business. Demand planning became a separate function of management, making it possible to optimize the working capital of a company while ensuring timely delivery and customer retention. Solving these problems with the use of electronics made it possible to reduce costs significantly. Since the late 1960s, companies began to apply computer technology for multiple objective planning (so-called value chains that included procurement, production, marketing and human resource management).

The advent of plastic payment cards and their wide dissemination by post, as well as the widespread acceptance of such cards for payment, resulted in all major banks becoming tied up in a digital network, and mass tourism and car rental were industrialized so that services could now be sold in one place and delivered thousands of kilometres away. After that, e-business transfigured the operation of stock exchanges.

Commercialization of the internet began in 1990; three years later, the first electronic money appeared and, another year later, the first electronic payment system; the first internet bank was launched still another year later.

E-commerce changed business, creating unimaginable cost reduction opportunities and introducing new services. The latter included additional services for clients generated from their online self-registration, which enabled targeted advertising of products and services and detailed market research. Ordering goods via the internet using electronic price lists became perfectly normal. This resulted in substantial savings in the time spent searching for goods and made the pricing process transparent. Corporate logistics acquired the modern digital look and plastic money, having become common, provided manufacturers in developed countries with a steady inflow of buyers from around the world, thus enabling the use of economies of scale as a serious economic advantage.

Initially available to customers through personal computers, e-commerce is now moving quickly to smartphones. Modern communication technologies are able to provide adequate technical conditions for their fully fledged use in e-business. This means that the global economy has involved the population of the poorest countries and even that of an entire continent, Africa. Modern smartphones will soon turn into purses, making numerous pieces of plastic with the logos of different banks unnecessary. A new, young and flexible technology can make entire industries redundant and occupy a dominant position in the market.

Today's civilization is different from those of previous civilizations in two main respects: abundant energy consumption and modern communications. These two components form the basis for all achievements in engineering and technology of our time. Having harnessed these, humankind has made itself much better off and more comfortable. With wellbeing growing and the quality of services improving, the essence of wealth has changed. In the past, land, gold and profitable securities were the main assets.

Today, human capital and intangible assets are becoming more and more important. At the same time, the value of information as such continues to grow progressively on account of knowledge gained! As a result, all business has become 'information' and global, while companies have evolved to fit in industry-specific frames.

The history of the last three revolutions promotes a simple thought: there are no sectors and industries, or any other invented entities or artificial restrictions; there are just inert, static companies that have no thirst for growth on the one hand, and lively, dynamic companies that are looking for such growth, and deserve it, on the other.

CHAPTER 11

HOW AN INNOVATION ECONOMY WORKS

"*Most importantly, do not listen to American economists, because they know nothing whatsoever about the specific institutions that have formed in the Russian economy...*"

– Douglass North,
an American economist known for his work in economic history,
a Nobel laureate in Economics, speaking after a conference
on the reform of the Russian economy in Moscow, 1990

INSTITUTIONS ARE ALL-IMPORTANT

In England, at the beginning of the 16th century, King Henry VIII was absolute monarch with unlimited power. However, some historical logic originating from seemingly minor events very soon led the country to the English Revolution, Cromwell and the Civil War. A constitutional monarchy emerged, where the king was already obliged to take the interests of society into consideration. The power of the king was undermined when the English parliament grew able to control the distribution of the country's finances and establish the Bank of England for the management of the national currency.

Anthropologist David Graeber writes about this period (Graeber 2011, 339): "It was only with the creation of the Bank of England in 1694 that one can speak of genuine paper money, since its banknotes were in no sense bonds. They were rooted, like all the others, in the king's war debts. This can't be emphasised enough. The fact that money was no longer a debt owed to the king, but a debt owed by the king, made it very different than what it had been before. In many ways it had become a mirror image of older forms of money."

The Habeas Corpus Act, an enactment adopted by the Parliament of England in 1679, which established procedures for arresting the accused and bringing them to trial, and gave the court the right to control the legality of the arrest and imprisonment of citizens, actually meant the introduction of privacy and private property as advanced values of the upcoming new time. Did the people perceive the importance of this key change? At that point in time, they did not. Indeed, the act provided that an arrested person shall be released on bail in the event of a delay in the judicial investigation, but poor prisoners could not use this provision for lack of money, while wealthy debtors were usually able to buy more or less decent conditions of imprisonment. And yet, this was a real, disruptive innovation – a time bomb or a powerful impetus to the development of society's latent 'business' energy.

The introduction of new technologies was impossible without establishing new institutions. Society could not progress while the structure of the state was outdated. The new institutions were called upon to select the most successful scientific discoveries and provide the resources required for further acceleration of innovative growth. Douglass North, John Wallis and Barry Weingast, very well known economists in the West and Russia alike, identified in their book *Violence and Social Orders* (North 2009) the three main reasons for Europe's prosperity – the three major disruptive innovations that led to the rise of the West above China and the Islamic world:

- Submission of elites to the rule of law, or the equality of all before the law;
- Presence of permanent organizations that were not dependent on the government or the power of a Great Man;
- Reduction of the risk of self-destruction and degradation of the existing social order by imposing public control over the armed forces and technologies for destruction and violence.

The social revolution and then the industrial revolution, both beginning in England in the 17th-18th centuries and then continuing to spread across Continental Europe, led to the establishment of new open procedures for access to the country's natural resources. These procedures were increasingly operated by invisible market forces, the forces comprehended and described by Adam Smith.

The finance evolution provided the world with new economic growth opportunities. Using leverage, entrepreneurs were now able to expand production, paying off the loans at the expense of subsequent profits from the development. But it was the invention of the limited liability company as a legal form of enterprise – at the end of the 19th century – that enabled business to evolve to the maximum extent. This legal tool caused the process of evolutionary business development to ascend to a completely new level.

Joint-stock companies, organizations that were independent of the state, became agents of this new order. These institutions emerged owing to the rule of law and the establishment of a reliable system of legal guarantees and freedoms. Companies organized on corporate rather than partnership principles appeared in England as early as in the 16th century.

Having proved successful, these disruptive innovations slowly and invisibly spread to other countries in Europe. Competition between secular and religious authorities in Europe resulted in the establishment of new institutions that strengthened the rule of law. This process directly determined the economic growth rate.

The increase of wealth through economic growth became a necessity for the elites of European countries; as it turned out, a better alternative to the old political game of rent distribution. Growth enabled the payment of interest on the loans and Europe's economy grew steadily at comparable rates. It became possible to accumulate new wealth.

Before the Rothschilds, it had only been land, real estate and trade that earned profit. Bankers introduced a new profit generation tool – securities (investment grade bonds), whose value was related to the activity of specific agents of change – joint-stock companies.

Since the British colonies in North America originally developed as sets of settlements founded by quite independent people, such as farmers and merchants, and scattered throughout the country, British North America was a special place where free trade flourished, ideas were exchanged and many religions were practised. The American Revolution (1765-1783) was founded on economic freedom and propelled by a folk culture that was wary of the Great Man and preferred equality to any hierarchy. A large and independent middle class of wealthy farmers had formed, which resulted in an unprecedented market economy success: by 1775, British North America's GDP had reached 40% of that of Great Britain, in contrast with the mere 5% it had comprised 75 years earlier. Thus, British America became one of the fastest growing economies in the world thanks to 'disruptive' social innovations.

By the end of the 18th century, new social institutions had laid the basis for the rapid development of market economies in England, Northern Europe and North America. The new social institutions ousted the Great Man from the process of selecting areas for business investment, which resulted in free enterprise coming into bloom. Another leaf of the lucky clover – science – also did not stand idle. It is in these countries that practical scientific knowledge took the deepest root, ensuring the start of the industrial revolution.

A continuous cycle of development of new social relationships and business rules resulted in further innovation and a long period of unprecedented economic growth. A 'positive feedback loop' formed between society, business and science. In the 19th and 20th centuries, the development of science accelerated significantly in search of new technologies and the markets that had emerged as a result of society becoming richer contributed to rapid evolution in technology, bringing about new products and services.

AN INNOVATION ECONOMY, JOSEPH SCHUMPETER

If innovation is intended to result in a commercial success, then what is an innovation economy? To answer this question, we turn to an invaluable source – the work of the outstanding economist and sociologist Joseph Alois Schumpeter (1883-1950).

In 1932, Schumpeter moved to the USA, where he worked as a professor at Harvard University and wrote his prominent books *Business Cycles* (1939) and *Capitalism, Socialism and Democracy* (1942) (Schumpeter 1942).

Schumpeter's predecessors considered primarily static objectives of economic development, focusing on two fundamental ones: how to ensure the best use of available resources and how to achieve balance between production and consumption. Schumpeter in his analysis drew attention to factors that disturbed the equilibrium of a market system, identifying them as new production combinations on which change in an economy depended. He regarded the following as new combinations of production factors:

- Creating a new product;
- Using new production technology;
- Using new production organization;
- Opening new sales markets and sources of raw materials.

It is precisely these new combinations of production factors that came to be called 'innovations'. In Schumpeter's book, *The Theory of Economic Development*, the overriding role is ascribed to the entrepreneur – a person who creates new combinations of production factors. An entrepreneur is the central subject of economic development. It is thanks to him that technological progress is achieved and the economy receives an impetus for development. Schumpeter demonstrated that revolutionary changes in production techniques and technologies and the creation of new markets and reorganization of market structures are inherent in capitalist production. Such constant innovations, being implemented in the production process, are the chief source of profits that cannot be generated in a situation of mere 'economic turnover', or simple reproduction. Profit can only be obtained in continuous motion, in dynamic economic development.

INNOVATIVENESS AS A KEY TO COMPETITIVENESS AND GEOPOLITICAL LEADERSHIP

According to the views of Schumpeter, innovations provide a new type of competition (effective competition), which is indeed far more effective than price competition. Thanks to innovations, it becomes possible not only to improve technologies and products, but also to influence the structure of demand and the price formation process. Schumpeter's theory also linked innovations with a new type of monopoly: an effective monopoly that enables an innovative entrepreneur to obtain profits that serve as a stimulus and reward for innovations. This effective monopoly is only temporary for any one company: it can be lost as a result of competition in that same sphere of innovation. In other words, Schumpeter's theory regards the effective monopoly as a component of economic development.

Schumpeter also attached great importance to the availability of credit resources in an innovation economy. By obtaining money from banks, innovators effectively initiate the redistribution of resource flows, that is, the redistribution of social capital. There occurs a change in economic structure, a transition to a new turn in the spiral of development. Thus, banks are an important component of economic development, and money serves not merely as a means to circulate and measure value, but is actually a catalyst for economic growth.

It is remarkable that, 30 years later, while observing the new economic reality in America, in *Capitalism, Socialism and Democracy*, Schumpeter noted a reduced role of credit in the development of an innovation economy. This development led to a situation where this "ideally bureaucratized, giant production unit" was so successful in rationalizing and simplifying the process of implementing innovation that the "most powerful engine of economic progress" was now the large-scale enterprise capable of using its own resources to finance innovative developments. Thus, scientific and technological progress was henceforth achieved through the efforts of not individual entrepreneurs but groups of well-educated specialists who could properly channel this progress. This phenomenon also poses a certain danger for the development of an innovation economy, in that the central figures in the business world are not the actual innovative entrepreneurs but the managers controlling these large corporations. In contrast to innovators, these managers typically have completely different qualities: instead of striving towards innovations, risk and independence, they are more inclined towards caution, towards actions that guarantee career advancement and towards coordinating decision-making on all levels. Nonetheless, if the entrepreneur disappears, the range of economic development possibilities narrows.

A modern innovation economy requires harmony in the relationships between all business entities. Small business should offer innovations and develop new services and products, while large companies should incorporate or buy those small businesses and multiply and enhance their economic effect. Overall, according to Carlota Perez, innovations have a farther-reaching effect on finances and on society than the mere adaptation of technologies by firms, and clusters of radical innovations and technological revolutions modify the entire structure of production (Perez 2003).

Naturally, since Schumpeter's time, his economic theory has been enriched with new scientific ideas that reflect the realities of modern-day life. Nonetheless, virtually all authoritative economists and sociologists (Alvin Toffler, Francis Fukuyama, Daniel Bell, John Naisbitt and others) have no doubt that it is precisely an innovation economy that ensures competitiveness and global economic superiority to the country that embodies it.

National competitiveness, or the competitiveness of a specific country, is usually determined as the capability of that country's institutions to ensure economic growth rates that are sustainable in the mid-term. There are methodologies for numerical determination of this crucial parameter (global competitiveness index) that were developed by the World Economic Forum, which also ranks various countries of the world in its annual reports that are prepared in conjunction with a network of leading research institutes and organisations that work in those countries. This ranking is based on generally available statistical data and the results of a survey of company managers. Such research provides abundant food for thought and analysis.

The World Economic Forum's global competitiveness index is compiled using 114 indicators that are integrated into 12 pillars:[159]
- The quality of institutions;
- The infrastructure and connectivity;
- The macroeconomic stability;
- The health of the population and the quality of basic education;
- The quality of higher education and professional training;
- The efficiency of the goods and services market;
- The efficiency of the labour market;
- The efficiency of the financial market;
- The level of technological maturity;
- The size of the market;
- The competitiveness of companies;
- The innovative potential.

INNOVATIVE COMPANIES' DEVELOPMENT STRATEGIES

In 1987, when *Forbes* magazine celebrated its 70th anniversary, it published information on the 100 companies that had topped its 1917 rating. As it turned out, 61 of those companies had ceased to exist over the past seven decades, 21 had dropped out of the top 100 and only 18 had remained in the rating, though not in the leading positions. By analysing this fact, as well as the history of over 1,000 corporations from 15 industries, Richard Foster and Sarah Kaplan of McKinsey & Company came to the conclusion that modern companies can preserve their superiority and remain competitive over a long period of time only if they master the strategy of discontinuous evolution and processes of creative destruction. Creative destruction is a term introduced to scientific circles by Joseph Schumpeter, meaning the formation and acquisition of new companies, as well as elimination of the least efficient business units, but without losing control of ongoing operations (Foster 2001).

Robert R. Wiggins and Timothy W. Ruefli, who have studied the history of 6,772 companies from 1974 to 1997, have discovered that the periods during which these companies occupied leading positions on the market lasted as follows:

10 years – 5% of the companies;
20 years – 0.5% of the companies;
50 years – less than 0.05% of companies (or, in other words, only two of them) (Wiggins 2005).

Moreover, the average duration of periods of competitive advantage tended to reduce over time. In conclusion, in order to be successful under present-day conditions, a company has to be innovative.

Analysis of business practices shows that a more or less workable solution to this problem must rely on identification of a number of quantitative parameters that characterize the innovativeness of companies. Such parameters designed to determine a company's receptivity to innovative solutions (let's provisionally call them 'input' parameters) include:
- The quantity of innovative ideas or concepts accepted for implementation by the company;
- The percentage of R&D in the company's revenues;
- The quantity of research projects developed by the company;
- The percentage of company personnel engaged in innovative projects.

Naturally, there are also 'output' parameters that can help us assess the effectiveness of an innovative activity. These include:

- The increase in profits as a result of producing the new products or providing new services;
- The client satisfaction with the company's new products/services;
- The increase in sales volumes due to deployment of the new products/services;
- The quantity of new products manufactured by the company for sale on the market;
- The return on investment from the production of the new products or the provision of new services.

It should be noted, however, that such a 'metric' for innovation is used not to characterize a company as being innovative, but to 1) determine the strategic direction of its innovative activities, 2) more precisely allocate available resources among innovative projects, and 3) obtain sufficient information so as to be able to identify shortcomings and improve the overall efficiency of innovative work.

The importance assigned to innovations by owners and managers of modern companies is shown in Table 6.[160]

	FIRST PRIORITY	AMONG THREE TOP PRIORITIES	AMONG TEN TOP PRIORITIES	NOT A PRIORITY
World	14	51	30	5
Asia	29	43	24	4
Europe	12	49	33	5
North America	16	54	25	6
Developing countries	9	52	35	3

TABLE 6. PRIORITY OF INNOVATION IN COMPANY ACTIVITIES, PERCENTAGE

As we can see, for most companies in the world (65%), innovations are one of the three main priorities in their development strategy. Economic statistics confirm that more than a third of companies active on the world market owe 30-60% of their growth to innovative activities.

TYPE OF INNOVATION	COMPANIES THAT IMPLEMENT INNOVATION	COMPANIES THAT "MEASURE" INNOVATION
Innovation in the manufacture of new products	71	54
Innovation in the provision of services	65	37
Innovation related to production process organization	62	37
Innovation in business modelling	51	28

TABLE 7. USE OF INNOVATION METRICS, PERCENTAGE

For objectivity's sake, it should be noted that by no means do all companies resort to quantitative measurement of parameters of their innovative activities, or 'innovation metrics' as they were referred to above. This is demonstrated by Table 7.[161]

The modern business community is convinced that only top-priority attention to innovative activity is capable of guaranteeing a company success and more or less long-term competitiveness on the market. Only by maintaining high vitality in everyday work on improving its products, introducing innovations, and preserving and expanding competitive advantages can a company guarantee itself a firm position in the modern market. Otherwise, they will be replaced by new companies that fill previous product niches, renew consumer demand and create markets for new products and services. In this respect, it is enormously important to merge the power of a corporate colossus with the flexibility of a newly created company. Thus, real success for a company today is defined not by achieving consistently high-performance indicators over a prolonged period, but by continuously forming many temporary advantages based on the requirements of 'the current moment' (Beinhocker 2006). It is precisely innovations that are capable of ensuring such advantages.

SUPPORTIVE AND DISRUPTIVE INNOVATION STRATEGIES

Returning to the concept of innovation, it is appropriate to distinguish between supportive and disruptive innovation in the modern theory of innovation (see Figure 14). Supportive innovation is focused on continuous improvement of the quality of goods and services that are already recognized in the market. A newly established company seeking to occupy a niche in a mature market has very little chance of success.

Disruptive innovation takes place when a principally new product appears on the market and the main problem its creators have with establishing it as an accepted commodity is not competition, but lack of demand for new, unusual merchandise. If successful, a disruptive innovation forms a new market. A disruptive innovation can also be successful in lower segments of the old market which are of little interest to large companies. Quite often, the creators of a disruptive product are able to offer it in such a segment at so low a price that leading companies find that the production of an alternative commodity would not bring them particular profits. In both of these cases, so-called disruptive companies begin their activity without going to battle against the old-timers of the industry. This lets them strengthen their position in the market and improve their product, which gradually becomes a necessary attribute of modern life.

The concept of disruptive innovation was introduced by Clayton Christensen (born 1952), an American expert on management, Professor of Business Administration at the Harvard Business School and author of a number of in-depth research studies in this field. Christensen argues that disruptive companies meet no resistance in the market from traditionally leading companies not because of the latter's lack of desire to react, but because objective reasons prevent them from undertaking such opposition. Their business, which has already become successful, dictates a certain configuration of goals, resources, processes and management procedures to their managers. Managers cannot freely reconfigure a long-established and successfully functioning system without losing their already occupied positions. They have no capability to compete with new companies that have launched a disruptive business.

This gives the advantage to a new company that does not need to discard long-established preconceptions about 'correct' approaches to running a business. It is precisely for this reason that disruptive strategies provide market newcomers with an excellent chance for success while posing a huge threat to 'old-timer' companies that would have to create an absolutely perfect system of strategic management to minimize such threats.

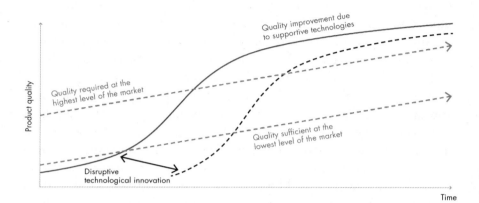

FIGURE 14. SUPPORTIVE AND DISRUPTIVE TECHNOLOGICAL INNOVATIONS (CHRISTENSEN 1997)

Some typical cases of disruptive innovation usually referred to as classic examples are the telephone (which replaced the telegraph), steamboats (which replaced sailboats), semiconductors (which replaced vacuum tubes), and email (which undermined the positions of traditional mail to a large extent). Disruptive innovations can be global, as is the case for the above-mentioned examples, or local in nature. Global disruptive innovations are capable of closing down entire business lines or opening new sub-industries, as happened, for example, when the technology for controlling the fission chain reaction of a nucleus of uranium laid the foundation for nuclear power engineering.

Local disruptive innovations do not bring such impressive changes to the economy as global ones: they transform the market only in narrow, sub-industry niches. World experience shows that newcomer companies that have dislodged recognized leaders from the market were able to do this largely by implementing local innovations. An example of this is the 50-year history of how the electric arc furnace steelmaking technology was able to steal the market from integrated steelmaking plants in the US, segment after segment. The mini-mills that entered the market with this kind of technology first manufactured rebar, which could be made of steel of any kind – even low-quality grades. Then they took over the shaped section segment, dislodged steelmaking plants from the construction steel market and took on steel sheet production (see Figure 15).

It is commonly known that metallurgy is a highly traditional, conservative manufacturing industry. Steelmaking plants employ integrated production, having their own raw material base, production of ore, coal and limestone, as well as their own blast furnaces and chemical coking batteries. Could all this be made more compact?

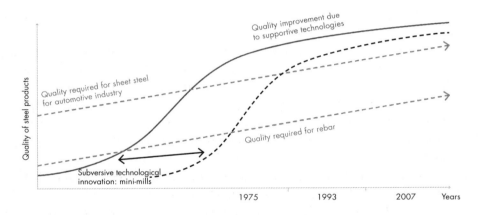

FIGURE 15. THE SUBVERSIVE STRATEGY OF METALLURGIC MINI-MILLS

At a metallurgic mini-mill, the whole technological process, from melting scrap metal in electric furnaces to the production of galvanised rolled metal, takes place in just one building. When the first mini-mill was built in the U.S. in the 1970s by SMS Group, the cost of its rebar (which is the least critical product since its external appearance has little importance, as it will be covered with concrete at the construction site anyway) was 30% lower than the cost of rebar manufactured at integrated factories. The high profitability of this new technology stimulated the construction of more and more new mini-mills producing rebar, while the traditional facilities whose operation had now become expensive began to shut down.

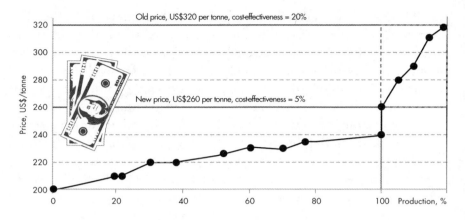

FIGURE 16. DEPENDENCE OF REBAR PRICES ON CAPACITY UTILISATION

The low cost of production at steel mini-mills initially allowed the companies to rake in high profits. However, the disappearance of old, high-cost production facilities from the market intensified competition between mini-mills; the cost-output curve almost flattened out, which meant a significant reduction in profitability. Thus, in order to preserve profitability going forward, they were forced to develop technologies and produce more and more sophisticated products (see Figure 17).

Truly revolutionary changes to American metallurgy occurred in 1993, when the team of Ken Iverson and John Correnti became the first to produce rolled sheet at a Nucor mini-mill. When John Correnti tired of the bureaucracy of Nucor, which by that time had turned into an enormous corporation, he decided to take part in the construction of a next-generation plant and thus the SeverCorr mini-mill was commissioned in 2007. The results exceeded even our wildest expectations. The start-up and full ramp-up of capacity was completed in a miraculously short time. Moreover, the highest manufacturing quality level was reached already in the third month of plant operation. The competitiveness of SeverCorr turned out to be so high that even when the crisis hit in 2008 and U.S. steel-making capacity utilisation dropped to less than 50% , SeverCorr was still working at full capacity!

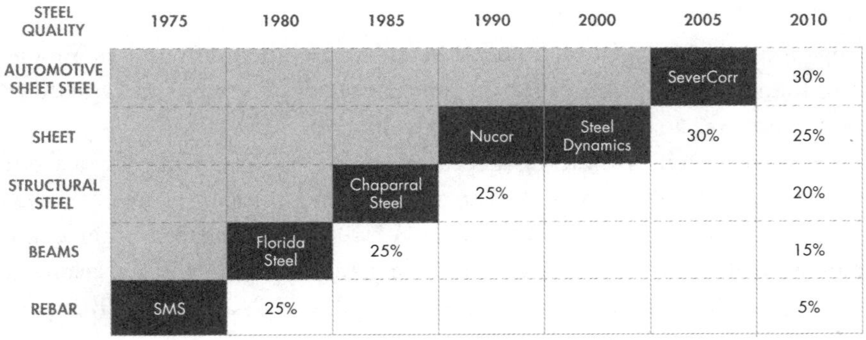

STEEL QUALITY	1975	1980	1985	1990	2000	2005	2010
AUTOMOTIVE SHEET STEEL						SeverCorr	30%
SHEET				Nucor	Steel Dynamics	30%	25%
STRUCTURAL STEEL			Chaparral Steel	25%			20%
BEAMS		Florida Steel	25%				15%
REBAR	SMS	25%					5%

FIGURE 17. TYPES OF STEEL (FROM SIMPLE TO MORE COMPLEX) PRODUCED AT MINI-MILLS AND THEIR OPERATING PROFIT, PERCENTAGE

But why don't all mini-mills in America operate profitably? It's all about correctly selecting a business model and quality of management. For example, at SeverCorr, a product sales specialist is immediately notified when a customer has a problem, for example, with quality. They receive this information directly from the manufacturer. And here, metal scrap is purchased not by the CEO or sales manager, but by the assistant manager of the shop. Everything else is purchased by the foreman: all repair services, bearings, spare parts and everything else they need.

Thus, SeverCorr shop managers and workers have received the appropriate powers and have actually begun to perform the functions of production managers. They have also been granted company stock options. Teams attached to shops have essentially become self-regulated. If it turns out that a certain worker is not meeting the team's standards and the income of other team members is suffering because of them, the team can take disciplinary measures against that worker and even fire them. In other words, all production participants have been inducted into a self-regulated system that evolves according to the plant's technological processes. Here, literally everyone understands what actually facilitates increased output of steel and improvement in its quality, so they don't need any outside consultants or power point presentations for this. It is all constantly under the watchful eye of the shop manager, who immediately responds to any red flags. After all, his bonus depends on production efficiency.

This business model enables them to harness the power of a workforce of fewer than 800 people, including subcontractors, to produce the same output as a workforce numbering two thousand at the integrated plants.

INNOVATIONS IN MANAGEMENT

For innovative companies, innovations in management are no less important than new technologies for the production, development and release of new products capable of conquering the market.

Why are such innovations necessary? What distinguishes them from innovations in other areas? What distinguishes companies like General Electric, DuPont, Procter & Gamble, Visa and Linux from other companies? A high output volume? Yes. Smart, competent and experienced employees? Without a doubt. Outstanding leaders? Of course. But perhaps there's something else?

Answering these questions, Gary Hamel, founder of the international consulting firm Strategos and director of the Management Lab, asserts that this decisive 'something else' is innovations in management (Hamel 2006).[162] In support of this view, he presents the following indisputable facts.

At the beginning of the 20th century, General Electric improved the most well known invention of Thomas Edison – the industrial research laboratory. The discipline of management was imported into the disorderly process of scientific discoveries and, as a result, General Electric obtained more patents over the next 50 years than any other company in America. GE registered small-scale inventions every 10 days on average, while serious achievements were patented every six months.

In 1903, DuPont was the first company to calculate comparative return on investment, in order to standardize comparisons of the work efficiency of its different departments, and thereby became a pioneer in developing methods for budgeting capital investments. By adhering to the principle of competition between investment projects under conditions of limited financial resources, the company became one of America's industrial giants.

The success of Procter & Gamble in the consumer goods industry began in the 1930s, when the company formalized its approach to brand management. At that time, management of intangible assets was something new and the company has augmented its intangible assets ever since. Right now, the company's portfolio includes 50 brands, of which 24 have a turnover of more than US$1 billion a year.

Visa, the world's first virtual company, achieved its success thanks to organizational innovations. By forming a consortium in the US, the banks/founders of Visa laid the foundation for the brand that is now known all over the world. Right now, Visa is a global network connecting more than 21 thousand financial institutions and 1.3 billion credit card owners. The annual transaction volume of Visa cards amounts to US$4.8 trillion.

Linux is the best example of innovations in management, as its software was developed based on open-source code. The kernel of the Linux operating system and its components are created and distributed according to a free and open-source software development model. This innovation became an effective mechanism for coordinating the work of globally dispersed software developers who are all focused on achieving the same goal.

These examples demonstrate that huge achievements in management provide companies with advantages and lead to radical changes in all of their activities. Hamel names three conditions under which innovations in management can create long-term advantages:

- The innovations are based on new principles that challenge traditional management;
- The innovations must be systemic, they must encompass a wide range of methods and processes;
- The innovations are part of a continuous process of new developments that lead to improvements over time.

As a typical example, he cites the experience of Toyota, which relied on its ordinary employees who, company management believed, were capable of solving problems, becoming innovators and improving production technologies. While their American competitors relied on specially staffed experts to improve production processes, Toyota made efforts to give each employee the appropriate skills and tools that allowed them to solve problems as they arose, as well as identify situations that had the potential to cause new problems. As a result, the company was able to receive more than 540 thousand innovative suggestions from the employees of its facilities. American automakers, following traditional management principles, tried all of the other methods until they finally came to the conclusion that the real advantage of Toyota was its utilization of the creative capabilities of ordinary employees.

Thus, realization of the necessity for management innovations should be followed by a search for new principles. No serious problem can be solved with obsolete methods. Just as scientists wanting to understand the subatomic structure of matter were forced to abandon Newton's laws in favour of the then dubious theory of quantum mechanics, new problems in management require new approaches to find solutions.

As the above examples show, innovative activities in management and, accordingly, the search for principles on which management work should be based, have a long history. In 1924, several forward-looking principles of management were proposed by the recognized management expert

Mary Parker Follett (1868-1933) in her book titled *Creative Experience* (Follett 1924). These principles are:

- Leadership is determined not by authority, but by the capability to strengthen trust in that leadership. The most essential job of a leader is to educate his/her followers;
- Problems are best solved not by imposing a single point of view in the absence of alternatives, but by fighting for an effective solution that encompasses all problematic issues;
- A large organization consists of an array of local communities. Individual and organizational growth occurs when those communities are self-governed.

Can we formulate practical recommendations for a person who has suddenly realized that their company's existing management processes only exacerbate the problem and hinder development? Gary Hamel proposes that we begin by answering the following questions as they relate to management:

- Who directly implements these processes?
- Who has authority to change them?
- What are the objectives of the specific process? How is success measured?
- On whom and how do existing management processes make an impact? Who takes part in these processes?
- What information is needed to implement a specific process?
- Which analytical tools are utilised?
- What are the intermediate and end results of the specific management process?
- What are the main performance criteria for the process?
- How and to whom are decisions communicated?
- How does the specific management process interact with other processes?

This will definitely require experiments that enable testing of the proposed innovations without changing the established organizational structure. In other words, construct a simulated problem situation and assess whether the new decision-making process will lead to an effective solution to the problem. Accordingly, new management principles must be applied in parallel with the old principles for a certain period of time. The goal of such work is to create a portfolio of bold proposals for managing the company that are capable of ensuring victory over the competition.

Scientific thought, represented by selecting and putting forward hypotheses and then subjecting them to criticism and verification, has given humanity freedom of creativity in science and has created new technologies. Modern society and government cannot exist without creating new institutions for the introduction of new technologies. Such institutions are designed to select the most successful scientific discoveries and give them the necessary resources for further rapid development. This process directly determines the economic growth rate in any modern country.

The accumulation of wealth through economic growth, being a better alternative than the previous form of economic development in humankind's history, namely the political game of rent distribution, has become a necessity for modern national elites. Such accumulation enables states to give away interest on their loans. Since the economy in this process grows steadily at a rate comparable to the interest rate, accumulation of new wealth has become possible as well. Formerly, it had only been land, real estate and trade that earned profit. Bankers introduced a new profit generation tool – securities whose value was related to the activity of specific agents of change, such as joint-stock companies.

The transition to the innovation economy was associated with disruptive innovations or creative destruction (by Schumpeter) and a change in existing institutions for property rights protection, financial markets development, education and innovation capacity building (acting as an analogue of biodiversity in biology).

Limited liability companies increased the variety of legal forms of business and means of utilizing creative entrepreneurial talent in addition to joint stock companies, existing for a long time. The domination of the new forms of combining capital made it possible to exclude the Great Man permanently from the process of adopting decisions on purely economic issues.

In the course of further development (evolution) of different limited liability companies, innovation will mean their survival. As Douglass North and John Wallis wrote in their book (*Violence and Social Orders*), supportive innovations (for established companies with a certain market share) and disruptive innovations (for beginners) will ensure competition and the development of advanced capitalism in an economy. At the same time, the ability to find market information about unused opportunities for business will be a crucial condition for success.

CHAPTER 12

GLOBALIZATION. HOW HIGH DEMAND FOR OIL CHANGES THE ESSENCE OF GLOBALIZATION

In the 20th century, the big ate the small; the 21st century will inevitably see the fast eating the slow.

– Thomas Friedman

According to Thomas Friedman, the pace of change is of crucial importance.[163] In 1972, the relations between China and the US were 'reset',
with negotiations on China's accession to the World Trade Organization (WTO) starting soon after Richard Nixon's visit to China. The
momentum enabled China to occupy firmly the position of a third
'global workshop' by 2000, surpassing many of Southeast Asia's countries (so called 'Asian tigers' – South Korea, Singapore, Hong Kong and
Taiwan) in the international division of labour and staying second only
to Japan. The countries China surpassed lost over time their advantages
as a result of their national currencies strengthening, labour costs growing and rapid urbanization.

For the US itself, things did not go as well as they did for China.
Starting from 1969, the US dollar started to inflate increasingly due
to the war the US had been fighting in Vietnam. The structure of the
foreign exchange reserves of many countries was changing, with gold
being 'washed out' (its shares reducing) and the US dollar portions
growing. In 1971, a year before his visit to China, US President Richard Nixon made a crucial step that led to the collapse of the entire
post-war monetary system based on the dollar pegged to gold at a fixed
price. Fearing an outflow of gold from the country as a result of it being
purchased by foreign central banks (for US dollars) after Charles de
Gaulle's démarche, he removed the fixed linkage of the US dollar to
gold, letting the currency go on a free-floating exchange rate course.[164]
On 15 August 1971, the entire post-war global monetary system,
based on the Bretton Woods Agreement, came to an end. This was the
agreement of the International Monetary Fund and it established the
rules for commercial and financial relations between the US, Canada,
Western Europe, Australia and Japan. This was the first example of a
fully negotiated monetary order intended to govern monetary relations
among independent states.

The US administration tried to extend the diplomatic success it had
achieved in China to other areas. The US has always strived for world
leadership, trying to change the world for its own benefit. However, the
implementation of the United States' global plans was hindered by a
second post-war global economic crisis that broke out in 1973-1974.

The crisis was precipitated by US banks which had been massively
lending money to Latin American companies, banks and governments.
Widespread defaults ensued, leading to a series of bankruptcies in the
US banking system, since the share of investments in Latin American

countries reached a third in the United States' aggregate loan portfolio at that time.

In 1973, another crisis broke out, an energy crisis this time, triggered by the OPEC (Organization of the Petroleum Exporting Countries) countries, which reduced the volume of oil production, causing oil prices to soar. On 16 October, 1973, the price of a barrel of oil rose by 67% – from US$3 to $5 – and went as high as $12 in 1974, thus showing a fourfold increase altogether.

In 1970, 61% of the world's oil production was controlled by the so-called 'Seven Sisters', another 33% was produced by smaller corporations and only 6% was produced by state-owned companies in developing countries.[165] In the 1970s, the situation changed dramatically. The share of the Seven Sisters sharply decreased to 25% (by 2.5 times), the share of the small corporations decreased to 20%, while the share of state-owned companies in developing countries rose to 55% (showing a ninefold increase!) As a result of this change, the oil-producing developing countries became a major player on the global oil market. At that moment, the term 'petrodollars' appeared on the global financial market as a new phenomenon, denoting the hottest, most movable and speculative capital capable of destabilizing whole financial markets and national economies.

In response to the emerging challenges, a non-governmental, non-partisan discussion group called the Trilateral Commission was founded by David Rockefeller and Zbigniew Brzezinski in July 1973 to foster closer cooperation among North America, Western Europe and Japan.[166] The commission proclaimed the transition to a new international order based on processes that we now call 'globalization'.

GLOBALIZATION 2.0 OS

George Soros, in the introduction to his book called *George Soros on Globalization* (Soros 2002), aptly noted that globalization is a term that is used all too often and may be assigned a variety of meanings. Indeed, universal notions, as is known from philosophy, often do not explain anything, but require explanation themselves.

Attempts to define globalization through in-depth economic research still do not clarify the situation. Here, for example, is what Diana Farrell, director of the McKinsey Global Institute, says in her article *The Truth about Globalization*: "Do not forget that the current boom in investment in developing countries is not the first in history.

But whereas the primary purpose of foreign investment during the so-called first wave of globalisation in the late 19th century was the exploitation of developing countries' natural resources, the expansion of multinational companies today is increasingly determined by the desire to expand markets and improve production efficiency." (Farrell 2003)

When attempting to highlight the essence of globalization as a concept yet one more time, we can identify two points of view:

1. Some people tend to view globalization as a natural historic process (directed towards the formation of a world government able to solve a variety of problems, such as eliminating the threat of nuclear conflicts, economic crises, environmental disasters, etc.);

2. Others believe that it is an artificial process initiated by the leading Western countries lead by the US, as well as by transnational corporations based in these countries.

For specialists, 'globalization' is a debatable term as well. Historians view it as one of the stages of development of capitalism. Economists believe it to be the result of the merger of financial markets. Political scientists are focused on the emergence and spread of democratic institutions. Culture scholars associate globalization with the 'westernization' of culture, meaning primarily American economic and cultural expansion. There are also information-technological approaches to the explanation of globalization processes.

I personally perceive globalization as the aggregate of various, diverse, divergent and contradictory processes occurring at the present time. Let's imagine our world as a computer controlled by a certain operating system (called, for example, Globalization 2.0). Let's open something like Task Manager and look closely at the running processes. We will see something similar to the list below.

Finance: Currency wars are waged where growing borrowings are acting as the driving force behind consumption growth, whose scale is unprecedented in human history.

Economy: Victory of the market economy (market liberalism) over the planned economy. Reforms in China (1978); Perestroika in the Soviet Union (1985). Emergence of the Chimerica economic symbiosis (Chimerica – a symbiotic term based on the relationship between China and the US).

Industry: Mineral resources redistribute the economic balance of power.

Management: Movement towards a multipolar world and further polarisation (strengthening of the poles).

Security: Widespread fighting: terrorism and separatism, with these two concepts becoming ambivalent.

Infrastructure (the influence of new technologies): Microelectronics, digital revolution, the internet, electronic transactions.

The origin of the word 'globalization' indicates that the rapid growth of international trade taking place at various stages in history plays the leading role in this process. Therefore, let's take a look at the elements of the lucky clover from this trade-induced perspective.

CURRENCY WARS
THE LOST DECADE (THE 1980s)

The floating exchange rate system in various countries did not remain a thing in itself, but was immediately subjected to an oil embargo and pressure from OPEC, which was now able to control energy prices. In the 1980s, this practice resulted in a series of economic crises, mainly in Latin America. Instead of doing good, surplus dollars, which could not have a direct effect on technological innovation, fuelled inflation and boosted interest rates on loans, which eventually led to a further increase in debt.

The inflow of capital, needed by developing countries to start an innovation cycle, was not used for its intended purpose. An inflow of money to a country from outside, as a result of some external shock, is considered by a national government first of all as a means of reducing the country's balance deficit. But since developing countries still did not have social structures that would ensure effective use of an inflow of money, the inflow of investment proved unpredictable and short-term. The lucky clover never bloomed.

The Federal Reserve System came to the rescue of US banks. It provided a line of credit to many troubled banks; however, this did not prevent a series of massive bankruptcies. In Europe, bankruptcy was not as widespread. Most often, banks suspended payments and then renewed activity a few months later, after restructuring their balance sheet.

It was at that point that Western European countries came up with the idea that currency fluctuations (which confused investors, who, as a result, reduced investment, causing a decline in economic growth) could be overcome through the creation of a single currency. We see today that it was a half-hearted decision. It enabled the European countries to combine their economies, but did not eliminate the fluctuation of the euro against other currencies.

The impact of the debt crisis manifested itself in the US and the UK by a renewal of interest in classical market ideas. The government, which according to Keynes's followers was expected to start a new innovation cycle by filling the country with money, moved to the background and conceded the role of growth generator to scientists and businessmen. These sentiments determined the course of the state after Ronald Reagan came to power in the US and Margaret Thatcher in the UK. State intervention in the economy, which was considered a boon until then, was gradually reduced.

Ronald Reagan led the country in a difficult period (1981-1989), when the whole world expected the US economy to collapse due to the above-mentioned crisis. The US economy had a negative growth (down to -5%) during that period and one third of the country's production capacity in the manufacturing sector worked at a loss. Inflation reached 12.5% and the unemployment rate almost 10%. Besides, the East-West détente policy and the flirting with the Soviet Union in the 1970s undermined America's role as a world leader.

The new economic policy of those years, called Reaganomics, was based on the theory that lower tax rates facilitate inflow of capital into the economy, which in turn leads to an increase in the number of jobs, economic growth and, consequently, an increase in tax revenues.

Monetarism was selected as a theoretical platform for these changes. The dominant paradigm in economic theory was once again the concept of general equilibrium, which considered markets in their relationship. Reagan's policy was based on two principles:[167]

1. Reduction of state intervention in the economy. Reagan argued that "the government does not solve problems, but creates them" and "the less government, the better".
2. The idea of a 'cheap state', where the costs of the public sector, with the state apparatus and social programmes, should be kept to a minimum.

Reagan reduced state control over the prices of oil, natural gas and community services, limited government intervention in environmental issues, and began to cut government expenditures. The entire post-war 'social state' model was dismantled. Whatever property there was still in public ownership was to be put up for privatization and uncompetitive enterprises were to be liquidated. Gradually, the country went through a technological restructuring of industry and foreign capital was invested more heavily in the US economy. Reagan undertook a large-scale and targeted tax cut.[168] This stimulated investment activity and allowed the middle class to improve their position.

Simultaneously however, this measure further increased the incomes of the richest Americans. The sharp reduction in the expenditure on social programmes resulted in the welfare of poor Americans falling back by 20%. It was the Protestant work ethic, according to which everyone is responsible for themselves, that saved America from a social explosion. Most people considered the reduction a just measure designed to fight social parasitism.

In America, this approach did work. By the end of Reagan's presidency, unemployment hit an all-time low (5.3%) in the country, there was virtually no inflation (4.5%), the average annual economic growth rate reached 3.2% and the average family income increased by US$4,000. The mass media announced that the US economy had entered a new era and that the old economic laws did not apply to this country anymore. But in actual fact, the state budget deficit had reached US$200 billion, the national debt had almost tripled (arriving at US$2.9 trillion), while tax revenues had fallen significantly after the reduction in tax rates and public spending had increased due to military expenditure.

In 1990, the US, a country that had had the highest gross national product (GNP) per capita in the world in the mid-1960s, lagged behind some 10 other countries on this score. Success was not obvious even with the standard of living, because the average salary after Reaganomics, by the early 1990s, was at its lowest level since the 1960s.[169] It was at that point that the US turned from a creditor into a debtor.

It was largely thanks to one of its main innovations that the US managed to keep the lucky clover. In the post-war period, the country was able to convert international trade to economic liberalism principles, which presumed self-regulation of markets and elimination of state intervention in the economy. These principles, unjust in trade relations between countries, prevented the lucky clover from blossoming where all the conditions had seemingly been established to this end, clearly demonstrated in the case of Japan.

JAPAN

By the mid-1980s, Japan's economy had gained such momentum that the country actually began to challenge the US as the world's largest producer of goods and services. Many will recall that in the 1980s, Japan fascinated the world and its economy was very successful, stable and, most importantly, highly dynamic. American businessmen openly feared Japanese competitors.

This confrontation resulted in a meeting of the finance ministers of the world's most developed countries in the autumn of 1985, where the US, threatening Japan with trade sanctions, forced it to sign an agreement which protected America's interests under the guise of the above-mentioned principles of non-interference of the state in the national economy. The agreement introduced measures to decrease the dollar-to-yen exchange rate. Hardly anyone doubted that Japanese products were better than analogous goods made in the US and, therefore, according to the American understanding of justice, the increase in price would make Japanese merchandise more expensive and thus equalize the positions of the two competing countries.

However, the agreement resulted in reductions in the sales of Japanese goods around the world. In several months, the yen rose by 40% and the prices of Japanese goods doubled. Japan's GDP growth fell by 50% next year. The Bank of Japan immediately began to take action. The Central Bank's decision was simple: if the economy is in a downturn, the borrowing costs need to be reduced – and the interest rate fell.[170] The stock market reacted by feverishly using loan funds to buy shares.

In 1987, Nippon Telephone and Telegraph (NTT), Japan's national telephone company, went public. As there were not enough shares for all who saw them as a good investment opportunity, they had to be raffled off. NTT's market capitalization exceeded US$376 billion! Following NTT, the stock prices of other Japanese corporations also rose.[171] Western investors, who were not totally overcome by the euphoria, began to sell shares. But in Japan, investors, analysts and economists engaged their imagination instead of doing sober calculation in an attempt to explain the exorbitant prices. The pressure of excessive monetary liquidity spread to the real estate market, where prices for property in Japan's major cities tripled in speculative expectations.

However, at the same time in 1987, the profits of Japanese corporations began to fall for the reasons already named. Wages grew at a moderate pace. From 1985 to 1990, the rising prices in Japan were driven by loans and the amount of bank loans increased by US$724 billion. But the Japanese did not take into account the trickiness of this invention: if you borrow a million, your standard of living rises up immediately, but your expenses give traders and industrialists the wrong signal that you have become richer and are able now to buy additional products. Under this false impression, they would also take out loans in order to produce and sell more products. But you cannot or do not want to borrow another million. Moreover, it is most likely that you will also be requested to return to the loan you have already got. And then everything falls into place!

The bubble created by the growth of debt did not just implode, but turned colossal savings to dust due to bankruptcies and write-offs of bad debts. The sudden external shock caused by the Iraqi invasion of Kuwait on 2 August, 1990 caused tension on all world markets, and the shares of Japanese corporations, which had already been falling, collapsed completely in a flash. The Japanese market fell from a peak Nikkei index of 39,000 points. The unprecedented mortgage bubble burst and the country's credit system fell into a coma. The debt burden of the population went out of control.

The long-forgotten phenomenon – deflation (appreciation) of the national currency – turned out to be the worst thing for the Japanese economy during those years, resulting in Japanese products completely losing competitiveness on world markets. Another negative aspect of a deflation is also well known: in a situation where money is appreciating while prices are going down, people stop making large purchases, reasonably believing that everything will be still cheaper tomorrow.

THE LESSON LEARNED

Japan's bad experience has served as an invaluable lesson for other countries. It has become clear that we live in a world where the financial systems of various countries are somewhat similar to communicating vessels. A simple way to strengthen a country's own production and economy is to either undervalue or 'drop' the national currency in relation to the dominant (anchor) currencies. Therefore, Western countries' attempts to impose 'currency targeting' agreements, on countries that demonstrate strong growth (countries that are faster and therefore more formidable competitors), have not been successful so far. The Japanese lesson determined in many respects the unprecedented growth of the Chinese economy in the last decade of the 20th century.

By now, China has accumulated huge foreign exchange reserves. They have been growing since the second quarter of 1998. Within the period from 2004 to the end of 2012, China's international reserves increased by 721% to reach US$3.3 trillion.[172] Thus, China's reserves grew faster than the price of gold.[173] The total reserves of the other BRIC countries (Brazil, Russia and India) increased during the same period by 'just' 400%, to arrive at US$1.1 trillion.

China now ranks first in terms of international reserves, followed by Japan, Saudi Arabia, Russia and Switzerland. The rapid growth of China's foreign exchange reserves during the last 10 years is associated with the country's rapid economic growth. The Chinese economy is second and, in terms of gross domestic product based on purchasing power parity, first in the world. China has recently overtaken the US, ranked first by the International Monetary Fund (IMF).

Other countries also make efforts to avoid following the Japanese scenario, which sometimes results in currency wars. The point of a currency war is to keep the exchange rate of a national currency at an artificially low level. In the course of such a war, nations that manage to drop their currencies most in relation to the currencies of their competitors find themselves in the best positions, since this enables them to make considerable cuts in export prices, thus earning a substantial profit.

Quite often, a country, finding it impossible to enhance radically the competitiveness of its national currency and economy, would undertake a massive financial intervention by buying foreign currency through its central bank. There is also another way to achieve the same end, though it is much more complex: it requires taking a range of measures to adjust the national legislation to make any transactions conducted in a currency other than the national currency unattractive.

In spring 2013, for example, the euro was the most disadvantageous currency, losing to all currencies in the world except the national currencies of Norway and Peru. Production in EU countries is becoming uncompetitive on world markets. The only EU country that has relatively high survival chances is Germany, as consumers from other countries are still willing to pay well for the high-quality commodities offered by its automotive, chemical and pharmaceutical industries (Hammer 2010).

The dollar was preferable to the national currencies of Russia, China and the European Union, but did not have much chance on the most promising markets – Brazil, India, Argentina and Australia.

The Japanese yen has started to regain against the US dollar. This has resulted in an increase in the sales of Japanese cars and a reduction in the sales of American cars in Japan. The Japanese industry now has, once again, a major advantage in cost due to the low exchange rate of the national currency. This has not been a miracle – at the beginning of April 2013, the Central Bank of Japan began to buy up massively the country's national debts, i.e. Japan has, for the first time in two decades, launched a campaign for so-called quantitative easing of its financial policy.

Meanwhile, the EU leaders seem to have decided to get their economies out of the crisis by taking a completely opposite course. Japan's decision to firmly depreciate its currency, maintain inflation and stimulate consumption has divided the world into two camps today, with the US and Japan taking one side and the EU and, partly, Russia, the other.[174] Japan's aim to keep inflation may result in a new round of currency wars.

Following these events, the famous American investor George Soros pointed out two clear alternatives: Germany is making too many concessions – far more than is necessary for the survival of the euro. This strategy is destroying the European Union. Furthermore, the main structural error of the single European currency system, according to Soros, is that it allows the risk of bankruptcy of its member countries as such (Malien 2013). Other developed countries, such as Japan or the US, having central banks of their own, run virtually no risk of bankruptcy, since their central banks can always print as much new money as is needed to pay off the national debt.

Fluctuations in the euro-to-dollar exchange rate in recent years have only confirmed these trends. For the euro, a currency war turns into a 'currency wave'. In relation to the dollar, the euro moves within certain boundaries all the time, the lower of which is parity between the two currencies. The difference in the value of the two currencies is the result of two emission reduction policies which have been alternately expanded and contracted by the US Federal Reserve System and the European Central Bank in recent years. The dollar becomes more expensive as soon as the Fed cuts emissions and the euro rises as soon as the ECB carries out a similar action.

FROM MARKET LIBERALISM TO CHIMERICA

Will globalization, as a process opening national markets to international trade, reach its climax as a result of the currency wars? Will further development proceed in the direction of protecting national markets?

The protection of local markets and industries at the expense of weakening the national currency does not undermine the already existing international division of labour which results from the trade processes we call globalization. Another, technical issue, takes priority. How well will the above-mentioned processes be managed? The question is important because uncertainty caused by currency wars will inevitably jeopardize the profits of transnational corporations.

In the days of Reaganomics, American economist Theodore Levitt used the term 'globalization' with reference to the processes that started to develop once national commodity markets around the world, influenced by transnational corporations, began to merge into one. In 1990, immediately before the dissolution of the Soviet Union, the Soviet bloc countries, which still had centrally planned economies in the early 1990s, occupied a territory of 34.3 million square kilometres, or about 25% of the world's terra firma, but produced, according to the World Bank, only 5.6% of the world's goods and services (worth US$1.2 trillion in total). The aggregate population of these countries was about 1.6 billion, with an average GDP per capita of US$818, or about 20% of the world average. In 2014, the total volume of production of goods and services in these countries already amounted to about US$14 trillion, or 18% of the global GDP, and the average GDP per capita in these countries was US$7,700, or about 72% of the worldwide mean figure. The expansion of the world's transnational corporations (Figure 18) did not take place in a vacuum and not so much because of the incompetent actions of the then leaders of the Soviet bloc. Today, when the Russian economy is a full-term part of the global economy, it is appropriate to elaborate on the process of globalization after the victory of the liberal economy ideas over the planned. The formation of the economic dipole called Chimerica was a consequence of these events.

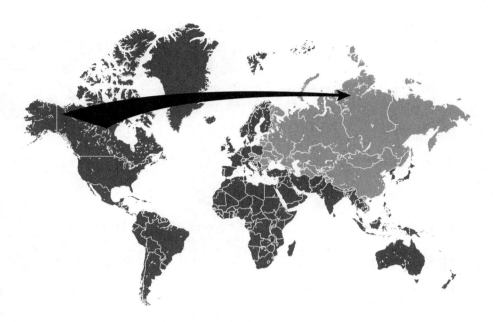

FIGURE 18. EXPANSION OF THE MARKET ECONOMY

Over the past 30 years, the total value of the global financial assets has been growing much faster than world GDP. Economists use the term 'financial depth' to refer to the ratio of financial assets to GDP, and attach great importance to studying the influence of this parameter on other macroeconomic indicators. To understand the meaning of this ratio, let's take and analyse, for example, the change in the structure of the assets in the UK for the period from 1688 (see Table 8). Data for this analysis was taken from two sources: *Premodern Financial Systems: A Historical Comparative Study* by Raymond William Goldsmith for the period before 1960 and national statistics published by the UK's Office for National Statistics for the period from 1960-2008. Raymond W. Goldsmith was a Belgian-American economist who was engaged in research of cash flows dynamics and balance sheet accounts.

NATIONAL ASSETS*	1688	1760	1800	1830	1850
1. Tangible assets, %	85	71	64	57	60
2. Financial assets, metals and net foreign assets, %	15	29	36	43	40
Total, %	100	100	100	100	100
Financial assets/tangible assets	0.17	0.40	0.57	0.76	0.68
1.1. Property, %	14	11	12	12	14
1.2. Agricultural land[175], %	58	43	31	24	14
1.3. Industry, %	14	18	20	21	32
1.4. Corporate capital (stocks, bonds, commodity loans), %	5	10	9	6	9
1.5. Precious metals, %	3.7	1 1.9	1.1	1.5	1.5
1.6. Net foreign assets, %	0	-2	0	3	3
1.7. Total debt, %	0	8	17	20	13
Total debt / GDP, %	0	89	199	233	157

TABLE 8. STRUCTURE OF THE UK'S NATIONAL ASSETS IN 1688-2008

For ease of comparison, the data in the table has been adjusted to the 2003 benchmark values using official deflators. The table clearly shows that the share of finance in the total assets has increased substantially over the last three centuries. In particular, this share increased from 15% in 1688 to 73% in 1937, having shown nearly a fivefold increase by the beginning of World War II. It is worth noting that a decrease in the share of financial assets by almost a third in comparison to the pre-war level was seen for several decades after World War II and the pre-war level was only restored by 2008. The table shows how the financial depth changed over time and the ratio of financial assets to

1875	1895	1913	1927	1937	1948	1977	2000	2008
52	34	34	29	27	36	47	31	28
48	66	66	71	73	64	53	69	72
100	100	100	100	100	100	100	100	100
0.93	1.96	1.96	2.45	2.70	1.77	1.11	2.26	2.63
10	8	9	9	9	13	16	18	19
18	8	4	2	2	2	2	0.4	0.2
24	18	20	18	16	21	30	12	9
12	25	22	21	23	17	10	25	19
1.1	0.8	1.0	0.3	0.6	0.4	0.2	0.0	0.0
10	15	18	11	9	0	0	0	0
7	6	5	18	17	20	9	19	26
65	57	46	179	170	182	108	278	401

Sources:
1688-1960: Premodern Financial Systems: A Historical Comparative Study by Raymond W. Goldsmith, 31 July 1987
1960-2008: National Statistics; Office for National Statistics; UK

tangible assets (GDP) increased from 17% in 1688 to 263% in 2008 – more than 15 times!

Analysis of changes in the share of real estate in the general structure of the UK assets leads to no less interesting conclusions. Thus, the table shows that the share of real estate ranged from 8-19% for over 300 years. This is the only asset that remained stable over the three centuries. Could it be the reason why real estate is still one of the most attractive and sought-after assets for investment?

Further analysis of the table shows how the share of agricultural land changed in the structure of assets. In particular, this indicator was

58% in 1688 and was down to 0.2% by 2008, a 300 times reduction! At the same time, the global population increased about 10 times over the same period. These figures clearly show how knowledge enabled people to reduce significantly their physical participation in food production without reducing the consumption of food per capita (and even increasing it).

Let's analyse the dynamics of the changes in the share of industrial production. In the period from 1760 to 1850, this indicator grew almost twice! Actually, it is not surprising, as this was the time of the Industrial Revolution in England. Afterwards, this figure remained relatively stable for a century and then started to decline significantly in the last decades of the 20th century. There is, however, nothing surprising about this either: 1979 saw the beginning of Margaret Thatcher's period in office as Prime Minister, during which she actively implemented a number of radical economic reforms. The key principles of her reformational policy formed an economic concept which was later called Thatcherism. This concept was founded on free enterprise, personal initiative and individualism. It was in those years that small and medium businesses became a new force in the structure of the British economy and, accordingly, the share of services in the structure of the economy began to increase. This trend also continued after Margaret Thatcher left office in 1990.

After the Industrial Revolution, there came a period during which businesses and corporations thrived. The joint share of stocks and bonds in the structure of assets reached 25% by 1895. For the next several decades, this indicator stayed practically unchanged, but then it went through a gradual decrease after World War II, to return back to the pre-war level only by the year 2000.

In 1688, share of gold was 3.7%, but then went down, to arrive almost at zero by 1977. In my opinion, this was due to the decision by US President Richard Nixon mentioned at the beginning of this chapter to abolish the gold dollar standard and introduce a free floating exchange rate.

The next line in the table, which represents the changes in the share of net foreign assets, shows a growth from 3% in 1850 to 18% in 1913. Addressing history, it is worth recalling the Opium Wars with China in 1840 to 1842 and 1856 to 1860 (which occurred at about the time when the period under review began and definitely had some impact on it) and the benefits the UK received as a result of those wars, with China having been practically subjected to economic colonization. If we think about the weight of this indicator (with net foreign assets occupying 18%

in the structure of the country's assets in 1913), the enormous importance of the additional colonial revenues to the British economy becomes
perfectly clear as they continued to be received for almost half a century.
This money could be invested to bring more profit. In comparison with
the profits from the net foreign assets which the UK possessed at that
time, the current Russian oil rent represents a much less important source
of revenue! However, after World War II, UK's largest colonies gained
independence, which led to the almost complete disappearance of net
foreign assets from the country's economy. And here history shows us
something of a sunset for the economic power of the UK, which seems
to have been taken over by the US.

Finally, let's look at the last two indicators in the table – the share of
the country's total debt and its ratio to the GDP. The UK's debt-to-GDP
ratio increased significantly during certain periods, namely the Napoleonic wars and World War II, when this index reached figures in the
region of 200%. Apparently, this was characteristic of wartime, whereas
in peacetime, as the figures show, the situation normalized and the index
went down to values in the region of 50-80%.

If we look at the overall dynamics of the financial depth indicator in
the global economy over the past few decades (based on data published
by the McKinsey Global Institute on the structure of global financial
assets in the period from 1980-2010), we can see that the financial assets
have grown faster than the world economy (see Figure 19). In 1980, the
total value of financial assets amounted to 108% of the global GDP; in
2010, the ratio already reached 375%. This became possible owing to
an unprecedented increase in the volume of general borrowings in the
US and the EU. The infusion of trillions of new dollars into the global
economy under the guise of market liberalism, and very low rates set by
the US Federal Reserve, resulted in the world being flooded with money
and financial assets being inflated. In this context, the market capitalization of leading multinational corporations increased tenfold within the
period from 1990 to 2000. That said, the labour productivity in these
corporations was higher than that at enterprises of centrally planned
economies. This was exactly where the advantage of Reaganomics and
Thatcherism lay: the implementation of these policies made whole
nations work more efficiently.

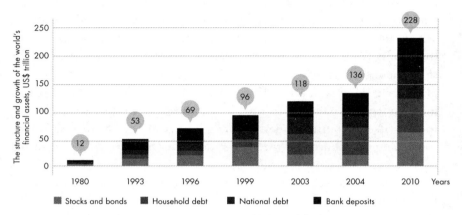

FIGURE 19. BORROWINGS IN THE UNITED STATES
AND THE EUROPEAN UNION

In 1978, China launched its major economic reforms.[176] Since then, China has had no significant recession or economic slowdown.

The reason for this was the successful combination of making wide use of international expertise and maintaining the national currency at a low exchange rate, which had a positive impact on the national economy. By 2008, the Chinese currency had depreciated to one fourth of what it had cost in 1980! In 2008, China had a multiple advantage over Japan whose currency had come to be three times stronger over the same period. This gave the Chinese economy a tremendous potential for growth. Let's consider this story of success in more detail and analyse the dynamics of the international division of labour system in Southeast Asia from 1960 to 2008 (Figure 20).

As you can see from the figure, Japan increased its GDP per capita from US$7,000 to US$36,500 over the years from 1960 to 2008, without a substantial growth in the population, and was one of the first global workshops in the second half of the 20th century, providing merchandise for the growing consumption in the US after World War II. The US was embroiled in the Cold War and the arms race, and its population was increasingly involved in service industries and new sectors populated by representatives of the creative class. Japan's good infrastructure and hardworking people enabled the country to show high GDP per capita figures. In the second half of the 20th century,

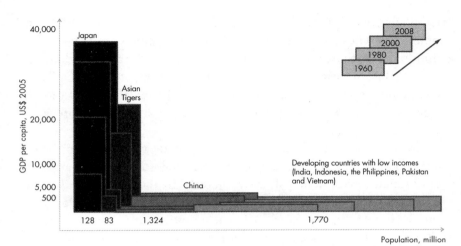

FIGURE 20. CHINA AS THE WORLD'S THIRD WORKSHOP IN INTERNATIONAL
SPECIALISATION OF LABOUR (1960-2008)

Source: World Bank

Japan was followed by the Four Asian Tigers – South Korea, Singapore, Hong Kong and Taiwan. Although China's population considerably exceeded that of Japan's in 1980, its GDP per capita lagged behind. At that time, many developing countries could claim the role of a new global workshop – Indonesia, the Philippines, Pakistan, India and Vietnam, whose GDP per capita exceeded China's almost twofold, while their aggregate population was slightly over that of China. Yet China pursued different economic and demographic policies. While the country succeeded in achieving a growth in GDP per capita terms, its population also increased significantly. Today, China's GDP per capita is higher than that of any of those countries, all of which dream of taking China's place and are trying to succeed it in the capacity of a global workshop, actively developing their infrastructure and intensively working on bringing their products to the world market in large amounts.

As a result, an amazing symbiosis of the largest market-based consumer economy (the US) and a market-and-planning producer economy (China) had developed in the world by 2008. However, this symbiosis is not devoid of serious problems. Despite China's growing economic power, there is a huge dependence by China's exports on US demand today.[177] China invests its export revenues in US government bonds (i.e. in the United States' national debt), and the US, respectively, depends on China as a key creditor.[178] Having a substantial positive trade balance, China exports much more than it imports. When the country switches to a different mode of development and starts consuming rather than saving, it will increase the capacity of its domestic market. This, in turn, will lead to a drop in the competitiveness of Chinese labour in the world and China itself will replace the US as the largest consumer of goods produced in other countries. This process is already gaining momentum.

However, despite China's impressive growth, the opportunities for investment inside the country are limited. The government's attempts to stimulate investment led to an increase in food prices and growing social discontent. China has to invest in the currencies of other countries, actually financing their consumption or production. If the Chinese leadership decides to prioritize domestic development and increase the standard of living of the country's population, this will mean increasing labour costs and wages levels.

And this is already happening little by little: earnings in Chinese industry have increased from US$1 per hour in 2000 to US$3 in 2012. According to the National Bureau of Statistics of China, the number of workers who had moved to developed areas of the country increased by only 3.5% in 2009, totalling about 145 million. Factories in eastern China lacked labour. In this situation, the only possible solution for many enterprises was to either stop production and go bankrupt or hire workers from Vietnam, Laos and Cambodia. The Chinese government turned a blind eye to illegal immigration into China, recognizing that it had no better solution to the problem yet, and set a new goal: putting the economy on a new innovation path. Dozens of innovative cities have already been built and now most of the GDP growth is expected to be achieved in the medium term by focusing on innovative products.

The resulting steady increase in the cost of labour in China has created an interesting trend, namely reindustrialization of the US, where much better conditions for industrial business have formed. For example, natural gas costs US$70 per 1,000 cubic metres, electricity costs 3–5 cents per kWh and the cost of labour (in the southern states bordering Mexico) is US$8 per hour, and is not growing, unlike in China. In these conditions, more and more businesses are returning to the US. And here the question arises: can the US become the next global workshop?

A MECHANISM FOR REDISTRIBUTION OF ECONOMIC POWER

The 'consumer dipole', where the US consumes and China produces, is most likely to survive for another decade. The workings of this symbiosis involve not only the two countries that act as producer and consumer, but also exporters of raw materials and energy, which supply the necessary process components. It is obvious that in order to satisfy the needs of the international community in products, China, as a global workshop, requires significant amounts of energy. In this regard, the growth of industrial production in China has long determined the escalation of the world prices for oil and other energy sources. Currently, demand for oil and, therefore, its price, is going down, owing to a slowdown in China's economy.

This is confirmed by the fact that the problem of forecasting oil prices has remained at the centre of the expert community's attention for many years, if not decades. One of the problems, for which economists still cannot provide an adequate solution, is that oil prices are determined not only by the conditions existing on the world market, but also by a number of political factors falling outside the purview of economic analysis. Nevertheless, some empirical generalizations (in the words of Vladimir Vernadsky) make it possible to discuss this topic in a constructive spirit. One of such generalizations is shown in Figure 21.

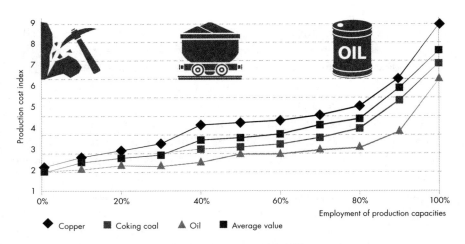

FIGURE 21. THE PRODUCTION CAPACITIES AND COSTS
OF KEY RAW MATERIALS IN THE WORLD

The curve that averages the cost indices for the three extractive industries shows that if 80% of the global production capacity is used, the average cost comes up to about three conventional points, i.e. three times the cheapest production cost. But once another 15% of the total capacity is employed, the average cost soars up to eight conventional points.

The employment of the most expensive 15% of the total production capacities began with the growth of the Chinese economy and the exponential increase in oil imports aiming to meet the needs of China's growing industry (Figure 22). It is largely due to this growth that the sharp increase in oil prices occurred on the world market from 2000 to 2014.

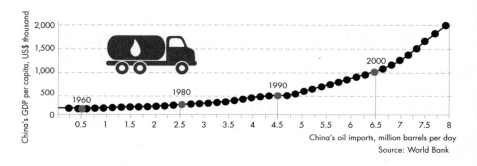

FIGURE 22. THE EXPONENTIAL DEPENDENCE OF OIL IMPORTS ON THE GROWTH OF CHINA'S ECONOMY

Thus, before the launch of the economic reforms in China, the situation on the world commodity markets was relatively stable and the commodity prices fluctuated in a relatively narrow range corresponding to the nearly horizontal sections of the curves shown in Figure 23.

The success of China's reforms is largely rooted in some imbalances that the US created earlier and is continuing to create today. More specifically, from 1945 to 1980, the United States' ratio of the total debt to the GDP was about 150%. However, this was not a public debt as such, but the total debt, including the domestic debt and the debts of households, corporations, etc. In the early 1980s, Ronald Reagan and Margaret Thatcher began to implement, as part of the market liberalism ideology, a number of programmes that led to an increase in the total debt of both the US and the UK. As a result, by 2012, the two states' debts already amounted to about 400% in relation to their GDPs.

These reforms stimulated consumption in countries such as the US and production in countries such as China. It was due to this process, despite all of its costs, that the Chinese economy began to grow at such high rates that would have been impossible without a capacious external market.

The following empirical generalization results from analysis of the dependence of oil consumption on the GDP per capita in different countries. This dependence is shown in Figure 24, where a few dozen points correspond to different countries.

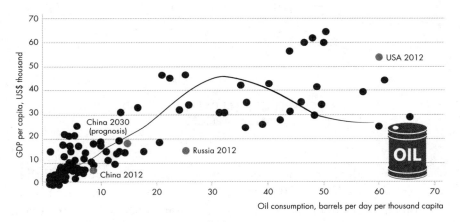

FIGURE 23. WORLDWIDE CONNECTION BETWEEN OIL CONSUMPTION AND GDP PER CAPITA

As we can see, in countries where the GDP per capita is about US$50,000 (such as the US), the average oil consumption is in the region of 60 barrels per day per 1000 people. At the same time, in China, where the GDP per capita was around US$6,200 in 2012, the oil consumption per capita was about 10 times less. But if the Chinese GDP per capita reaches US$15,000 to 20,000 (which is, according to some projections, possible as soon as 2030), the country's oil consumption per capita will increase two to three times compared to the current level – provided, of course, that China does not carry out large-scale energy-saving programmes.

But it is not China alone that is responsible for the above changes. If not China, other countries would have produced goods demanded in the world market and the global industrial energy consumption would have amounted to about the same figure as it does today. And here we make use of a third empirical generalization.

Figure 24 shows the dependence of oil prices (in US dollars per barrel) on daily oil production (in millions of barrels).

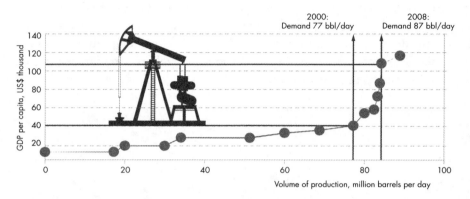

FIGURE 24. CORRELATION BETWEEN OIL PRODUCTION AND OIL PRICES

This dependence is typical for the period from 2000 to 2014. Within the period from 2000 to 2008, the daily oil consumption increased from 77 million to 87 million barrels, i.e. by 10 million barrels a day, as the USA reduced its consumption by 1 million barrels a day, China increased its consumption by 4 million, the developing countries increased their consumption by 5 million and the OPEC countries cut their production by 2 million barrels a day. This resulted in an increase in oil prices from US$40 per barrel to US$105.

Oil production in the US fell by 0.5 million barrels per day within the period from 2000 to 2008, but then, starting from 2008, came to grow by about 7% annually on average, reaching an annual increase of 14% in 2014, primarily due to the active development of shale oil production. Altogether, oil production in the US increased by 65% during that period!

Starting from 2015, the OPEC countries also began to increase oil production at a rate of 2.5-3% per year, after a 0.5% reduction in their aggregate oil production during the period from 2008 to 2014. As a result, global oil production showed a 1-2% surplus over oil consumption in 2014, which led to oil prices going down to a minimum level of US$32 per barrel in January 2016.

The US Energy Information Administration predicted that oil production in the US would decline by about 4% by the end of 2016.

However, the reluctance of OPEC countries to reduce their production volumes, plus growing oil production in Iran after trade and economic embargoes imposed by the US and other Western countries were lifted recently, as well as the slowdown in industrial production growth in China, do not favour predictions about changes in the oil production-to-consumption ratio. Without understanding clearly the correlation between demand and supply, no-one is likely to make predictions as to what the price of oil will be in the foreseeable future.

It is important to understand that the world economy is now consuming, on a daily basis, about 2 million barrels of biofuels produced using green technologies. If the world did not have these capacities, the price of a barrel of oil would be higher. That is why industrialized countries (and the US first of all) express growing concern about the dependence of their economies on imported oil and develop plans to overcome this dependence, including the development of shale oil production technologies.

The pursuit of these objectives is being generously financed from the US budget. For example, in 2009, US$2.2 billion were spent to fulfil the task of stimulating consumer interest in the use of energy-efficient equipment and technologies alone.

Thus, the US economy, creating high demand for material goods, ensures their production in China which, in turn, requires resources from economies that are catching up with it. Incidentally, there used to be an analogue of this economic engine in the world: the UK, being a global workshop, ensured high economic growth rates not only for itself, but also for Australia, which supplied it with raw materials, being its colony at the time.

THE FAST VERSUS THE SLOW

Redistribution of resources has resulted in the emergence of new types of investors on the global financial market. A significant shift has occurred in the structure of accumulated global wealth: economically developed countries do not have the undivided financial power they have had until recently anymore. New large centres of capital accumulation have emerged: oil-producing countries and the central banks of Asian countries. Even growing interest rates and the fall in oil prices cannot hamper their increasing influence.

A study carried out by the McKinsey Global Institute in 2006 showed that the assets of investors based in the four BRIC countries had nearly tripled since 2000, coming close to US$10 trillion by the end of 2006, which was approx. 5% of the world's financial assets. The GDP and stock market growth rates of the BRIC countries were significantly higher than those demonstrated by the 'Big Three' economies (the US, the EU and Japan). From 2000 to 2008, the BRIC stock indexes rose 3.5-4 times; from 2000 to 2007, the value of their assets grew annually by 17% and the value of real estate in these countries grew by 7.8% each year.

Of course, if our world was more predictable, then oil prices could be stable. But there is always a lot of 'ifs' in this world. If we could stop the hurricane season, defeat international terrorism, stop world inflation, restore the destroyed Iraq and Syria, make the development of oil companies predictable, do something about the European economy whose businesses are particularly vulnerable to increases in energy prices and find more new oil fields, then oil prices would certainly stabilize. In practice, it is hardly possible to eliminate uncertainty and humanity is spending energy much faster than it finds new sources of it. So is it possible to replace oil?

The developed countries are unlikely to return to the use of coal-fired power stations and the construction of nuclear power stations, which could in principle solve all energy problems, will cause tension in society after the Chernobyl and Fukushima accidents. Recent interest in green technologies has been caused by the eagerness to find substitutes for oil. After all, oil prices are unpredictable: they can rise sharply and then quickly fall due to lack of elasticity in demand.

How much time may be required to switch to the commercial use of new sources of energy? Some estimates may be made if we consider the shift in energy supply towards natural gas as an example. Natural gas is in many ways superior to oil, but still lags behind it in terms of consumption on the world markets, although technologies enabling the use of natural gas became available back in the 1970s.

Scientists agree that the full transition to any substitute fuel requires a time lag of at least 25 years. And the reason for such delay is not the need to develop and adapt technologies for the use of the substitute – the problem is that the technical and investment requirements for the production and transportation of a new fuel greatly exceed those required for the use of the 'previous generation' resource. In other words, the main reason for such a lag is the lack of infrastructure.

It is clear that the mass introduction of new oil-displacing technologies into daily life is already a question of tomorrow. But the world is not standing still – changing under the influence of innovations, it is radically changing the content of the concept of globalization as well.

IS THE WORLD TO BE MULTI- OR SINGLE-POLAR?

In the table opposite, we will try to summarize the trends which are typical of the current level of globalization and then take a closer look at each of them separately.

CONSUMPTION IN EMERGING MARKETS: AN ADDITIONAL INCENTIVE TO GLOBAL GROWTH?

In the 2000s, the massive production of inexpensive Chinese goods resulted in a global consumption boom. The Western world readily passed the role of global workshop on to China. However, the situation changed dramatically in the last few years, with the economies of the developed countries experiencing difficult times. In view of this, China has set the goal of shifting the focus of its production on to its own, domestic consumers. Consumption is always a growth stimulus. The growth of China's urban population and its earnings facilitates the attainment of this goal. China has more than 60 cities with a population of more than 5 million, where earnings have been growing at higher rates than anywhere else – by 15-20% each year.[179]

A strong consumer demand formed in other BRIC countries as well. From 2000 to 2008, bank deposits in Brazil had been growing at an annual rate of more than 29%; the respective figure in India was 18.5%. India's middle class is already over 400 million. Russia's foreign exchange reserves were third in the world until recently.[180]

SHOULD THE EMERGENCE OF A NEW GLOBAL PRODUCTION CENTRE BE EXPECTED?

China's fight for a place in the sun is a struggle for servicing global financial flows and for intellectual property rights. In the area of finance, processes are so complex, that the calculation of the expected effect of any of them is a very time-consuming task.

Today, information is transmitted within seconds. This is true not only of events taking place on stock exchanges and currency and commodity markets, but also of scientific discoveries and their areas of use. Such technical capabilities were unthinkable just 50 years ago. Financial engineering, having formed over this time, resulted in the emergence of new risk management techniques which seriously affect the movement of capital from country to country. Countries whose institutional and financial infrastructures are underdeveloped in comparison with those of developed countries are particularly vulnerable to this. It is no secret that investment

LONG-TERM TRENDS	I. MARKET LIBERALISM, 1980-2000	II. GLOBALIZATION, 2000-2009	III. NEW TRENDS, 2010-2020
1. The driving force behind global consumption growth	An accelerated increase in the US and EU borrowings	Global imbalances and trade in oil and raw materials generate cash flows	Consumption in emerging markets: an additional incentive to global growth?
2. International specialisation	Japan and the Four Asian Tigers are the first and second global production centres	China is the third global production centre and is rapidly building up its superiority	Should the emergence of a new global production centre be expected?
3. Market liberalism	Market economy principles defeat central-planned economy principles (economic reforms in China and the Soviet Union)	A global economy based on capitalist principles is formed	Free floatation of the yuan: to become reality, but when? What are the prospects for regional markets and currencies?
4. Shift in the global balance of power	A shift from a bipolar world to a unipolar one. The Big Three control 90% of global wealth	High development rates shown by the BRIC countries whose wealth had tripled since 2000	The East and the West: will a historical balance be reached?
5. Measurement of the level of wealth	A shift from the gold standard dollar to a commodity dollar, supported by the economic might of the US	The dollar and the euro, the yen in part	A set of several currencies, dominated by the dollar, the euro and the yuan?

TABLE 9. CURRENT GLOBALIZATION TRENDS

capital is actively leaving countries with a backward infrastructure.[181] It does not go to Europe since the conditions there (low growth rates) are not very attractive. Currently, it is flowing out to the US economy.

But it's not so simple. To be beneficial, capital flows must fulfil certain conditions, and must be predictable and long-term. Governments use such capital to fill large holes in the balances of payments of their countries. Most financial flows, being short-term transfers of capital (whether in the form of shares or in the form of loans), create problems for most developing countries.[182] Most countries are small and open economies in financial terms, and they simply do not have the time, or are not prepared, to use properly modern financial instruments for their own benefit. The problem lies not so much in the inefficiency of investment in developing countries as in the speed of capital flowing in and out.

Leading economists are convinced that in order to be able to 'seize and digest' inflows of short-term capital, recipient countries must have well-functioning institutional structures – well-adjusted markets of financial instruments, as well as good and effective laws in the areas of insolvency and protection of property rights. Otherwise economic mistakes will be inevitable, followed by deepening social inequality and potentially explosive political situations fraught with crises and general chaos.

The high speed of processes, characteristic of the modern financial industry, would be inconceivable without the mass penetration of information technologies into society. International transportations are mass-scale technologies too. Unified containers move first by sea and then by road and rail. Optimization of global logistics results in continuous reductions in production and transportation costs. Labour employed in production is reducing all the time, while the physical volumes of goods and services are steadily on the increase. The need for people who have no substantial education is diminishing.

The remaining jobs move to where labour is cheaper and the conditions are more attractive. Thanks to globalization, today's planet is a giant single factory and market. The movement of financial services and capital generates movement in another key resource – the labour force. The importance of migration is growing, since people settle for unskilled work, but in developed countries.

The fight for a global-scale privilege – for the right to build a certain new global hierarchy – has escalated. And what will countries do to win this privilege? How should a country change the structure of its economy so as to get hold of the lucky clover?

The answer is that developing countries should stimulate domestic demand, since this is the most significant factor for global corporations making investment decisions and deciding where to set up production on the globe. What developing countries around the world should do is increase their output (GDP) and thus ensure economic growth. Following the same logic, we should expect a wave of new industrialization in developed countries, although this will be a new type of production, one in which intellectual activity and production as such are closely intertwined. The placement of such new production centres around the world located at considerable distances from invention centres proves to be ineffective, because everything is tied to innovation.

It appears that in today's world, any sector of the economy can be either high-tech or outdated. The sectoral structure of an economy cannot serve as an indicator of the country's technological base being either backward or advanced, but there is another indicator that is more important: speed. Faster companies that are able to enter a market and take it quickly will begin to jostle with large and unwieldy industry giants, former leaders. A country that provides effective support to emerging economies ahead of others will become a new global workshop.

The further development of China, which started to revitalize its economy by setting a favourable rate for its national currency against the US dollar as the worldwide currency, will depend on whether it can modify its relations with the US as its main trading partner without a loss. Of course, it will be extremely difficult to challenge China for two obvious reasons.[183] Firstly, free access to advanced technologies was an important factor in China's rapid growth. Foreign companies moving high-tech production to China in effect advanced technologies there and China quickly learned how to copy and use them. China received, quickly and virtually for free, technologies whose development by the Western world took decades and hundreds of billions (if not trillions) of dollars. In addition, China has now the most powerful and efficient transport infrastructure in the world. In the last decade, an extensive network of highways was built in China, connecting its major cities, and overall the country has built a network of world-class airports.

Infrastructure investments make a double contribution to the development of an economy. First, the construction of the infrastructure creates jobs, and later the operation of the infrastructure increases the productivity of labour and capital. China's progress through the active part of the first phase, which will be completed in the next decade, has already led to some reduction in the country's economic growth rate. Now the Chinese are planning to benefit from the operation of the infrastructure they have created by developing their economy.

Recently, the US has been secretly promoting the idea of using other countries as production sites alternative to China, choosing between the Philippines, Indonesia, India, Thailand, Laos and even Japan.

FREE FLOATATION OF THE YUAN: TO BECOME REALITY, BUT WHEN? WHAT ARE THE PROSPECTS FOR REGIONAL MARKETS AND CURRENCIES?

On 22 January 2009, US Treasury Secretary Tim Geithner accused China of manipulating its national currency. Geithner stated that President Obama would "use aggressively all the diplomatic avenues open to him to seek change in China's currency practices". *The Financial Times* reported on this subject: "The euro is not the only possible candidate for replacing the dollar. The rapid development of China and the shift of focus towards Asia may well end up with the yuan becoming a reserve currency."

The growing role of China in the global economy has caused many countries to consider including the yuan in their sets of reserve currencies.[184] All economies are worrying about how long China will keep its colossal dollar reserves, because the cost of keeping these reserves is only growing. Exchange rate differences and inflation of China's currency result in the country incurring huge losses. However, if China sold its dollar reserves, this would lead to a global economic disaster. China has chosen a more peaceful way of changing the structure of its reserves, diversifying it by buying euro assets so as not to bring the dollar down. Will the US, together with the EU, be able to force China's leadership to repeat the Japanese scenario? I think that the yuan will not compete with the dollar as long as China is not confident that its currency is as stable and reliable as the globally dominant currencies.

THE EAST AND THE WEST: WILL A HISTORIC BALANCE BE REACHED IN A MULTIPOLAR WORLD?

On 7 June 2009, financier George Soros, speaking at Fudan University in Shanghai, said: "When the (Chinese) government orders the banks to lend, the banks lend. As a result, it is easier for China to recover from a recession and this is what is actually happening." Russian economist Mikhail Khazin has delved into China's key problem: "China has not become an independent technology centre. For this reason, it cannot even benefit from what it already controls, for example the funds it has invested in US securities. To put it crudely, China produces intermediate raw materials while falling short of becoming an independent technology centre. And if the US disappears, China will sink automatically. If the Chinese had been developing technologies during the last 20 years while, possibly, refraining from raising the standard of living and other things too quickly, everything would be great for this country now" (Khazin 2009). The balance of power is such that if the US had a major crisis, China would find itself on the threshold of a major crisis too. A crisis in China means a reduction in the oil consumption market, which has been the fastest growing market in recent years.

But China's points of growth are not limited to merely buying energy resources. Since 2002, the average number of applications for registration of trademarks has been increasing in China by about 100,000 each year.

By mid-2009, China already had 10 million companies (an order of magnitude more than Russia) and about 30 million private farms.

China has begun to support actively a wide range of countries, including the poorest. China's largest agricultural project in Africa is being implemented in Malawi, a country in Southeastern Africa. China-Africa Cotton Development Ltd is carrying out projects in many African countries. China is also actively investing in projects in Latin American countries. Thus the Chinese economic power may soon start to dominate the whole region, increasing China's national wealth.

A SET OF SEVERAL CURRENCIES, DOMINATED BY THE DOLLAR, THE EURO AND THE YUAN

China's GDP is gradually becoming less and less dependent on foreign countries (the country's exports and imports have tended to reach a balance in recent years), and thus the fate of the yuan depends solely on domestic demand (investment and consumption). If China is able to expand its domestic demand so that it can be compared with that of the US, then there will be strong demand for yuan.

However, a process of erosion of the dollar as the main world currency is already underway. After China and Japan agreed not to use dollars in their mutual trade exchange, as well as in view of the fact that China pays for Iranian oil in yuan and settles accounts with Turkey in gold, the trend seems clear. Beijing is actively introducing a new monetary policy based on revaluating the national currency and increasing investments abroad.

Currently a covert internationalization of the yuan is being undertaken in order to make it an instrument for forming other countries' foreign exchange reserves. At the same time, China is continuing to rely on two institutional levers: the banking system and the industrial companies in backbone industries – metallurgy, chemistry and construction. Moreover, both the former and the latter are either state-owned or controlled by the state.

GLOBALIZATION: ARE WE UNDER THREAT OF LOSING JOBS DUE TO INNOVATION?

The speed of processing information directly determines safety issues, which means that this area is becoming increasingly dependent on innovations in the field of hardware. It was the transistor that became the element base that provided key innovations in this area. According to Moore's Law, the cost of transistors reduces by half every two years. In 1968, a transistor cost a dollar; today, a transistor costs 10 orders of magnitude less! The number of transistors in a chip has increased from 1 to 25 billion. When the military and the US government connected computers to make systems which were prototypes of the World Wide Web, we became totally dependent on computers and digital technology.

The statistics tell us that while only 15% of US households had computers in 1989, the respective percentage was 51% in 2000. In 2008, the total number of internet users exceeded 1 billion and the number of mobile telephone users exceeded 3 billion people.[185]

The use of PC software is widespread. A company may give a commission to do some work requiring the use of PC software to a professional located anywhere in the world and receive the output instantly in their office once the job is done. Manufacturing has become fast, flexible and mobile, and does not require the immediate presence of the labour force at the actual production site anymore. Thus, a new practice, called outsourcing, has come to be widely used by many companies, resulting in a reduction in their size. In the US, where outsourcing and cuts are practised most widely, the innovation sectors of the economy have, moreover, been able to maintain a stable downward trend in the unemployment rate until recently.

The wide spread of online trading changes our world no less significantly. China's success in this field is especially notable. In 2012, China's total annual amount of online commerce reached 3.1 trillion yuan (about US$440 billion), showing an increase of 43% on the 2007 figure.

Does this mean that the information revolution is becoming a panacea for humankind's ancient diseases? As with all of the good brought by the information revolution, this, like any other revolution, is double-edged. It is not only capable of creating additional value amazingly fast, but can also destroy wealth at no slower a speed. Examples of this are plentiful.

From 2000 to 2010, global online music sales grew 1,000 times, whereas global sales of music recorded on physical media shrank 2.5 times. The aggregate sales of music fell by 40% – from US$25 billion to US$15 billion. Roughly speaking, each dollar earned by selling music online caused, within this segment of the information revolution worldwide, the loss of three dollars in the sales of music recorded on physical media.

A similar fate has befallen the global news publishing industry. In 2000, 425,000 members of staff were employed by all US newspaper publishing houses and only 40,000 by US news online portals. Both had high qualifications and were paid very well. By 2009, however, only 150,000 members of staff remained working for all US newspaper publishers, as employment in this segment had shrank almost threefold! The number of employees of internet portals had increased, but only by half, to make 85,000 professionals. A total of 235,000 jobs were thus lost over a decade in the US news industry. Most of the remaining employees had lower qualifications, including the employees of internet portals.

This is a fundamentally new situation, when new technologies destroy venerable industries without creating adequate substitute employment for the people they have made redundant. It took time (25-30 years) for the car, the TV and the internet alike to progress from an invention to a mature product offered on the mass market. For example, many online media outlets replacing print media are already 10 to 15 years old, but most of them have never been able to create added value, staying unprofitable for all these years.

Quite often, it is the absence of an idea capable of generating added value that poses the main problem. Some kind of imitation of innovation is taking place instead. How do then such businesses that stay unprofitable for years find funding? Why are the 'fast' companies that have replaced the 'big' ones not always successful?

Just a few years ago, more than 90% of the broker companies in the leading stock markets were actively managing stocks and searching for points of growth, unique success stories, undervalued securities, and young and promising companies with great ideas. Only 10% were 'index' companies that just bought shares at their index value.

The situation today is exactly opposite: 90% of the money goes into index funds and only 10% into active management by professionals. More than 90% of all trading in the stock market is run by trading robots, which do not care about the investment characteristics, business ideas and corporate culture of the companies they deal with. Apparently, information technologies have only exacerbated the situation in the problem areas that usually lead to the inflation of financial bubbles and full-scale crises of the entire system.

———————————

Globalization has come to mean 'universality' of the global economy. However, according to the law of uneven development of complex systems, wealth accumulates unevenly around the world. America during the presidency of Richard Nixon made an important step by withdrawing China from the orbit of Soviet influence. The financial sector has finally become central to globalization. Money flows, huge in power and amplitude, have formed. Inflows of foreign capital are now followed by outflows during crises. Inflows of capital into a country are often significantly affected by the exchange rate of the country's currency in relation to the base currencies.

To generate growth in an era of a global 'information' economy, a global economic engine is required. During the last half century, the 'financial dipole' Chimerica has been acting in this capacity. China has been producing, and the US consuming, borrowing more and more at the expense of the public debt, which is helpful when faced with difficulties during crises. But during all these years, China has been stepping up its economic strength and foreign exchange reserves.

Wealth is flowing rapidly towards Asian countries, where the 'new middle' class is rapidly growing, expected to exceed the 'old middle' class of the West within the next two or three decades. This means that the East will get hold of the lucky clover again. But will the East make it flower this time? After all, 'a right is a privilege'.

Can anything stop this trend? To prevent it, Western companies will have to be very 'fast', because they will no longer be sufficiently 'large' in comparison with Asian companies. The right to have a share in the global wealth will have to be earned anew. Only 'live and fast' companies can provide a promising economic growth.

CHAPTER 13

A CRISIS OF COMMUNICATING VESSELS. HOW BUBBLES ARE INFLATED AND DEFLATED

Blow a soap bubble and observe it.
You may study it all your life and draw one lesson
after another in physics from it.

– William Thomson,
1st Baron Kelvin, a great British scientist

A CRISIS OF COMMUNICATING VESSELS

In the language of the Romans, the fluidity and mobility of water as its main properties came to be used with reference to 'good' money (and thus the Latin word 'liquidus' came to mean 'free of debt'). The word evolved in English, where the financial term 'liquidity', i.e. the ability of an asset to sell quickly at a market price, was coined. Literally translated, this word means 'fluidity'. The term is so good at conveying the essence of one of the most essential properties of assets that the principle of communicating vessels can be used now with reference to financial transactions, meaning that a pressure created by excessive liquidity (excess of money) in one local market immediately affects all other financial markets.

At the beginning of the last crisis, the money pressure from oil exporters became apparent. According to the McKinsey Global Institute, the worldwide cost of such assets as shares, private and corporate loans, and bank deposits soared from US$12 trillion (108% of the global GDP) in 1980 to US$195 trillion (355% of the global GDP) in 2007. The oil exporting countries, including Russia and Norway, Asian governments, and hedge funds and private equity funds, had accumulated enough capital and began to push aside traditional Western investors in their own markets.

The ratio of the value of the financial assets to the nominal GDP is called the 'depth' of the financial market. The growth of this index from 110% to 355% was a result of the swelling of the volume of bank deposits, shares and debt obligations, including government bonds, which stemmed from stimulated lending and increasing total debts.

Within the period from 2000 to 2008, the growth of the aggregate wealth of the BRIC countries and the mineral resource exporters, in conjunction with the increase in the total debt of the Big Three countries (the US, the EU and Japan), led to the creation of tens of trillions of dollars of additional financial capital. Where was this money put? The answer is obvious to the market: into liquid financial assets, such as shares, deposits and bonds, all denominated in US dollars.[186] In 2007, the US dollar was used as the key currency in international settlements, although it had begun to give up its dominating position. Payments for energy commodities accounted, and still account, for a quarter of all international trade transactions, of which 51% were conducted in dollars. The dollar is used in the accounting and valuation of foreign exchange reserves and assets and property, and also as the typical means of accumulation and preservation of wealth. The loan capital market is founded entirely on the dollar, which acts as a universal means of expressing wealth. The 2007 lending market was also typically estimated in dollars and all sales of oil and many mineral resource commodities were also carried out exclusively in dollars.

The resulting surplus of financial capital caused a significant reduction in yields on the US financial market and other markets related to it. The 2007 Dow Jones index remained at the 2000 level, while the interest rate on short-term US and European bonds fell to almost zero. Finance capital desperately needed liquid assets that would give higher returns. It became necessary to find a new communicating vessel and connect it to the system before any of the existing vessels burst (Figure 25) from the increased pressure. Of course, the word 'burst' is used in a figurative sense here.

The phenomenon of excessive capital liquidity is extremely controversial. On the one hand, excessive capital brings about delays during its circulation, prompting capital to transform into stocks, reserves and treasures. In this form, part of the savings and securities inevitably loses its value and cost. On the other hand, excess of capital inevitably creates a feeling of euphoria: capital loses the sense of risk and heads for hazardous activities, where proceeds are generally higher but losses are more likely to occur too.

We can assume that the participants of the financial market lost sharpness of risk perception at that point and their ability to assess reality reduced. Entrepreneurial intuition was replaced by technical analysis of stock quotes and extrapolation of current market trends. You will remember that it was during this period that so-called 'high-frequency' trading was brought into action, with computers making decisions in place of brokers with their intuition. Loans became more available and thus the engagement of a huge asset that had not yet been engaged by the financial sector – the global private housing market – was perfectly logical.

Totalling US$54 trillion in 2000, this market reached US$91 trillion by the beginning of 2008. The most active was the US real estate market, where millions of private homes were bought and sold with minimal difference in price. A minimum initial instalment was required to purchase a house, which had come down to 10% or below by the beginning of 2008. The new owners paid out the rest by taking out a loan secured by the acquired real estate. Such loans were given for 10 years at interest rates under 5% per annum and with the possibility of short-term financing at 1% per year! Building their judgment on statistics for the previous decade, rating agencies gave high investment-grade ratings to such obligations.

Deft investment banks grasped at the chance to take advantage of favourable market conditions and augment their investment in a growing market. 'Synthetic' products were created, in which the investor put part of the money in the purchase of structured financial products, took out a short-term loan at minimum interest (say, 1%), and then bought 5% yield mortgages with that money.

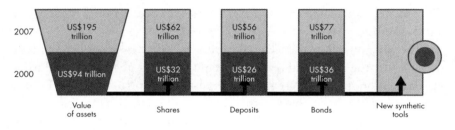

FIGURE 25. THE SYSTEM OF COMMUNICATING VESSELS IN THE US STOCK MARKET IN 2007

The new vessel in this 'magic system' kept the liquidity pressure well, but soon began to fail: people paid their mortgages as long as prices in the housing market were growing. Once the growth had slowed, prices began to fall and mass bond payment defaults occurred. Since the initial instalments for the purchase of homes were often less than 10%, and the interest on the mortgages was not required to be paid at first (it was accumulated and then distributed on future payments), it became in some cases more profitable to 'forget' about the initial instalment and purchase another, very real but greatly devaluated house. The liquidity pressure found this weak link, whose failure triggered the outbreak of the financial crisis. Already in 2008, the excess liquidity turned from an advantage into a disadvantage, virtually immobilizing numerous assets which had previously been liquid.

Still, there are some questions to be answered. How could a property market crisis have caused such a reduction in consumption and production? Why did the crisis that erupted in September 2008 become international? How could the bankruptcy of a number of investment banks, including Lehman Brothers, and defaults on several dozen thousands of home mortgages in the US (out of millions of such mortgages) have caused such turmoil in global financial and commodity markets? Let's use Lord Kelvin's advice: take a magnifying glass and look closely at the bubble.

HOME SWEET HOME

Housing in the 20th century had political significance in the US; in fact, this was the starting point for any politician at local and federal level alike. Work, car and home are the three pillars of the American way of life, the three components of the American Dream. By the beginning of the 21st century, wages and cars were good in the US, but housing proved to be the Achilles heel of the American prosperity concept.

It is important to note that the severity of the problem was that the housing market was critically short of affordable housing. In 1970, the nationwide demand for low-cost housing was almost completely satisfied: 6.5 million housing units were available for rent to 6.2 million low-profit tenants. But the volume of affordable accommodation remained at the same level, while the number of low-income tenants was steadily increasing and, by 2003, 14.4 million US households with very low incomes were in need of better housing conditions. More than 27% of all accommodation in the US was rented. This was rather a considerable figure – more than 33 million homes. But that was only half the problem. More than 15 million homes were put up for sale in anticipation of buyers, or were in poor condition and thus assigned for demolition and reconstruction first. The problem was acquiring political significance. For this reason alone, 2.2 million low-cost homes disappeared from the US market between 1973 and 1993.

The US authorities have been trying to solve this problem for a long time, though without much success. Huge subsidies simply remained undistributed because of low-income citizens lacking financial literacy and awareness of their rights and opportunities. Needless to say, the attachment of the real estate market to the financial system took place with the blessing of the US authorities and financial regulators. The US authorities required a point to apply economic forces to and they chose the US real estate sector.

In 2001, the policy of the US Federal Reserve System (an independent federal agency established on 23 December 1913, to perform central bank functions and exercise centralized control over commercial banking) caused a real estate boom by taking an unprecedented reduction in the discount rate: from 6.5% in May 2000 to 1% in June 2003. Cheap mortgages and a huge outflow of free funds from a low-yielding stock market provided the real estate business with previously unprecedented financial injections, which the government reinforced by a series of additional incentives: the procedure for granting loans to people who had bad credit histories and unconfirmed incomes was simplified, a long-term (40 years) mortgage was introduced, etc.

The result was not long in coming. A cursory glance at the Case–Shiller index chart overleaf (Figure 26) will be enough to see that what it depicts is the formation of a classic financial bubble.[187] The size of mortgage loans in the US grew from US$5.5 trillion at the end of 2001 to US$11 trillion by 2008. If considering the structured debt notes, the total soared to tens of trillions of dollars (Silver 2012, 33).

We see that the Case–Schiller index grew continuously from 1987 to 2006, resulting in a huge pyramid scheme building up over two decades. The ease of taking out a mortgage, the continuous reduction in the down payment percentage and the falling short-term rates made buying a home very similar to purchasing an option. You could pay as little as 10% or even less of the total price of a house, immediately take out another loan at a very low rate, pledging the house which you have not yet bought, and then resell the house two years later at a good profit guaranteed by constantly rising prices.

That initiated a whole mythology according to which personal success in life could be achieved without making special efforts at your main job: first you buy and resell houses (using tax breaks on interest payments) and then get a huge and unencumbered house at retirement, whose price is increasing every day. Then you sell the house and buy a property at half the money in the south, for example in Miami, and live off the other half nicely for the rest of your life! The myth proved attractive and robust and began to spread like a virus.

Many low-income earners enthusiastically plunged into the exciting process of real estate speculation, taking out mortgage loans without a second thought about their own financial capabilities and wholly relying on a quick resale. An army of mediators provided services in partial pre-payment of property, necessary for obtaining a mortgage loan, in exchange for a share in the acquired property. And, despite the daily warnings of an impending collapse, the homeowners still blindly believed that property prices would continue to rise!

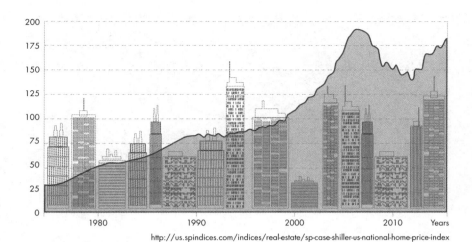

http://us.spindices.com/indices/real-estate/sp-case-shiller-us-national-home-price-index

FIGURE 26. THE CASE–SCHILLER INDEX, AN INDEX OF HOUSING PRICES IN
THE US' 20 LARGEST CITIES ACCORDING TO STANDARD & POOR'S

The abundant money supply at low interest rates set by federal funds (1% until 2004), considerably weakened lending standards and the household savings rate dropped from 3% to 0%!

The profits of Moody's Investors Service increased sharply owing to the inflow of liquidity into the market. The agency's proceeds from rating structured finance products grew from US$200 million in 2000 to US$900 million in 2007 (from 33-50% of the agency's aggregate earnings). And the company was expected to monitor the situation and inform the public, by ranking borrowers fairly, about the growing threats.

The multi-level bond market, secured by so-called synthetic products (credit default swaps, or CDSs) grew even more spectacularly than the mortgage loan market: from US$632 billion in 2001 to US$62 trillion in 2007 (Barnett-Hart 2009).

This surge in the amount of issued CDSs occurred exactly due to the connection of the whole US mortgage sector to the system of communicating financial vessels. Since real estate prices only grew, insurance companies, investment banks, mutual investment funds, pension funds and hedging companies, as well as private speculators, all took to selling and buying CDSs (Sorkin 2009). The largest numbers of such securities were issued by AIG insurance group and Lehman Brothers investment bank.[188] [189]

HOW CDSs WERE CREATED

The increasing complexity of the financial system resulted in the US banking system deciding to shift the traditional risks of payment defaults entirely onto insurance companies. This enabled the banks to make more loans without creating additional reserves in special government funds. To circumvent the state's requirements, the banking community and the insurers organized a conspiracy. Normally, a bank would have to insure its loan repayment default risks and the cost of such insurance would be quite high. Insurance companies were not keen on indemnifying loan repayment, because of having to be prepared to face an insurance case until full expiration of the term of the loan, and the insurance premiums were high.

In 1994, to promote the interests of financial groups and insurance companies, JPMorgan Chase, a US multinational banking and financial services holding company, created a new financial instrument which made it possible to separate credit risks from loan interest and to insure loans cheaper than under the traditional scheme, and so CDS (credit default swap) was developed. Company A produces a promissory note in the form of a corporate bond. Bank B buys the bond from Company A, but, receiving regular payments, the bank accepts the risk that Company A might go bankrupt. Then Bank B signs a deal with Insurance Company C, under which Bank B (the CDS buyer) regularly pays Insurance Company C (the CDS seller) a premium for all default risks related to the business of Company A.

If Company A ceases to fulfil its debt obligations, a so-called credit (insurance) event occurs and Bank B gives Company C the debt obligations of Company A, receiving the full value of the bond from the seller in exchange. This whole scheme relies on an incorrect mathematical model based on the assumption that all individual debtors are not linked to each other. As a result, the risk of default on securities was undervalued about 20,000 times.

The credit default swap is special in that it resembles a traditional insurance policy while not being one in reality. A CDS may insure any obligation (a supply contract, a bond, a promissory note, or a mortgage loan contract). As a result, the buyer and seller have in effect no relation to the subject of insurance. The unregulated status of credit default swaps made it possible to sell and buy a CDS an unlimited number of times without restriction, both at the stock exchange and privately.

DOWNHILL

If we go back to the Case–Schiller index (Figure 26), we can see that in 2006 real estate prices stabilized briefly and then rapidly declined. The fact of the matter is that while demand for new homes was growing (until the end of 2005), the stock market did not manage to recover from the recent crisis. And since the two were interconnected, the total pressure remained normal. All this time, property replaced proceeds from the once profitable stock-market.

With the recovery of the stock market, the Federal funds rate rose and all other interest rates followed, including mortgage lending rates. This instantly broke the on-lending scheme and lending costs increased. Borrowers could not even manage current payments. Defaults cascaded, followed by housing being put up for sale.[190] Sub-prime borrowers realized that their debts significantly exceeded the value of the homes they had mortgaged.

The first signal that the situation was becoming really serious came in 27 February, 2007, when the Dow Jones index fell. On 13 March, 2007, a second collapse occurred on the market. Its exact cause was established immediately: the NYSE administration had removed the shares of New Century Financial Corporation from trading.[191] Since the beginning of 2007, the company's shares had fallen by 90%. By that time, it was already quite clear for experts that the US property market had caused a 'financial earthquake'.

Other private companies and banks, seeing the example of New Century and realizing that a similar fate awaited them too as a result of the mass sub-prime loan payment defaults, first tightened their mortgage lending policies and then stopped mortgage lending almost completely, unless provided with 100% guarantees by the government. The situation had become critical: the cost of the debts had exceeded the value of the mortgages. In this situation, it was easier for borrowers to give up the homes rather than pay the monthly payments.

The mass refusals to repay loans were followed by bank interest rates starting to rise in order to take account of the new risks and this, in turn, caused a further increase in the size of monthly mortgage fees. The rush of non-payments caused another wave of defaults. Banks raised lending rates again, thereby contributing to a new increase in monthly payments. The system had established a strong positive relationship and it was now impossible to stop the impending avalanche.

A loan insurance system was supposed to act as a 'safety valve' for the mortgage sector. This is exactly how it had worked before. The sector was connected to the system of communicating vessels: a bank provided a loan to a client and, if the client stopped paying the fees, the bank simply took the house for sale on another, disconnected market. But things changed dramatically in 2006. Together with mortgages, all the derivatives of these securities became problematic too. Those who sold CDSs suddenly found themselves obliged to buy impaired securities at their full original value. Since CDSs were securities, not insurance policies, their value was determined by supply and demand on a regulated and unregulated market, a market whose trading volumes were several times greater than the amount of mortgage loans. CDS dealers were unable to meet their obligations and banks received worthless pieces of paper instead of houses.

In August 2007, the entire US financial market entered a spell of hardship, which was immediately identified as a period of 'market dysfunction'. The sharp rise in interest rates for short-term commercial papers and interbank loans led to a contraction of the money supply and a sharp deterioration in liquidity. All financial communicating vessels turned out to be connected to CDSs and an unprecedented systemic crisis erupted – a crisis that was now affecting a whole system of communicating vessels.

In these circumstances, even reliable clients (e.g. manufacturers) had difficulty in obtaining short-term financial resources. After the money market, the crisis affected other markets and institutions, prompting now longer-term problems.

In September, it was the turn of such financial giants as Lehman Brothers, one of the oldest financial investment companies in America, AIG, America's major insurer and, finally, Washington Mutual to go bankrupt. It became clear that the financial vessels, which had for many years served the system faithfully, had sprung a leak and the market was experiencing another shock, comparable with the greatest stock exchange disasters in history. The Dow Jones lost 504 points and the crisis began to spread outside the United States.

The Federal Reserve System – the last giant vessel in the system of financial communicating vessels – had to allocate US$85 billion to nationalize AIG, but confidence in the market was undermined and the Dow Jones Industrial Average fell another 450 points. By the end of 2008, the Fed had provided support to a number of credit institutions which had lost their money to the amount of US$1.5 trillion. In exchange, US banks provided the US government with securities whose value on the market did not exceed US$62.5 billion. Later, Henry Paulson (who was Secretary of the Treasury in 2006–2009) carried out the last operation: he convinced the US Congress to allocate another US$700 billion.

That was how the bubble that formed in the property market and developed into a global financial crisis burst. Let us ask a few simple questions.

Was there a chance to prevent the crisis? Was there a person who knew the weakness of the system and could have prevented the development of the crisis?

This may seem strange, but we know the exact answer to this question. On 18 February 2009, Reuters circulated a prognosis made by Alan Greenspan, former head of the Federal Reserve.[192] Greenspan said that the current financial recession would be the longest and deepest since 1930, and would require huge cash injections into the national economy from the government. Asked whether the US government could have done anything about the mortgage bubble that had formed shortly before the crisis, Greenspan said the following: "I think it would have been good to find a way to suppress the bubble. But I am sceptical about this possibility" (Tuccille 2002). Among the key points of the crisis, the ex-head of the Fed highlighted the following: destruction of the economy, unstable real estate prices, falling stock prices, unprecedented financial assistance to the private sector and fear of the future on a scale unknown by a whole generation of Americans. Greenspan forgot to mention one thing in that interview: it was not only Americans that had to pay for the outbreak of consumer spending in the United States. It was primarily paid for with foreign money and this is why the crisis acquired a planetary significance. Huge numbers of new global financial market players, who had suddenly become wealthy owing to soaring commodity prices (oil, metals, etc.) sought to invest "in the most reliable economy in the world" and thus promoted the American consumers' reckless spending.

History teaches us that few learn from the mistakes of others'. Since the 'tulipomania' in 17th century Holland, the first well-documented and thoroughly described financial bubble, humankind has been looking for a clue as to why markets sometimes overheat and then fall. One of the first attempts to analyse the problem was *Geschichte der Handelkrisen* (The History of Trade Crises), a book by Max Wirth, published in 1877. Based on historical documents, the author tells us about many crises of which at least two are worth considering here.

TULIPOMANIA 1634–1638

At the end of the 16th century, tulip bulbs were imported to the Netherlands from Turkey, to be grown by floriculturists and gardeners. The bright colours of the flowers fascinated the main trendsetters of Europe, such as the court of Louis 13th, which meant that the proliferation of the flowers all around Europe was just a matter of time.

The Dutch managed to grow more than a thousand varieties of this flower, different in shape and colour, over a short period of time, due to a certain virus which caused the tulips to react by mutation.[193] As a result of the mutation, unique and hence expensive flowers appeared.

This set of circumstances resulted in tulip bulbs becoming a commodity that fetched good earnings and tulip bulb prices began to rise steadily in 1630. New varieties were bred very slowly at first and tulips were rare flowers for the Dutch until 1630.[194] In 1630, the demand for tulip bulbs rose sharply due to a sudden increase in the welfare of the country's population.

There was a shortage of labour in the Netherlands (due to a recent plague that had struck the country), which led to an increase in wages and accumulation of cash by the ordinary people. The Netherlands were a union of provinces that was experiencing one of the first major economic upswings in its history. An influx of silver from America and great success in trade and crafts created unique conditions for the emergence and rapid development of a financial sector. The ample money supply created an atmosphere in which speculation and investments were critically needed, and the tulip trade gave vent to these aspirations.

The pragmatic Dutch quickly noticed the growth and began to invest in the inconspicuous flower bulbs. Investing in flowers turned into a profitable business which did not require much starting capital. Anyone could do it.

Very soon, a positive feedback mechanism had formed in this peculiar market. The bigger the demand for flowers, the higher the prices went, and more people were willing to put their money in the purchase and resale of flowers. Before long, bulbs were traded by weight, measured in units borrowed from gold traders.

As the market grew, payments in kind – with clothes, dishes, poultry, cattle – came to be accepted. Tulip bulb prices had reached dizzying heights. Historical records report that in the peak of the tulipomania, 2,500 guilders was paid for a bulb. That was the cost of two wagons of wheat, four wagons of hay, several oxen, twelve sheep, two barrels of butter and 500 kilograms of cheese!

Real passions raged around tulips. Alexandre Dumas described the intrigues of those years in his novel *The Black Tulip*, asserting that the Dutch had begun to worship the flower and to make more of a cult of it than naturalists ever dared to make of the human race for fear of arousing the jealousy of God himself (Dumas 2000).

At a certain point, something happened that usually happens in an artificially overheated financial market: a bulb put up for sale brought its owner only 1,000 guilders instead of the expected 1,250. This news quickly spread throughout the country and the market crumpled overnight.

Despite the impoverishment of large numbers of people, the tulip market crash did not seriously affect the economic development of the Netherlands – the country did not fall into a depression or stagnation. Before the financial bubble was inflated, tulip bulb prices were low, but volatile. The tulip fever clearly demonstrated that the lower the starting capital threshold and the softer the contractual terms, the higher the price of the commodity may rise.

Keeping a financial pyramid intact requires a continuous influx of new members and money. Once this source dries up, a collapse is inevitable. In January 1637, all possible derivatives which the improvised Dutch stock market could come up with had been used. Even the cheapest varieties of tulips became so expensive that no new stakeholders could enter the market.

All financial bubble mechanisms always involve the same stages. First, rampant enrichment achieved by fraud; then, when the fraud is revealed, the victims demand revenge. Why do investors have good sense before the bubble has begun to inflate and lose it when the bubble is already inflated and the price of the asset is clearly absurd? The answer is simple: a loan taken out to maintain speculation clouds the mind. Why think when the assets are growing in value? Credit inflation is encouraged by all market participants until it reaches such a grotesque level where the 'clever ones' start to take their money out of the superheated market. A big boom is always followed by a boom in either technology or business.

**STILL LIFE WITH
SPRING FLOWERS,
JEAN BENNER.**
Gouache on brown paper

TULIPOMANIA REINCARNATED

The Dutch tulipomania is not a unique phenomenon in history. In 1838, a narcissus fever broke out in France. At that time, the narcissus was, just as the tulip had been in its time, a new flower in Europe: it had been brought from Mexico in 1790. At the peak of the narcissus fever, a beige narcissus cost as much as a middle-sized diamond. In 1912, a gladioli boom broke out, originating in Holland again. In 1985, a similar situation occurred in China with a lily variety known as the red spider lily. This flower was grown in Africa and was introduced to China in the 1930s. The mania broke out after the economic reforms in China proved successful and massive foreign investments ensued. In 1985, the price of a red spider lily reached 200,000 yuan, or US$50,000. Red spider lily prices collapsed after a Chinese newspaper published an article about the tulipomania in the Netherlands in the 17th century.

THE FALSE LOGIC OF JOHN LAW

John Law was one of the most famous Scotsmen in history. From an early age, Law had a passion for risk and an eagerness to win. He was big-hearted, generous, extravagant and ready to put millions to the wind at any moment. He was extremely fortunate during the first half of his life, being loved by beauties and incredibly lucky at the card table and in throwing dice. That was rather a questionable luck, but still the death penalty was replaced by imprisonment, from which he was again lucky to escape by jumping from a 10-metre tower and getting away safe and sound, only slightly injuring a leg.

He later served as minister of finance of the most powerful country in continental Europe and finished his life in exile, under a hail of curses. His legacy, which went down in the history of world finance as Law's system, best characterizes his short but very active five-year financial endeavour (1716-1721).

JOHN LAW'S INNOVATIONS

It was in France during the Regency, when Philippe d'Orléans ruled the country, that Law conducted his financial experiments. By that time, the country's financial system had been utterly devastated: as a result of con-tinuous wars, the extravagance of Louis 14th, and extortion and outright theft on the part of tax farmers (tax agents), the second half of the reign of Louis 14th had seen the country lose nearly half of its national wealth. Louis 14th died in 1715, leaving his great-grandson (Louis 15th) a legacy consisting of a 2-billion public debt and thoroughly empty national cof-fers. The great-grandson was a seven-year-old boy and the country came under the rule of the regent of Louis 15th, Philippe d'Orléans. He was a clever man, though prone to vices, extravagance and laziness.

When he arrived in Paris, John Law became acquainted with d'Orléans, as the two men had the same vices. Law's financial talents were already legendary in the Netherlands, even before his escape from England. Then he was fascinated by the idea of creating a new type of bank, the principles of arranging which he outlined in his work *Money and Trade Considered*. Seeing the lack of money as the main problem of a national economy, he believed that the amount of cash – and the national wealth too – could be increased by replacing precious metal with something less rare.

But it was only in France of all countries that his idea found support. Philippe d'Orléans was so enthused with Law's project that he permitted him to open a bank and start printing paper money. Having obtained, by intrigue and thanks to a happy coincidence, the position of Comptroller General (the cashier of the King), Law used paper money to develop industry and remove trade barriers.

To understand Law's real innovations, let's turn to a few historical facts. In the days of Louis 14th, Law's predecessors, seeking to replenish the royal coffers, had established a complex hierarchy of new official posts. Hundreds of thousands of financial commissaries, treasurers and royal secretaries had entered the king's employ. Obviously, trading activities were depressed by continuous extortions practised by this army of bureaucrats.

Law's reform took full control of the payment of various direct and indirect taxes. A company founded by Law managed the collection of all taxes through the efforts of just 30 directors. Instead of fiddling around with a legion of independent and unreliable financial agents, the government had now to deal with Law's company only.

Both the country and the royal purse immediately benefited from this change: the taxes were now levied under less pressure and paid with greater accuracy. With the stroke of a pen, a variety of onerous duties which had been levied by the king's agents on grain, bread, meat, coal, etc. were abolished. Trade began to grow quickly and taxes were paid on time. The trust in government bonds had been restored and Law's banknotes were now valued more than gold coins.

A BANK AND A COMPANY

Through the efforts of his enemies, John Law was soon obliged to switch to the establishment of a company which was to play a central role in the development of Louisiana (the French province in the basin of the Mississippi River, named after Louis 14th).

Law suggested creating a joint-stock company whose shares were intended for sale to the widest range of people and could be freely traded on stock exchanges. In August 1717, the Mississippi Company began to prepare an issue of 200,000 shares on offer. As Law was already well known and trusted, many people were eager to buy shares in the new enterprise. Soon, the company was granted an exclusive right to trade with 'both Indies' (the US and India) and was renamed the Company of the Indies. This spurred demand for its stocks.

Law's house, where the shares were distributed, was besieged by a throng of people who wished to have a share in the Mississippi riches. The success brought Law fame and popularity. Agitation also reigned on the Company of the Indies' secondary stock market. On Rue Quincampoix in Paris, a stock exchange was spontaneously formed whilst the share prices continued to grow. Some people were killed for shares in the company and some even committed suicide, while John Law enjoyed nationwide recognition and respect, because everyone who wanted to get rich could do so quickly thanks to his two great innovations: the bank and the company.

Never before had so many luxury goods been sold in Paris. Statues, paintings and tapestries, which had previously been the privileged property of the nobility, moved now to the homes of middle-class Parisians. The whole situation had taken such a serious turn that edicts had to be issued for employees to return immediately to their places of work on pain of dismissal, since masses of people had stopped working and plunged into speculation. John Law's authority had grown so much that he was soon appointed Controller General of Finances of France.

THE BANK THAT WENT BUST

While Law was fully engaged in the establishment of the company, his bank, which had become France's de facto central bank, continued to issue paper money, or loans. People spent these loans mainly to buy shares in Law's company, which were also issued continuously. The proceeds were used to buy government bonds. After some time, Law's company became the largest and, finally, the only creditor of the treasury.

Of course, not only aristocrats, traders and dealers became millionaires, but also many members of the general public, such as merchants, shoemakers and servants. Soon, the most intelligent of them realized that it would be wise to materialize their profits by buying tangible assets. Actually, it was Law himself who set an example of such action by buying numerous estates in France.

Soon, some people realized how the whole progression would end, visited the bank and demanded that their paper money be exchanged for coins. These people were becoming more and more numerous and exchanged millions in paper money for gold and silver. The gold and silver reserve of the Royal Bank was melting away quickly. As Controller General of Finances, Law issued decrees to limit such exchange, but this did not improve the situation. All subsequent actions taken by Law in order to stabilize the exchange rate of the paper money bore the unmistakable imprint of confusion. Prohibitions to exchange banknotes for jewellery or precious stones followed. The nation's love for Law, which had reached its utmost limit, was now rapidly turning into hatred.

A revolutionary situation formed, where no one wanted to defend the authorities. It was only by fleeing that Law saved himself.

FINITA LA COMEDIA[195]

In December 1720, Law fled from Paris to Brussels. Law's own possessions had been confiscated, and all he was able to take away was a small amount of money and a large diamond. He made a living by gambling. On many occasions, he had to pawn his only diamond, but his luck never ran out and he always managed to redeem the jewel.

John Law spent the last years of his life in Venice, where he wrote a voluminous book titled *The History of Finance during the Regency*, where he attempted to justify his doings.

Law died from pneumonia in 1729, but his idea of a central bank is still alive. Since then, the world has repeatedly forgotten about the dangers of issuing money, and many economists, top managers of central banks and politicians accepted the idea of monetarism so irrevocably that they started to believe it themselves, arguing that prosperity can only be ensured by means of monetary pumping up.

Law's logic inevitably led to the acquisition of new assets in the form of paper money and, furthermore, gave birth to the persistent myth that it was possible to solve any problems by simply printing money. And this myth is still alive and will never die, but will continue reappearing as an unlucky clover in history many times, in different countries and in different eras.

DEMOGRAPHY MATHEMATICS

Why do people invest their money on a short-term rather than long-term basis? Why do they often act so recklessly? The short answer is that the opportunity to make money today outweighs the risk of losing it tomorrow. There is also a more detailed and more scientific answer to this question, the essence of which is that demography is the reason for everything. Let's turn once again to the 'perpetrators' of the last global financial crisis – the aged generation of US baby boomers.

The 1980s demographic surge produced rather a surprising result: there were too many baby boomers and they were hardly able to reach the standard of living their parents had enjoyed. This was the first generation that preferred to borrow instead of making savings for old age. By 1999, more than half of this generation had a credit card debt of more than US$10,000, while the debt burden of the average American family exceeded US$8,000 (Bonner 2000).

But the overall economic effect seemed to be a panacea for the economy. By 2001, this line of action resulted in every percentage point of the GDP growth being matched by 4.8% of new debts. Thanks to this historically unprecedented credit expansion and due to the baby boomers increasing their personal debts, the US economy was booming. The reason for this phenomenon is well known. Observing their own stock portfolios advancing in price, the Americans developed a false sense of their wealth increasing. Little attention was paid to the unprecedented level of arrears.

At the turn of this century, American economist, Harry S. Dent Jr., made a number of predictions about the future of the US economy, which proved to be correct in many respects. He predicted that a span starting in 2008 would see deflation of the economic bubble that had been growing with the support of the baby boomers' generation. The deflation was expected, quite naturally, to be accompanied by a sharp reduction in spending. As we know now, the actual amount of real estate transactions did fall by 70-80% as a result of measures taken to correct the uncontrolled growth of the country's sovereign and private debt.

The method Dent used to make his predictions (the Dent Method) is a long-term economic forecasting tool based on demographic trends. It is used to predict the long-term development of an economy. According to this method, the behaviour of a consumer is determined by his/her age (the stage of life they are in). During certain phases of our lives, our expenditures are very predictable. Information about how we spend money today and what we buy at different stages of our lives is used to predict how the aggregate expenditure will change over the next few decades.

Private consumption accounts for about 70% of the US gross domestic product and has the most significant impact on the country's economic wellbeing. When a large group of a country's population spend more, the economy grows. Once such a group has passed its peak of expenditure, the economy starts to experience a slowdown. Waves of demand generated by different generations 'roll in' every 40 years. Consequently, it is not too difficult to predict the development of an economy by analysing its spending and saving cycles, as such cycles are largely defined by demographic factors. The peak of a citizen's personal expenditure usually takes place between the ages of 40 and 50, when the children have grown up and are either studying at university or already working (Figure 27).

According to Dent's logic, total expenditure in an economy correlates with the population that has reached 40 years of age but has not yet passed the 50-year milestone.

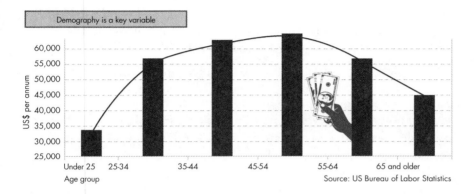

FIGURE 27. THE AVERAGE EXPENDITURES OF AMERICANS DEPENDING
ON THEIR AGE (AS OF LATE 2014 – EARLY 2015)

Using the Dent Method to forecast is simple: all you have to do is examine how a demographic situation develops along the timeline. For example, since fewer babies were born during the 1929 Great Depression than years earlier or later, the number of middle-aged people 40 years later, i.e. between 1968 and in the early 1970s, also dropped, owing to which consumption fell and the economy began to stagnate.

The next wave of expenditure, caused by the baby boom that had taken place in the 1950s and the early 1960s, was seen over the years from the late 1990s until 2008. It was this unusually large post-war generation of baby boomers that made the stock market work.

But 40 years after 1968, i.e. the year when the previous recession started, everything repeated again, following an already well known scenario. The consumption in the population group with the highest personal consumption, aged 40-50 years, fell again, the housing market crumbled and a global financial crisis broke out.

The expenditure in the dominant and largest group of population at the peak of its revenues stimulates economic growth. This, in turn, provides companies with profits and, ultimately, causes share prices to go up on the stock market. Of course, stock market fluctuations are caused by a great number of other factors which are psychological in origin and very volatile in the short term, but in the long term, all trends average out and add up to produce a clear picture.

Today, Dent's conclusions are shared by many in the US.[196] The country is at a crossroads (Dent 2011). Will it be able to revise its lifestyle, characteristic of the 'tumultuous 2000s'? Will it be able to get rid of the impressive debt, or will America be faced, like Japan was in the 1980s, with a lack of economic growth and high debt? Who will be holding the four-leaf clover?

———————

Having observed the evolution of finance over several centuries, humanity has learned many ways to attract capital and invest it so as to promote economic growth – and has achieved great heights in this art.

Today, as we see, the financial market is based on expectations, since the evaluation of any company with a view to making investment decisions is based on expectations of future profits. It is clear that the reasonably expected accuracy of a business plan does not go beyond a few years, and it is only within these limits that an investor can roughly predict and estimate the expected amounts of dividends, cash flows and financial results. Today, however, this amount makes up no more than 30% of the future value of the company and the remaining value is based on expectations of earnings over the next 20 years of its operation.

It turns out that the financial system is based on market expectations and on investors' belief that this or that company will make a profit, rather than on the company's actual financial performance. After all, leading US companies operating on a global scale, such as Tesla, Google and Facebook, do not earn substantial profits. Their huge capitalisation has been formed on the basis of expectations of their future profitability. It appears that by selling their shares, an investor may, as it were, take money from the future.

As a result, developed countries can thrive while having huge budget deficits and external debts that exceed their annual GDPs. Indeed, their stability and success instil more confidence than the stability and success of other countries, and, consequently, their economies see more investment. In fact, this phenomenon is driven by the belief that the financial and economic systems of these countries will do with the investors' money what they have been able to do before: invent new technology chains which will once again bring about economic growth.

Huge amounts of money have accumulated in deposit accounts around the world. This is the result of people's belief that they can get the money back with interest on the one hand and the US and Europe's willingness to borrow the money and secure further economic growth on the other.

In such a paradigm, wealth becomes dependent on the expectations of people, and expectations are known to form the basis of knowledge which enables the assessment of business and its prospects. However, the problem is that there is no such thing as absolute knowledge of the future.

CHAPTER 14

KALEIDOSCOPE OF INNOVATION – HOW TO LOOK BEYOND THE HORIZON

" It is those who risk nothing who risk the most... "

– Ivan Bunin

It was English physicist David Brewster who first created the kaleidoscope in 1814 as a spin-off from his experiments in the polarization of light. Brewster was quick enough to realize that the device was more than a mere optical toy and patented it in 1817 under the name 'kaleidoscope' (from the Greek words meaning 'beautiful', 'form', and 'see'). Even today, all kaleidoscopes resemble the prototype: they always include mirrors that are arranged at an angle to each other and divide a circular object field into a number of parts, and the observer's eye is positioned as close as possible to the seam between the mirrors, where the picture is evenly lit. Any objects that occur in the space between the two mirrors are reflected in them, and so are their reflections and the reflections of the reflections. A symmetrical pattern is thus formed, which, moreover, comes alive with each shake of the kaleidoscope.

The history of humankind, presented in the preceding chapters, can be seen through a four-leaf clover prism. As the tube turns, the newly formed pattern suggests that a particular stage of development will focus on innovation. As the device is given a stronger shake, the old pattern is destroyed and a new one comes in its place. In this way, you can even look into the near or distant future. Let's just imagine the four-leaf clover model as part of a more complex design – an imaginary kaleidoscope where the clover's petals have turned into beads of glass to refract the light of future events.

Two centuries ago, Brewster failed to make money from his invention, despite its enormous popularity. His patent described two mirrors put inside a tube. Manufacturers and traders found it profitable to add a third mirror in order to avoid paying royalties and get around Brewster's patent. Consequently, the kaleidoscope went beyond laboratory walls, conquering both America and Europe and paving the way for other optical toys, which in turn brought about the invention of animation and cinema a few generations later.

The world can be perceived through an imaginary kaleidoscope, divided it into two parts: the history that has taken place and is visible, and the future, consisting of our images and thoughts that are expected to channel the flow of life in the best possible direction.

The image of a mirror is always a reflection of our way of life, of our behaviour and aspirations. The content of our world is a reflection of our own selves, a consequence of our desires, preferences and actions. We ourselves shape the future, and shape it at this very moment, by turning the kaleidoscope!

Pushing off from the current moment, like a reflection off the surface of a mirror, I will modify the history issues referred to in previous chapters as if 'mirroring' them, in order to discern the contours of future innovations by adding a third mirror to our kaleidoscope (Table 10). For convenience of presentation, let's group the 'mirrored' issues in three broad categories:
- Finance and globalization;
- New industrial revolution and future technologies;
- Artificial superintelligence and new traps set up by progress.

HISTORY ISSUES	MIRRORED QUESTIONS
A communicating vessels crisis: How bubbles are inflated and deflated	1. How do we avoid bursting with a new financial bubble?
Globalization: How high demand for oil changes the essence of globalisation	2. How will the universal craving for innovation change the content of globalisation once again in the future?
How innovation economy works	3. How will new wealth be created? How does the evolution business work?
Scientific, technological and information revolution: How nuclear and space technology, aided by the Creative Class, brought innovation to the fore	4. How does innovative economy bring the Creative Class to history's fore? The future of work
Technological revolution: How electricity, the automobile, oil and nitrogen created our prosperity	5. What do 'green' technologies promise?
Industrial Revolution: How the steam engine 'advanced' the capitalist West towards the East	6. New industrial revolution. Industry 4.0
The great geographical discoveries and colonization: How the old world and the new world collided	7. Great space voyages: Colonising planets

HISTORY ISSUES	MIRRORED QUESTIONS
Commercial and banking revolution: How wars were financed	8. How will new conflicts and wars be financed?
Scientific revolution: How the world changed owing to the printing press	9. A new paradigm: knowledge as a source of wealth
The power of empires: How the power of gold emerged	10. How do we find a replacement for gold?
Neolithic revolution and the first civilizations: How to get out of traps set up by progress	11. How shall we discern new traps set up by progress?
Separation of man from biological evolution	12. Evolution of synthetic biology. Creativity of artificial intelligence

TABLE 10. HISTORY ISSUES AND CORRESPONDING
NEW ISSUES OF THE FUTURE

HOW TO AVOID BURSTING WITH A NEW FINANCIAL BUBBLE

The 2008-2009 global financial crisis only aggravated the problems and contradictions inherent in the global financial system, but did not change its essence. Any change in the current expectations of the future (that future being, by definition, uncertain and multivariate) still affects to a large degree the estimates of expected cash flows and will, therefore, continue to contribute to the emergence of financial bubbles. Apart from figures and ratings, risky investment decisions need to be counterbalanced with common sense.

MINSKY MOMENT[197]

It is a widely known postulate in the corporate finance world that the managers of heavily indebted companies, when acting in the interests of their shareholders, often favour risky projects (Brealey 1980). With the debt leverage growing and the prospects of future financial flows becoming vaguer, the managers' predisposition towards risk becomes ever greater.

Recently, venture capital, which is an integral part of the financial market, has been increasingly used to finance such risk. The basis of any financial system is the observance of clear rules based on mutual confidence established between financial market participants. But what if the rules are broken?

Then clients do not trust banks and funds anymore and take away their money, while banks do not trust clients and refuse loans. All parties are 'sitting', as it were, on their money.

As the recent financial crisis has shown, governments choose the simplest possible way to make up for a lack of money in their countries' economies by simply printing more of it. As former US President Ronald Reagan aptly noted on one occasion, "…the Government does not solve problems, it finances them." The global crisis, that broke out 2008-2009, was successfully 'quenched' with money. Having noticed a fall in the monetary aggregate M2, Ben Bernanke, the then head of the Federal Reserve System, compensated for the lack of money in the economy with printed dollars. The alternative would have been a repeat of the Great Depression.

But as soon as the crisis of confidence in the banking sector was over, money gushed once again into the system from banks and funds resuming their operation and started to raise the pressure. Once again, the architects needed to find a connected pot to keep savings in safety. Some of the industries, based on the technologies of the future, will, no doubt, act as the new pot and the pressure will be brought back to normal. Meanwhile, the number of start-ups is growing, and so are the numbers of risky and adventurous projects that have found funding. The excessive liquidity is manifested in the form of debts made by venture capital funds and equity raised by high-risk start-ups. But the general economic conditions are the same for both start-ups and established companies. They are cyclical in nature, which means that after receiving money injections for some time, many high-risk companies will only be able to pay interest alone, as a result of which companies and funds, trying to avoid going bankrupt, will have to take new loans regularly in order to repay old ones. The top management in such circumstances will go for more and more risky projects which will mainly benefit shareholders as a result of capital reallocations made as part of modifying the financing structure.

This process may even be relatively smooth for a while, but just as long as interest rates do not go up. A slight rise or drop in a high-risk firm's cash flow will be sufficient to turn inevitably its financing into a financial pyramid. In that case, there may not be enough money even for the regular payment of interest. A Minsky moment comes.[198] The inflated bubble must burst and the pressure in the 'financial pot' drops, together with the market participants' confidence.

Generally speaking, it is quite possible that the 2008 crisis could have been predicted. However, it only became evident at the very last moment that the economy would collapse and the central banks of developed countries would have to take unprecedented measures.

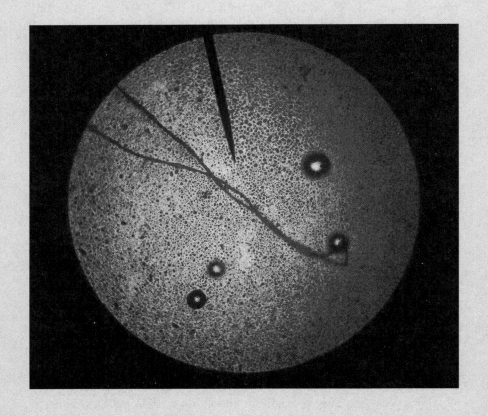

AN 'ILLUMINATING' MOMENT

To illustrate the point, I chose, at random, Illumina, a company specializing in genomics. In 2012, the company invented a next-generation sequencer, capable of providing a full transcript of the genome of a particular person for just $1,000.

In 2013, Illumina invested almost half a billion dollars in Verinata, a start-up company with a unique technique that made it possible to decipher the DNA of an unborn baby. Verinata at that time made virtually no profit.

The investor (Illumina), whose book value totalled $3 billion with long-term debts amounting to $800 million, had a market capitalization of $23 billion, while its annual receipts made just over $300 million. It turns out that the company's P/E (stock price to earnings) ratio was not some 10 or 20, but 97!

In other words, the price of one share was 97 times greater than the current annual profit made by the company on each share! This means that the current rate of return on invested capital, excluding future growth, was 1%. What would a company do in such circumstances? It would most likely get involved in more risky projects, constantly stirring up interest in itself, because anyone investing $97 per share would want to capitalize on its price growing further rather than on innovation! The mechanism will work accurately until a certain point, the Minsky moment, or until the expectations of future profits are reduced.

The Minsky moment reminds us that it is not enough in breakthrough areas to gather engineers, scientists and entrepreneurs in a company. It also has to be ensured that the capital structure of the emerging innovative company is strong enough to survive a fall in the 'financial pressure'.

CONCENTRATION OF COMMON SENSE

Of course, not every high-risk company is a poorly estimated speculation, not at all. Verinata, for instance, has a great idea behind it: to decipher the DNA of unborn babies through quite harmless manipulation involving taking the maternal blood and finding the foetal DNA. The company operates in the highly attractive personalized medicine industry which, once successful, will enable doctors to recommend each particular patient a course of treatment and prevention based on their genetic data. What threats might confront this business, as the population (and hence the number of potential patients) is increasing daily? The main risk to the success of such a company is not posed by the particular market it operates in, but by the condition of the common financial market, i.e. by the current financial 'pressure'.

How do investors reduce such risks normally? They act on the well known advice given by Paul Samuelson (author of *Economics*): "Since we cannot predict the future, we diversify." The trick of substituting uncertainty by the concept of risk, proposed by Frank Knight long ago, does work to some extent (Knight 1921). By putting eggs in different baskets, investors reassure themselves that they eliminate the risk of loss, even when investing some of their funds in the most risky projects (explicitly reckless undertakings to a certain extent).

The high-water mark of this approach was formulated by William Bernstein. According to his concept (Bernstein 2000), an investor who has invested 25% in reliable bonds, 25% in large companies' shares, 25% in high-risk shares (these exactly are found in innovative industries), and 25% in well known foreign companies' shares, is highly likely to have protected himself from potential losses.

Bernstein's main idea was to concentrate common sense and use arrays of information available to us today. His approach to processing information required in selecting businesses (ones based on competitive business schemes) resembles the four-leaf clover model. Though, instead of four leaves, he distinguishes four types of knowledge: knowledge of the theory of finance, knowledge of the history of markets, knowledge of investment psychology and knowledge of how the industry in which money is to be invested works.

This proves to be sufficient for many companies and even individuals, to manage their money effectively or earn a decent pension.

That said, for a particular investor, it is sufficient, as it safeguards them against losing to the market. As the GDP per capita in the world is increasing in real terms by 2% annually, 2% of real earnings, purified from inflation, are required in order to guarantee a 'sufficient' level of wealth preservation. However, this approach is based on the assumption that there will be those who provide the 2% growth (Bernstein 2000). Will the technologies designed to ensure new growth be 'supportive' or 'disruptive'? Will they undermine the basics of the existing 'fundamental economics', or will they support it?

OVERCOMING DECREASING RETURNS ON CAPITAL

The persistent pursuit of sustainable growth by financial institutions has already resulted in the appearance of a number of impressive theoretical insights. A little-known economist, Paul Romer, authored an article (Romer, 1986) in which he formulated the thesis that it is possible to overcome diminishing returns on capital if the capital is considered as a broad term and includes human capital (Sharaev, 2006, p.91).

An increase in workers' capital-to-labour ratio creates opportunities to train workers and gain and accumulate new knowledge. New knowledge is thus converted into productive force and is accumulated in the same way as financial capital.[199]

Some interesting and very important consequences are derived from Paul Romer's approach. The first was formulated by Romer himself and states that, with the capital-to-labour ratio growing, the total output of the economy increases as well, and does so at an accelerating pace, which, in its turn, leads to even higher capital-to-labour ratios. This 'economic perpetual motion machine' may seem amusing at first, but think about it for a second: how many times have you changed your computer or operating system over the last 10 years? With each such change taking place, the content of your work (not your performance) is likely to have remained the same. This model explains the increase in the sales of such companies as Microsoft or Apple.

The second consequence logically derives from the first. To ensure economic growth, it is necessary to re-equip existing jobs, but also to increase their numbers. To do this, it is necessary to increase the frequency of sales (of products or services), thus making them less material. Global companies charge a relatively small but constant rental fee, annually releasing updates and new product versions. If you think that this only applies to software for office computers and CAD tools and machines for developers, you are mistaken. An increasing number of modern machines and mechanisms are provided with 'intelligence', and then the performance of the hardware is improved further by updating its 'brain' or installing more advanced replacement parts.[200]

The apotheosis is reached with the appearance of a new phenomenon – reinvention. It is about trying to 're-embed' inventions that are already well known in the economy. Apple is making another attempt of this kind with its iWatch and as the company turns to electric vehicles. Everything will be enmeshed in sensors, until we get to the last level – the sensory world level where absolutely all things and people are interconnected and act as a supernet, 'a network of networks'. It is the supernet, or 'the fluid net', that will limit further growth of population, as education does today. For example, the average woman in Nigeria gives birth to six children over the course of her life, but, according to recent research, around 50% of Nigerian women aged 20-24 have high school education today, which immediately reduces the figure by two thirds – down to two children.

In March 2014, Intel, the world's largest IT company, announced that its strategy would be focused precisely on the internet of things. Jason Waxman, Intel's senior project manager for cloud technology, stated that Intel wanted to focus on 'smart' things and wearable and automotive electronics. In his opinion, there will be a market for about 50 billion 'smart' devices in the coming years. The profit, as you might have already guessed, will come with the development of the software. Waxman himself asserts that one can be sure that every dollar of royalties paid on the software will bring four dollars for the hardware.

HOW THE UNIVERSAL CRAVING FOR INNOVATION WILL CHANGE THE CONTENT OF GLOBALISATION ONCE AGAIN IN THE FUTURE

Let's get back to the question of who, or what, will ensure global economic growth. This task is expected to be carried out by the market, an arrangement which an individual investor, even a very powerful bigwig, is unlikely to be able to beat. Or modern global capitalism, in the broadest sense of the term. The only question is what part of it will ensure accelerated growth.

About five centuries ago, the West pressed the East, developing a dynamic society on the basis of the scientific and industrial revolutions.

Will the East be able to exact historical revenge and how soon will this happen?

A NON-ZERO-SUM GAME

If global growth takes place at a 2% rate, it means that the game is still being played as a non-zero-sum game.[201] In view of the increased efficiency of human capital, financial markets engage intelligent and capable people all over the world for cooperation. Their combined experience weighs no less than that of an individual investor, even such a lucky one as Warren Buffett or George Soros. By the way, their achievements are largely based on their ability to 'play long'. Long process cycles exist objectively. They show, for example, that US companies' shares were very cheap in the mid-1970s and became very expensive in the late 1990s. This means that the mid-1970s were a good time to buy for successful investors and that today, on the contrary, many companies' growth prospects may be subjectively overvalued.

For investors, who, in contrast to governments, finance concrete projects rather than problems, ensuring total world growth in percentages, financial globalization is something like the tides in the world-wide ocean. But the reaction to the momentum of globalization that came from developed countries is increasing year after year. At the moment, the action and reaction forces have reached their peaks, with closed trade unions and quite real trade wars coming to replace the World Trade Organization (WTO). Having begun with 'westernization' and dissemination of free trade ideas, and having integrated the economies of the former socialist countries, world capitalism has aggravated the contradictions between expansion and its opposite, stimulation of import substitution and protection of domestic markets.

War serves as a strong catalyst for innovation processes. Acting on the advice given by Keynes, the US did not reduce the army after the end of World War II (thus avoiding the possibility of re-plunging into the pre-war crisis and unemployment) and secured a breakthrough in space exploration (a responsive one) through embarking on massive and long-term public expenditure and increasing its public debt.

But attempts to replace private sector initiatives in innovation with public programmes are unlikely to be successful, simply because the state has a rather vague idea of where to look for innovation (remember that according to Reagan, the state merely finances problems rather than solving them). The world has become more complicated, and the growing interdependence of national economies around the world ensures a non-zero growth, making full-scale clashes and armed conflicts rather unprofitable.

The search for specialization in Western economies is conducted solely on an experimental basis and in different directions, where innovative private businesses create 2% global growth (Heston 2013). Therefore, there have to be numerous private businesses which have significant international financial support. Once new promising areas open for business, leading investment companies rush there, followed by other investors around the world.

The alternative development option brings a negative result. A return to a state-run economy in the modern world, overflowed with financial debts as it is, would result in the next systemic or national crisis.

The search for development is now taking on an intensified zeal, since the desire to live comfortably is embedded in human nature. As recently as 10 years ago, the average European was more than four times better off than the average Chinese, but today, they are only two times better off. Russia, China, India and Brazil want to develop quickly and be independent. Every nation needs nothing other than breakthrough technologies and large-scale projects.

The developed countries, on the other hand, 'burdened' with accumulated capital, are forced to spend a significant portion of their GDP to maintain a 2-3% growth of their national economies. Stability is valued highly in a modern economy. Inflation control and low interest rates ensure that economies run smoothly. The most notable macroeconomic innovation in recent years is inflation targeting.[202] But low interest rates impel players to resort to financing more risky projects. In the West, with its capital reserves, rapid economic growth (7% or more) is unlikely.

HOW THE EAST WILL PRESSURIZE THE WEST

China remains the world's growth driver, with more than 20% of the world's population living there. The growth in Chinese citizens' incomes over the past decade has significantly increased the demand for food, but the country's domestic production is already close to the limit. According to Bloomberg, China needs about half of each kilogram of wheat or meat produced in the world. But arable land comprises just 9% of China's territory. Furthermore, more than 3.3 million hectares of arable land in China are contaminated with pesticides and are thus unsuitable for farming – notably, this is mostly typical of north-eastern Chinese regions, where environmental concerns have also led to a decrease in fresh water supplies.

And still, China's population will continue to grow in the medium term. However, China has learned from the past. A few centuries ago, problems with food supplies to the Chinese capital acted as a catalyst for unrest in the country; to solve the problem, the country began to construct ships and channels. Today the government will keep trade and production in its own hands.

Such actions are a part of a long-term national anti-globalization strategy. This is based on the Chinese population's growing concerns that imported genetically modified foodstuffs cause harm to human health and the environment and recently, China's Minister of Agriculture banned the import of genetically modified foodstuff from the US. Therefore, China will seek to meet the population's demand for foodstuffs, primarily rice, using its own resources. For this purpose, China is continuing to buy agricultural producers from around the world. So far, the country has spent about $12.3 billion to this end.

Apart from food production, similar patterns can be found in other sectors as well. Over the past decade, China has spent more than $200 billion to buy mines and oil fields around the world. The expensive (worth more than $40 billion) acquisition of oil assets around the world by PetroChina actually paved the way for achieving energy independence for the country. China has already partially won the world battle for resources.

But the main battle between the West and the East is starting, and it is about the future principles that the global financial system will be based on. Only a century ago, the UK was the world's first power provider, and even lent money to such large countries as India and China. The high-water mark of British supremacy was reached some years before World War I, when a system based on the gold standard, advantageous for the country, prevailed in world trade.

The two World Wars changed the balance of power. The US (which had previously borrowed money from the UK) became the leader. The Bretton Woods agreements were, in fact, a deal between two countries, entered into to formalize the status quo of the moment: where the US became the world's main creditor and the UK the largest debtor. Later, the US agreed to help other countries to fight their current account deficits, while the latter agreed to discard the practice of competitive devaluation of national currencies.

Today, the situation is entirely different again; the world's largest creditor is China, the largest debtor is the US. Describing the situation with reference to the 'China–US dipole', it may be worth noting that Asian economies have already imported business schemes created in the West to organize industrial processes, purchased technology and acquired clients, brainpower and even advanced education techniques. Now it's trade's turn to play the ball. What is there still left to be done?

There's the last element of the four-leaf clover that remains to be added – financial innovation, designed to maintain and increase capital. If China fails to borrow and adjust in some form the essential elements of a developed financial market, the country may fall into a 'middle income trap'.

As a result of having a long-standing positive trade balance, the Eastern countries have much higher savings rates, or share of investment in GDP. They have better long-term prospects for extensive economic development by means of bringing in low-cost labour force reserves – both in the present human workforce form and in the future, silicon-based, robotic form, easily available due to being cheaper than in the West. Meanwhile, having low household consumption rates and rather embryonic social institutions (such as pension systems), the East is delaying the rematch it will serve on the West. The Western countries in their turn are trying to find 'disruptive' innovations that would slow down welfare growth and give rise to demographic problems in the East, thus eliminating the imbalance between the two macro-regions' rates of development and impeding the process of reducing the existing welfare gap between them.

HOW NEW CONFLICTS AND WARS WILL BE FINANCED

At all times, leading countries of the world have listed other countries as the ones on the wrong side of history. Access to advanced business models and technology is very limited for a country listed in this way. Foreign policy practice shows that such an innovation as oral agreements between the leaders of states cannot replace such long-established and customary instruments as treaties, conventions and agreements.

POSSIBLE AREAS OF FUTURE CONFLICTS

No 'peaceful' exploration of oil and gas reserves in many areas, e.g. the Arctic Region, would be possible without the United Nations Convention on the Law of the Sea, which has not been signed by the US, as there would be no legal basis for such activity. The US, Denmark, Norway, Iceland, Finland, Sweden, Russia and Canada would not be able to go beyond their 200-mile exclusive economic zones in that case.

The US' position on the issue is reminiscent of the old story of fighting opponents with patents, or the more recent one of blocking technological development – only this time, the blocking is done by means of deliberate refusal to develop new rules of conduct in the Arctic. Meanwhile, private US-based companies (ConocoPhillips, ExxonMobil, Statoil, etc.) have already planned the allocation of huge investments in the development of various parts of the Arctic. Scott Borgerson wrote about this in an article published in *Foreign Affairs*: "The Arctic is warming up faster than scientists predicted, and now it's only a matter of time before the region will be available for large-scale exploration and development. Viewed from the top of the globe, the region sits at the crossroads of the world's most productive economies.

Thanks to new realities and good geography, such cities as Anchorage and Reykjavik could someday become major shipping centres and financial capitals – the high-latitude equivalents of Singapore and Dubai. Converted tankers may someday ship clean water from Alaskan glaciers to southern Asia and Africa. Icelandair has started offering circumpolar service between Reykjavik, Anchorage and St. Petersburg.

The Arctic's high latitudes make the region a good place to expand existing ground stations for satellites in polar orbits. With some of the world's most powerful tides, the Arctic has spectacular hydropower potential and its geology holds tremendous capacity for geothermal energy, as evidenced by Iceland's geothermal-powered aluminium smelting industry" (Borgerson 2013).

The Arctic is neither the only nor the first region where there are global interests. Some time ago, African countries hoped that cooperation with the US would bring them considerable dividends, as it would facilitate the integration of Africa's small and medium-sized enterprises into global value chains. The US was expected to support advisory service programmes, provide access to marketing information and some technologies, and promote foreign direct investment in agricultural produce processing. Yet the US has done little to benefit Africa.

Africa itself is a region for potential future conflicts, with its rapidly growing populations, uneven development across the continent, plentiful natural resources (including mineral deposits), and an abundance of diverse elites proclaiming different attitudes to war.

The proliferation of mobile devices will turn Africa into a patchwork of areas, some of which will remain outdated, but some will come to the forefront of the new digital payment and money transfer technology. The lack of legal precedents with reference to digital currencies will not only provide great opportunities for African entrepreneurs, but also transform the continent into a kind of testing ground and new battlefield for financial confrontation.

In the next five to seven years, Sub-Saharan Africa will develop well enough to use crypto-currencies (e.g. Bitcoin) and witness aggressive growth in private property. Crypto-currencies will encourage an entrepreneurial boom in the same way as mobile communication technology today. So far, the complexity and costliness of cash movement constitute a serious barrier for African entrepreneurs. However, this will be overcome through the development of communication and information networks.

ON THE NATURE OF WAR

Scientists have long debated the nature of war. Some see it as something intrinsically natural to our kind, referring to the fact that even chimpanzees exhibit behaviour resembling human warfare. Others argue that war is an example of adopted, rather than innate, behaviour and is based on a gregarious mentality. Proponents of the theory formulated by Karl Marx believe that modern war is merely a kind of political manoeuvre that has developed together with that of civilisation, and that war is not to be taken as a rejection of diplomacy but rather as the continuation of trade relations by other means.

Indians in medieval America waged wars with the financial aim of imposing an indemnity on the defeated enemy. But things changed places in the last century.[203] Today, the winner is found out in a financial battle first. Then the defeated side is obliged to fight another opponent in order to weaken the financial standing of the latter (whereas the defeated side's own currency and economy have been brought into complete submission at best, or totally ruined at worst). Such controlled action is also, in a sense, an indemnity paid by the defeated side to the winner.

But some things remain the same. Wars are still waged for control over territories, with importance attached to the resources and critical infrastructure. Today these are not limited to water, gas and electricity supply systems, but also include the information infrastructure. Availability of telecommunications is the most important part of modern warfare, since it is electronic space that becomes the primary battlefield – here the West has the most significant advantages in 'armaments' – and it is only once a victory has been achieved in the media sphere that the war may be taken into its extreme phase involving direct military action. Why is that?

Because war is, in fact, another form of competition for 'getting embedded' in the market. Financial globalisation suggests that a more subtle wealth extraction mechanism has come to replace brute force and that people all over the world are working to strengthen the global financial system with a much more serious motivation, and not under duress. The combination of debt and telecommunications is truly a great invention!

Scientists have calculated that the murder ratio (the ratio of the average number of murders committed per unit of time to the population in a society) in 20th century Europe was 10 times lower than that in hunters and gatherers' tribes (Pinker 2011). We almost got out of progress' ancient trap. In the 21st century, according to consistent data provided by the UN and WHO, there are fewer murders than suicides. Warfare has become less military, as it were, and more informational in nature, propagated by the media with the help of a widespread telecommunications infrastructure.

HOW TO FIND A REPLACEMENT FOR GOLD

Recent events in the world have offered us some hope that there is still a long way to go to a 'Fukuyama' end of history (Fukuyama 1989). Any crisis is primarily a crisis of confidence. Specific groups of people cease to trust each other, their neighbours, governments, banks, peacekeepers, the UN and so on. At such moments, as soon as instability starts mounting, investments in gold tend to intensify. Gold still allows people to convert a large part of their savings into a reliable asset.

Apart from incurring buy/sell losses and storage costs, there are other disadvantages, one of which is that gold is not a very liquid commodity. Banks give very low offers. It takes finding buyers willing to pay a fair price, arranging the deal, delivering the gold safely and deciding which currency should be exchanged, not to mention the fact that gold is rather difficult to use as a means of payment.

CRYPTO-CURRENCY

Each generation is obsessed with the creation of a 'new gold'. Now, in our time, there is an alternative. It still cannot compete with gold as a physical commodity, of course, but at least it's nearly perfect as a means of saving the earnings of the new creative class.

So-called digital cash systems have emerged recently (the most famous of which is Bitcoin). These are fully fledged payment systems whose reliability is guaranteed by strong cryptography rather than by the state or a private company (i.e. they are safeguarded by fundamental laws of mathematics and transparency of transactions).[204] While the governments of developing countries are struggling to cope with money substitutes such as Bitcoin,

Western countries, having realized that crypto-currencies are the thing of the future, have come close to the development of laws designed to regulate crypto-currency circulation. Lawmakers are arguing about the rules required for businesses eager to use Bitcoin and its derivatives.

Western governments realize that they cannot control new currencies solely by means of restrictions – this would be simply impossible from a technical point of view. Instead they have decided to introduce state licensing and... purchase new money. Interest in the subject on the part of public authorities is confirmed by the fact that more than 2% of all bitcoins are held by the US government which, in fact, controls the Bitcoin rate. The governments of Spain, Poland, the Czech Republic and Iceland have already launched national analogues of the peer-to-peer electronic payment system Bitcoin.[205] A peer-to-peer system is based on equality of its members and has no dedicated servers. Unlike a client-server structure, a peer-to-peer arrangement makes it possible to maintain the network operational with any number and combination of available nodes.

Given the fact that a virtual currency has no emission centre, it is not prone to inflation: Bitcoin in particular is programmed to periodically reduce the volume of its issues, as demand grows. Since the quantity of newly issued bitcoins will be reducing by half every four years, the value of this currency should only increase in time.

The appearance of Bitcoin generated a lot of investment activity and research, as well as completely new and specific risks. Bitcoin today is a paradigmatic electronic 'Wild West' where you can be robbed in broad daylight and with impunity. One in 10 issued bitcoins has been stolen. However, if successful in eliminating scams and providing at least minimal safety for bit currency operations, society would receive a huge and growing market with the lowest possible transaction costs and more rapid cash transfers. This would create further leverage: people would be attracted to the system and the profits of companies doing business in or with crypto-currencies would grow. Bitcoin is attractive because it is very simple: the entry barriers are low and the potential payoff is huge. As a result, the administrations of such large cities as New York will soon permit Bitcoin and similar currencies to be used. This, in turn, will create an additional revenue channel for municipal budgets and create an infrastructure for new private money used by the creative class.

Of course, there is a very small possibility that Bitcoin will disappear just as it appeared. Experts, however, believe there is quite another possibility. Something very similar to Bitcoin may appear one day, able to replace the dollar, the euro and all other currencies. This may happen if an official authority responsible for monetary emission in a state simply writes a crypto-currency client program of its own and launches a peer-to-peer network.[206] It will not be difficult to regulate such a program. Since management in modern economy is normally exercised by regulating money supply, it will be possible to control the amount of currency existing in circulation by simply withdrawing certain amounts. The US, Russia, India, China and many other countries may create their own 'artificial' crypto-currencies.

The most interesting thing about the new digital cash is its emergence. We already know how conventional paper currency came about as a result of John Law's experiments. The story of the emergence of Bitcoin is no less exciting and is still being written before our very eyes. But the most important thing is how the new currency is produced. It is produced by means of calculation. The printing press is replaced by a set of mathematical problems whose complexity increases exponentially with the passage of time and the growth of the quantity of already 'mined' bitcoins. This computation process is called crypto-currency extraction, or mining.

DATA PROCESSING CENTRES

Today, Bitcoin mining has moved to specialized data processing centres (data centres), and niches for new innovative companies have been created in the data processing market. In 2013, a network was formed within the Bitcoin system, whose computational power is 150,000 petaflops per second.[207]

The Bitcoin start-up market is developing in several directions simultaneously, creating bizarre combinations. This new gold rush means that the data centre market is undergoing significant changes and, as a result, so is the market for 'normal' cloud computing.

The emergence of a separate class of data centres has resulted in displacement of some of the traditional players that, apparently, simply failed to realize the danger in good time because of their corporate unwieldiness. Once again, the fast prevailed over the large. The Bitcoin fever has also provoked amazing changes in chip production. To achieve better results and reduce costs, crypto-currency miners have even developed a new architecture based on the so-called 28-nanometer ASIC chips without the participation of major IT companies.

This story is reminiscent of a concept formulated by Russian economists in the 1920s, according to which the gold standard would be replaced by an energy currency rather than the commodity dollar (which proved to be incorrect). With the advent of Bitcoin and its clones, we in fact have come back to that concept: in mining, energy is directly and immediately converted into cash. If desired, one could even calculate the Bitcoin-to-kWh conversion factor.

INFRASTRUCTURE AS A SERVICE

This, however, does not mean that conventional data centres will be out of work. Modern facilities of this type are rapidly gaining strength everywhere, expected to solve a wide variety of tasks. The concept of cloud computing has virtually evolved into that of a computing hypermarket, where individual users or corporate employees can buy not only computing capacities, but also time to work with specific software applications. This approach has been given a conventional abbreviation, IaaS (Infrastructure as a Service). In other words, it is based on a 'cloud' model that implies the use of virtual servers with software provided for rent.

Furthermore, as practice shows, existing conventional information systems are unable to scale up in order to meet the rapid development of information technology. Conventional enterprise resource planning systems (ERP systems) do not include data models that would make it possible to run a company in accordance with new management trends. Therefore, flexible cloud systems containing standards relevant to a specific industry will start to displace conventional players in this market in the near future.

In fact, computing resources function as a fuel that brings companies' business processes to the next level by means of automating processes that used to be performed exclusively by people. This is very similar to what happened during the Industrial Revolution. Society ceased to be agricultural and became industrial, not least because there was a possibility to replace the energy of man, who tended to get tired of monotonous work, with steam power.

Accumulated piles of data and amplified computation capacities, in conjunction with libraries of algorithms, have produced such a modern phenomenon as big data. For example, the multinational company Shell has in the last few years been laying fibre optic cables on its oil and gas rigs, in addition to installing the standard equipment, and fixing sensors that continuously collect a wide variety of data. Such extensive data can enable the company to predict how long oil or gas could be extracted from a well which, it would seem, has run dry. How exactly Shell engineers do it is unknown, but what is known is their ultimate goal:

to build a detailed model of the structure of the Earth at depths of 1 to 12 km – a kind of underground Google Map.

Making it possible to handle terabytes easily, big data processing technologies have already contributed towards reducing time and money expenditure on DNA decryption and analysis. IBM experts believe that the next breakthrough will be made using so-called cognitive systems (this term refers to analogues of the IBM Watson supercomputer), which can be of great help in the treatment of cancer, heart disease and stroke.

David Friedberg and Siraj Khaliq, founders of a start-up called the Climate Corporation, demonstrated another promising area for the use of enhanced digital capacities, which fetched them $1.1 billion. In 2013, when the company was sold, it employed two hundred scientists who processed some 50 terabytes of data daily. The Climate Corporation's servers bring together pictures of areas, weather data and field sensor readings. This extremely valuable information is essential for any farmer making the most important decisions: when to sow and when to harvest. That's how IT solutions profoundly affect the course of biological evolution on our planet.

In 2013, the start-up was acquired by Monsanto. This biotech giant, holding patents on genetically modified crops, has developed a technique whereby agricultural seeds are not sold to farmers, but made available seasonally... for rent. The company's technological tool kit includes a specifically designed 'terminator' gene that can make seeds of crops sterile under specific conditions.

Big data opened up attractive prospects for Monsanto. Under the guise of advice given to farmers on how to improve crop productivity, the company may trick them into buying seeds of some varieties, as well as proprietary fertilisers and equipment. Agricultural machinery fitted with a host of sensors collects data, in addition to its main function, on areas under cultivation and fuel and time expenditure. Monsanto successfully sells all this data as additional services through their online service desks, along with information about soil types and recommended crop distribution patterns.

The company obtains information about actual seed application rates by means of another innovative piece of technology: drones. Commercialisation of data went successfully: the advice given by the company through its service desks brought the subscribers (the largest US agricultural companies) additional revenue in the range of $85 to $127 per hectare in 2013. The company itself has begun to sell two and a half times more maize seed over the past nine years, displacing and absorbing smaller competitors. Today, this scheme is already applied on a global scale.

Ten agricultural companies control a commercial seed market fetching $23 billion each year, while five of them control virtually everything related to genetically modified crops.[208] Before long, control over the entire agricultural infrastructure of each country in the world will be concentrated in the hands of a few companies. Penetrating into the domestic markets of sovereign countries, they buy up cheap shares of local competitors and then sell these assets in an attractive casing at a totally different price.

I have already mentioned that the US financial system is based on expectations entertained by markets and people, in their belief that a particular company will bring them a profit. Many US-based global companies, such as Tesla, Google and Facebook, make no profit and their enormous market capitalisation is based on the common expectation that the company will be profitable in the future, because it is continuously growing and will one day beat all its competitors. They manage to attract financing easily, because each of their investors can, selling their shares today, take, as it were, money from the future by exploiting buyers' expectations of future growth.

So, synthesis of new knowledge, the use of which creates new technology platforms and provides further improvement in our wellbeing, is probably worth more than gold.

NEW INDUSTRIAL REVOLUTION. INDUSTRY 4.0

In 2000, Jeremy Rifkin proposed a concept of a new industrial revolution. The concept was supported by the European Parliament. In subsequent years, a number of research centres developed this hypothesis. According to the concept, a new single infrastructure will emerge as a result of consolidation of five components: 1) renewable energy sources; 2) power-generating buildings; 3) hydrogen-based and other energy storage technologies; 4) intelligent networks (so-called smart grids), or 'energy internet'; and 5) electric, hybrid and other vehicles.

ALL IN DIGIT

In 2010, a strategic initiative proposed by the German Government, called Industry 4.0, was adopted as part of the EU's High-Tech Strategy 2020 Action Plan. Its implementation will result in the emergence of new cyber-physical systems, integrating the internet of people, things and services, linking people, objects and systems. It is expected that the quantitative effect of the application of Industry 4.0 elements in the next 5 to 10 years will be quite substantial and include a productivity rise of 20-30%, and an increase in revenue and employment.

The new industrial revolution has already begun and even passed its most difficult phase, which involved the selection of key directions of development of new technologies. It is based on three technological shifts: 'all in digit', materials with new properties, and management technology based on digital modelling and design.

German, Korean and Japanese companies have achieved a significant breakthrough in the development of 6D projects, successfully carrying out 3D (three-dimensional) object modelling, time scheduling, procurement management and 3D construction. The production process will be lined up as follows: 6D design, scanning (the structure and material composition), and layer-by-layer additive manufacturing. 3D modelling will be more and more widely used in production. Real time data generation will make it possible to combine a virtual model and the real world: machines, products and workers.

Companies are just beginning to use additive layer-by-layer printing technology, so far mainly for prototyping. MIT has announced a plan to create, in 15 years' time, a 3D printer able to work with 10 different materials. Aerospace companies are already using layer-by-layer printing techniques to manufacture certain components for their products. Airbus's road map provides for a shift from printing small details to 3D printing of entire aircraft by 2050. This will result in reductions in weight, time, waste, energy and so on.

This will lead to a complete change in principles used to locate industrial facilities. Products will be printed on demand. Thousands of various details can be printed at one production site, thus eliminating the need to co-operate with hundreds of different suppliers. Designs, not products, will travel around the world as digital files ready to be printed out at any place, with just materials and cartridges required.

Analysis of big data sets, having come to actual use in production relatively recently, makes it possible to achieve higher quality in production, improve energy efficiency and make decisions in real time.

INTERACTION OF PEOPLE AND MACHINES

All systems designed for capitalization of human resources will undergo a complete overhaul. Education will be focused on the needs of the individual. Companies will seek to develop well-structured individual training programmes for their employees and develop service infrastructures based on these platforms. Some countries are even planning to include training in the use of the Lego Mindstorms educational kit in their school curricula.

As a result, people will acquire skills in using 3D technology. It is much easier to train a person to think and work in 3D terms right from the start than to retrain a designer experienced in 2D modelling to work in a 3D environment.

At the end of the twentieth century, individual businesses and even large multinational corporations lost their potential for being the main repositories of technical and organisational knowledge. The new industrial revolution is bringing with it a fantastic increase in the complexity of operation systems on the one hand and a continuous specialisation of knowledge on the other.

Knowledge management systems are trying to solve the problem of involving the companies' employees in a knowledge-sharing process. This requires awareness of where the relevant knowledge is and how to decipher it.

During the first Industrial Revolution, innovative companies changed the course of history by not only accelerating the pace of economic growth, but also by creating conditions for a continuous increase in job numbers. Steam power provided new opportunities in transport, heavy industry, agriculture, medicine and urban infrastructural development.

We know that the invention of new technologies as such does not guarantee immediate success. Commercially successful 'embedding' of innovation can only be achieved with new companies. And it is much more important to have skilled people who would be able to create and lead such companies. Modern power engineering needs leaders such as Richard Branson and Elon Musk for modern space technology. It is difficult to effect such fast recombination by creating breakthrough innovations without figures of this calibre and companies able to bring the necessary resources and the right people into the industry. Without new leaders, no rapid progress in world power engineering is possible. Hydrocarbon energy giants can only be overtaken by fast and investment-attractive companies. But these will not arrive if there are no bright leaders.

AUTONOMOUS ROBOTS

It is quite possible that a humanoid robot will be created to work alongside humans. Such beings may be shaped as drones or micro-drones – unmanned aircraft the size of a fly, which can take pictures, listen in and even take DNA samples without your knowledge. A miniature robot, called RoboBee, has been created at Harvard, which weighs only 80mg. Since 2014, the so-called Robot Olympics have been held annually under the auspices of the US military agency DARPA.

Baxter, an industrial robot developed by Rethink Robotics (US), may prove to be capable of revolutionising work on assembly lines around the world. The robot is skilled enough to replace a worker in industrial assembly: it has a camera, sensors and sophisticated software; it can 'see' objects, 'feel' force, 'understand' tasks and automatically adjust to changing conditions. Baxter is able to do what is usually expected from a worker. Additionally, it has a face with moving eyes. It is adaptable, easy to train and, while conventional robots can only perform certain tasks, Baxter has only to be given the right grips and shown what to do. But the most important feature of this android is its price: $25,000. The robot can work 24 hours a day and scrupulously observes labour safety regulations.

The marine division of Rolls-Royce announced in 2014 that it had for a long time been carrying out research and development to create unmanned cargo ships. The rationale for creating an unmanned cargo vessel is obvious: the maintenance of the crew on board a ship accounts for more than 40% of all operating costs, and the presence of the crew as such requires a lot of space and is fraught with the risk of accidents. The rapid development of robotics means that in some 10 years, robotic technology will gain access to defence, health, education and transport, and likewise fill our homes on a large scale, even finding its way into our children's toys.

Robots will be helping people every day. They will be widely available for sale to the public and easily customizable to suit users' needs. We will face the need to develop and discuss new laws. In all likelihood, we will begin to think about the social consequences of the interaction of children with toy robots and elderly people with medical robots, about some new sexual practices and so on, as a move towards a close intertwinement of our biological evolution with the oncoming techno-wave becomes evident.

Advances in robotics could result in robots performing human labour, even in such fields as surgery. Experts expect that no less than 320 million people will be employed in modern technological industries paired up with intelligent robots. According to an estimate made by McKinsey, 250 million robot sales are made annually, fetching some $2-3 trillion. Machine operation will begin to displace more expensive human labour even in the most labour-intensive and high-tech industries.

However, according to Michio Kaku, a well known American visionary and physicist, the introduction of robots has been held back by two main problems: robots are able to see and hear much better than humans, but they do not understand what they see and hear. Moreover, unlike humans, they have no common sense. According to Kaku, the main problem is that

huge numbers of code lines would be required to create a software analogue of human sense in order to simulate human thinking. These factors
do not allow robotics to integrate fully into the existing market.

To store massive amounts of obtained data, new storage facilities will be
required. Data accumulation and storage on the basis of old technology will
be ineffective, as people and organizations will no longer be able to manage
their sprawling 'digital history'. Humankind will face a dilemma: to delete
the data or to invent a non-burdensome medium for their eternal storage.

Hitachi (Japan) recently presented a prototype for a novel optical
medium capable of storing data practically forever – hundreds of millions
of years! In physical terms, the model is a mere set of thin plates made of
transparent quartz glass, able to withstand temperatures of up to 1,000°C.
Moreover, the plates are water- and chemical-resistant. The binary code is
recorded with a laser beam in four layers of points which are visible under
an ordinary optical microscope.[209]

Once inexpensive means of storing and visualizing information are
designed and manufactured, this will inevitably cause serious changes in the
modern social structure, where the judiciary plays a key role. Today, a situation
where a person who has received a speeding ticket is able to pay the fine using
their telephone or to present a DVR record in court is considered the highest
point of perfection. With the advent of new data storage media, the judicial
process itself will change: holograms of incidents may be studied and the outcome of a court case may be predicted by computing. Big data processing
technology will make it possible to predict the outcome of a case and estimate the due amount of compensation, and it is quite possible that the sides
involved in the conflict will prefer to resolve their dispute without a legal trial.
Physical courthouses may appear as anachronistic to the next generation as fax
machines and typewriters appear to us today. The presence of high-capacity
and low-cost storage media will open up access to public digital repositories.

ENERGY ENGINEERING IN THE FUTURE, ELECTRIC VEHICLES AND UNMANNED DRIVING

Each technological platform is founded on a certain energy basis. Thus,
in 17th century Holland, forests were grown, peat burned and windmills
were built along canals. In 18th-19th century England during the Industrial
Revolution, coal was mined to produce steel and operate steam engines.
The energy basis of the technology revolution consists of oil and gas, electric power and nuclear power. What can serve as the basis for the new
industrial revolution?

A NEW ENERGY PLATFORM

The new industrial revolution is expected to be based on green energy and, possibly, thermonuclear fusion in the future.

The development of manned cosmonautics and the creation of a lunar base will make it possible to launch the production of Helium-3, a new and environmentally friendly source of energy. Helium-3 is a rather rare and expensive isotope, practically unavailable on Earth (according to some estimates, no more than a tonne of it can be found on our planet), but present abundantly (in a quantity of some half a million tonnes) on the Moon, to which Helium-3 has been brought by solar wind since it was formed. Helium-3 is an ideal matter for launching fusion reactors. Most importantly, it does not produce radiation and as little as 30 tonnes of Helium-3 would be required to cover the Earth's energy needs (in terms of current energy consumption) according to estimates made by scientists of the Russian Vernadsky Institute of Geochemistry and Analytical Chemistry. To have these plans implemented, however, a base would have to be set up on the Moon and about one billion tonnes of lunar soil would have to be processed. Nevertheless, according to experts, the establishment of mining on the Moon can solve the task of providing humankind with energy for another thousand years at quite earthly costs.

However, the implementation of these plans in this field will most likely depend on legal issues. The point is that the current international space law is based on the Outer Space Treaty, an agreement that was signed back in 1967, according to which outer space, including the Moon, is not subject to appropriation, and the exploration and use of outer space shall be carried out for the benefit and in the interests of all countries and shall be the province of all humankind. Following the letter of the law, it turns out that one can engage in mining operations beyond the Earth's atmosphere, but any resources one would obtain would have to be shared with all the member states of the treaty (and that is about half of the world's nations).

Nevertheless, a completely new bill was originated in the US Congress in a special hearing recently, the American Space Technology for Exploring Resource Opportunities in Deep Space Act, or the so-called Asteroids Act. The idea is clear: to withdraw from the international legal framework in order to extend private ownership principles to the results of exploration, production, delivery and sales of extra-terrestrial resources.

The financial statistics of recent years indicate that investment in solar energy (or PV, photovoltaics) has increased from $2.5 billion in 2000 to $150 billion in 2015 globally.

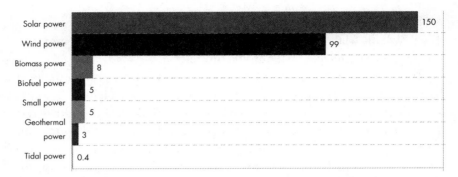

FIGURE 28. GLOBAL INVESTMENT IN RENEWABLE ENERGY
IN VARIOUS AREAS IN 2014, $ BILLION

Figure 31 demonstrates that wind power has also shown results similar to those produced by solar power and reached total investments of $99 billion in 2014 (for comparison: it was only $4.5 billion in 2000). China is making a crucial contribution to the development of these industries (Table 11).[210]

COUNTRY	INVESTMENT VOLUME ($ BILLION)
China	83.3 (+ 39% to 2013)
EU Countries	57.5 (2013 level)
USA	38.3 (2011 level)
Brazil	7.6
India	7.4
South Africa	5.5
Indonesia	1
Chile	1
Mexico	1
Kenya	1
Turkey	1
Rest of the world	65.4
Total	270

TABLE 11. STRUCTURE OF THE UK'S NATIONAL ASSETS IN 1688-2008

Another question is bound to become more and more acute: how much energy will be required to create accumulated capacities connected to the network? Will the total power required to ensure the functionality of the wind and solar power sectors be less than the power they will produce?

Analysing the situation in its entirety, scientists from Stanford University (US) found that investment decisions are based solely on average estimations, since statistics in this field are rather scarce. Solar batteries have an efficiency of 12% and wind turbines slightly over 25%.

It turns out that the sun cannot be relied on alone and we can expect wind to blow for more hours per year than the sun shines. But wind power generation is fraught with difficulties too, one of which is that progress in the battery market is dramatically lagging behind the growth rate shown by renewable energy. The capacity of current energy storage facilities is a very important factor. The world has large-scale energy storage technologies. These include pumped storage power plants and 'great walls' of megawatt-capacity lithium batteries. Experts argue that the construction of a pumped storage plant requires 26 kWh of 'power investment' per accumulated kilowatt, while batteries require 153 kWh.[211]

It turns out that in order to save a three-day amount of wind-generated energy, PSPs (which are the cheapest type of power accumulating facilities today) require as much energy as it took to build the wind turbines whose energy they are designed to store.

Integration into the existing market is the main problem for alternative power engineering. Lack of power cannot be eliminated within the paradigm "more eco-friendly energy and less conventional energy", or "less conventional energy and more micro-energy". The energy conservation law cannot be waved away and, if no fundamentally new sources of energy are found, we will very soon face the necessity to limit our power consumption, which will result in a reduction in humanity's material wellbeing and, therefore, in a dilemma: either the world economy slows down its forward movement, or people turn back to nuclear energy, having once again overestimated the benefits and risks of the new endeavour.

In the near future, we will learn the answer to a question that puzzles even the most insightful energy analysts today: what technologies (either disruptive ones or supportive of already-established conventional technologies) will gain the most weight in this century (Figure 29)?

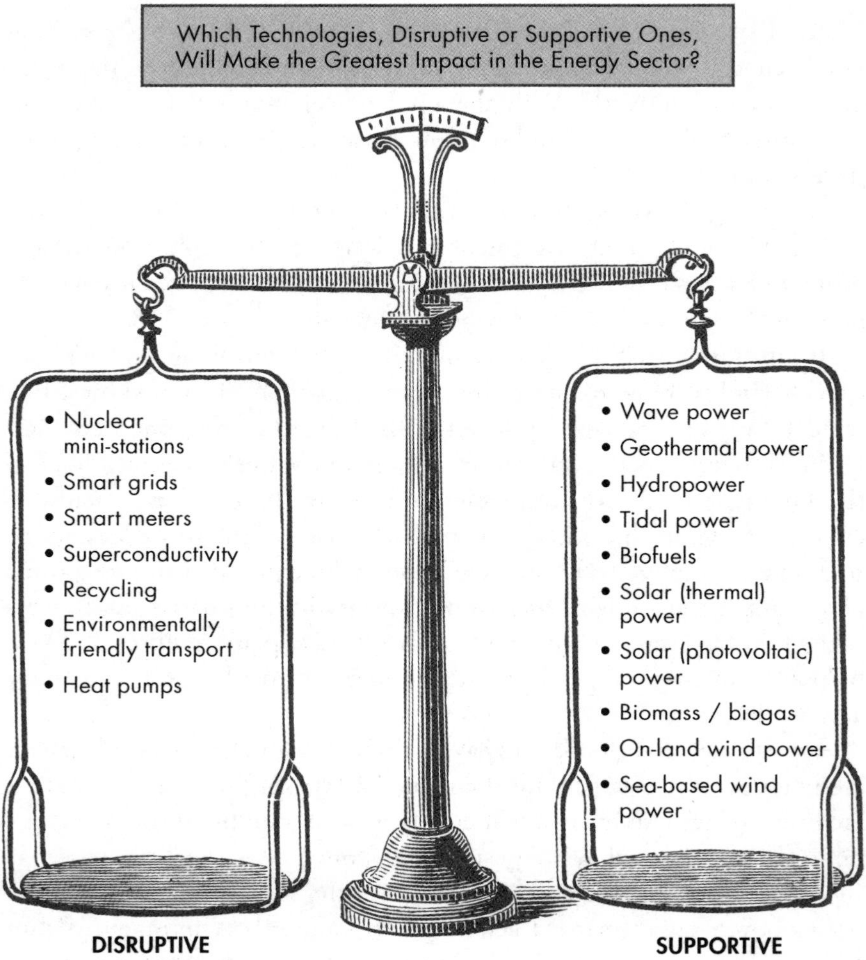

Which Technologies, Disruptive or Supportive Ones, Will Make the Greatest Impact in the Energy Sector?

DISRUPTIVE

- Nuclear mini-stations
- Smart grids
- Smart meters
- Superconductivity
- Recycling
- Environmentally friendly transport
- Heat pumps

SUPPORTIVE

- Wave power
- Geothermal power
- Hydropower
- Tidal power
- Biofuels
- Solar (thermal) power
- Solar (photovoltaic) power
- Biomass / biogas
- On-land wind power
- Sea-based wind power

FIGURE 29. WHAT KIND OF POWER ENGINEERING WE CAN EXPECT TO MATERIALISE IN THE NEAR FUTURE

Throughout history, it has not been technical factors that have played the decisive role in this matter. The so-called disruptive technologies are called disruptive because they require, apart from a fundamental change in the structure of power generation, a substantial change in the structure of energy delivery and distribution networks. So far, electricity and heat have flowed to our homes from large power and heating stations. All systems within power grids and, moreover, all accounting and taxation systems in the industry, are designed to provide for this one-way flow of energy.

The emergence of new technologies makes advanced power grids more similar to telecommunications networks. To this end, devices called FACTS (Flexible AC Transmission Systems) have been designed. These are power routers of some kind, able to send quickly the required amounts of electricity to the right places. Their introduction is hindered by their costliness, certain taxation difficulties, lack of a unified system of standards and state protectionism provided for conventional energy producers.

Besides, the development of new technologies raises questions which seem to have been forgotten since the time of the dispute between Tesla and Edison. With the advent of the digital era, devices that use direct electric current have begun to proliferate. New disruptive technologies (particularly wind and solar power stations) generate direct current, unstable though due to their dependence on natural conditions. A situation where double conversion of electric current is required could be resolved either through the creation of more powerful batteries or by means of an explosive growth in the numbers of DC 'microgrids' able to operate with reliability comparable with that of existing power transmission systems. These aspects make it impossible to give a clear answer to the question of what technologies – supportive or disruptive – will prevail in the near future.

Alternative power generation (including such power as solar, wind, geothermal and tidal) is suitable as a source of power supply for domestic use, but is categorically unsuitable for industrial purposes (where enormous amounts of energy are consumed).

Alternative energy is discontinuous and presents huge problems owing to the need to accumulate it for further use. The use of hydropower as the cheapest form of energy is very limited since the creation of artificial reservoirs is not economically feasible on smooth terrain.

The situation will not change even with a growth in new or improved conventional oil and gas extraction techniques. Sources of non-renewable fossil fuels are being depleted and fuels still emit, regardless of the method of their production, carbon dioxide during their combustion, which places a new burden on the planet's biosystem – 'the big cleansing tank' according to Altshuller.

However, from an environmental point of view, biofuel could replace oil as a source of energy for humanity. Today, the world economy is already using, on a daily basis, up to two million barrels of biofuel produced using so-called green technology. Recently, depletion of oil reserves spurred demand for biofuels as an alternative source of energy. If biofuels had been unavailable in the world, the price of oil could have exceeded $150 per barrel in peak demand!

But environmental degradation, climate change and plain competition for farmland for crop production – all these factors in combination have brought about the fact that the energy problem has turned into a food problem. In the near future, acreage suitable for agriculture will only shrink due to climate change.

Does this mean that green technologies will not help us out either? Let's not be so pessimistic. As it has been already noted, evolutionary change in newly established industries has often led to serious disruptive innovation. Experts believe that it is possible to distinguish four generations of biofuel. It is no exaggeration to say that green energy has huge potential for innovative development.

First-generation biofuel is conventional ethanol produced by fermentation, usually from grain. It is the large-scale production of this first-generation fuel that causes shortage of farmland. The production of second-generation biofuel involves a higher level of processing of biological raw materials, making use of such sources of primary stock as wood pulp (cellulose, etc.), agricultural waste, less valuable agricultural crops and straw. These techniques result in bioethanol produced from cellulose, biodiesel produced using the Fischer-Tropsch[212] method, biomethanol, biohydrogen and many other commodities. The advantages of second-generation biofuels in comparison with first-generation ones are diversity of biomass suitable for processing, higher production efficiency and a significant (up to 90%) reduction in greenhouse gas emissions if compared with fossil fuels. Experts in the market believe that the total volume of biofuel produced globally is in the range of 34 to 160 billion barrels of oil equivalent per annum.

Third-generation biofuel is not yet produced on an industrial scale. Its production, however, once set, is expected to be based on algae, a potentially low-cost and high-yield resource, as the main raw material. In theory, 30 times more energy per unit of farmland can be acquired from algae production than from the production of such crops as soya. But production techniques for this type of biofuel do not exist yet.

Fourth-generation biofuel is an alkane mixture, similar to diesel fuel, obtained directly from special bacteria that are constantly reproducing themselves, consuming carbon dioxide and releasing an alkane product. So far, the main problem with this biofuel as a finished product is its very low price, while the artificial catalysts required for its production (bacterial enzymes seem to be insufficient for setting a stable production process) are very expensive. This unfavourable combination of prices makes it difficult to attract investment to the development of relevant production techniques.

Figure 30 shows projected prices for biofuel of all four generations, with reference to the cost of a barrel of conventional fuel in oil equivalent.

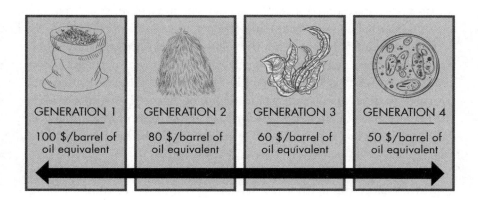

FIGURE 30. FORECAST OF PRICES FOR BIOFUEL OF FOUR GENERATIONS SUBJECT TO FULL INDUSTRIALISATION OF THE PRODUCTION PROCESS

The economy of using biotechnology for energy is such that the production of bioethanol and biodiesel from maize is economically viable at oil prices upwards of $100 per barrel. The production cost of second-generation biofuel is $80 per barrel in Europe or the US and even less – $60 – in Brazil. The production of third- and fourth-generation biofuel is expected to be even cheaper, at $50 per barrel. The cost may be substantially lower if deploying production in countries such as Brazil or Russia. Experts expect the biofuel industry to grow from the current $56.4 billion to $113 billion in 2020.

An important feature of biofuel is the possibility of its production from food waste. In other words, used foodstuffs and food waste are not waste – they are a valuable raw material, and its processing both has a positive impact on the environment and provides business opportunities for enterprises.

As a result of the temporary absence of a dominant production technique and a leader in this field, the competitiveness of biofuel is de facto dependent on the availability of arable land. Some countries, such as Russia, could eliminate the lack of power generation capacities by involving significant resources of arable land (currently idle) in biofuel production, which could contribute to accelerating the development of the agricultural sector.

Waste management in its turn should be combined with biofuel production too.

Furthermore, biofuel has a significant export potential. In terms of wholesale prices, it has not yet reached parity with electricity in 'expensive markets', which means that niche production techniques for such commodities as first- and second-generation biofuel will find a buyer simply because they are already integrated into the market.

However, biotechnology is not the solution alone, since humanity should be making better use of what it already has. For example, at present, 7% of generated electricity is lost over wires in transmission. This can be prevented with the use of cryogenic superconducting cable, whose throughput capacity is 100 times greater than that of similarly applicable copper cable with practically 'zero' losses at the same time. But unfortunately, energy companies have long ignored scientific research that demonstrates this.

However, it is not only transmission losses that can be reduced. We can also save energy through energy-saving opportunities. In motor vehicles only 20% of fuel consumption produces energy of movement, while the rest is converted into heat and emitted through the exhaust pipe (Figure 31).

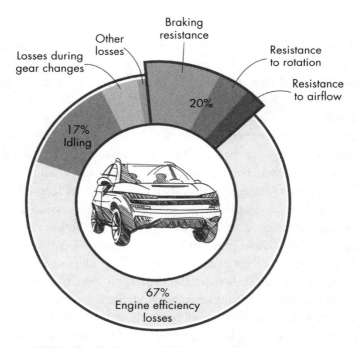

FIGURE 31. ENERGY LOSSES IN A MODERN CAR

Leading automobile manufacturers (GM, Ford, BMW, etc.) develop thermoelectric systems that use heat absorbed from the cooling system and exhaust. However, it is quite possible that these efforts may soon prove to be redundant as we see innovations such as those introduced by Tesla Motors in electric vehicle manufacturing. The merits of this company's electromobiles are numerous, including their high environmental friendliness due to no emissions being produced. There is also no need for fuel, antifreeze, oil and filters, which means that such a vehicle poses a minimum fire hazard in case of a traffic accident. Electric cars are easy to maintain and have no transmission, and therefore allow more mileage between routine services, and higher reliability and durability of the case. The possibility of charging the battery via a household outlet makes it possible to find the 'fuel' wherever there is electricity (Figure 32).

Electric vehicles are also characterized by their relative quietness due to having fewer moving parts and mechanical gears, smoothness of movement, the ability to recover charge (recharging during braking), the ability to brake by the electric motor (in electromagnetic brake mode), and the ability to recharge the battery from solar energy (while driving and during periods of inactivity).

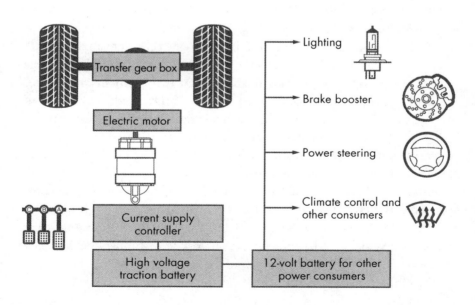

FIGURE 32. WHAT AN ELECTRIC CAR IS

It is most likely that humankind turned off the highway called 'progress' at the beginning of the last century, finding itself on a country road called 'petrol and oil'. Mass production and the use of electric vehicles can contribute to solving the problem of 'peak power consumption' by recharging car batteries at night. For example, the recharging stations Tesla Motors is already building will sell electricity into the power grid on sultry afternoons, when there are few customers. Quite naturally, a question arises: how much will it cost to recharge the battery of an electric car?

It all depends on how successfully innovation will be integrated into the existing market, since the creation of networks of recharging stations will incur significant costs. Such large-scale changes are only possible in leading countries, where the substantial costs deliberately incurred in the initial phase of such a major project are expected to be refunded through distribution of the new scheme on a global scale. According to analysts, only China, the US and possibly the European Union can become global leaders in the field of 'green' or 'clean' energy.

However, electric cars are not the only forgotten and then revived concept. As I said at the beginning of the chapter, so-called 'supergrids' are becoming a fashionable topic, reviving some of Thomas Edison's ideas. High-voltage DC power lines can efficiently transport electricity over distances of thousands of kilometres, surpassing AC power lines that currently dominate in power transmission grids. The currently existing technologies were developed because high DC voltage could only be used for point-to-point transmission. It would be impossible to embed the new technology in the market and create integrated direct current grids required for establishing a stable power supply system while using the old process base (without computers).

Both computer systems designed to manage DC grids and advanced energy storage systems will be key technological elements in the proliferation of solar and wind power systems as sources of alternative energy and their integration into the market. Without these elements, the integration of alternative energy into the market is evidently stalling: despite the fact that the cost of conventional batteries has dropped by almost 40% in comparison with 2009, this course is still extremely costly.

The fate of another fundamental forthcoming innovation – moving unmanned vehicles – depends on the success of disruptive technologies. There is no need to provide examples of the rapid spread of this innovation. In the US, enthusiasts of unmanned electric car driving are already testing Tesla's products at full speed in real-world conditions, crossing the country from east to west. Apple is preparing to enter the market of unmanned electric vehicles in the coming years. US army trucks and Russian Kamaz trucks are already equipped with technical solutions that pave the way for the creation of automated unmanned vehicles.

AUTOMATED UNMANNED DRIVING

Nevertheless, vehicles without drivers, familiar to us thanks to such films as *Minority Report, I, Robot* and *The Fifth Element,* will come to exist very soon owing to information gathered by the Google Street View service and the launch of the self-driving car project by Google. The project involves cars of 10 different brands. In a similar project, Volvo has recently developed and successfully tested a caravan technology of its own. Unmanned projects have been launched and are now being carried out at full speed by Honda and Mercedes. Tesla has unveiled plans to launch a serial manufacture of Model III robotic electric cars by 2020, which will be cheaper than Model S cars and will be able to travel 320km on a single charge.

All such vehicles will be literally filled with electronics and video cameras, and the information from these will be easily readable by equipment installed on police patrol cars. The New York City Police already has such experimental cars. Cameras installed at each corner, huge databases and facial recognition systems – these are all part of today's reality.

The next phase of automated unmanned driving is developing actively. Some vehicles already have cruise control systems designed to automatically maintain a set speed without the driver's involvement. So far this is only possible on motorways and acceleration lanes provided for vehicles to merge into the main flow of traffic, as well as on motorway exit lanes. This means that caravans of unmanned trucks on motorways will be part of reality in the not too distant future.

Google is currently making considerable efforts to bring its self-driving cars to a new level of development – to teach them how to move in urban environments. The purpose of these efforts is to make people passengers rather than major participants in the urban traffic. The developers of Google self-driving cars note that their cars are now able to detect and identify hundreds of different objects simultaneously. The identification system can make out moving pedestrians, buses, road signs, traffic lights and traffic controllers, and even cyclists gesturing to inform others of their intention to execute a manoeuvre. Unlike a person, an automatic control system never gets tired or distracted.

Practically all major car manufacturers have announced road tests to be conducted on automated versions of their vehicles. But it can be complicated to create a technology capable of making a car fully autonomous, since it is necessary to establish effective communication between all road users. The main difficulty is that a human driver may sometimes ignore road traffic regulations. Pedestrians also add to this complexity. Unlike conventional drivers, an unmanned vehicle will never commit a conscious violation of the traffic rules. One of the major stumbling blocks to bringing unmanned vehicles to public roads is the legal responsibility for a traffic accident caused by such a vehicle. So far there is no legislation to define which party would be found guilty of an accident of this kind. Despite all of this, the introduction of unmanned vehicles is only a matter of time.

To sum it up, I would like to emphasize that it is not individual technologies that win and lose, or the discovery itself. The fate of new technologies is solved by the configuration of integration in the market (which technologies will complement each other and which will compete) and the relative speed of processes (those showing a better development rate).

The ability to see the perspective configuration before it is fully completed is strategic vision. If you possess it, you simply know the outcome. If you do, it is time to act.

HOW INNOVATIVE ECONOMY BRINGS THE CREATIVE CLASS TO THE FORE OF HISTORY. THE FUTURE OF WORK

To implement revolutionary ideas and have a good return on their investment, innovative companies greatly need a world market consisting of well-trained users – the Creative Class. Creative people create new knowledge, invest in technologies of the future, and then distribute and consume the products of innovative companies.

CREATIVE MERITOCRACY

To a large extent economic wealth is created most efficiently in conditions where meritocratic principles of society management are adhered to, according to which leadership positions must be occupied by the most capable people regardless of their social background and financial prosperity. The level of economic progress made by this or that society is most adequately reflected by the size of its GDP per capita. The higher the level, the more pronounced the intensive (innovative) nature of development of the society and the more significant the role played by the Creative Class. A country's leadership in the global market largely determines its possibility to exert geopolitical influence; as a result, political systems undergo transformation. This process is also promoted by close cooperation between countries and peoples, achieved in the conditions of globalisation through free exchange of information, improvements in transportation systems, more and more ample opportunities for international tourism, various types of exchange, ever increasing flows of exported and imported goods, and so on.

Societies that have achieved a sufficiently high level of development and comprehended the reasons for their success become increasingly interested in harmonizing their living conditions, expanding the Creative Class's ability to function, and promoting more intensive circulation of new productive ideas that give rise to the next generation of innovation.

A new type of commerce will grow stronger and a peer-to-peer economy will emerge, i.e. an economy where homemade things are produced and their manufacturers become key elements. These new economic relationships will have a significant impact on society.

Education will become more and more creative and learning methods will be adapted to students based on their innate abilities. Our world is rapidly moving towards specialization and transformation of public education. Soon robots will take over much of the routine work. People's outlook on their creative skills will change rapidly. The new education system will train people who have never considered themselves especially creative. Increasing adaptability and specialization of education will result in the emergence of an entire generation of pragmatists who will learn disciplines that are quite distant from one another, such as programming and art. Significant changes will take place in the national school curricula of many countries. Such subjects as painting, drawing and geometry may be replaced with virtual design using 3D spatial software.

We live in a time of a great demographic transition. Future epochs will be so short that people may fail to notice one replacing another immediately. If a kingdom of 'mature humankind' comes 50 years from now, this will mean that social norms and attitudes towards innovation processes will also change significantly. The creative class (leading artists, scholars and intellectual leaders who understand this major trend) will have to instruct national authorities regularly in order to enable the slowly adapting governments to understand the upcoming grand transition and realise the approaching radical change in society.[213]

Today's governments continue to use the concept of work or employment while implying that it is something that people go to or something that they are paid for. But the nature of work is changing. People today actively use combinations of their skills and any existing markets that can pay adequately for those skills. They come to occupy a variety of niches and change society itself, turning from design developers into design assemblers.

Since the essence of work is changing, demand for money and the requirements to be met by banks are changing too. The so-called peer-to-peer money (take, for example, the peer-to-peer payment system using Bitcoin as the unit of account) becomes more real once people move away from the conventional concept of work and employment. How can governments, democracy and systems of taxation work if there are no conventional currencies and no conventional transactions? Governments banning 'money substitutes' cannot solve the problem.

THE FUTURE OF WORK

However, as Erik Brynjolfsson and Andrew McAfee, the authors of *Race Against the Machine*, state, people will soon have to compete for jobs not only with their own kind, but with their own creations – robots (Brynjolfsson 2012)! This is quite possible: just remember that not so long ago, in the 19th century, half of the US population was employed in agriculture and now it is less than 2%.

Brynjolfsson and McAfee, both researchers at MIT, are convinced that many occupations are already losing the race against new technologies. However, while attempting to find out whether people can cooperate rather than compete with machines, they came to the conclusion that the development of technology opens up many possibilities where man and machine complement each other.

"Digital progress is so fast and inexorable that people and organizations find it difficult to keep up with it," Brynjolfsson says. "Machines can become our allies, but only if we change the mode of work." Brynjolfsson and McAfee base their statements on the fact that rapid technological progress destroys jobs faster than it creates them. The scholars provide graphs in their book showing the relationship between growth in labour productivity and the overall employment in the United States. In the past, productivity growth used to cause an increase in the number of jobs. Starting from 2000, the lines began to diverge: labour productivity has grown significantly, while the overall employment has dropped unexpectedly. Brynjolfsson and McAfee called this phenomenon "the great separation" (Brynjolfsson 2012).

Process automation is gradually but steadily replacing human labour with computers. Reports presented by the International Federation of Robotics in 2013 stated that the industry would create, both directly and indirectly, 2-3.5 million jobs by 2020 and each robot would require 3.6 service technicians on average. In the autumn of 2013, futurists from Oxford University published a study called *The Future of Employment*. Taking the study conducted by Brynjolfsson and McAfee, they suggested that services and robots would gradually master unconventional occupations. The conclusion was shocking:

over the next 20 years, up to 47% of all professions, including lawyers, doctors and teachers, were expected to find themselves in the risk zone.

For many of our contemporaries, technologies have come to be hardly distinguishable from magic. What will the digital future give people: enormous opportunities or huge disappointment? The answer depends on us, as any evolutionary development in any technologies, whether biological or informational or communicational, depends on decisions we make today.

HOW NEW WEALTH WILL BE CREATED. HOW THE EVOLUTION BUSINESS WORKS

In the future, new technologies and globalization will bring about the creation of a novel wealth. The future economy will transform the very pattern of innovative business, turning it into a living evolutionary organization.

HOW NEW WEALTH WILL BE CREATED

Thanks to the McKinsey Global Institute, we may expect the total contribution of new technologies to the world economy to vary in the future (starting from 2025) from $14 trillion to $33billion.[214] This is comparable with half the current global GDP that, for reference, totalled some $72 trillion in 2013, while the GDP of the US, the wealthiest country in the world, amounted to about $15 trillion that year. What can give such a great effect? According to the McKinsey Global Institute, it will be breakthrough technologies, the most promising 12 of which are:
- Internet of things:
  1) Mobile internet;
  2) Internet of things;
  3) Cloud technologies.
- Artificial intelligence:
  1) Automation of knowledge/data;
  2) Advanced robotics;
  3) Autonomous vehicles.
- Energy:
  1) Accumulation and storage of energy;
  2) Modern methods of oil and gas exploration and production;
  3) Renewable energy.
- New industrial production:
  1) 3D printers;
  2) Advanced materials.
- New generation genomics.

**ROBOT BAXTER, CREATED BY RETHINK ROBOTICS INC.,
DEMONSTRATES ITS OPERATION AT THE OPENING OF THE
ASIA-PACIFIC INNOVATION CENTER (APIC) ON DECEMBER 9, 2015**

ROBOTRADE ECONOMY, OR WILL PEOPLE BE AFRAID OF COMPETITION FROM ROBOTS?

There will be no threat to skilled workers by robots yet. But those who were paid $1 per hour for their work, i.e. the lowest wage workforce, will be the first to be displaced. Wages of about that size are paid to employees at Foxconn (China), where iPhones are assembled and where management is planning to replace four of each five workers with robots. A simple calculation shows that for a robot to be able to compete with a Chinese worker, it has to be able to do what the worker does and cost less than $9,000 ($1 × 24 hours × 365 days a year = $8,760). One robot will be able to replace three workers (employed in

8-hour shifts) whose tasks involve loading and unloading operations or assembly line inspection. Foxconn is the 10th-largest company in the world in terms of numbers of employees. It employs one million people. The world's nine largest employers that rank above Foxconn in this respect are the armed forces of various countries, led by the armies of China, India and the US. Although I do not know the exact plans for robotics in the military sector, I believe these to be no less radical. Vast numbers of auxiliary military occupations may disappear overnight.

The engineering automation market has produced a number of giant manufacturers of specialized industrial robots, including Swisslog, Kuka, Fanuc and ABB. Their main clients are engineering monsters – such as GM, GE and Tesla – that employ huge numbers of robot operation engineers. To these companies, each ordinary shift-work employee costs no less than $8,000 per year and a fully fledged staffing position costs no less than $24,000. The replacement of staff with robots in these companies means that the expected return on the investment (ROI) made in robots and humans is roughly comparable with the cost of Robot Baxter.

According to experts, our civilization will soon acquire a 'new energy land-scape' (renewable sources, energy storage, new mining technologies, etc.). The total contribution made by this trend to the global economy could reach $1.4 trillion a year, while the minimum estimate is $0.4 trillion. Although McKinsey & Company base these figures on the assumption of a 200% increase to be achieved in North American oil production by 2025, owing to the use of hydraulic fracturing and horizontal drilling technologies, this, strictly speaking, has nothing to do with either new or 'green' technologies. I will explain this point below.

Next is the 'digital world', (internet of things, cloud technologies, 'smart' cities and so-called big data). According to McKinsey, the potential economic effect to be achieved by 2025 through automation of mental labour alone is estimated to be $5-7 trillion. The total contribution made by this sector to the global economy will range from $8.1 to $23.2 trillion a year.

Another sector designed to change our lives is automation (total robotization and autonomous vehicles). By 2025, more than 1.5 million potential deaths caused by drivers can be avoided. The cost advantage to be achieved by introducing unmanned driving will range from $7.1 to $13.1 trillion a year. This is a very significant effect, given that today's robot market totals about $30 billion or 0.05% of the global GDP, while the worldwide GDP of the manufacturing industry amounts to $11 trillion. Advanced production technologies and previously unavailable technology engineering (robotics, new materials and 3D printing) may fetch from $0.4 to $1.1 trillion a year.

Medicine of the future (genetic engineering, further 'digitisation', personal healthcare and biomedicine) may contribute from $0.7 to $1.6 trillion to the world economy each year. Diagnosis will become less expensive. This is impressive, though even today the global healthcare costs are estimated to total $6.5 trillion.

According to McKinsey Global Institute experts, all these rapidly developing breakthrough technologies have some characteristics in common: they will affect practically every aspect of life and have a serious impact on important economic values.

There is, however, one important issue. Benefits obtained from technologies are unevenly distributed between developed and developing countries. Not all technologies are of interest to developed countries. Thus, cloud computing, renewable energy and mobile internet will have a greater impact on the economies of developing countries. This is due to a significant growth in the population and therefore the numbers of new users in these countries. In renewable energy, such distribution in favour of developing countries is due to large projects in China and Africa.

Recent economic research in the EU and the US has shown that investment in intellectual capital by business organizations results in a 20-30% increase in productivity on average. It is exactly this increased productivity that ensures 2% growth in global GDP. Economic statistics show that countries that invest in intellectual capital more than others are more efficient in redistributing resources (in favour of innovative enterprises). This is a very important aspect, because it is not so much imports of means of production as foreign direct investments that serve as a critical factor in strengthening the innovative potential of a nation. Foreign direct investments result in knowledge accumulation and ensure technology transfer to national companies both directly (through licensing) and indirectly (through accumulation of expertise by local personnel). When explaining the four-leaf clover model, I noted that it takes designs, components and assemblers to create an innovation. During interaction with foreign investors, countries accumulate and develop knowledge of design, standards and quality requirements, and develop principles for cooperation in joint ventures, as a result of which new products get an opportunity to integrate into the world market.

There is no point anymore in distinguishing individual carriers of innovative change, as Schumpeter did, considering the business class first and then corporations. What an outstanding personality, an innovative firm and a striving corporation have in common today is that they do not accept 2% annual growth, because their ideas cost more! It is not individual inventors and entrepreneurs that become agents of change, but teams of diverse and dissimilar people 'infected' with a particular idea. Even the most advanced management technology would not be sufficient on its own to ensure success for an innovative company. A creative team requires skilful management from within the organization (Jeston 2015), since the inertia of the entire organization will over time extinguish the innovation flame, turning the organization from a living being into a dead one (Stuart-Kotze 2006, 107).

THINGS BUILT BY EVOLUTION

Businessmen, economists and management gurus have for many decades been searching for an answer to the question of whether there is a formula for success and what differentiates one great company from another.

Not surprisingly, numerous books have been written on the subject 'Why great companies fail'. In the 1980s and 1990s, emphasis was made on core competencies possessed by great companies. Then the focus was shifted to disruptive innovations and novel product niches that are filled with fast start-ups defeating giants. Today, more and more research is devoted to exploring a new idea: the evolutionary essence of great companies.

It is asserted that the success of many thriving companies is rooted in the use of an innovative, evolutionary model of business development. This model employs certain algorithms that use previously accumulated data and take account of the current circumstances in order to reach the most rational decisions. The same evolutionary development principle is employed in the management of new companies. Before, corporations mostly relied on managerial experience and intuition; today's business uses some or other mechanisms that enable it to adapt to diverse conditions and avoid making sudden and hasty decisions.

Life is full of chance and contradiction. Let's recall the famous aphorism by Helmuth von Moltke, the 19th century Prussian General, who said that "strategy is a system for evading predicaments". Since a carefully developed plan usually fails, an optimum strategy should provide at least three ways out of difficult situations.

In their best-selling book *Built to Last*, Jim Collins and Jerry Porras come to the following conclusion: "Visionary companies make some of their best moves by experimentation, trial and error, opportunism and – quite literally – accident. What looks in retrospect like brilliant foresight and preplanning was often the result of 'Let's just try a lot of stuff and keep what works'. In this sense, visionary companies mimic the biological evolution of species. We found the concepts in Charles Darwin's *Origin of Species* to be more helpful for replicating the success of certain visionary companies than any textbook on corporate strategic planning" (Collins 1994).

Modern conditions require speed and sobriety in decision-making in various fields. Despite this, only a few realize the advantages offered by the evolutionary model of development and put its principles into practice systematically. Meanwhile, the absence of an evolutionary mechanism capable of continuous improvement increases risks and costs. Collins and Porras describe the evolutionary process as branching and pruning. The idea is simple: by continually adding sufficient numbers of branches to a tree (change) and removing dead branches correctly (select), you are sure to develop it into a plant with healthy branches, well adapted to thrive in an ever-changing world. The complex adaptive systems theory plays an important role in the study of the evolution of most various items, ranging from space objects to social matters. At present, biologists, sociologists and experts involved in studying management problems, including those related to innovation, actively use this theory. It is high time we got to know a few of its basic concepts.

CONCEPTS EMPLOYED IN THE COMPLEX ADAPTIVE SYSTEMS THEORY

The first concept to mention is that of an active element (agent) of a system, whose behaviour is determined by certain consistent patterns and rules. In various systems, various agents can act as active elements (e.g. atoms, computer programs, or people).

Another important concept is that of recombination (i.e. connections practically realizable in a system, interactions between the system's active elements). It is the possibility of such recombination that leads to innovation. A typical and striking example of recombination is the combination – quite unexpected at its time – of the properties of a wing capable of developing lifting power, a bicycle wheel providing acceleration and an internal combustion engine as the necessary source of energy. The result was the invention of the airplane by the Wright brothers in 1903 (not to mention the persistent and truly titanic research efforts Wilbur and Orville Wright made with their engineering research and dangerous test flights, i.e. everything that preceded the first flight of an aircraft, which opened modern aviation).

The concept of selection in the complex adaptive systems theory serves, as it does in Darwin's natural selection theory, to denote processes that determine which elements of a system will be the most viable and will be able to participate in further recombination.

Naturally, the concept of adaptation, i.e. that of self-adjustment and self-tuning, is one of the central notions in the complex adaptive systems theory. It is known, for example, that animals can, subject to changes in climatic conditions, change their behaviour patterns from generation to generation and thus preserve themselves as a species. In a market where the conditions are changing, companies may change their behaviour patterns too. Obviously, only those companies that are able to grasp accurately the market trends and restructure their operation to meet these trends in the best possible way obtain an advantage over others.

The tool kit of the complex adaptive systems theory includes the concept of joint evolution. This results from interaction, cooperation and competition taking place between them.

The essence of this concept is well illustrated by the development of such companies as Google, Apple, Microsoft and other software developers. Operating in one and the same market, they adapt to each other and determine the development of not only the sector they belong to, but the entire industry as a whole.

Finally, there is the concept of an ecosystem. It is known to have been formulated in the life sciences but, thanks to the development of the complex adaptive systems theory, is now used to adequately describe numerous social and economic phenomena. For example, modern science cannot predict with certainty what a complex and vulnerable ecosystem such as modern tropical forests will be like 100 years from now. It's a similar situation trying to predict how the aggregate of personal computers, mobile phones and other means of telecommunication, which may in their entirety also be represented as a kind of ecosystem, will evolve in 100 weeks.

It can be said with certainty that the creation of evolutionary development mechanisms will be an important component of the operation of most companies in the near future. Innovation is increasingly becoming a norm of conduct for a living organization rather than something unusual and new. To make evolutionary progress, a company needs to incorporate a certain algorithm in the structure of its operation and strengthen the following areas of its activity:

- Creativity is necessary to encourage initiative, forgive staff for failures and analyse the current situation, even if it seems to be stable, as well as set new tasks and develop mechanisms for rapid response to change in the environment.
- Mechanisms for continuous testing of products throughout their lifecycles and for receiving feedback. It is necessary to use various sources of information to analyse the situation and predict its development.
- Flexibility in resource allocation can be achieved through outsourcing certain functions. Resources should be reallocated regularly.
- Constant monitoring of the market should involve monitoring both the market in which the company operates and adjacent markets in order to be able to use novel technologies, whether concerned with new materials or IT systems, in the company's products.

In Chapter 1, the evolutionary algorithm acting as part of biological evolution was examined. Of course, it would be wrong to apply this algorithm to business mechanically. We need to adapt these principles when applying them to evolutionary business, seeing as it differs significantly from biological evolution. In the words of David Deutsch, humans differ from other species in what knowledge they can use (explanatory rules rather than rules of thumb) and how this knowledge is created (by putting forward hypotheses and criticising ideas rather than by variation and selection of genes) (Deutsch 2011).

Biological evolution has no specific goal – it just grinds trillions of design options, creating organisms and selecting the most competitive options in the ever-changing ecosystem. However, as we have already noted, it is not organisms that are selected, but designs encoded in the genes. Businesses set clear ambitious goals and business models, once built, create products that compete in the market. In this process, it is not products as such that are selected, but elements of designs – business models that make it possible to produce these products. Successful elements of a business model are amplified by financial markets' expectations.

Figure 33 demonstrates the functioning principles of an evolutionary algorithm built on four key actions: create, embed, compete and select.

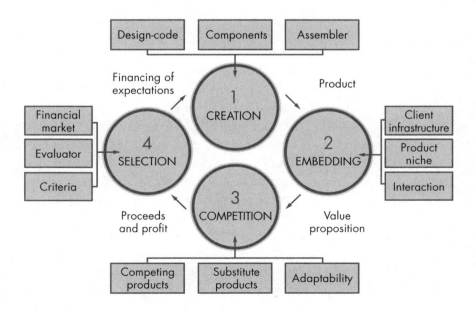

FIGURE 33. EVOLUTIONARY BUSINESS MODEL

EVOLUTIONARY PROGRESS:
LET THE STRONGEST... DESIGNS SURVIVE

To gain a better understanding of how this evolutionary mechanism works, let's consider the following example.

Let's imagine that a theme contest is held for the best truck assembled from Lego toy parts. Let's imagine that the competitors are requested to assemble a truck that will be ideally suited to the task of transporting goods from warehouse to warehouse. Loading and unloading will be performed by a loader that is also collected from Lego parts.

Creation. Using a set of 200 Lego pieces of four colours, some 10^{100} objects could be assembled – more than the number of atoms in the universe (about 10^{80})! A catalogue representing all these objects, with each page devoted to one design option, would have to have more than 10^{100} pages. In other words, the whole universe would not be enough to create such a catalogue, even if every page consisted of a single atom!

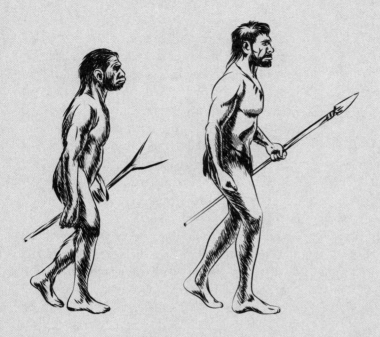

To assemble a truck following one of the design options presented in the catalogue, a skilled reader and assembler of designs would be required, who would be able to assemble the object precisely and accurately according to the design using the given Lego pieces. In reality, however, assemblers sometimes fail to put such products together exactly according to plan: some extra parts may be left unused, or, for example, some pieces may prove to be joined to one another in a different way. These inaccuracies are called variations.

Incorporation. The finished truck must be incorporated into the operation system of a construction factory that is also constructed using Lego parts, i.e. into the client's infrastructure. In this system, the truck and infrastructure, which consists of the loader, the cargo and the cargo handling area, form an interconnected ecosystem, in which the truck has a niche of its own — the optimal transportation niche.

This means that the truck should conform in the best possible way to the task of carrying construction parts (i.e. match the parts' size and weight), to the cyclic operation of the loader and to the distance which it has to cover moving from the loading area to the unloading area and back. All elements of this ecosystem are interlinked, interdependent and interactive with each other. For example, an expansion of the capacity of the construction factory may require the loader to be replaced with a more efficient one. The requirements to the truck would have to be adjusted accordingly.

Competition. The truck competes with trucks of other models in terms of efficiency, quality, cost, fuel consumption and other parameters. It is possible that the entire subsystem would be more efficient if the truck was equipped with a lifting mechanism that would perform loading and unloading operations instead of the loader. It is possible that it would be more efficient to load the truck with construction parts of a slightly larger or smaller size. Then the truck would able to compete for the right to occupy another niche in the subsystem, i.e. the cargo loading and unloading niche. In this example, the truck competes with representatives of other species within its ecosystem. There is yet another important aspect to mention: economic cycles, within which there are fat and lean years. This aspect affects competition profoundly. During recession years, the company that manufactures the trucks will need a cash reserve and, possibly, support from the shareholders. A vital issue is whether the company will be able to adjust its output to a change in demand quickly, i.e. how quickly it will be able to adapt to a changing market.

Selection. Let's imagine that our contestant presents their truck for the contest and that this truck competes with the trucks presented by other participants. Refereeing is done by a professional jury which, prior to the contest, produced and distributed among the contestants the criteria for selecting the winners who will go through to the next round of the contest. For example, the criteria may specify the maximum number of parts that a truck must be able to transport and unload during a certain period. As a result, the best specimens that meet these criteria to the utmost extent are selected at the first stage of the competition.

The object of selection. Let's try to understand what is going to be the object of selection. At first glance, the object is a truck that better interacts with the loader, moves faster and unloads cargoes quicker. But is it really? Let's see what happens if this criterion is modified as a result of the eco-system evolving over time. For simplicity's sake, let's imagine that a bigwig comes to replace the qualified professional jury. It may happen that the bigwig just likes yellow and has little interest in other parameters. Then, with our contestant completing one development cycle after another, we notice that our truck becomes more and more yellow. It will be no surprise if the black wheels suddenly disappear altogether, to be replaced with yellow skids, and the truck is no longer able to move. Actually, now the jury selects design components. After that the jury gives additional time and resources (new Lego parts) to some of the best participants and requests them to modify and improve their models, while taking into account additional criteria according to which the best machines will be selected. Finally, if the truck proves to be truly innovative and surpasses by far all existing analogues, then the financial market comes into action. Its expectations may raise the company's value very high by including forecast profits to be earned in the future in the assessment of the company's market value. This may give the company additional resources to enhance its operation and a significant gain in time.

Evolutionary business is the key to building a truly living organization!

GREAT SPACE TRAVEL. COLONIZATION OF PLANETS

Let's turn the kaleidoscope once again and look at the stars, or rather at what we actually see – their reflections. Here we leave the comfortable and safe position of an observer of facts (which we have invariably occupied until now) and enter the realm of an unknown distant future. Nobody knows what it will look like exactly. Five centuries ago, Christopher Columbus set out to find a sea route to India, but discovered America! Although it is quite possible that we are making discoveries that will prove to be very different from what we expected, this does not render them less exciting or great in any way.

However, humanity does not have to create old-style colonies, where one, more developed society, exploits its less-developed fellow men and creates intolerable conditions for them. Colonies could be created on uninhabited planets found nearby, which would make it possible to populate them in the future.

The Moon, because of its proximity to the Earth (within three days' journey) and owing to the fact that it has been well studied for over half a century, is regarded as the main candidate for the role of launching a base from where space colonization could start. The Moon has large quantities of minerals and, in particular, vast reserves of Helium-3, which could be an indispensable fuel if the fusion project proves to be successful. According to most conservative estimates, the already found reserves of Helium-3 on the Moon are sufficient to provide the Earth with all the energy it may need during the next 150 years or more! The Moon is also viewed as a unique base for developing future space technologies and thus gaining access to more distant planetary systems.

Konstantin Tsiolkovsky, in his famous 1926 book *Exploration of Outer Space by Means of Rocket Devices*, presented a detailed timetable for conquering outer space, according to which the first research base on the Moon was scheduled to exist by 2015. Tsiolkovsky proved to be a little overly optimistic, because we have still not created space transport systems, high-capacity power plants and long-distance transcosmic power transmission lines required for carrying out the task. Modern scholars have moved industrial development of the Moon and Mars, as well as that of Venus and Mercury, towards much more distant points in the future. Some parts required to 'assemble' the design we have developed are still missing.

But the main obstacle in the way of colonization of the Moon is that the satellite has neither an atmosphere nor radiation belts similar to those that protect the Earth from cosmic radiation. People would be defenceless against galactic radiation on the Moon. Astronauts can reach the threshold dose of radiation within just 100 hours on the lunar surface.

Other candidate planets for human colonization are Mars and Venus. However, for missions to these heavenly bodies to be successful, more than mere radiation problems, similar to those existing on the Moon, will have to be solved. For example, a radio signal sent from Mars reaches the Earth within four to 20 minutes, depending on the relative positions of the planets. As a result, colonization of planets becomes a matter for the very distant future. Concepts of 'sowing' or 'controlled initiation' of life on other planets by Earthlings are becoming increasingly popular and enjoy active development. It must be said, however, that we are only taking the first steps in this direction. Terraforming means changing the climatic conditions of a planet, a satellite, or another celestial body in order to bring all of its parameters and environmental conditions to a state that would make it suitable for habitation by terrestrial plants, animals and humans. Despite the fact that many large-scale programmes have been announced in this area, the answer to the question of whether we can change the environment of an entire planet, making it comfortable for people, remains rather obscure.

As for the other planets in the Solar System, conditions suitable for life cannot be created in principle: Mercury faces the Sun with one of its sides, a result of which is that any gas would be immediately blown away from its surface, with one side being sizzlingly hot and the other cosmically cold. Jupiter, Saturn, Uranus and Neptune are gaseous planets where there is no surface even to step on. The gravitational fields of these planets are strong enough to crush a human, while powerful magnetic fields are sure to bring down any electrical equipment.

It turns out that the Moon is the most suitable candidate for colonization. At the beginning of this century, the US launched a lunar programme expected to result in the establishment of bases on the Moon. Since then, a number of advanced space powers – Russia, the EU, China and Japan – have also announced plans to establish bases on the Moon in the 2030s and 2040s. However, such plans tend to shift gradually further along the timeline into the future.

I will quote physicist David Deutsch (Deutsch 2011):

"…The Moon has essentially the same resources of mass, energy and information as the Earth has. The fact that humans living on

A POSTER FOR 'A JOURNEY TO MARS',
A SOVIET 1926 SCIENCE-FICTION FILM
(Source: Russian State Library, Moscow)

CAN PEOPLE LIVE OUTSIDE THE EARTH?

The modern perception of the possibility of creating conditions for life on other planets is still far from perfect. It rather resembles the advancement of science fiction hypotheses. For example, a theory has been put forward, according to which an atmosphere could be created on Mars either by using water available on the planet itself, or by pumping over ambient gases from Venus to Mars via a laser beam. One more theory suggests that water could be obtained from a passing comet by shattering its core with a laser beam and then focusing the resulting vapour in the right direction. But most scientists believe that colonists would have to live in caves or bunkers.

Another planet that appears to be more or less suitable for colonization is Venus, where there is an atmosphere, though very poisonous and pressurized to nearly a hundred atmospheres. But scientists still believe that Venus could be refined much quicker than Mars. According to Carl Sagan, a famous American astrophysicist, algae could be pulverized over the planet, binding nitrogen, utilizing carbon dioxide and releasing oxygen. But would we be able to carry out a massive biological outreach while the course of our own biological evolution is still a mystery to us? In any case, such insemination of Venus, if it ever took place, would be fraught with many uncertainties. It could only be controlled partly by means of penetrating radiation from the orbit. But we would still need to know exactly the composition of the second, third and subsequent landings made up of other microbes, and this would be a long paramilitary mission. An error could result in irreparable damage. After a disastrous experiment, the atmosphere of an entire planet cannot be slopped down the drain like an inedible soup.

the Moon would have to make their own air is no more significant than the fact that laboratories on Earth have to make their own vacuum. Both tasks can be automated so as to require arbitrarily little human effort or attention.

...Setting up self-sufficient colonies on the Moon and elsewhere in the solar system – and eventually in other solar systems – will be a good hedge against the extinction of our species or the destruction of civilization and is a highly desirable goal for that reason among others."

Another outstanding physicist, Stephen Hawking, has verbalized Deutsch's thoughts with the utmost clarity: "I think that humanity will become extinct in another 1,000 years unless it populates space. There may be many threats to existence on a single planet. But I am an optimist. We can make it to the stars" (Highfield 2001).

In the Age of Travel, discussed in Chapter 6, the discovery of new lands would have been impossible without the scientific revolution, a shift in the paradigm and the use of new knowledge. The colonization of planets, apparently, can only become a reality once we reach a fundamentally new level of technology based on new, yet unknown, knowledge. This, in turn, may require major changes in our worldview.

A feasible and pragmatic solution to the problem of lunar exploration proposed today suggests that the Moon could be explored and colonised by robonauts rather than astronauts. NASA has drawn up the so-called Project M, a project conceived to send a robot to the Moon, rather than a human. Scientists located on Earth would have their sight and other senses synchronised with those of a robonaut operating on the Moon, and thus be able to walk, as it were, on the lunar surface and carry out research. The project has a budget of $0.5 billion, or about 1,000 times less than the estimated cost of the lunar station project Lunar Oasis ($550 billion).

NEW PARADIGM:
KNOWLEDGE AS A SOURCE OF WEALTH

Having made up its mind to preserve and disseminate knowledge, humankind invented cuneiform first, then other forms of writing, followed by books, then carried out a revolution in the dissemination of knowledge by introducing the printing press and, ultimately, made the exchange of knowledge instantaneous by bringing in the internet. These 'jumps', 'transitions', or 'shifts' in the paradigm are already well known to us. It is unlikely though that the evolutionary process will leave it at that. It will be humankind that will cease to develop once it has reached

**SPACEX DRAGON COMMERCIAL CARGO SPACECRAFT,
PHOTOGRAPHED A MOMENT BEFORE CANADARM2, THE ROBOTIC
ARM OF THE INTERNATIONAL SPACE STATION, RELEASES IT FOR
A SPLASHDOWN IN THE PACIFIC OCEAN**
May 18, 2014

HOW VIRGIN GALACTIC AND SPACEX
ARE 'WARMING UP' GLOBAL GROWTH
IN SPACE INDUSTRY

Thanks to Richard Branson and his Virgin Galactic, anyone who has $250,000 to spend can make a space trip on Space Ship 2 today. To go into space, one does not have to be an astronaut any longer – what one really needs is money, good health and enough patience to wait in a queue of 400 people.

Elon Musk has committed himself to more serious undertakings. His company SpaceX is successfully testing a reusable vertical take-off system, Grasshopper, and a giant rocket, Falcon Heavy, capable of delivering tonnes of payload on a projected mission to Mars.

a certain level in its progress as a species that is rather tangibly constrained in terms of channelling and processing information. Even today, to make another leap forward, we need something extraordinary.

And what about future leaps that could bring about new ways of gaining knowledge? Futurist Ray Kurzweil heralds a new era by arguing that the next transition will be that to technological singularity. In his opinion, we have already taken the first step by starting a process in which computation speeds, bandwidths and memory capacities are continually increasing. Then it will be up to appropriate software to select suitable replicators. We do not know how soon computers will acquire analogues of our neurons. However, we do know that in theory this is possible.

In the coming decades, two important trends will unite: progress in the development of trainable software and progress in the use of biological paradigms in computer systems. It is quite possible that at first this will result in some kind of 'information farms' (as suggested by Stanislaw Lem), where pure information will be 'grown', somewhat similarly to the way nuclear explosions or protein interactions are simulated on computers today, creating a virtual environment abiding by certain laws. Though looking at conventional data centres, these farms will be the place where, according to Kurzweil, technological singularity will occur and artificial superintelligence will emerge.

This will be the key point, because today we are superior to the computers we have created in that we can think creatively. In other words, we can perform a task in various ways, while a computer, if set to do the same, will always use one and the same algorithm. This is so because it has no intelligence – yet.

However, we will actively assist machines in acquiring intelligence. In pursuit of knowledge, people actively use computers as intellectual amplifiers. We assume that the possession of a more intelligent computer than ourselves will be the key to success. A computer that is more intelligent than we are and provided with artificial intelligence (subject to reasonable restrictions, in our view) should be able help us to solve our complex problems.

In reality, the internet is already an integrated man-machine tool. The development of the World Wide Web is similar to that of the biosphere, being different from the latter in that it is taking place a million times faster and involves hundreds of millions of intelligent human beings.

Systems are being created everywhere, either dependent on control by biological life or existing under the laws of biological life –

laws that we ourselves do not quite understand but still are eager to recreate in hardware. Direct brain-computer interfaces are already part of commerce and therefore the creation of neurosilicon transducers to be used to download knowledge directly into the brain is a matter of the not-too-distant future. What do we need it for? To generate new knowledge out of knowledge!

Recently, global media that share Kurzweil's optimism have relished the parameters of the Chinese supercomputer Tianhe-2, pointing out that its processing speed, 33 petaflops per second, is comparable with that of a human brain (about 1,016 operations per second).[215] They forgot to add that this supercomputer is the size of a small town and consumes as much energy as a medium-sized city with its environs. A human brain consumes power measured in watts and does not exceed the size of a volleyball.

Owing to technological progress, people will soon be able to connect special chips to the human brain. Whole organs, designed, for example, to provide an isolated brain with all essential nutrients, can be printed out today, cell by cell, on 3D printers. To prevent a science-fiction scenario in the style of that described in *Professor Dowell's Head* (a 1925 novel by Alexander Belyayev), we need the highest morals and ethics as a safety catch, because such a diabolical machine can only be driven by a program code written by a human. It is morality that directs progress along a more humane path.

In technological terms, another scenario is also possible. Today, routine biotechnology procedures make it possible to copy genes to computer memory, where they can be stored in a different physical form. It will soon be possible to incorporate such records into the DNA chains of various animals to ensure their survival. No doubt biotechnology will eventually acquire enough experience to be able to create a database containing information about the function of each gene. This means that in the future we will be able to rewrite, quite consciously, our own genetic code, thus enabling our functionality to make one more leap.

For 'ordinary' people, good treatment is in the making. A golden age is not a utopia at all if the problem of immortality is solved and progress in a post-singular world (as seen by Kurzweil) is provided by superhuman beings owing to their ability to communicate with us and with each other at different speeds. It will be possible to copy parts of superhuman beings and increase the volume of their consciousness in proportion to the complexity of the problem to be solved. This world will go beyond

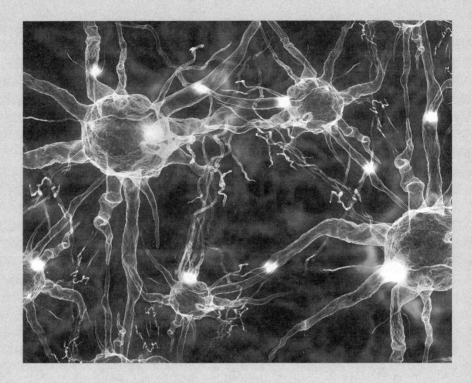

HOW TO REWRITE THE GENETIC CODE
OF A HUMAN BEING

In fact, we do not have to rewrite our genetic code. What we need is to learn how to activate necessary genes and deactivate unnecessary ones. As theoretical physicist Michio Kaku noted, "Stem cells are 'mother cells of all cells', as they are able to change their structure and turn into any type of cells. Every cell in a human body contains the full genetic code required for the construction of the entire body" (Kaku 2011). However, as the author stresses, a cell, while maturing, grows to specialize, so that many of the genes it contains become inactive, switched off, as it were. "A skin cell, for example, has all the genes required for its conversion into a blood cell, but they are switched off; all unneeded genes are switched off when a germ cell becomes an adult skin cell," he writes.

the boundaries of good and evil as we know them. Ultimately, our pursuit of knowledge will cause us to create a mind that has outgrown the limits of our understanding. Is this the ultimate meaning of the long journey towards knowledge?

EVOLUTION OF SYNTHETIC BIOLOGY.
CREATIVITY OF ARTIFICIAL INTELLIGENCE

The rapid development of synthetic biology will enable us to design biological systems that do not exist in nature. This can be done by assembling DNA out of 'bio-bricks'.

Attempts to teach artificial intelligence how to think creatively and feel will become more successful. The key to success is the creation of a multi-level hierarchical system based on a set of rules that make it possible to study the world and develop as a species by means of an evolutionary algorithm.

Progress in these areas may enable us to create beings that are capable of producing new knowledge along with biological evolution. Let's hope that humankind's choice in creating these new beings in the image and likeness of man will be great and correct. It is morality and the basic principles of social interaction of humans with such future beings that will determine the real contours of a new and yet unknown world. May this new world, created by humankind in cooperation with the new creatures, be surprisingly beautiful and wonderful!

THE POTENTIAL OF SYNTHETIC BIOLOGY

Synthetic biology, also called SynBio, is a new direction in genetic engineering, a field of biology that is being actively developed in more than a hundred laboratories worldwide. The term 'synthetic biology' appeared in 1980 thanks to biologist Barbara Hobom, who described bacteria that had been genetically modified by a recombinant DNA.

The practice of synthetic biology originated in 1989, stemming from a study conducted by Steven Benner and Peter Schultz in Zurich, as a result of which a DNA was created which had two more 'letters' in addition to the four already known 'letters' of the genetic alphabet. Synthetic biology is based on designing biological systems by encoding or re-encoding DNA and therefore constitutes a set of methods for creating 'synthetic' biological material that does not exist in nature.

This area makes use of achievements made in such disciplines as chemistry, biology, information technology and engineering. The achievements of genetic engineering erase the borders between living organisms and machines, enabling people to program the functionality of living things. An extensive bank of genetic data is currently being created, where it will be possible to select bio-bricks featuring appropriate functions, somewhat similar to selecting components to construct an electronic circuit. A bio-brick is a DNA fragment with well known functions, which can be introduced into a cell's genome in order to synthesize a predetermined protein. All selected bio-bricks must have such properties so as to ensure their easy production, storage and incorporation into the genetic chain, as well as smooth interaction with other parts of the bio-code.

Colonies of bacteria will synthesize foodstuffs, medicines and synthetic fuels. The existing achievements are impressive. In 2010, American engineer and biologist Craig Venter synthesised the first cell with an artificial genome assembled on a supercomputer. American chemical engineer Jay Keesling developed a genetic program comprising 12 new genes, and successfully used it to alter the metabolism of ordinary yeast to receive artemisinin (a medication for treating pinworm infection). Evolva, a Swiss company, has created a compound surprisingly similar to vanillin, which is also grown on synthetic yeast. I have already mentioned the prospects of commercial use of fourth-generation biofuels. This technology is a direct way to produce an alkane mixture, a fuel similar to diesel, through the use of modified bacteria which, when placed in specially designed conditions, absorb sunlight and carbon dioxide and produce an alkane substance. The production of fourth-generation biofuels, unlike that of biofuels of previous generations, does not require biomass and therefore needs no farmland. Another advantage of this technology is that the resulting fuel does not need processing (like, for example, oil refining, which in itself is a very energy-intensive and costly process). Joule Unlimited successfully conducted experimental trials of an alkane production method and then launched alkane production in November 2012 at its Sunsprings demonstration plant in Hobbs, New Mexico, US. The purpose of this plant is to prove that the unique modular system developed by the company is capable of providing reproducible results regardless of whether it is installed on a site of one hectare or on a thousand times greater area.

The prospects for synthetic biology are absolutely dazzling. The already pending acute antibiotics crisis can only be eliminated by using synthetic biology techniques. Biologists claim that vaccines against influenza and AIDS will soon be created.

Moderna is a company pioneering the development of an informational RNA that produces human proteins, antibodies and completely new protein structures within a patient's cells, which, in turn, are secreted or are activated intracellularly. This impressive platform keeps the focus on currently incurable diseases and suggests the best alternatives to existing medicines.

Synthetic biology will become absolutely indispensable during nearest outer space exploration. To illustrate this point, I will quote David Deutsch (Deutsch 2011):

"In some environments in the universe, the most efficient way for humans to thrive might be to alter their own genes. Indeed, we are already doing that in our present environment, to eliminate diseases that have in the past blighted many lives. Some people object to this on the grounds (in effect) that a genetically altered human is no longer human. This is an anthropomorphic mistake. The only uniquely significant thing about humans (whether in the cosmic scheme of things or according to any rational human criterion) is our ability to create new explanations and we have that in common with all people. You do not become less of a person if you lose a limb in an accident; it is only if you lose your brain that you do. Changing our genes in order to improve our lives and to facilitate further improvements is no different in this regard from augmenting our skin with clothes or our eyes with telescopes."

The thought expressed by Deutsch is simple and straightforward: if you want to survive as a species on other planets, modify your genetic code. Notably, Deutsch refers to modification rather than to switching on or off individual genes or gene sequences, as suggested by Michio Kaku.

Chris Adami, a physicist and a professor at Michigan State University, upholds interesting views on the nature of our genes.[216] His main assertion is that life is purely information a living organism receives about the world that surrounds it. To Adami, our genes are just a repository of everything that humankind has learned about its environment over the millions of years of the species' existence.[217] Our repository contains information about everything we need to know to survive. For example, how to convert sugar into energy, how to hide from a predator in a savannah and, what is most important for evolution, how to reproduce an organism similar to yours – a replica of your own.

Such information enables a person to predict future events around them with much greater accuracy than that resulting from blind biological combinations. This informational approach to life makes it much easier to explain many changes in the course of evolution. For example, the mass extinction of the dinosaurs appears to have been inevitable, since an abrupt change in ambient conditions in the outside world suddenly made these beings' internal encyclopaedia useless. The dinosaurs' repositories had no records applicable to the new state of the environment. Similarly, information available in our repository would be useless to us in the unusual conditions found on Mars or Venus. But we may be able to solve this problem through a combination of SynBio and our space rocket technology. This is what Michio Kaku writes in his other famous work, *Hyperspace*, about the Astrochicken project by Freeman Dyson:

"Dyson has proposed to use what he calls the *Astrochicken*. Small, lightweight and intelligent, Astrochicken is a versatile space probe that has a clear advantage over the bulky, exorbitantly expensive space missions of the past. It will weigh a kilogram and will be grown, not built. It could be as agile as a hummingbird with a brain weighing no more than a gram. It will be part machine and part animal, using the most advanced developments in bioengineering" (Kaku 1994, 280). It is assumed that the Astrochicken will be small but powerful enough to explore the outer planets, such as Uranus and Neptune. It will be bred and programmed to consume ice and hydrocarbons and transform them into chemical fuel. "The Astrochicken's key features will result from technological breakthroughs in genetic engineering, artificial intelligence and solar-electric propulsion. Once its appetite has been satisfied, it will then rocket to the next moon or planet" (ibid).

CREATIVITY OF ARTIFICIAL INTELLIGENCE

Ray Kurzweil, an advocate of the technological singularity concept, according to which a moment will come sooner or later when all further progress will be made by artificial superintelligence, says that by 2029, the chasm that separates computers and humans today (i.e. the difference between logical and emotional intelligence) will disappear. His notion is based on the fact that we have already acquired a deeper understanding of how the human brain works. Our knowledge is growing continually, and today we can literally look inside a living brain and see how ideas are generated in real time. Kurzweil believes that deep learning techniques employing multilayer neural networks could successfully replace conventional ones. The point when this happens will be the point of no return, after which we, humankind, will be unable to comprehend progress and will perceive each new advancement made by artificial superintelligence, not by us anymore, as something akin to magic.

In his book *The Singularity is Near*, Kurzweil cites an example in which a monkey could mentally control the behaviour of a program by using a chip implanted in its brain. That chip was already capable of updating its software independently.

In a human brain, transitions between levels (neocortex films) take from a few hundredths to a few tenths of a second. It has been established experimentally that the recognition of a human face takes a few tenths of a second. This speed is achieved owing to all recognition modules in a biological brain functioning simultaneously. If our brain functioned as a typical computer and recognised all images in sequence and in a hierarchical order, it would have to make millions of cycles while going from one level to another. That is why, despite the fact that computers operate a million times faster than biological systems, the human brain is still superior to computers of all models in terms of universality.

Kurzweil sees no contradiction and does not separate biological evolution from technical. Human history appears to him to consist of six epochs. The first of these, Epoch One, is 'Physics and Chemistry', an epoch that came within a few hundred years after the Big Bang. Several billion years ago came Epoch Two, 'Biology and DNA', the period when the first self-replicating organisms emerged. Epoch Three, 'Brains', was the period when organisms emerged that were able to automatically detect and process information. Currently we are going through Epoch Four, 'Technology', in which our technology is evolving with us, developing from steam engines to fully self-sufficient nuclear reactors. After a few decades, according to Kurzweil, Epoch Five will come, called 'The Merger of Human Technology with Human Intelligence', in which the human mind – liberated from our biological limitations – will be able to alter the matter of the Universe. After that, the last epoch, Epoch Six, will come, called 'The Universe Wakes Up'. As we can see, Kurzweil is not anxious about the prospect that artificial intelligence will come to dominate in all spheres of human life as soon as in Epoch Four.

Artificial intelligence is already trying its hand at creation. In March 2016, a novel written by a robot titled *The Day a Computer Writes a Novel* reached the final of the Japanese Shinichi Hoshi literary contest. The project was supervised by a group of researchers lead by Professor Hitoshi Matsubara at Future University Hakodate. In the experiment, a computer program was given a certain set of parameters, including the sex of the central characters, some keywords and so on. Complying with these, the artificial intelligence created a completely coherent and unique text. Hitoshi Matsubara said he hoped they would be able to expand the potential of the software, so that it could demonstrate virtually real human creativity.

SOUTH KOREAN PROFESSIONAL GO PLAYER LEE SEDOL ANALYSES THE FOURTH GAME (IN A SERIES OF FIVE GAMES) AGAINST ALPHAGO, AN ARTIFICIAL INTELLIGENCE PROGRAM DESIGNED BY GOOGLE DEEPMIND. SEOUL, 13 March 2016

GO, THE MOST ANCIENT AND COMPLICATED GAME IN THE WORLD, FALLS UNDER PRESSURE FROM ARTIFICIAL INTELLIGENCE?

Go, the most intricate intellectual game in the world, originated in ancient China. In a game of Go, two players put game pieces, called stones, on the board one after another, each aiming to surround more territory than the opponent. The winner is the player who is able to surround the largest area. Despite its relatively simple rules (which can be expressed in nine simple sentences), Go is a highly complex game, which requires the players to be able to combine skilfully complex calculations with mental images and associations, logic with intuition, and tactics with strategy. Go teaches how to find the most important points in a problem and select the key to its solution, to see what is concealed and to find a means to control events. In other words, mastering Go requires the player to have advanced creative thinking.

Until today, it has been believed that even the most powerful computer would not only be unable to defeat a high-profile player of Go, but could not play this game against a human on equal terms even in theory, as the number of possible unique games totals 3×10511 (with the average, standard game counting 200 moves). In chess, for comparison, this number is 1×10120 (with the standard game counting 80 moves). However, in March 2016, Google DeepMind, a UK-based artificial intelligence start-up, announced that its program, AlphaGo, had inflicted, for the first time in history, a crushing defeat on Lee Sedol, one of the best masters of the game and an 18-time world champion, in the very first game in a five-game match. AlphaGo beat Lee Sedol in the first three games consecutively and thus earned victory in the tournament. But then the program made a mistake in the fourth game and lost, after which Lee Sedol noted that AlphaGo had some vulnerable areas.

What makes AlphaGo different from all other previous Go programs is that it is not just equipped with a powerful search component, but is also able to learn to play. Compared with a human, AlphaGo learns much faster, resting its skills on the available database of games it has played and playing against itself at a silicon speed.

During a game, the program is guided by human opponents' probable moves generated by a 'network of rules' – a simulator of the actions of real Go masters in different situations. But when the 'evaluative' neural network is activated in order to start an in-depth analysis of a situation, the program can make creative moves.

Unlike chess, Go has no simple guiding principles for players to follow and to evaluate the progress of the game. As a result, computers are traditionally bad at playing it. But AlphaGo proved to be an order of magnitude better than anyone could ever have imagined. Demis Hassabis, DeepMind co-founder, commented on the program's efficiency as follows: "AlphaGo plays in a very human style, because it's learned in a human way and then got stronger and stronger by playing, just as you or I would do. It has taught itself to master the game by using general-purpose machine learning techniques. Ultimately, we want to apply these techniques to important real-world problems like climate modelling or complex disease analysis, right? So it's very exciting to start imagining what it might be able to tackle next..."

However, expert opinion says that a victory scored by a computer in Go, a game for two players with clearly defined rules, does not mean that the time has come for the machines to take over the humans. "Today, artificial intelligence copes fairly well with many cognitive tasks that could only be performed by people before," says Babak Hodjat, co-founder of Sentient Technologies and the company's chief researcher. "Still, it will take years for artificial intelligence to reach the human level of abstract thinking." This is the next milestone to be reached, but how far are we away from it?

HOW TO DISCERN NEW TRAPS SET UP BY PROGRESS

Civilizations often happen to collapse, only to be followed by degradation. This means that the four-leaf clover model is not a mechanism that will work in all conditions. In the past, the Chinese were far ahead of all other nations in invention, technology and art. However, as a result of limiting contacts with the outside world, China ceased to develop for several centuries and is only catching up now, before our very eyes. Information technology, with its growing cultural influence in society, is expected to save us from conflict and confrontation.

DIVERSITY REDUCTION

Our planet is going through a biodiversity crisis. In total, 16,000 species of animals are endangered today.[218] Things are worse in the case of plants. What is more, the process is taking place at a tremendous speed: Earth is losing one plant or animal species every 20 minutes, which adds up to 26,280 species within just one year (De Greef 2013). By the time humanity is prepared to make the transition to its mature phase, over a quarter of the Earth's plant and animal species may have disappeared for good, together with all the information links humanity fails to decipher to be used as food for future innovation.

Additionally we are also losing our own heritage, our historical memory. Of the 6,000 languages that form the planet's logosphere (a linguistic analogue of the biosphere) today, only 500 to 3,000 will remain in 100 years (Noack 2015).[219] It looks as if all important information can be expressed using just one dominant language (e.g. English). The fact that thousands of small languages have disappeared, together with a large part of common knowledge, has simply been ignored. The loss of languages deprives humanity of the ability to make future discoveries and reduces the chances of creating conceptually new things.

David Harmon, the specialist who shed light on the relationship between biological and linguistic diversity in 1996, argued that language connects us with the environment more closely than we can imagine. For example, according to Nicholas Evans, a linguist at the Australian National University, humankind owes the discovery of one of the first anti-HIV drugs to a conversation that had taken place between tribal healer Samonas Epensea Moigo and ethno-botanist Paul Allen Cox about the healing properties of a rare plant, Homalanthus Nutans (Evans 2010). This discovery was made only because Cox could speak Samoan.

Reduction in diversity is a way to monotony. Monotony is always about control and, ultimately, total control, a forerunner of death for every living thing in the long run. In the conditions of strict control over living matter, a living mind will just have nothing to build new combinations from.

CLIMATE CHANGE

Another trap the human race is currently under threat of falling into is a dramatic increase in the amount of energy spent to maintain an individual in the modern world. A hunter-gatherer, though physiologically similar to a modern human, consumed just enough food to receive 3,000-4,000 kcal per day on average, to be spent to sustain him.

A peasant who lived at the time of the agricultural revolution already consumed more energy than he required. His domestic animals also consumed energy. His home needed wood to be burnt in the stove (a single household consumed 30,000 kcal daily for heating). Just to get to work, a modern-day person uses two to three litres of petrol (whose caloric value is about 25,000 kcal) obtained from crude oil.

Cooking and heating with natural gas requires another 3,000 calories, or thereabouts. Home appliances, such as the refrigerator, the vacuum cleaner, the TV, the computer, the washing machine, the air conditioning, the lighting and the elevator, together account for another 15,000 kcal. This calculation shows that we take from the environment and consume on a daily basis some 40,000 kcal. But people still need more and more energy, while producing less and less economic effect. To achieve a 2% growth in global economic welfare, we borrow (or rather appropriate) several times more from nature. That is not only about energy. The huge and still-growing population of the planet is bound to bring about environmental problems and, particularly, climate change, which scientists are seriously talking about being caused by humankind rather than by anything else. Nature's response to the human population growing out of any reasonable proportion will include an omnipresent climatic impact on human life and we must be ready to adapt to this.

Climate is global and difficult to predict, so no one will dare to assert that droughts, storms, or floods will hit specific corners of the globe at any specific time. But there are some trends that can be predicted today: it will be hotter in Europe, Australia is in for more frequent droughts and the sea level will rise due to ice melting in the Arctic. Whatever we do, the temperature and sea levels will rise at least until the end of the century.

This means that coastlines will have to be strengthened everywhere and that cooling will be a major problem on continents.

In the northern part of the European continent, warming will result in a reduction in energy costs, while southern Europe will, on the contrary, require additional expenditure of energy for cooling. Grain production techniques will change, so will grapevine cultivation methods and even fishing practices. The biosphere will be changing rapidly. As a result, even tourist flows may be reoriented by the mid-century. Innovation that increases energy efficiency will be in demand. New types of property insurance will be created. Demand for new crops that can grow in drought conditions will strengthen and so will demand for new ways of growing plants, such as capillary irrigation in Israel or greenhouse systems in the Netherlands. Reliable flood warning systems will be much sought-after, as the damage caused by severe floods will increase tenfold by the end of the century.

Asian countries may become highly interested in innovations developed in New York and Norfolk (Virginia), where programmes to raise boilers above expected water levels are being implemented and inner-city walls, resembling gateways, are being built to minimize the effects of floods. If glaciers melt in the Andes, the Australians and the inhabitants of Central and South America will be faced with droughts. According to forecasts made by some scientists, northern Brazil will lose 22% of its annual rainfall by 2100, while in Chile, in contrast, floods will spread and the annual rainfall will increase by 25%.

Change is coming to continental Europe too. Recent studies have shown that the previously average flood cycle of 12 years is reducing, with floods affecting more densely populated areas now. The Rhine and the Danube, as it has been discovered recently, may be considered communicating vessels that make part of the same water basin (Source: RIA Novosti 2013). An unfavourable situation of a similar kind may occur in Siberia, in the Amur and Lena basins, albeit these areas are as yet less densely populated.

All these threats, quite foreseeable and multiplied by continued population growth, generate demand for innovation in 'green' technologies, modelling natural phenomena and the means of controlling those natural phenomena. These, in turn, create additional demand for computation capacities. Consequently, attention to quality of life and quality of the environment will come to the fore and will be supported by conventional small-scale energy technologies, latest-generation digital networks, and special functions in personal devices. Companies, services and applications will emerge, which will, in addition to their primary functions, be able to warn populations about other critical events, such as earthquakes, gas attacks, and terrorist and insurgent offensives. New interfaces will be developed for more effective cooperation between population and emergency and first aid services, through which citizens will be able to report accidents, show wounded people, clarify victims' conditions and even remotely accompany emergency services to incident locations.

As a result of climate change, the focus in urban development worldwide will be shifted towards the construction of new 'smart' cities and villages with a high degree of autonomy, where innovative companies' products will emerge, 'settle down' and develop. What have been seen as deficiencies before may turn out to be significant advantages. Low temperatures in northern regions, which are still the key factor in keeping the population density low there, have already made the Arctic an attractive place to set up computer data storage centres (thus avoiding huge computer cooling costs). Facebook is already building its largest data centre in the north of Sweden. Still further north, hundreds of thousands of seeds of various plants are kept in vaults under a Svalbard mountain.

But to take advantage of the new opportunities, more than just new business plans are needed – we also need new materials for their implementation. Everyone knows that steel, the principal construction material, becomes brittle as glass at low temperatures. So, we need something more stable. Perhaps this something has already been invented.

A group of biologists led by Professor Don Jarvis[220] at the University of Wyoming has developed transgenic silkworms that produce a silk thread whose strength per unit of weight is comparable with that of steel. Though unsuitable as a substitution for steel in construction, the silk will certainly find use in healthcare and be of interest to military organizations. In construction, change may come from a completely different direction. For example, Enrico Dini was obviously envious of the glory of Joseph Monier, the inventor of concrete, whom I mentioned in Chapter 8. Dini has created a printer, D-Shape, capable of 'printing', using sand and an inorganic compound as the base, a two-storey building complete with rooms, stairs and partitions. The strength of the 'print-out' material, which looks like marble, is comparable with that of reinforced concrete. Most importantly, the speed of printing is such that a house can be erected in just a quarter of the time required for constructing a similar structure using conventional techniques. The modern world creates endless combinations of unprecedented or previously unimaginable assortments of all possible technologies.

However, sometimes such an active combination of inventions unavoidably raises a suspicion that people are trying to copy nature in its 'blind evolutionary process'. Combinations are numerous and the economic impact is, as yet, negligible. This idea was expressed by economist Robert Gordon. He noted that the time span characterized by rapid economic growth, usually perceived as the age of innovation and technological progress, was, in fact, very short in human history (Gordon 2010).

One can see that this surge occurred in the late 19th and the first half of the 20th century. The rapid economic growth was brought about by electrification, proliferation of internal combustion engines, breakthroughs in the chemical industry, and the emergence of new forms of communication and new media, particularly film and television. Modern electronics, the internet, robotics, and all other similar sectors are important, in Gordon's view, to a much lesser extent than the achievements made in the past epoch (Gordon 2010). He writes that "electricity, internal combustion engines, telecommunications and chemical engineering were a much more powerful source of productivity growth than anything that has appeared in recent years. Most of the inventions we can see now are 'derivatives' of older ideas. For example, video recorders have combined the features of television and film, but the fundamental impact of their emergence cannot be compared with the effect produced by the invention of one of their predecessors. Similarly, the proliferation of the internet also basically results in mere replacement of one form of entertainment with another and nothing more than that."

The rationale behind Robert Gordon's arguments is that progress was necessary in the conditions of constant growth of the population. Humankind needed progress in order to survive, to be able to cope with old threats or traps, such as hunger and war. Having learned to combat these plagues, we seem to have lost the passion for reaching new horizons. This means that we may soon get into new traps set up by progress, to which the internet and electric vehicles will not be enough to combat.

ARTIFICIAL SUPERINTELLIGENCE

Today, many prominent scientists involved in solving the problem of creating artificial intelligence as a potential remedy capable of ensuring continued progress of modern society, are wondering about the future relationship between humans and their cybernetic opponents. By giving artificial intelligence human qualities, humankind will inevitably bring it into its social field, which implies a degree of dependence. In this case, the question will be which race will come to dominate in this interdependent system, managing the opponent to its advantage.

In his work *The Phenomenology of Spirit*, the German philosopher Georg Hegel studied a similar problem arising in connection with building relationships in human society, using the relationship between a master and a slave to illustrate his thought. Hegel's main idea was that both the master and the servant are depersonalised in their relationship, since a human being's desire to dominate is one of his most important driving forces in his social behaviour. Power relations account for many human actions, laying the foundation for psychology and ethics and manifesting themselves in legal, ideological and religious relationships. But a master who owns a slave and has an unlimited power over the latter is, in turn, also dependent on the slave's physical efforts or the results of his labour. This interdependence makes both equally dependent, despite the difference in their social status.

Alan Kay, a modern American scientist, has put forward the hypothesis that long-term programmes for future carriers of artificial intelligence have to be developed in advance in order to make it possible for such carriers to function as human beings' colleagues, not servants. Indeed, having created new intelligent assistants, civilization may become directly dependent on them, giving up its ability to think independently. Artificial servants, in turn, may in the future be able to concentrate power over humankind which has chosen the easiest way to solve its pressing problems. As a result, humanity is presented with a creative disability problem: it cannot tackle complex issues through looking for algorithms, as the very intellectual ability to develop such algorithms has been lost.

Randy Komisar, an author and well known venture capitalist, made a statement on this subject while speaking at the presentation of Google Now, a new Google service. He said that the modern world has literally turned upside down for young people, who have lost the ability to make essential deductions from their life experience because they are now completely immersed in a 'virtual cloud'.

Today, people use the internet in a variety of real-life situations – from ordering pizza to searching for a partner in life. If this trend goes on, people will, gradually and imperceptibly for themselves, begin to lose the natural ability to find ways to gain vital and socially indispensable skills.

TRANSHUMANISM

Genetic modification of bacteria brings with it a risk humankind is well aware of – the risk of losing control over the evolution of deadly and dangerous bacteria and viruses. Considering this, the prospect of creating a genetically modified human, or superhuman, being looks even more unpredictable. A superhuman being might prove to be a transitional stage between normal human beings and a post-human variety, whose abilities will be so much superior to the abilities of the ordinary human that a fundamentally new species will emerge.

Despite the vagueness of the scientific approaches practiced in this field and the existence of many cultural myths, ranging from ancient legends to the latest Hollywood masterpieces, there is already a science-based concept of improving innate human abilities with the help of synthetic genomics. Scholars have set about creating a superhuman being quite seriously. Back in 2004, *Foreign Policy* magazine published a report, titled *The World's Most Dangerous Ideas*. In it, professor of International Political Economy Francis Fukuyama described the very idea of 'transhumanism', i.e. the creation of a superhuman, as one of the most dangerous and disgusting products of social activity. According to Fukuyama, a superhuman with a claim to supreme power, based on the grounds of having excellent health and appearance, a sharper mind and a longer life, will inevitably require 'improved' or non-standard rights for itself.

Such ethics are unacceptable to a caring society, where it is viewed that those with severe disabilities must be granted 'improved' rights to a greater extent. Furthermore, scientists have long ago come to the paradoxical conclusion that genius and madness are often combined in the same individual. A person's talent in one area is accompanied by a natural compensatory defect in another.

In view of this, another question arises: whether there is a potential threat in creating a super-genotype that would combine excellence in some respects with a variety of unknown dysfunctions that may represent a danger to society. Indeed, an individual possessing greater intellectual power may prove to be outstandingly successful in creating technologies intended to destroy other species, as well as living beings of their own kind. However, here there is also quite a perceivable restriction: in addition to the content, the form is of great importance too. This is what Michio Kaku says about it in his book *Physics of the Future*: "Should a person be offered to move into a new body, it would only have to be one that would make the person attractive to the opposite sex and increase their reputation among peers. No one would want a new body otherwise. What teenager would want to gain superpowers at the expense of their appearance?" (Kaku 2011, 114).

In other words, the creation of a superhuman, or the willingness of a human being to undergo a transformation, will largely depend on our actual ideas about... beauty.

PROHIBITIONS

However, no anti-Frankenstein ban would resolve the problem. Social prohibitions on innovation can only result in temporary delays in progress. Given the current pace of progress in information search, processing and transmission technologies, a total ban on research and development in synthetic genomics looks absolutely unrealistic. Apart from any risks it may hold, synthetic genomics has numerous tangible benefits in store. The ban would only motivate the emergence of a black market run by illegal laboratories, which would mean loss of control over scientific research and its implementation in everyday life.

In 2006, Kevin Kelly, former editor of *Wired* magazine, closely examined the effect of bans that have been imposed on various technologies over the past 1,000 years. He found that some technological restrictions had only a negative deterrent effect on progress. Though capable of delaying the development of new technologies, social bans are powerless outside their areas of action. Thus, in 1971, representatives of 79 nations signed the *Convention on the Prohibition of the Development, Production and Stockpiling of Bacteriological (Biological) and Toxin Weapons and on Their Destruction*. However, in 1996, US intelligence sources stated a very unpleasant fact: the spread and development of biological weapons had continued outside the signatory countries. If ineffective, prohibitions prove counterproductive and eventually increase the likelihood of adverse effects.

The idea of opposing progress is still very popular in some parts of society. In 2010, the bicentenary of the Luddite movement was marked, whose supporters were opposed to industrial mechanisation and automation, correctly fearing that their jobs were in danger. But all the uprising added up to was violence and the destruction of machines. The Luddites failed to bring in anything constructive. The real driving force is still new technology. It has radically changed humans' natural ability to perceive and interact with the universe and given humanity numerous superhuman qualities. Thus, the tendency towards 'transhumanism' will only increase in the near future. The point is whether it is going to be our conscious choice.

———————

However, choice is always fraught with risk. There is at least one thing that humanity has firmly grasped over the time of its existence: it is those who risk nothing who risk most!

EVOLUTION IS THE ROUTE THAT WE CHOOSE

*Change always causes fear.
But no one will change your life for you.
You realize what choice you must make
and move forward despite your fear.
This is the main rule of success.*

– Paulo Coelho

A person perceives information better when it's grouped. For the sake of convenience of perception in this conclusion of the book, I have divided the chronological continuum of human history into four key stages:

1. Humankind's departure from biological evolution;
2. The emergence of civilization and natural states;
3. The advent of enlightenment and dynamic states; and
4. The future.

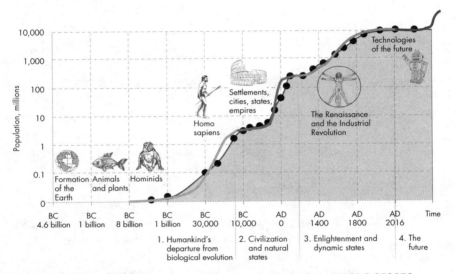

FIGURE 34. RELATIONSHIPS BETWEEN EVOLUTIONARY PROCESSES IN THE HUMAN ENVIRONMENT

Figure 34 uses logarithmic scales to represent time along the horizontal axis and population along the vertical. Why do we need logarithmic scales? With regular scales, this chart would look like a hyperbolic curve where the global population would first be close to zero for a very long time and then soar dramatically towards infinity.

The logarithmic graph clearly shows that each stage represents a clear S-shaped curve, a kind of life cycle with birth, growth, maturity and stagnation, the latter providing for accumulation of vital energy or resources for the beginning of a new stage.

The figure reflects changes in the human environment over time as a result of the evolution of constituent elements of this environment. These elements changed following certain historical events brought about by some results of humanity's creative thinking.

EVOLUTION OF MAN

Within the prehistoric period, there is no point considering the evolution of mankind outside biological evolution in general. Humanity developed in the same way as other large mammals, and its population was proportionate to the populations of other animals of similar size. However, once people, using the capabilities of their mind, began to use sticks and then axes, spears, traps and fire, and began to build shelters, they were able to cope with practically any type and any pack of animals and began to kill much larger animals for food. Humankind secured an abundance of food resources, thus enabling an increase in its population.

At that point, in my view, the evolution of the human mind began (i.e. the accumulation of knowledge), enabling humankind to continue to develop further and further. The noosphere, the sphere of human thought, is likely to have emerged at that time.

EVOLUTION OF SOCIETY

Man, as we know, is a biosocial being. Society is a key part of the human environment, the creation and development of which is carried out by humanity as a whole on the one hand but is virtually independent of the will of a single individual on the other. And, as has been said, society is one of the leaves of our lucky clover and thus its evolution is of particular interest to us. When did the evolution of society begin?

Hunter-gatherers lived in social groups, which could be defined as the first communities, though essentially they did not differ much from groups of apes, packs of wolves or prides of lions, and were certainly not as highly organized as multi-structured communities of bees and ants. Social groups of that time had no specific nature that would be fundamentally different from the nature of animal communities. Completely new, social evolutionary processes began with the beginning of the Neolithic revolution, which brought about the first settlements and gave rise to the rapid development of social institutions.

Given the importance of these institutions, the evolutionary development of man should be considered separately. In Figure 35, the evolution of society as an integrated network of thinking minds is analysed in terms of changes that took place in the organization of its structure and in its size and density.

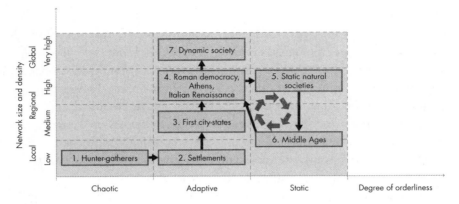

FIGURE 35. THE EVOLUTION OF SOCIETY

1. It is easy to notice that the hunter-gatherer society was chaotic and had a low network density, with its size enabling it to be present on a local level only. As a result, any ideas people might have had were lost without receiving proper development. Further in the figure, we can observe a stable relationship between the network density and bursts of innovative activity in society.

2. The first signs of substantial innovative growth appeared with the beginning of the Neolithic revolution, which resulted in the formation of the first settlements, characterised by a certain societal orderliness or adaptivity. In this type of society, new ideas began to consolidate and develop. It was then that the evolutionary development of society began – which is also well demonstrated in the drawing.

   During the epoch of the first settlements, society already showed an adaptive nature, i.e. already had certain features of statehood represented by mechanisms for administration and coercion, which, however, could be quickly and easily transformed under the influence of both external and internal factors emerging within society itself.

3. The first city-states, and later the first democratic societies of ancient Rome and Athens, which preserved adaptivity in their principles of state building, were characterized by an increasingly high network density. Ideas were passed on from person to person and thus saved for future generations.

4. In ancient Rome, the urban democracy, the size of society, and the network density and adaptability resulted in the efflorescence of culture and the prosperity of the population. Adaptive high-density

networks also provided better conditions for the emergence of innovation, as well as helped to keep the accumulated wisdom of human culture by means of literature and books.

5. Later, however, power in the Roman Empire was factually concentrated in the hands of military commanders. The empire froze within its borders. The centralisation of power in the hands of a small group of rulers, an increase of control over the population, the imposition of tough mechanisms of state coercion and suppression of initiative made Roman society static. Sources of innovative development were suppressed. In static societies, also called natural societies, whose economies are characterized by the dominance of the Great Man (GM), a business lives or dies according to political factors. In dynamic societies, where market economies typically prevail, a business lives or dies depending on whether the customers like its products and whether they are ready to pay for them.

In natural states, society provides resources for businesses that fill the pockets of the GM better than others. In a market economy, resources are allocated to venture capital firms that make the best economic use of them. The economy of the hunter-gatherer society was guided by a fairly straightforward selection process: the more efficient a tribe is at hunting and the more rationally it spends the calories on food production, the greater chance it gets to give birth to a new generation. With the economy and society growing and their relationships deepening, the existing rigid and direct natural selection feedback became less significant. The first collision between the economy and society occurred when the GM said "Let's allocate this good piece of fertile land to my third wife's cousin" (though he was a pretty mediocre farmer) rather than proposing to allocate the plot to the best farmers of the tribe. Such decisions give preference to poor business plans (stuck to by mediocre farmers) and not to good business plans (worked out by the best farmers of the tribe). Society, therefore, was faced with a huge challenge: the GM began to distort the function of natural selection!

Market relationships may be good, although they are not always perfect, and, if they work, they are more efficient than any alternatives. Traditional economics holds that markets are the best way to allocate resources and optimize the level of social welfare through attaining market equilibrium. From an evolutionary point of view, markets provide incentives for deductive research and differentiation. They perform the natural selection function which reflects the needs and preferences of the entire population, not just a single GM. Furthermore, they are a means of moving resources from less competitive business models to more competitive ones. Evolution, as a rule, turns out to be smarter than the GM. The GM cannot select business plans as efficiently as evolution does by means of market mechanisms. Markets defeat a single GM and overcome tight control not only because they are more efficient in the distribution of resources, but also because market innovations break existing rent-generating schemes by creating new product niches. Markets are evolutionary machines. Most of the modern world's technological and social innovations came from market economies, and only a few originated in GM-lead economies where they were created mainly to strengthen the nations' military power. People vote with their feet and, in global migration, outflows from GM-lead economies to market economies prevail. This is the strong side of the market, since it gives a lot of opportunities for innovation and growth. One of the hallmarks of a market economy is that a market is more efficient in the selection of business plans.

DYNAMIC SOCIETY

After a few centuries, the first commercial cities appeared in northern Italy. Around the market squares, new societies formed, distributing decision-making powers through human networks whose scale was much larger and which were more closely interconnected than those found in castles and monasteries. No matter how smart the power represented by a GM may be, if the number of people in the market is a thousand times larger, there will be more good ideas in the market than in a feudal castle. This, however, does not magically result in an increase in the level of collective consciousness, but simply expands the opportunities for minds capable of creating interesting ideas.

Along with this, the economic system moved from the feudal structure to newly emerging forms of contemporary capitalism and became less hierarchical, gaining and developing network qualities. The Renaissance finally broke the old information shackles and provided opportunities for the free exchange of ideas, enabling great Italian innovators to breathe new life into the collective European mind. The circle was closed. Society returned to the same state in which it had been in the days of the Roman democracy.

Interestingly, society has gone through this cycle more than once in its evolutionary development. Thus, the golden enlightenment and democracy age in the city-state of Athens ended in 404 BC, when a tough, heavily militarised Sparta crushingly defeated Athens and established an authoritarian form of government in the city. Athens ceased to be a place where progress was fast and unimpeded by restrictions.

Another case of enlightenment, a short-lived one, took place in the Italian city-state of Florence in the 14th century. It was an era of brilliant innovation, known as the Golden Age of Florence, deliberately encouraged by the Medici, a family which is already well known to us. They promoted a new philosophy, humanism, which prioritised knowledge, intellectual independence and curiosity. Florence of that time was a place where new ideas gave rise to more new ideas. But progress did not last long. A charismatic monk, Girolamo Savonarola, began to speak against humanity, urging the people to return to the medieval values and predicting death to Florence if it continued to follow the path of humanism. Many believed him and, in 1494, Savonarola was able to seize power and re-impose restrictions on art, literature, thought and behaviour. Ultimately, Savonarola was also deposed and burned at the stake. It took a long time for Florence afterwards to recover from that anti-cultural upheaval.

Since prehistoric times, human society has many times tried to reach a new stage in its development, but every time progress brought it to a new level, something happened to return it back to stagnation and static existence.

The phenomenon that finally enabled humankind to break out of this vicious circle was a scientific revolution that brought about a system of scientific worldview approaches based on putting forward hypotheses and subjecting them to criticism. Consequently, knowledge began to grow like a snowball, enabling humanity to improve significantly the standard of living, to settle in new territories and to build up communication networks. As a result, a dynamic and adaptive society with a very high density network formed, providing ideal conditions for consolidation, development and dissemination of new ideas and, therefore, innovative growth.

EVOLUTION OF FINANCE

The Italian Renaissance and the Medici family, as we recall, gave the world a banking revolution which in turn boosted the rapid development of financial instruments. This, in my opinion, marked the beginning of financial evolution – the evolution of new mechanisms for payment, accumulation, investment and, perhaps most importantly, debt capital engagement.

Over centuries, financial evolution has provided humankind with numerous tools designed to assist in raising funds and attracting investment, contributing to economic growth. This process has now reached heights unthinkable for our forerunners. Particularly, today's financial market is based on expectations. In fact, a company, when making investment decisions today, builds its assessments on expectations of a profit in the future.

More or less accurate business plans are drawn up for periods of about five years, for which an investor can roughly predict and estimate the dividends, cash flows and financial results, though this makes, as a rule, no more than 30% of the future value of the company. The rest of the value is estimated on the basis of profit expectations for the sixth year and the subsequent 20-30 years.

It appears that this financial system is based on expectations held by the market, i.e. other people and their belief that this or that company will make a profit. As a result, at the macro level, there are countries today with huge budget deficits and external debts exceeding their annual GDP, such as the US, Western European countries and a number of others. These countries, however, have the highest ratings, and their success and stability instils most confidence and trust, encouraging further investment in their economies.

The world's leading companies, such as Tesla, Google and Facebook, have no profit today and their huge market capitalization has been formed on the basis of future profit expectations. It turns out that by selling their shares, an investor has the opportunity to take, as it were, money from the future, or, in fact, trade expectations.

Huge amounts of money have accumulated on deposits worldwide and, were it not for the people's belief that this money can be taken back and the US' and Europe's willingness to incur these debts, there would be significantly fewer assets. In fact, this is a belief that the financial and economic systems of the countries that are keeping that money will come up with new technologies that will bring about new growth.

The global financial colonization has resulted in financial capital penetrating into all aspects of society (e.g. in housing), making it possible to borrow money and buy financial assets in any country. This is what financial globalisation is about: to make it possible for business to take whole countries' wealth away safely without enslaving or destroying them, while making the people work with strong motivation and not under duress. A truly great invention!

BUSINESS EVOLUTION

The financial evolution has given the world new opportunities – economic growth opportunities. Using credit leverage, entrepreneurs were able to expand their production capacities, paying off debt from subsequent profits resulting from development. In my opinion, though, the event that ramped business evolution up most considerably occurred much later, in the late 19th century. This event was the invention of the limited liability company as a legal organizational form of business incorporation. It was this invention that enabled the evolutionary business development process to come up to a whole new level.

To understand this phenomenon better and to realize its importance for the further development of humankind, let's analyse the history of the changes that took place in the price of errors. In the agrarian society of the first settlements, land and other natural resources were the main assets that generated profit (in kind at the time). If a community waged war on other communities or seized their lands and resources, any captives were just killed. Keeping prisoners alive was economically inefficient, as slaves could not produce a surplus product, being only able to feed themselves. At the time of the first settlements, representatives of ruling dynasties, whose percentage of the total population was apparently rather small, acted as the main recombination agent – the class that made decisions and implemented changes, or the Creative Class.

With the development of society and economic relations, as well as with the introduction of gold as a means of payment, the structure of people's assets changed. Human labour became the main profit-generating production factor and slavery became the main price that people could pay for their mistakes. The main driving force behind decisions was war.

The course of history resulted in people paying for their mistakes by simply losing personal freedom or having it restricted (going to jail, as opposed to losing freedom and independence totally when enslaved). Thus, if failing as entrepreneurs, market capitalists were incarcerated, with restrictions imposed on their personal freedom. Entrepreneurs risked all their personal property, freedom and honour.

Up to that point, the price of an error, as we can see, had been quite high and often not commensurate with the benefits that people could get if successful in venturing. But then limited liability companies were invented. From that point onward, anyone who invested in some business risked neither their life, nor their freedom, nor even their personal belongings. Naturally, this immediately resulted in a growth in business activity and, as a consequence, positively affected the economic development of those countries that had introduced this innovation in their economies.

Nowadays, business opportunities have advanced even further. In a number of countries, law does not permit making a company bankrupt just because it is insolvent. In other words, if a business itself is cost-effective and can make money, but cannot cope with the debt load it has accumulated, it only loses some of its market capitalisation and is rehabilitated;

its debt is restructured and ownership changed, while the business as such remains alive and continues to operate with a clean credit history.

THE FUTURE

Our world is the consequence of our realized desires, preferences and actions. Reflecting our thoughts and filling the world with energy and visions of a future reality enables us not only to build the future, but also to change life for the better. We ourselves are shaping our future and we are doing it now!

In the coming decades, a new technology platform will actively be built upon, expected to produce new cyber-physical systems that combine the internets of people, things and services by linking people, objects and systems.

The new industrial revolution is founded on three technological shifts: 'all in digit', materials with new properties, and management technologies based on digital modelling and design. The energy base is expected to be provided by green power engineering and, possibly in the future, nuclear fusion. Electric vehicles that outdo their petrol fellow carriers have been created. They are already able to move safely in unmanned mode on motorways. Huge efforts are being made to bring self-driving electric vehicles to the next level by teaching them how to move in urban environments.

It is safe to say that the creation of evolutionary development mechanisms will be an important component in the activity of most companies in the near future. The innovation business is increasingly becoming not something unusual and new but a rule of behaviour in a living organization.

For many of our contemporaries, technology is already indistinguishable from magic. What will the digital future bring to people – enormous opportunities or huge disappointments? This depends on us, as any evolutionary development, whether biological or information-wise, depends on decisions we make today.

People will soon have to compete for jobs not only with others of their own kind, but with their own creations – all kinds of robots. Services and robots will gradually master unconventional professions. Scientists predict that within the next 20 years, up to 47% of all professions, including lawyers, doctors and teachers, will face the risk of robotization. Robots already offer us serious competition, even in space exploration. One possible and fairly realistic scenario today is that the Moon will be explored and colonised by robonauts rather than astronauts.

It is assumed that the creation of a machine that is more intelligent than we are will be the key to our success. A more 'intelligent' machine with artificial intelligence is expected to help us in solving our complex 'natural' problems. Attempts to teach artificial intelligence to think creatively and 'feel' are becoming increasingly successful. The key to success is the creation of a multi-level hierarchical system that would be able to explore the world and develop itself using an evolutionary algorithm based on a set of rules.

The rapid development of synthetic biology will enable us to design biological systems that do not exist in nature. This can be done by assembling DNA out of bio-bricks, structural modules of types known to mankind, the total number of which makes up several thousand today.

Genetic modification of bacteria brings with it a risk humankind is well aware of – the risk of losing control over the evolution of deadly and dangerous bacteria and viruses. Considering this, the prospect of creating a genetically modified human, or superhuman being, looks even more unpredictable. A superhuman being might prove to be a transitional stage between normal human beings and a post-human variety whose abilities will be so much superior to the abilities of the ordinary human that a fundamentally new species will emerge.

When we look two or three decades ahead and make decisions on the basis of vague images, our brain puts together a vision of the future, in a way somewhat similar to how an image forms in a kaleidoscope out of four pieces of glass that represent today and yesterday. Of course, we all may be wrong. We risk losing money. But success comes not to those who accept change as a fait accompli and pay for it after the fact, but to those who take risks today as soon as they perceive how things will end in the reflected light of the kaleidoscope. By facing this risk, we step on the path of innovation. After all, it is those who do not risk embarking on a new and unexplored route that risk most!

In today's world, all the elements of the lucky clover, having come into existence and begun to evolve thanks to creative human thinking, have reached heights that had not yet been seen in human history. The combination of these elements will result in hitherto unimaginable achievements and events. The explosive growth of knowledge that we can already see around us opens up truly incredible opportunities for our civilization. At the same time, this new knowledge, like a thermonuclear reaction, represents a considerable threat and poses a question of survival, for both humanity and the Earth as a whole. The question is what kind of path we choose for ourselves...

WORDS OF
GRATITUDE

Dear reader! You are holding now a book that I began to work on back in 2009. I am happy to have shared with you the results of my research and my reflections concerning evolution, our future and the interdependence of the levels of innovative development, the economy and the social climate. The book is based on the scientific research I conducted and the practical experience I gained while working at large industrial corporations, as well as in the field of venture capital and direct investment.

This project is very important for me and the fact that I have been able to undertake it is thanks in many respects to having a unique team of like-minded associates, each of whom has invested a great deal of time and intellectual effort into their work. While working on the book, I was fortunate enough to communicate and work with outstanding scientists of our time and exceptional representatives of the business community. Among them is Alexander Auzan, PhD (Economics), Professor, Dean of the Faculty of Economics of Lomonosov Moscow State University and a member of the Russian Federation Presidential Economic Council, whose views on economics are presented in this work in the form of concise statements. Not only did Alexander become one of the first readers of my book, but he also wrote a brilliant foreword to its Russian-language edition. I am deeply grateful to Professor Andrew Kakabadse, Professor of Governance and Leadership at Henley Business School, for his precious advice and wise thoughts, as well as for continuous discussions of the problems which formed the basis of this book. In addition, Andrew wrote an intriguing foreword to this English-language edition.

I owe a great deal to Professor Alexander Abramov, who looked through drafts of this book more than once, expressing some criticism and suggesting improvements, and thus contributing greatly to its publication. I would also like to thank Serguei Beloussov, CEO of Acronis International GmbH, who shared with me his vision of the functions of a venture company and the role of an entrepreneur in Russia. Furthermore, it is thanks to him and his company that David Deutsch's book *The Beginning of Infinity*, material from which I used in my work, has been published in Russia. I would also like to express my special thanks to Daniel Yergin, a Pulitzer laureate and a recognised authority in the field of energy, international politics and economics, for his unique works on energy resources. I am deeply grateful to Alexei Antipov, scientific editor of my previous book. As many of the considerations I presented in it are still relevant today, I reused some parts of our joint work with Alexei in this book too.

While working on this book, I received substantial help from some great experts and top professionals, including Yermolai Solzhenitsyn, Nikita Mishin, Svetlana Nikolaeva, Irakli Mtibelishvily and Thomas Verasto.

I would like to warmly thank my art editor, Alexander Kiryanov, who has provided an invaluable contribution to this book by making every effort to render my thoughts into creative language while making the text of the book as simple and understandable as possible, and exciting and fun to read at the same time.

I am sincerely thankful to Kirill Sidorov, Maria Kosheleva and Maria Rybakova, who helped me in preparing historical references and searching for rare literary sources, offered their ideas and plot twists, and also tirelessly worked to make each word of the book perfectly perceptible. Their criticisms have helped me in expressing my thoughts most precisely and clearly.

Many thanks go to the whole creative team of LID Publishing and especially to Editorial Director Sara Taheri, Art Director Caroline Li, and Assistant Editor Liz Cooley. I am also sincerely grateful to Maria Pinto-Peuckmann, my literary agent, and the team of Alpina Publisher, the publishing house that issued the Russian edition of the book, for their intensive efforts in searching for opportunities to publish the book in the English-speaking world. All of them made every effort to make the book available to all those to whom it may be of interest and use.

I am deeply thankful to Moscow School of Management SKOLKOVO and especially to its Dean, Marat Atnashev, for their support in the publishing and promotion of the book. They approached the work with the manuscript quite informally, saw it as an interesting project for the market and provided substantial support for the book to be published outside Russian borders.

I express my heartfelt and most sincere gratitude to my parents, Alexander and Albina, for their love, care and warm-heartedness, and for giving me all the support I might need at any time. I am thoroughly convinced that it is in the family that a love for science, knowledge and comprehension of new things is instilled in one's heart.

I am eternally grateful and deeply indebted to my wife, Anna, and my children, Dennis, Olga and Svetlana, for the endless inspiration, caring and understanding they keep on giving me. They show complete understanding of my nomadic life, of the constant necessity for me to work away from home and of the weariness with which I usually return.

At last, I would like to express the most profound gratitude to my teachers. Without them, this book would certainly have not been written. Our teachers teach us to think, to look for and find information, and to formulate an opinion on different issues. This is how science develops, and our society and our world with it. I express my appreciation to all the people to whom I have spoken in person, by telephone, or by e-mail, either with direct reference to this book or otherwise, over the many years of our collaboration. Of course, it is impossible to mention all of them personally in this brief address, but I still infinitely appreciate the attention devoted and experience shared by each of them.

I hope you will enjoy the book!

BIBLIOGRAPHY

Altman, E. J., Sinfield, J. V., Johnson, M. W., Anthony, S. D. *The Innovator's Guide to Growth: Putting Disruptive Innovation to Work*. Boston: Harvard Business Press, 2008.

Andreev, Arkady. Modernisation and the State's Industrial Policy. *Free Thought*, No. 5, 2010.

Azarenkov, N., Orlov, V., Slipchenko, N., Udovitsky, V., Farenik, V. Nanosciences and Nanotechnologies: Achievements, Prospects, Problems, and Development Objectives. *Physical Surface Engineering*, Vol. 3, No. 1-2, January/June 2005.

Baglay, Valentina. *The Aztecs: Their History, Economy, and Socio-political System*. Moscow: Eastern Literature Publishers (RAS), 1998.

Banville, John. *Kepler: A novel*. London: Martin Secker & Warburg Limited, 1981.

Barnett-Hart, Anna Katherine. *The Story of the CDO Market Meltdown: An Empirical Analysis*. Cambridge, Massachusetts: Harvard College, 2009.

Beinhocker, Eric. *The Origin of Wealth: Evolution, Complexity, and the Radical Remaking of Economics*. Boston: Harvard Business School Press, 2006.

Bekhteev, Sergei. T*he Results of Forty-Five Years' Economic Development, and Measures to be Taken for Economic Improvement*. St. Petersburg, Russia, 1902-1911.

Bely, Yu. A. *Johannes Kepler, 1571-1630: At the Origins of Modern Astronomy*. Moscow: Librokom, 2013.

Bergson, Henri. *The Two Sources of Morality and Religion*. Paris: Felix Alcan, 1932.

Bernal, John Desmond. *Science in History*. London: Watts & Co., 1954.

Berners-Lee, Tim. *Weaving the Web: The Original Design and Ultimate Destiny of the World Wide Web by Its Inventor*. New York: HarperCollins, 2000.

Bernstein, Peter L. *The Power of Gold: The History of an Obsession*. New York: John Wiley and Sons, Inc., 2000.

Bernstein, William J. *The Intelligent Asset Allocator: How to Build Your Portfolio to Maximize Returns and Minimize Risk*. New York: McGraw-Hill, 2000.

Bolkhovitinov, Nikolai N. *The Russian-American Relations and the Sale of Alaska, 1834–1867*. Moscow: Nauka Publishing House, 1990.

Bolman, Lee G., Deal, Terrence E. *Reframing Organisations: Artistry, Choice, and Leadership*. San Francisco: Jossey-Bass, 1991.

Bonner, W., Wiggin, A. *Financial Reckoning Day: Surviving the Soft Depression of the 21ˢᵗ Century*. Hoboken, New Jersey: John Wiley and Sons, Inc., 2003.

Borgerson, Scott G. The Coming Arctic Boom: As the Ice Melts, the Region Heats Up. *Foreign Affairs*, July/August 2013.

Bratchenko, E., Dmitriev, A. Economic Theory in Peter Struve's Enterprise and Price Study. *The School of Economics*, No. 4, 1998.

Brealey, R., Myers, S., Allen, S. *Principles of Corporate Finance*. New York: McGraw-Hill, 1980.

Breasted, James Henry. *Ancient Records of Egypt all 5 Vols*. Chicago: The University of Chicago Press, 1906.

Brynjolfsson, Erik, McAfee, Andrew. *Race Against the Machine: How the Digital Revolution is Accelerating Innovation, Driving Productivity, and Irreversibly Transforming Employment and the Economy*. Digital Frontier Press, 2012.

Burke, James. The Pinball Effect: *How Renaissance Water Gardens Made the Carburetor Possible – and Other Journeys Through Knowledge*. Boston, New York, Toronto, London: Little, Brown and Company, 1996.

Buzdalov, Ivan. Intensification of Russian Agriculture. *Economic Issues*, No. 12, 2013.

Cameron, R., Neal, L. *A Concise Economic History of the World: From Paleolithic Times to the Present*. New York: Oxford University Press, 1993.

Carbajales-Dale, M., Barnharta, C., & Benson, S. Can We Afford Storage? A Dynamic Net Energy Analysis of Renewable Electricity Generation Supported by Energy Storage. *Energy Environmental Science*, 2014, 7, 1538-1544, http://pubs.rsc.org/en/content/articlepdf/2014/ee/c3ee42125b.

Chernyak, Leonid. *Vannevar Bush, the Inventor of Hypertext*. URL: http://www.computer-museum.ru/galglory/4.htm.

Childe, Gordon V. *The Dawn of European Civilization*. London, Routledge & Kegan Paul, 1950.

Chizhov, Fyodor. *Steam engines: History, Description, Use*. St. Petersburg, Russia: Edward Praz and Co. Print, 1838.

Christensen, Clayton M. *The Innovator's Dilemma: When New Technologies Cause Great Firms to Fail*. Boston, Massachusetts: Harvard Business School Press, 1997.

Clark, Gregory. *A Farewell to Alms: A Brief Economic History of the World*. Princeton: Princeton University Press, 2007.

Collins, Jim. *How The Mighty Fall: And Why Some Companies Never Give In*. New York: HarperCollins, 2009.

Collins, J., Porras, J. I. *Built to Last: Successful Habits of Visionary Companies*. New York: HarperBusiness, 1994.

Connolly, Peter. *Greece and Rome at War*. London: Macdonald Phoebus Ltd., 1981.

Crosby, Alfred W. *The Columbian Exchange: Biological and Cultural Consequences.* Praeger, 30th edition, 2003.

Csikszentmihalyi, Mihaly. *Flow: The Psychology of Optimal Experience.* New York: Harper & Row, 1990.

D'Efilippo, V., Ball, J. *Infographic History of the World.* London: HarperCollins, 2013.

Dawkins, Richard. *The Selfish Gene.* New York: Oxford University Press, 1976.

De Greef, Thierry. Tous les 15 jours, une langue meurt. *Le Huffington Post*, 8 October 2013. http://www.huffingtonpost.fr/thierry-de-greef/tous-les-15-jours-une-lan_b_4064797. html?utm_hp_ref=international.

De la Mare, Albinia Catherine. *Vespasiano da Bisticci, Historian and Bookseller.* London: London University, 2007.

Delong, J. Bradford. *Estimates of World GDP, One Million B.C. – Present.* Berkeley, CA, USA: University of California Press, 1988.

Dent, Harry S. *The Great Crash Ahead: Strategies for a World Turned Upside Down.* New York, USA: Free Press, 2011.

Deutsch, David. *The Beginning of Infinity: Explanations That Transform the World.* New York: Penguin Group, 2011.

Diamond, Jared. *Agriculture: The Worst Mistake in the History of the Human Race.* 1997. http://primitiv.anho.org.

Diamond, Jared. *Collapse: How Societies Choose to Fail or Succeed.* New York: Penguin Group, 2005.

Diamond, Jared. *Guns, Germs, and Steel: The Fates of Human Societies.* New York: W. Norton & Company, Inc., 1997.

Dugin, Aleksandr. *Social Science.* Moscow: Books on Demand, 2007.

Dumas, Alexandre. *The Black Tulip.* New York: Oxford University Press, 2000.

Durant, Will, Durant, Ariel. *The Story of Civilization.* 11 Volume Set. New York: MJF Books, 1993.

Ehrlich, Paul R., Brower, David. *The Population Bomb.* New York: Buccaneer Books Inc., 2011.

Eisenstein, Elizabeth. *The Printing Revolution in Early Modern Europe.* Cambridge: Cambridge University Press, 1993.

Elvin, Mark. *The Pattern of the Chinese Past.* Stanford University Press, 1973, 348 pages.

Engel, Louis; Boyd, Brendan. *How to Buy Stocks.* Boston: Little Brown and Company 1953.

Enis, B. M., Cox, K. K., Mokwa M. P. *Marketing Classics: A Selection of Influential Articles.* Englewood Cliffs, N.J.: Prentice Hall, 1969.

Evans, Nicholas. *Dying Words: Endangered Languages and What They Have to Tell Us.* Malden & Oxford: Wiley-Blackwell, 2010.

Farrell, D., Lund, S. New Players in the Global Investment World. *Vestnik McKinsey*, 2007.

Farrell, D., Remes, J. K., & Schulz, H. The Truth about Globalisation. *Vestnik McKinsey*, No. 3 (5), 2003.

Ferguson, Niall. *Empire: How Britain Made the Modern World.* New York: Penguin Group, 2003.

Ferguson, Niall. *The Ascent of Money: A Financial History of the World*. New York: The Penguin Press, 2008.

Florida, Richard. *The Rise of the Creative Class: And How It's Transforming Work, Leisure and Everyday Life*. New York: Basic Books, 2002.

Follett, Mary Parker. *Creative Experience*. New York: Longmans, Green and Co, 1924.

Ford, Henry. *My Life and Work*. New York: Double Day Page & Company, 1922.

Foster, R., Kaplan, S. *Creative Destruction: Why Companies That Are Built to Last Underperform the Market – And How to Successfully Transform Them*. New York: Currency, 2001.

Fukuyama, Francis. The End of History? *The National Interest* (Summer 1989), pp. 3-18.

Galilei, Galileo. *The Assayer*. Saarbrücken: Alphascript Publishing, 2011.

Gerasimenko, A. *Financial Reporting for Managers and Young Specialists*. Moscow: Alpina Publisher, 2015.

Goldstone, Jack. *Why Europe? The Rise of the West in World History, 1500-1850*. Boston: McGraw-Hill, 2009.

Golubev, A. V. Post-crisis Agricultural Development in Russia. *Economic Issues*, No. 10, 2009, pp. 131-135.

Google_Books_Ngram. (1880-1984). *Graph: Globalisation*. Retrieved from Google Books Ngram Viewer: https://books.google.com/ngrams/graph?content=globalisation&year_start=1800&year_end=1980&corpus=15&smoothing=3&share=&direct_url=t1%3B%2Cglobalisation%3B%2Cc0.

Google_Finance. *Moody's Corporation Profit Statement Quarterly Data*. Retrieved from Moody's Corporation Financials (NYSE: MSO): http://www.google.com/finance?q=NYSE: MCO&fstype=ii.

Gordon, Robert J. Okun's Law and Productivity Innovations. *American Economic Review*, vol. 100, issue 2, 2010, pp. 11-15.

Graeber, David. *Debt: The First 5,000 Years*. New York: Melville House, 2011.

Hamel, Gary. The Why, What, and How of Management Innovation. *Harvard Business Review*, February 2006.

Hammer M., Hershman L. *Faster Cheaper Better: The 9 Levers for Transforming How Work Gets Done*. New York: Crown Business, 2010.

Harford, Tim. *Adapt: Why Success Always Starts with Failure*. London: Little, Brown 2011.

Heston, A., Summers, R., Aten, B. *Penn World Table Version 7.1*. Pennsylvania: Center for International Comparisons of Production, Profit and Prices at the University of Pennsylvania, 2013.

Hicks, John. *A Theory of Economic History*. London, Oxford, New York, Oxford University Press, 1969

Highfield, Roger. Colonies in space may be only hope, says Hawking. *Daily Telegraph*, 16 October 2001.

Horn, Ede. *John Law: Experience of Studying the History of Finance*. St. Petersburg, Russia: 1895.

Hudson, Michael. *Super Imperialism: The Economic Strategy of American Empire*. 2nd ed. London: Pluto Press, 2003.

Hummel, Charles E. *The Galileo Connection: Resolving Conflicts between Science and the Bible*. Downers Grove: InterVarsity Press, 1986.

Jared, C., Schmidt, E. *The New Digital Age: Reshaping the Future of People, Nations and Business*. New York: Alfred A. Knopf, 2013.

Jaruzelski, B., Loehr, J., Holman, R. The 2012 Global Innovation 1000 Study: Making Ideas Work. *Strategy+Business*. 27 November, 2012. https://www.strategy-business.com/article/00140.

Jeston, J., Nelis, J. *Business Process Management: Practical Guidelines to Successful Implementations*. Burlington: Elsevier Ltd., 2006.

Kaku, Michio. *Hyperspace: A Scientific Odyssey Through Parallel Universes, Time Warps, and the 10th Dimension*. Oxford: Oxford University Press, 1994.

Kaku, Michio. *Physics of the Future*. New York: Doubleday, 2011.

Kapitsa, Sergei. *Paradoxes of Growth: the Laws of Human Development*. Moscow: Alpina Non-fiction, 2013.

Kapitsa, Sergei. The History of Ten Billion. *Snob*, No. 6 (46), 2012.

Keram, C. W. *The First American: the Riddle of Pre-Columbian Indians*. Moscow: Progress, 1979.

Khazin, Mikhail. Five Kilos of Drugs for the Sick Economy. *Krasnaya Zvezda* newspaper, 14 March 2009.

Klyashtorny, S., Sultanov, T. *States and Peoples in the Eurasian Steppes: From Antiquity to the Middle Ages*. St. Petersburg: St. Petersburg Asian Studies, 2004.

Knight, Frank. *Risk, Uncertainty, and Profit*. New York: Riverside Press, 1921.

Kokorev, Vasily. *Economic Failures*. Moscow: Russian Merchants and Industrialists' Society, 2005.

Konfederatov, Ivan. *Ivan Ivanovich Polzunov*. Moscow, Leningrad: Gosenergoizdat, 1954.

Korotaev, A., Malkov, A., Khalturina, D. *Laws of History and Mathematical Modelling of Historical Macro-processes. Demographics, Economics, Wars*. Moscow: Lenand, 2015.

Kostinsky, A. Markov, A. *Humankind has Reached the Limit of Its Growth*, 2006. http://www.svoboda.org/content/article/131474.html.

Krugman, Paul. *Competitiveness: A Dangerous Obsession*. Foreign Affairs, March/April 1994.

Kryukov, M., Sofronov, M., Cheboksarov, N. *The Ancient Chinese: Ethnogenesis Problems*. Moscow: Nauka Publishing House, 1978.

Kuhn, Thomas. *The Structure of Scientific Revolutions*. Chicago : The University of Chicago Press, 1962.

Kukal, Zdeněk. *The Earth's Great Mysteries*. Moscow: Progress, 1988.

Lal, Deepak. *Reviving the Invisible Hand: The Case for Classical Liberalism in the Twenty-first Century*. Princeton: Princeton University Press, 2006.

Maddison, Angus. *Contours of the World Economy 1-2030 AD: Essays in Macro-economic History*. Oxford: Oxford University Press, 2007.

Makhov, Vadim. *Innovators Take Over. Battlefield: Heavy Machinery Engineering*. Moscow: Ladomir Scientific Publishing Centre, 2013.

Malien, J. Soros: Issue Eurobonds or leave the Eurozone, *InoPressa*, April 10, 2013, http://www.inopressa.ru/article/10apr2013/handelsblatt/soros.

Marean, Curtis. The Most Invasive Species of All. *Scientific American*, Volume 313, No. 2, 2015.

Marfunin, Arnold. *The History of Gold*. Moscow: Nauka Publishing House, 1987.

Matonin, Evgeny. *Nikola Tesla*. Moscow: Young Guard, 2014.

McNeill, William H. *The Rise of the West: A History of the Human Community*. Chicago: The University of Chicago Press, 1963.

Meliksetov, A. V. *The History of China*. Moscow: Moscow University Publishing House, Supreme School Publishing House, 2002.

Mellaart, James. *Earliest Civilizations of the Near East*. London: Thames and Hudson, 1965.

Mill, John Stuart. *Principles of Political Economy*. London: Longmans, Green and Co., 1848.

Moiseev, Nikita. *Humanity and the Noosphere*. Moscow: Young Guard, 1990.

Naisbitt, J., Naisbitt, D. *China's Megatrends: The 8 Pillars of a New Society*. New York: HarperCollins, 2010.

Natitnik, A., Auzan, A. How to Bring the National Economy Out of the Coma. *HBR Russia*, June - July, 2015.

Nazarova, Natalia. *Russia's Creative Class as a New Social Phenomenon*, 2012. http://www.mirvboge.ru/2012/06/novyj-socialnyj-fenomenrossii-ee-kreativnyj-klass/.

Nezhelskiy, Yuriy. The Pages from the Nuclear Bomb Creation History. *The Issues of Radiation Safety*, No.3, 1999.

Nikolaeva, I. P. (editor). *The World Economy*, 3rd edition, updated and revised. Moscow: Unity-Dana, 2006.

Noack, R., Lazaro, G. The World's Languages, In 7 Maps and Charts. *Washington Post*, 2015, http://www.washingtonpost.com/blogs/worldviews/wp/2015/04/23/the-worlds-languages-in-7-maps-and-charts/.

North, D., Wallis, J., Weingast, B. *Violence and Social Orders: A Conceptual Framework for Interpreting Recorded Human History*. Cambridge and New York: Cambridge University Press, 2009.

O'Neill, John J. *Prodigal Genius: The Life of Nikola Tesla*. New York: Ives Washburn, Inc., 1944.

Ogden, Christopher. *Maggie: An Intimate Portrait of a Woman in Power*. New York: Simon and Schuster 1990.

Okun, S. On the History of the Sale of Russian Colonies in America. *Historical Records* (Vol. 2), 1938.

Oldstone, Michael B. A. *Viruses, Plagues, and History*. Oxford University Press, USA, 2000.

Pelevin, Victor. *S.N.U.F.F.* Moscow: Eksmo, 2011.

Perez, Carlota. *Technological Revolutions and Financial Capital: The Dynamics of Bubbles and Golden Ages*. Cheltenham: Edward Elgar, 2003.

Perkins, John. *Confessions of an Economic Hit Man*. San Francisco: Berrett-Koehler Publishers, 2004.

Peterson, Peter G. *Gray Dawn: How the Coming Age Wave Will Transform America – and the World*. New-York: Three Rivers Press, 2000.

Pinker, Steven. *The Better Angels of Our Nature. Why Violence Has Declined*. New York: Kindle edition, 2011.

Pištalo, Vladimir. *Tesla: A Portrait with Masks*. Moscow: Azbuka-Klassika, 2010.

Popper, Karl R. *The Logic of Scientific Discovery*. Abigdon: Routledge Classics, 2007.

Pratchett, Terry. *Night Watch*. New York: Domino, HarperCollins, 2002.

Pringle, Heather. The Origin of Human Creativity. *Scientific American*, Vol. 308, Issue 3, 2013.

Ramonet, Ignacio. *Geopolitics of Chaos*. New York: Algora Publishing, 1998.

Rand, Ayn. *Atlas Shrugged*. New York: Dutton, 1957.

Rasiel, Ethan. *The McKinsey Way: Using the Techniques of the World's Top Strategic Consultants to Help You and Your Business*. New York: McGraw-Hill, 1999.

Razdorskaya, I., Shchavelev, S. *Essays in the History of Pharmacy, the first issue: The Advent of the Healer and His Pharmacy: Ancient Civilizations*. Kursk: Kursk State Medical University Publishing House, 2006.

RIA Novosti. *Major Floods in Europe in 2008-2013*. June 2, 2013, http://ria.ru/spravka/20130602/940857207.html.

Romer, Paul M. Increasing Returns and Long-Run Growth. *The Journal of Political Economy*, Vol. 94, No. 5, 1986.

Rozman, Gilbert, Bernstein, Thomas P. The Modernisation of China. *Free Press*, 1981, 551 pages.

Ruban, Olga. Blow It in the Right Place. *Expert*, No. 41 (582), November 5, 2007.

Rzhonsnitsky, Boris. *Nikola Tesla*. Moscow: Young Guard, 1959.

Saidasheva, A. Ivan Fyodorov and His Apostle: The Fate of a Man and a Book. *Book Industry*, No. 9, 2014.

Sanger, David E. *Confront and Conceal: Obama's Secret Wars and Surprising Use of American Power*. New York: Crown Publishing Group, 2013.

Sannikov, V. Forward to the Past! *Popular Mechanics*, No. 124, February 2013.

Schumpeter, Joseph A. *Capitalism, Socialism and Democracy*. New York: Harper & Brothers, 1942.

Schumpeter, Joseph A. *The Theory of Economic Development: An Inquiry into Profits, Capital, Credit, Interest, and the Business Cycle*. New Brunswick, New Jersey: Transaction Books, 1934.

Sharaev, Yuri V. *Economic Growth Theory*. Moscow: Higher School of Economics Publishing House, 2006.

Sherwood, Dennis. *Seeing the Forest for the Trees: A Manager's Guide to Applying Systems Thinking*. London: Nicholas Brealey Publishing, 2002.

Silver, Nate. *The Signal and the Noise: Why Most Predictions Fail – but Some Don't.* New York: Penguin Group, 2012.

Smirnova, N. A. (editor). World History. *Encyclopaedia*, Vol. 6. Moscow: Socioeconomic Knowledge Publishing House, 1959.

Smith, Adam. *The Wealth of Nations.* London: W. Strahan and T. Cadell, 1776.

Sorkin, Andrew Ross. *Too Big to Fail: The Inside Story of How Wall Street and Washington Fought to Save the Financial System – and Themselves.* New York: Viking Press, 2009.

Soros, George. *George Soros On Globalization.* New York & London: PublicAffairs, 2002.

Soros, George. *The Crisis of Global Capitalism: Open Society Endangered.* New York & London: PublicAffairs, 1998.

Spence, Michael. *The Next Convergence: The Future of Economic Growth in a Multispeed World.* New York: Farrar Straus Giroux, 2011.

Spengler, Oswald. *The Decline of the West: Essays on the Morphology of World History in 2 Volumes.* Volume 1: The Image and the Reality. New York: Alfred.A Knopf, 1926.

Stannard, David. *American Holocaust: The Conquest of the New World.* Oxford University Press, 1993.

Stepashin, Sergei. Russia's Competitiveness in a Globalisation Context: A View from the Accounting Chamber of Russia. *Russia's Competitiveness in a Globalisation Context.* Moscow: RAGS, 2006.

Strathern, Paul. *The Medici: Godfathers of the Renaissance.* London: Jonathan Cape, 2003.

Stuart-Kotze, Robin. *Performance: The Secrets of Successful Behaviour.* London: Pearson Education, 2006.

Studensky, P. *The Revenues of Nations: Theory, Measurement, Analysis, Both in the Past and Today.* Moscow: Statistics, 1968.

Tarle, Evgeny. *The Crimean War: A History in Two Volumes.* Moscow, Leningrad: 1941-1944. http://militera.lib.ru/h/tarle3/index.html.

Toynbee, Arnold J. *A Study of History.* Volume 1. London: Oxford Univercity Press, Amen House, 1934.

Tuccille, Jerome. *Alan Shrugged: Alan Greenspan, the World's Most Powerful Banker.* Hoboken: John Wiley & Sons 2002.

Twigg, Graham. *The Black Death: A Biological Reappraisal.* London, England: Batsford, 1983.

Vanshtein, S., Kryukov, M. A Saddle and a Stirrup. *Soviet Ethnography*, No. 6, 1984.

Vasiliev, A. *The History of the Byzantine Empire: Times before the Crusades.* St. Petersburg, Russia: Aletheia, 1998.

Velikhov, E. Taming Thermonuclear Reactions. *Science World*, Special Edition, 2015.

Vernadsky, Vladimir. *Things Experienced and Thought Over.* Moscow: Vagrius, 2007.

Vernadsky, Vladimir. *Works on the World History of Science.* Moscow: Nauka Publishing House, 1988.

Vishnyatsky, L. *The Neanderthals: The History of a Failed Humanity.* St. Petersburg, Russia: Nestor-History, 2010.

Vvedensky, B. Watt's Parallelogram. *BSE*, Vol. 43, 1957.

Ward, Peter. What Will Become of Homo Sapiens? *Scientific American*, January 2009, p. 56.

Warnecke, Hans Jürgen. *The Fractal Company: A Revolution in Corporate Culture*. Berlin: Springer-Verlag, 1993.

Warsh, David. *Knowledge and the Wealth of Nations: A Story of Economic Discovery*. New York; London: W.W. Norton & Company, 2007.

Webster, David. *The Fall of the Ancient Maya: Solving the Mystery of the Maya Collapse*.

London; New York: Thames & Hudson, 2002.

Wiggins, R., Ruefli, W. Schumpeter's Ghost: Is Hypercompetition Making the Best of Times Shorter? *The Strategic Management Journal*, Issue 10, Vol. 26, October, 2005.

Yagodyn B., Zhukov, Yu., Kobzarenko, V. *Agricultural Chemistry*. Moscow: Mir, 2004.

Yergin, Daniel. *The Prize: The Epic Quest for Oil, Money & Power*. New York: Simon & Schuster, 1990.

Zerzan, John. *Agriculture: Demon Engine of Civilization*. 2016, http://svonz.lenin.ru/articles/Zerzan-Agriculture.html.

NOTES AND FURTHER READING

1. In a broader sense, innovation is either something new, or a new way of doing something old, so that a new utility function is acquired as a result. In economics, innovation causes an increase in the value of goods in consumers' eyes. Furthermore, leading to an increase in productivity, innovation is the main source of enhancing nations' economic wellbeing. Speaking in macroeconomic terms, innovation transforms the production function (the production potential) of a country.

2. A DNA molecule (a molecule of deoxyribonucleic acid) is one of the three major types of macromolecules (the other two are RNA and protein molecules) that ensure the storage, transfer from generation to generation, and implementation of the genetic programme of development and functioning of living organisms. DNA contains information about the structure of various types of RNA and proteins (Source: Wikipedia).

3. Sapropel: centuries-old sediments formed in bodies of fresh water out of dead aquatic vegetation, the remains of living organisms and plankton, and particles of soil humus, and containing large amounts of organic matter.

4. Source: Jared Diamond, *Guns, Germs and Steel: The Fates of Human Societies.*

5. Egalitarianism is a concept that suggests the creation of a society whose members are given equal political, economic, and legal rights (Source: Wikipedia).

6. The theory formulated by Karl August Wittfogel, German-American historian and political philosopher.

7. Nome, nomos (ancient Greek νομός, Latin nomos) – the Greek and Roman name for an administrative unit in ancient Egypt, established in the Hellenistic period and used in science today with respect to earlier periods of Egyptian history, when the regions of the state were called sept, spat, or sepat (Source: Wikipedia).

8. Thomas Hobbes (1588-1679) – English philosopher and mathematician, one of the founders of the social contract theory and the sovereign power theory (Source: Wikipedia).

9. Apparently, they invented it twice – first as a whole wheel, and then as a wheel with spokes.

10. The Sumerians were the first to love Egyptian gold. According to Herodotus, the Ziggurat of Babylon was crowned with a statue of Sumer's supreme deity Marduk that was cast in pure gold and weighed about 24 tonnes! Of course, such an addiction on the part of Sumerian rulers to gold, a metal that was absent in Mesopotamia, can be explained by its rarity.

11. The Egyptian civilization lasted from the 4th millennium BC to 405-342 BC.

12. *Knowledge is Force* No. 6, 2011, p.76-84.

13. 'Nub' means 'gold'.

14. About 2050 BC the country reunited, and the power of the leaders of nomes was limited. Egypt increased its territory, especially in the south. According to Sergey Kapitsa's estimates, no more than 43-47 million people populated the world at that time.

15. The essence of such a state of affairs is best conveyed by a French saying: "The more things change, the more they stay the same."

16. In contrast to Western countries where primary education was universal and available to all.

17. The first known instance of conducting the Koto as demanded by the Chinese took place during the reception of the ambassador of Caliph Al-Walid by Emperor Xuanzong of Tang in 713 AD.

18. China's population grew together with the development of new lands. If the conquest of the Siberian territories by Russia had been supplemented with population of these areas following China's example, the Russian population would be substantially greater today.

19. There is a theory suggesting that the Mesopotamian civilisation was destroyed by a bicentennial drought.

20. Tikal was the capital of one of the kingdoms of the ancient Maya. A settlement in what is now Guatemala existed since the 7th century BC. In the 1st-9th centuries AD, the city was one of the most important centres of the Maya civilization.

21. The conventional name of a region in the Middle East. In current usage, the Fertile Crescent includes the territories of modern Lebanon, Israel, Syria, Iraq, southeast Turkey, and northwest of Jordan. Together with the valley of the Nile, the region is considered the cradle of modern civilization.

22. Zod – 2,160 years.

23. Stoicism and Epicureanism are ancient Greek philosophies. The idea of stoicism is about striving for moral perfection, which is reached through living in harmony with nature, submitting your will to fate, meeting the high demands of morality, and adhering to the principles of dignity and honour. The main obstacles to achieving harmony with your fate are passions – these have to be avoided or subjected to mental control. For epicureans, of most importance is the world of senses, and the main ethical principle is pleasure. The supreme good for them is peace of mind, which is achieved by virtue. Many see the essence of Epicureanism in satisfying passions. It appears that Will Durant tried to communicate the idea that civilisations arose where people began to live according to the principles of morality, and died once people began to pay more attention to satisfying their desires.

24. It is possible that in the 13th-14th centuries, during the internecine wars, the stone 'disguise' was put on the statue to hide the gold, shortly before the fall of the Ayutthaya kingdom in order to prevent the statue falling into the hands of the Burmese invaders.

25. German scientists A. Zetber (in 1879), and then Heinrich Quiring (in 1948). These materials on gold extraction in the past have been recognised as classical.

26. These statistics do not include data for the Commonwealth of Independent States countries.

27. Nubia was a historical region in the Nile Valley between the first and sixth rapids, i.e. south of Aswan in Egypt.

28. Altogether from 500-1494 AD, 571 tonnes of gold were produced in Europe, 903 tonnes in Asia, and 838 tonnes in Africa. Thus, although gold mining in medieval Europe was written about much more than that in the ancient world, its volumes were significantly smaller.

29. John Law was a Scottish economist, who established the Banque Générale and created the so-called 'Law's financial system' (Source: Wikipedia).

30. The ancient Greek historian Herodotus reported that the Lydians, or the Meiones, were an extinct people. They lived in the land of Lydia in western Anatolia (the Asia Minor peninsula), and were the dominant people there until Lydia was conquered by the Persians, who turned the country into a colony.

31. In terms of wielded power, Lydia at that time could be compared with Babylon and Egypt.

32. He reigned in 558-529 BC.

33. Which was a perfectly logical thing to do for a monarch who called himself the 'king of kings'.

34. Dishoarding: release precious metals from private savings into the market.

35. His contemporary citizens of Athens thought him just an upstart from the provinces.

36. To educate his heir, Philip invited Aristotle from Athens, asking him to teach his son Alexander from 13-16 years of age. This act can be compared with sending a teenager to Harvard, Cambridge or Oxford for higher education in our day.

37. Thrace: a historical region in the east of the Balkan Peninsula, divided between present-day Turkey, Greece, and Bulgaria.

38. Apparently, the creation of a road network becomes a critical factor for the protection of state borders at a certain stage of state development. Independently of Rome, the Inca civilization did the same in the New World.

39. According to various estimates, the entire global population by the beginning of the Christian era added up to 200-225 million, i.e. some 22-24% lived in the Roman Empire.

40. Most likely, these were pandemics of diseases of Asian origin.

41. The most essential and annoying shortage for the Bibliotheca Alexandrina was the lack of originals of Aristotle's works in its depository. The library did not succeed in buying his manuscripts from his heirs, who had received them as bequests.

42. Pliny wrote that Rome's balance of trade with Southeast Asia was broken. Silk and other oriental luxury commodities were now coming in smaller quantities, and the prices rose from one quarter to one half. The Roman Empire's gold and silver began to flow away to Asia.

43. In the lower right corner we see an already divided empire. This was part of Constantine's legacy. In his will, he divided the Roman Empire between his three sons: Constantine II (337-340) was given Britain, Spain, and Gaul (France); Constantius II (337-361), Egypt and Asia; and Constans (337-350), Africa and Italy.

44. Its population would once again reach the half a million mark only in the twentieth century.

45. A Christian legend says that the emperor himself was tracing the boundaries of the prospective capital with a spear, when his courtiers, astonished by the magnitude of his design, asked him, "Lord, how long will you keep going?" To that, Constantine replied: "I shall keep going until the one who walks ahead of me stops."

46. He adopted Christianity during the last year of his life. Constantine was a supporter of the cult of the sun, but it is not known exactly which deity in particular he worshiped. However, this solar religion gained him enormous popularity throughout the empire.

47. 1,484 / 31.103 (grams per troy ounce) × 4.55 × 0.98 = US$212.75 per coin. Today, a solidus would take pride of place in any collection of ancient coins. Some numismatists prefer to collect only solidi, which, I would say, should be a well-justified preference in economic terms.

48. The Byzantines.

49. Byzantium was connected with Southeast Asia through Persia: products from Ceylon, India, and China came via trade routes that went through the Persian Gulf. The main item of import from China was silk. Later, several monks and one Persian, having deceived the Chinese customs inspectors, brought silkworm cocoons to the empire and taught the Greeks the art of breeding silkworm pupae.

50. Greece, for example, was going through an economic decline at that time.

51. In Western Europe, such strata were successfully formalized by municipal charters which legally secured their freedoms.

52. Uneducated Arabs demanded only a minimum tribute, and this caused a further increase in the popularity of their power.

53. Yongle Emperor (1403-1424) Zhu Di named himself Yongle (literally meaning 'eternal happiness') after becoming emperor. He was the last really strong ruler in the dynasty, after its founder. During his rule, the Chinese empire achieved prosperity and power, expanded its international relations, and strengthened its international influence in Indochina and Southeast Asia.

54. As a result of a military conflict in the 1580s, Korea recognized its dependence on China.

55. Such relations with the outside world were very different from those maintained by Mongolian dynasties, whose objective was to conquer the world, and Yongle probably felt the need to restore a more attractive image of the Chinese civilization.

56. The open society concept was originally created by philosopher Henri Bergson, the winner of the 1927 Nobel Prize in Literature (Bergson 1932). Then the concept was further developed in detail by Karl Popper, who in his work *The Open Society and Its Enemies* united Bergson's philosophy of open society with his own philosophy of critical rationalism.

57. A monetary unit designed for comparing macroeconomic indicators of different countries, proposed by Roy Geary in 1958 and developed by Salem Khamis in 1970-1972.

58. "The written letter remains" (Latin), a saying which means "it is difficult to argue against written evidence", or "what is written cannot be renounced".

59. Anatoly Bakhtiarov, *Johannes Gutenberg: His Life and Work in Connection with the History of Printing, a Biographical Sketch.* This biographical volume was published about 100 years ago as part of *The Lives of Remarkable People*, a series initiated by Florentiy Pavlenkov (1839-1900).

60. By 1514, Copernicus sketched an outline of his new work on astronomy, which came to be known in a shortened form as *Commentariolus (Little Commentary)*. Taking his cue from the Italian school of the Pythagoreans, he distributed several hand-written copies among his close friends without mentioning the author's name. In the *Little Commentary*, he criticised Aristotle and Ptolemy's traditional geocentric world system, saying that "the centre of the Earth is not the centre of the world".

61. Copernicus worked on the mathematical axioms included in his *Little Commentary* for 30 years, postponing the publication of his main work for a number of reasons. Copernicus was afraid that people would laugh at a theory that was contrary to what they saw with their own eyes. Being away from the centres of science, he did not have the chance to discuss his system with other scientists. Moreover, he had no connection with major publishers that would be able to print such a large and complex book.

62. Awareness of the value of his work came much later: it was only in 1828 that the prohibition to publish his writings about the heliocentric system was lifted, and monuments in his honour were erected in his native Poland some years later.

63. In spite of the dual authorship of the theory, Kuhn's presentation is accepted as the primary one in the world.

64. The term 'Scientific Revolution' was introduced by Alexandre Koyre, a philosopher and historian, in 1939.

65. The peoples of Asia on the whole started using watches only in the 1970s, when Seiko, a Japanese company, flooded the mass market with cheap electromechanical models. In Europe, watches enjoyed mass distribution three centuries earlier.

66. Tycho Brahe (1546-1601), a Danish astronomer, astrologer, and alchemist of the Renaissance era (Source: Wikipedia).

67. Grosso (Italian): thick.

68. In 13th century England, Italian merchants replaced the Jews, who had been driven out of the country by the English. The Italians were engaged in lending money, cargo insurance, and currency exchange. At that time, as usury was outlawed, they would call a loan a temporary gift that would be returned with gratitude (i.e. interest) at a later date.

69. It is not surprising that the morals and manners of the first bankers resembled those of thugs. Until the 1390s, even the Medici were more bandits than bankers. From 1343-1360, five members of the Medici family were sentenced to death for crimes.

70. Literally, 'the secret book', secret records which are still kept in the State Archive of Florence.

71. The banks owned by the Bardi, Peruzzi, and Acciaiuoli families.

72. Literally, letter of exchange. Bills of exchange were initially used to exchange coins. With each municipality minting its own money, there was a great variety of coins in circulation, which differed in their origin, weight, denomination, and metal. Only professional money changers knew how to deal with this assortment. A merchant setting out on a journey and being in need of foreign money while away would seek to avoid the dangers and inconveniences associated with the transportation of cash. He would be more comfortable with a letter that would entitle him to receive an equivalent amount of money in the relevant currency. An innovation was thus created – a promissory note that made a new kind of transaction possible: hard cash could be exchanged for non-existent money. Bills of exchange became a commodity that could be bought for money.

73. Very often, secret deposits were required, as customers could be senior representatives of the Catholic clergy.

74. Thus the Medici received their nickname: 'God's Bankers'.

75. Under ecclesiastical law, interest was permitted to be paid in compensation for actual or hypothetical costs associated with mandatory investment.

76. Banco della Piazza di Rialto in Venice was established by decree of the Senate of Venice on 11 April 1587. However, being a state-owned enterprise, the bank was run by a manager licensed by the city and obliged to follow rather rigid guidelines. Tightly controlled by the senate, the bank gradually lost the confidence of traders. Very soon, transactions were conducted in Venice mostly as transfers between accounts within the bank. In 1614, Piazza di Rialto was renamed Banco Giro and began to specialize in payments in coins and securities issued by the bank itself.

77. Affaitadi and Gualterotti.

78. Charles V and Philip II.

79. During one of the Antwerp fairs held in 1536, an agent of this merchant desperately needed liquidity. He sold a long-term acknowledgment of debt, which contained a provision saying that the debt was "to pay the bearer on demand", "a third party" before the due date of payment, at a price below par. Documents found in the archives of the English merchant showed that in the 1530s, this practice was usual solely in the Antwerp market.

80. Middelburg (Holland, 1616), Hamburg (1619), and Rotterdam (1635).

81. Some scholars believe that this happened when connection by land between Asia and America was washed away – about 13,000 BC.

82. Today it's for the most part Southern Mexico, and partly Guatemala, Honduras, Belize, and El Salvador – up to Panama.

83. This is confirmed by the fact that Cortés's flag bore the Latin motto 'In hoc signo vinces' ('In this sign thou shalt conquer'), borrowed from Byzantine Emperor Constantine I.

84. In Tabasco on 19 March, Cortés received gifts from local rulers: a large amount of gold and 20 female slaves, including La Malinche, a Nahua woman who later became Cortés's official translator and concubine. She was immediately baptised, and the Spaniards called her Dona Marina.

85. The Triple Alliance was an Aztec union of three city-states, the principal of which was Tenochtitlan. Acamapichtli (1376-1395), who was elected ruler of Tenochtitlan in 1376, strengthened the state's external and internal positions considerably.

86. It was not the Aztec Empire's gold reserves that Cortés took under control, but their equivalent. Special pieces of cotton fabric, called 'quachtli', played an extremely important role in the empire's commodity exchange. The imperial coffers are most likely to have been represented by special quachtli storage facilities. If a court imposed a fine, it had to be settled in quachtli.

87. According to the conquistadors, Montezuma was killed on 27 or 30 June 1520 by the insurgents; Aztec sources suggest that Montezuma was killed by the Spaniards who no longer needed him as a hostage.

88. The Spaniards' bloody retreat on the night of 30 June became known as La Noche Triste ('the Night of Sorrows'). All the artillery and gold that had been plundered in Tenochtitlan were lost.

89. The Incan Empire occupied an area of 2,754,000 square kilometres and stretched for 4,800 km from north to south along the west coast of South America. The empire's territory covered the territory of present-day Peru, Bolivia, Ecuador, and Argentina, as well as part of the territory of today's Chile.

90. The names of the two brothers, Atahualpa and Huascar, meaning 'wild turkey' and 'sweet hummingbird' respectively, went well with their characters. The war was unleashed by Huascar, who lost it to his brother and was imprisoned.

91. When meeting with the envoy, Pizarro had presented gifts for the emperor and talked much about peace. In response to criticism of their actions the Spaniards praised their martial skills and suggested that the Supreme Inca should use their military services. This seems to have been the reason why Atahualpa agreed to visit Pizarro at Cajamarca.

92. The combat was nothing but a brutal massacre of unarmed Indians. Within hours, 6,000 Inca soldiers were slaughtered, but not one Spaniard was killed. Pizarro himself was wounded, shot by his own men while trying to capture the emperor alive.

93. The Native Americans' attitude towards gold differed from the Europeans'. The Indians did not turn gold into a bargaining chip, did not fight for it. In the Incan Empire, gold represented gifts of the goddess Pachamama, and gods' gifts could only belong to those who were close to the gods or related to them.

94. This fundamental military innovation enabled the Mongols to carry out a massive series of successful invasions.

95. In 1545, rich deposits of silver were discovered in Potosi (now part of Bolivia). Masses of local people were driven by the Spanish to the sites to mine the metal, and died there.

96. As a consequence of backbreaking hard labour on plantations and in mines, brutal suppression of frequent revolts, epidemics, and hunger, the native population of Hispaniola decreased from one million to a mere 10,000-15,000 within 20 years of Spanish rule, and had died out completely by the mid-16th century.

97. In their books, the well known historians Alfred Crosby (Crosby 2003) and William McNeill (McNeill 1963) provide numerous facts that enable us to assess the importance of the biological consequences of contacts between different cultures and continents.

98. Arnold J. Toynbee (1889-1975), a British historian, philosopher of history, culture specialist, and sociologist; the author of *A Study of History*, a multivolume work on the comparative history of civilizations.

99. Speaking figuratively, a 'penalty loop' like in biathlon – a forfeit for missing the mark.

100. A bushel is a unit of volume in the imperial system of weights and measures, equal to 36.51 litres and traditionally used to measure amounts of grains and fruits.

101. An acre is a unit for measuring area, equal to 4,047 square metres or 4,840 square yards, used in a number of countries as part of the imperial system of weights and measures (in the UK, the US, Canada, Australia, etc.).

102. The mechanism of the seed drill consisted of a box filled with seeds, and several pipes extended from the box to the ground. As the drill was pulled along, the seed dropped through the pipes and was planted into the ground in straight rows. Tull's innovations were gradually assimilated by prominent English landowners, which assisted in the evolution of the technological foundation for modern agriculture.

103. Source: The *Encyclopaedia Britannica*.

104. When in the 15th and 16th centuries the English woollen cloth industry began to develop and the prices of wool began to grow, grazing lands became especially valuable. It was precisely for the purpose of expanding grazing lands that lords and landowners confiscated land from the peasants and rented it out to farmers. The expropriated land was enclosed from the plots left to peasants, which is how this process came to be known as 'enclosure'.

105. Watt began to compress steam not in the cylinder, as had been done before, but in a capacitor, a special vessel he had invented. Soon, Watt carried out a second improvement, which was about using the elastic force of steam instead of atmospheric pressure in the working stroke of the piston.

106. Steam hammer. Source: http://the100.ru/inventors/steam hammer.html.

107. Henry Cort (1741-1800) was an English ironmaster. He noted the poor quality of English iron supplies in comparison with iron imports. Cort studied the issue and invented methods for producing iron of higher quality (Source: Wikipedia).

108. The first rolling mill, furnished with wooden rollers, was designed by Leonardo da Vinci. The first rolling mills for the production of flat steel and merchant mill commodities were constructed as early as in the 18th century, and were driven by waterwheels.

109. In 1808, Trevithick built a locomotive and demonstrated it in the outskirts of London. The locomotive developed a speed of up to 30 km/h at a ring road park he built at his own expense. However, having received no support from major financiers, Trevithick went bankrupt.

110. Murray/Blenkinsop 1811 rack and pinion locomotive.

111. Revolution in transport.
Source: http://telarian.ru/?r=history&id=354.

112. Steamboat (the story of the invention).
Source: http://istoriz.ru/paroxod-istoriya-izobreteniya.html.

113. Ibid.

114. Leblanc immediately initiated the construction of the first synthetic soda plants and thus laid the foundations of the chemical industry.

115. Chinese were forbidden, on pain of death, to teach the Chinese language to foreigners. Moreover, even export of books was banned, since books could also be used to learn Chinese and obtain information about the country.

116. India (the Mughal Empire) had always been a producer of opium.

117. Both in England and in China, the public opinion held opium trade as an immoral business. The management of the East India Company prohibited distribution of opium in British India, but its export to China was seen as the personal affair of the merchants who traded with that country. Drug trade met sharp criticism from representatives of the opposition in the British parliament. The import of opium was repeatedly banned in China.

118. In November 1839, the first major clash between the British warships and the Chinese navy took place. Formally, however, neither party ever declared war on the other.

119. Most of all, Europeans resented the need to recognize the superiority of the Chinese and the dreadfully shameful ritual associated with it: any European had to crawl into the forbidden city on all fours with a disgraceful sign hanging around his neck, and then lick the floor in front of the Chinese emperor.

120. The Treaty of Amiens was a peace treaty signed on 25 March 1802 between France, Spain, and the Batavian Republic (the Netherlands) on one side and Britain on the other. The treaty ended the 1800-1802 war between the French Republic and Great Britain (Source: Wikipedia).

121. Initially, flour milling, and meat processing and canning, grew as industries most closely related to agriculture. Then textile production and metal processing began to develop rapidly.

122. The development of railway networks in the north of the US ensured growth for heavy industry.

123. This revolutionized the food processing industry, of which we are only reminded when having the occasional blackout.

124. Menlo Park was a small village where Edison moved in 1876. The location soon became a centre of attraction for scientists, actors, artists, and inventors. By the beginning of the twentieth century, it had developed to become the first embodiment of the 'think tank'. There, the world's first electric power station lit a whole village with electric light, and the first electric locomotive made tours around Menlo Park.

125. The director of the US Patent and Trademark Office put it this way: "Young Edison's steps will not let the path to my door cool down."

126. One of them, Elisha Gray, brought his application to the patent office a mere two hours later than Bell. Afterwards, Gray sued Bell, but the dispute was settled out of court, with Bell paying Gray compensation. And who remembers Elisha Gray today?

127. Nikola Tesla came to New York in a shabby suit, half-starved, and without money. He was saved from a tight corner by a stroke of luck. Passing by a shop window, Nicola saw an elderly man who was unsuccessfully trying to fix a small generator which, evidently, was used to illuminate the workshop. Tesla offered his services. Though sceptical, the shop owner let the foreigner try his hand at the machine and was soon amazed by Tesla's skill. When the generator was fixed, the owner compelled Tesla to take a small amount of money. This random earning enabled Tesla to pay for a room at a hotel.

128. Such machines, though close to perfection in terms of their engineering by that time, were still unfit for large-scale production of electrical energy.

129. This effect was named the 'uniformly rotating magnetic field phenomenon'.

130. Up until the early 1920s, horse-drawn traffic was predominant.

131. Ford started manufacturing the Model T on 1 October 1908. In his words, only high quality materials were used to manufacture the vehicle, and it was affordable for people with high enough earnings. The first four-cylinder water-cooled engines weighed 545 kg and enabled the vehicles to build up speeds of up to 65 km/h.

132. There is a conspiracy theory, according to which the failure to start production was a result of pressure from oil companies, and that an arson attack on the laboratory in West Orange was their last warning to Ford and Edison.

133. Hence Ford's famous phrase: "Any customer can have a car painted any colour that he wants so long as it is black."

134. www.zerosottozero.it/2013/12/20/centanni-di-refrigerazione-domestica/

135. The Ford Trimotor, nicknamed the Tin Goose, was an American passenger aircraft, an all-metal strut-braced monoplane powered by three engines, manufactured by Henry Ford's company in 1927-1933.

136. A new Ford Model A car sold for US$525 then.

137. In the US, road vehicles account for more than 60% of oil consumption today.

138. Only two natural processes can break down nitrogen and make its atoms reactive: thunderstorms and biological immobilization.

139. Chemists were able to synthesize some nitrogen-containing compounds, such as lithium nitride (Li_3N), from atmospheric nitrogen, but the amounts of such production had to be measured in grams.

140. Another Nobel laureate. Haber and Bosch won the Nobel Prize in Chemistry in 1931 in recognition of their contributions to the invention and development of chemical high-pressure methods.

141. Chaim Weizmann, a chemist and the future first president of Israel, offered him a job in his lab at the Palestinian Daniel Sieff Research Institute.

142. The first test of the first Soviet atomic bomb was attended by Lavrentiy Beria, who supervised the project, and Igor Kurchatov, the director of the Soviet atomic bomb project himself. Beria proposed that Kurchatov give a name to the project. Kurchatov replied that it already had a name, RDS-1 (the abbreviation stood for 'Russia does it itself' in Russian). For several years, the bomb prototypes were indeed called RDS-2, RDS-3, etc.

143. Abram Ioffe (1880-1960) was a Russian and Soviet physicist and scientific administrator, and as such he was commonly referred to as 'the father of Soviet physics'. He was an academician and Vice-President of the Academy of Sciences of the Soviet Union, and the founder of a scientific school that gave the country many prominent Soviet physicists, such as Anatoly Alexandrov, Matvei Bronstein, Yakov Dorfman, Pyotr Kapitsa, Isaak Kikoin, Boris Konstantinov, Igor Kurchatov, Nikolay Semenov, and Yakov Frenkel.

144. Heavy water (also referred to as deuterium oxide) is a form of water that contains a larger than normal amount of the hydrogen isotope deuterium (also known as heavy hydrogen). Heavy water has the same chemical formula as ordinary water, but contains two atoms of deuterium, the heavy hydrogen isotope, instead of the usual two atoms of protium, the light hydrogen isotope. Externally, heavy water looks like ordinary water – a colourless liquid that has no taste or smell. The most important property of heavy water is that it practically does not absorb any neutrons, and for this reason it is used in nuclear reactors to moderate neutrons, and as a heat transfer fluid.

145. In 1954, this company produced the first commercially viable colour TV.

146. Joint Picture Expert Group – a group of experts on still image compression.

147. Motion Picture Expert Group – a group of experts on moving image compression.

148. To understand and accept this thought, read, for example, Ayn Rand's *Atlas Shrugged* (Rand 2016).

149. Thus, the term 'obsolescence' appeared in economics. To understand its meaning, look at your private cemetery of home electronics. All these video recorders, film cameras, and old mobile phones still work, but no one needs them anymore.

150. It is appropriate to recall here the Veblen effect, which results in conspicuous consumption.

151. Goodwill is an accounting term used in trading operations to reflect the market value excluding the value of the assets and liabilities. When a company is bought, the goodwill represents the difference between the cost of the investment made and the net fair value of its assets and liabilities. The goodwill of a company is equal to its actual purchase price less the fair market value of its net assets and liabilities.

152. Florida is often called the modern Marx for this assertion.

153. Actually, he needed the machine only so as to assert himself among the members of the computer club, who were just as ardent electronics fans as he was.

154. Before that, only computer assembly sets for techno geeks had been manufactured.

155. An acronym for Advanced Research Projects Agency Network.

156. The Arpanet ceased to exist in 1991, but the internet lived on as an already well-established international association of networks.

157. The first web site was info.cern.ch, which went online on 6 August 1991. The site contained information about what the World Wide Web was, how one could get a browser, and how to set up a web server.

158. It was then that American Airlines and IBM started to develop an electronic air ticket reservation system which enabled American Airlines to manage proactively the profitability of their operations by adjusting ticket prices based on the availability of seats on board aircraft.

159. The Global Competitiveness Report 2015-2016. URL: http://reports.weforum.org/global-competitiveness-report-2015-2016.

160. Assessing Innovation Metrics. McKinsey global survey results, November 2008.

161. Ibid.

162. The following is a loose representation of only a few ideas of Gary Hamel and examples he provided to support his conclusions and recommendations.

163. Thomas Friedman is an American journalist, and three-time Pulitzer Prize winner, and a bright critic of Israel's policies. In the 1980s, he worked as a correspondent for *The New York Times*.

164. In 1965, President de Gaulle of France undertook to strengthen the country's economy. The republic's gold reserve totalled a mere 500kg at that time. The general sent two shipments of dollars to the US, and simply exchanged it for gold at a rate favourable for France. De Gaulle collected US$750 million throughout France and received 825 tonnes of gold bullion for this money. Washington regarded this action as unfriendly, as the French currency intervention set a dangerous precedent for America.

165. Exxon, Shell, BP, Gulf Oil, Texaco, Standard Oil of California, and Mobil.

166. The commission was composed of 300 members from North America, Western Europe, and Japan, who were representatives of academia, business, the media, and political elites.

167. In the United Kingdom, a similar policy, known as Thatcherism, was pursued by Margaret Thatcher.

168. The maximum income tax rate was reduced from 50%-8%, and the federal corporate income tax rate from 48%-34%; 6 million low-income Americans were exempt from all taxes.

169. The average hourly payment rate for workers is US$14.8 in the US and US$21.5 in Germany.

170. In 1986, the official discount rate was lowered four times, down to 3%.

171. Shares of Japan Air Lines, as well as those of some fishing and timber firms, traded at 400 times their annual profit!

172. This would be enough to buy the gold reserves of all other central banks in the world twice!

173. Source: Bloomberg, referring to its own estimates. The agency reported that Chinese international reserves amounted to 30.2% of the world reserves, compared to 14% in early 2004.

174. Of course, the latest, post-Crimean events have changed the situation significantly.

175. The figure includes the number of livestock.

176. The reforms started after the death of Mao Zedong, when Deng Xiaoping proclaimed his famous maxim that "being a Communist does not mean being poor".

177. In 2014, China left the US behind in terms of GDP at purchasing power parity, reaching US$18 trillion against the United States' US$17.4 trillion, and becoming the de facto largest economy in the world.

178. China is the largest US creditor, holding US debt securities for more than US$1.1 trillion.

179. In 2012, China's share in the global consumption of luxury goods came to 40%.

180. According to the World Bank's forecast, Russia was able to increase its total assets to €800 billion until recently.

181. This trend has been explained by geopolitical reasons recently, but the real reason for capital leaving such countries is low economic growth rates and low expectations of growth rate increases.

182. During the 1980s debt crisis, capital flows turned out to be a trap for many developing countries and caused damage to a large part of the global economy afterwards.

183. Three or four countries have the potential to bite off a significant part of the Chinese pie: India, Indonesia, the Philippines, and Pakistan, but probably not before 2025.

184. Belarus included this currency in its currency reserve list in September 2007, becoming the first to do so among the CIS countries.

185. Many experts believe the mobile telephone to be even more of an innovation than the internet.

186. This situation is characterized best by the term 'monetary hegemony', which Michael Hudson introduced in his book called *Super-Imperialism*, first published in 1972 (Hudson 2003). The theory implies a strong slant of the global monetary system in favour of the US dollar.

187. Published by Standard & Poor's rating agency (Harold McGraw III).

188. AIG issued CDSs to a total amount of US$440 billion.

189. Lehman Brothers issued bond guarantees worth US$700 billion.

190. Foreclosure.

191. Once the second largest mortgage lender in the United States.

192. *The New York Times*, 18 February, 2009.

193. In the middle of the 17th century, people were unaware of the virus, but this did not matter.

194. As a rule, only two bulbs can be grown from one bulb in a year, four bulbs in two years, eight in three years, and so on, i.e. in a fixed geometrical progression.

195. This Italian phrase, meaning 'the comedy is over', is borrowed from *Pagliacci*, the famous opera by Ruggero Leoncavallo.

196. In his latest book, titled *The Great Crash Ahead*: (Dent 2011), Dent tells us how to make smart, forward-looking investments and to avoid 'high risk – high profit' investment schemes which have ruined the global economy.

197. A Minsky moment is a sudden major collapse of asset values as a result of the combined effect of the debt and credit cycles (Source: Wikipedia).

198. According to Hyman Minsky (1919-1996), an American economist, contemporary economy has a complex monetary nature, within which the credit system acts as a powerful internal destabilising factor.

199. Macroeconomists describe this process in their models using the same mathematics!

200. Today, the internet traffic generated by people accounts for a mere 38.5% of the whole informational content, the rest being the result of the activities of computer systems.

201. A non-zero-sum game is a situation where both players can win more through interaction and cooperation with each other (in contrast to the concept of a zero-sum game where one player wins strictly at the expense of the other).

202. Inflation targeting: a set of measures taken by public authorities in order to control inflation in the country. Inflation targeting is carried out in several stages: 1) A planned inflation rate is set for a certain period (usually a year); 2) Appropriate monetary tools

are selected to control inflation; 3) The monetary tools are used according to current requirements; and 4) The factual level of inflation at the end of the reporting period is compared with the planned level, and the effectiveness of the monetary policy is analysed.

203. John Perkins, the best-selling author of *Confessions of an Economic Hit Man*, describes this openly: "There are two ways to conquer and enslave a nation. One is by the sword. The other is by debt" (Perkins 2004).

204. A payment system of this type differs from PayPal or Yandex. Money in those transactions and the impossibility of spending the same amount of money several times are guaranteed by the system itself rather than by the company that owns the system. The system has no central hub and no guarantor company. All users' money is represented by files stored on computers. A transaction simply consists of transferring a file that contains information about the quantity of money sent and received, which immediately becomes known to numerous users of the system. The guarantor of each Bitcoin transaction is transparency.

205. Bitcoin: a peer-to-peer electronic payment system. Its monetary unit bears the same name. On the system's own website, Bitcoin is described as a 'digital currency'.

206. Bitcoin was created by a person known under the nickname Satoshi Nakamoto. In 2008, he published an article titled *Bitcoin: A Peer-to-Peer Electronic Cash System*, where he described the principles of a virtual payment system. In 2009, he presented a client program for such a system, following which the system was launched. So far, no one knows who is disguised under this Japanese name. Nakamoto used to communicate with other supporters of the idea on discussion forums, but then disappeared in 2011. Before disappearing, he handed over management of the system to a developer by the name of Gavin Andresen. The latter is still in charge of the Bitcoin Foundation, the official body, as it were, of this anarchist payment system.

207. This is 600 times more than the combined power of all Top 500 supercomputers.

208. Monsanto, Novartis, Zeneca (former AstraZeneca), Aventis, and DuPont.

209. So far, only 25 megabytes can be stored on one such plate, measuring 2×2 cm and 2 mm thick.

210. Based on the report *Global Trends in Renewable Energy Investment 2015*, prepared by the Frankfurt School of Finance & Management in collaboration with Bloomberg New Energy Finance.

211. A PSP employs either a set of generators and pumps or reversible hydroelectric units that can operate in both generator and pump mode. During the night drop in power consumption, a PSP receives cheaper electricity from the grid and uses it to pump water upstream (i.e. works in 'pump mode'). During the morning and evening peaks in energy consumption, the PSP discharges water to produce more expensive peak-time electricity and release it into the grid (working in 'generator mode').

212. The Fischer-Tropsch process is a chemical reaction in which carbon monoxide (CO) and hydrogen (H2) are converted into a number of liquid hydrocarbons used as synthetic lubricating oil or synthetic fuel. The process takes place in the presence of a catalyst usually containing iron and cobalt.

213. The idea of democratising working processes is already in the air: starting from 2015, Generation Z (the people who were born between the early 1990s and the early 2010s) will enter the labour market. By 2035, this generation will reach career heights and take power.

"These people will have an amazing faith in their abilities. They will enter the labour market with impudence and self-confidence, unusual for their age," a report produced by KPMG (*Letting Go to Grow*) said.

214. McKinsey & Company has recently published an analytical report that includes a new list of 12 breakthrough technologies which, according to analysts of the McKinsey Global Institute, will fundamentally change people's private lives, business, and the global economy over the next decade.

215. The name is translated as the Milky Way. The computer was built at the National University of Defense Technology of the People's Liberation Army of China.

216. Christoph Adami, a professor of Physics and Astronomy, a professor of Microbiology and Molecular Genetics at Michigan State University. He is no less popular and known in the West than Michio Kaku, Elon Musk, or Nassim Taleb.

217. Repository: a storage location, a place where data of any kind are stored and maintained. Most often, data is kept in a repository in the form of files available for distribution over a network (Souce: Wikipedia).

218. According to biologist David Suzuki, who gives a detailed layout of the problem, including 12% of the birds, 23% of the mammals, and 32% of the amphibians that inhabit the planet today.

219. According to Michael Krauss, a linguist at the Intergovernmental Panel on Climate Change. Today, 60% of all languages on our planet are accumulated in 17 countries that account for just 27% of the global population and 9% of the Earth's surface.

220. Don Jarvis, an acclaimed researcher of glycoproteins and glycosylation, a process of modification of proteins. Glycosylation is an enzymatic process during which sugar residues are attached to organic molecules.

ABOUT THE AUTHOR

VADIM MAKHOV has a PhD in Economics, and is a well known entrepreneur and expert innovator. He has taken an active part in many innovative projects, carried out by various Russian and foreign companies, and initiated the development of many new products. He founded the Bard Worldwide Investment Fund, which is concerned with the development of future technologies.

The leading private business school in Russia and the CIS

SKOLKOVO BUSINESS SCHOOL

Established by the elite members of the local and international business community in Russia in 2006

2 000
alumni

>18 300
attendees
of corporate
education
programmes

150
world-class
professors

10
types of
educational
programmes

1 300
guest speakers
and lecturers

>100
published research
papers

150
client
companies

LID
ANNIVERSARY

Sharing knowledge since 1993

- 1993   Madrid
- 2008   Mexico DF and Monterrey
- 2010   London
- 2011   New York and Buenos Aires
- 2012   Bogotá
- 2014   Shanghai